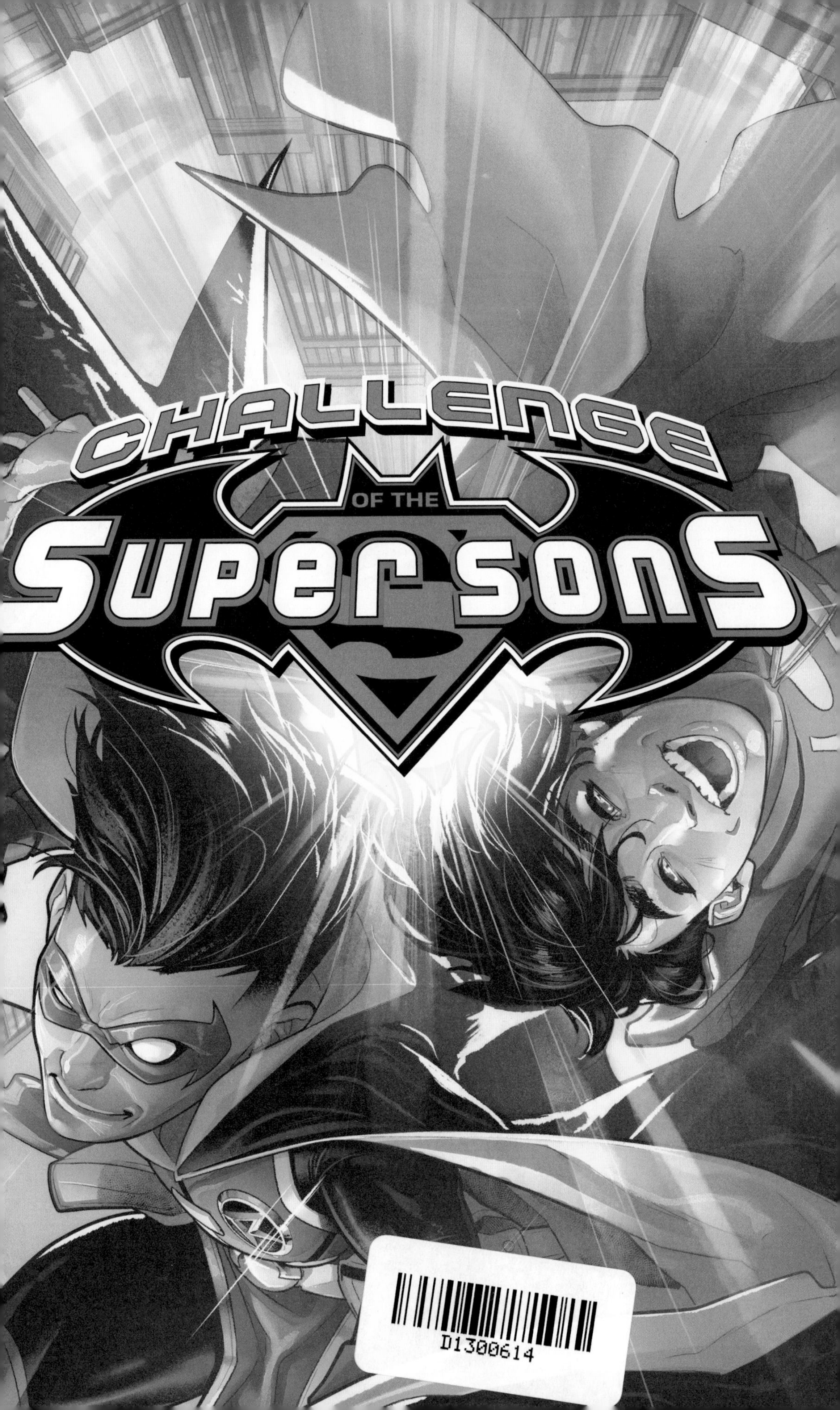
CHALLENGE
OF THE
SUPER SONS

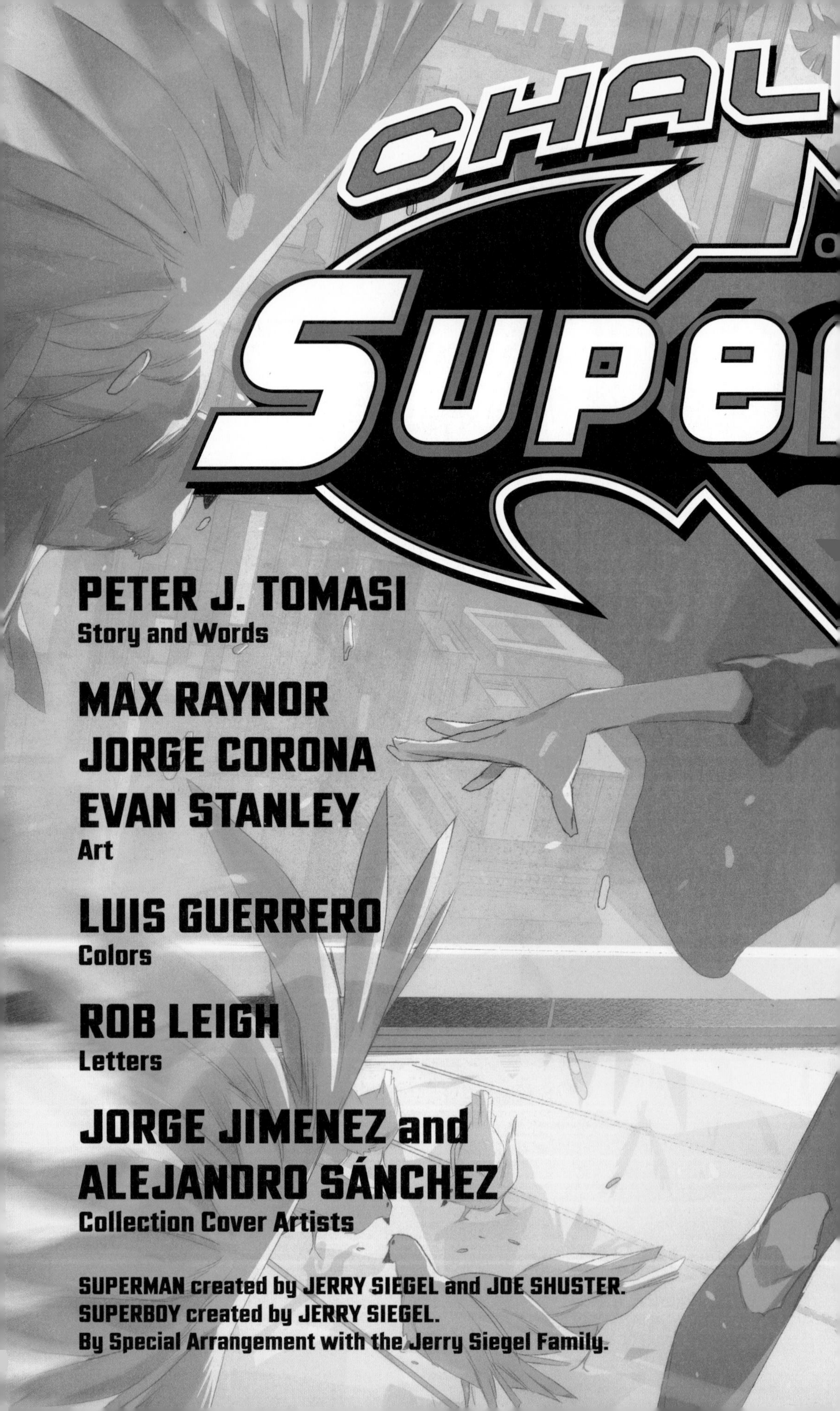

PETER J. TOMASI
Story and Words

MAX RAYNOR
JORGE CORONA
EVAN STANLEY
Art

LUIS GUERRERO
Colors

ROB LEIGH
Letters

JORGE JIMENEZ and
ALEJANDRO SÁNCHEZ
Collection Cover Artists

SUPERMAN created by JERRY SIEGEL and JOE SHUSTER.
SUPERBOY created by JERRY SIEGEL.
By Special Arrangement with the Jerry Siegel Family.

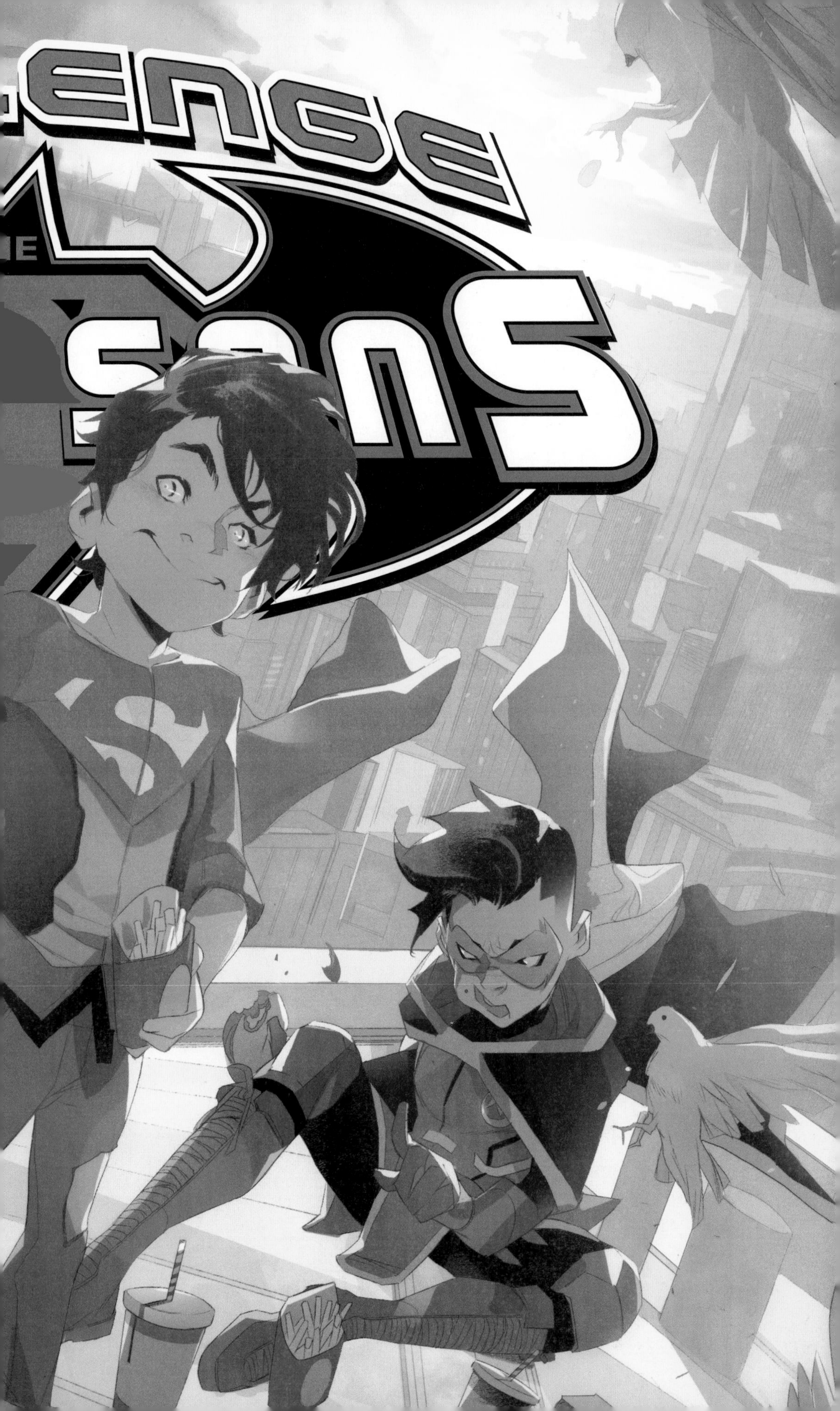
ENGE
SONS

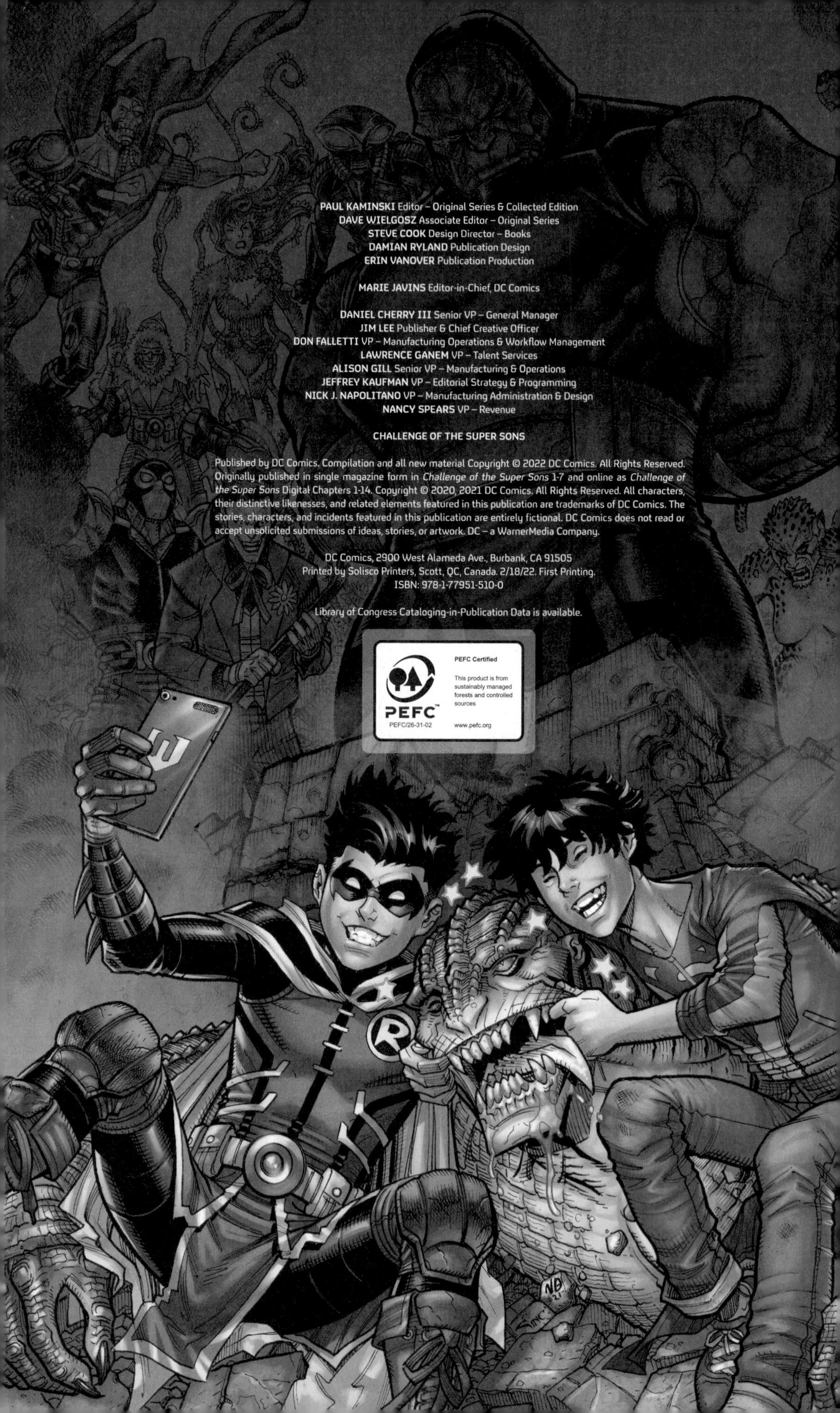

PAUL KAMINSKI Editor – Original Series & Collected Edition
DAVE WIELGOSZ Associate Editor – Original Series
STEVE COOK Design Director – Books
DAMIAN RYLAND Publication Design
ERIN VANOVER Publication Production

MARIE JAVINS Editor-in-Chief, DC Comics

DANIEL CHERRY III Senior VP – General Manager
JIM LEE Publisher & Chief Creative Officer
DON FALLETTI VP – Manufacturing Operations & Workflow Management
LAWRENCE GANEM VP – Talent Services
ALISON GILL Senior VP – Manufacturing & Operations
JEFFREY KAUFMAN VP – Editorial Strategy & Programming
NICK J. NAPOLITANO VP – Manufacturing Administration & Design
NANCY SPEARS VP – Revenue

CHALLENGE OF THE SUPER SONS

DC Comics, 2900 West Alameda Ave., Burbank, CA 91505
Printed by Solisco Printers, Scott, QC, Canada. 2/18/22. First Printing.
ISBN: 978-1-77951-510-0

Library of Congress Cataloging-in-Publication Data is available.

PEFC Certified
This product is from sustainably managed forests and controlled sources
PEFC
PEFC/26-31-02
www.pefc.org

Challenge of the Super Sons #1 cover by
JORGE JIMENEZ and **ALEJANDRO SÁNCHEZ**

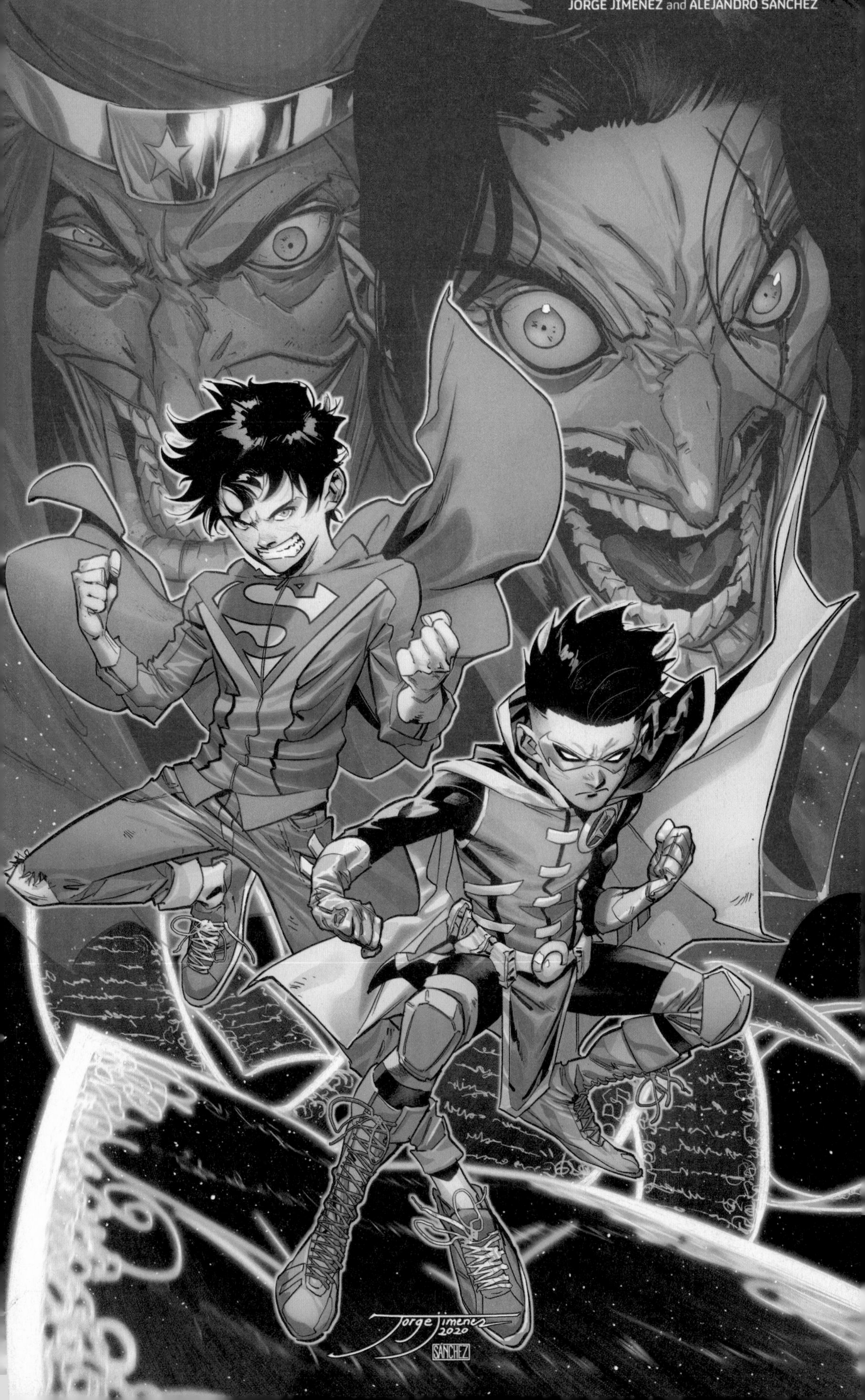

Jorge Jimenez 2020
SANCHEZ

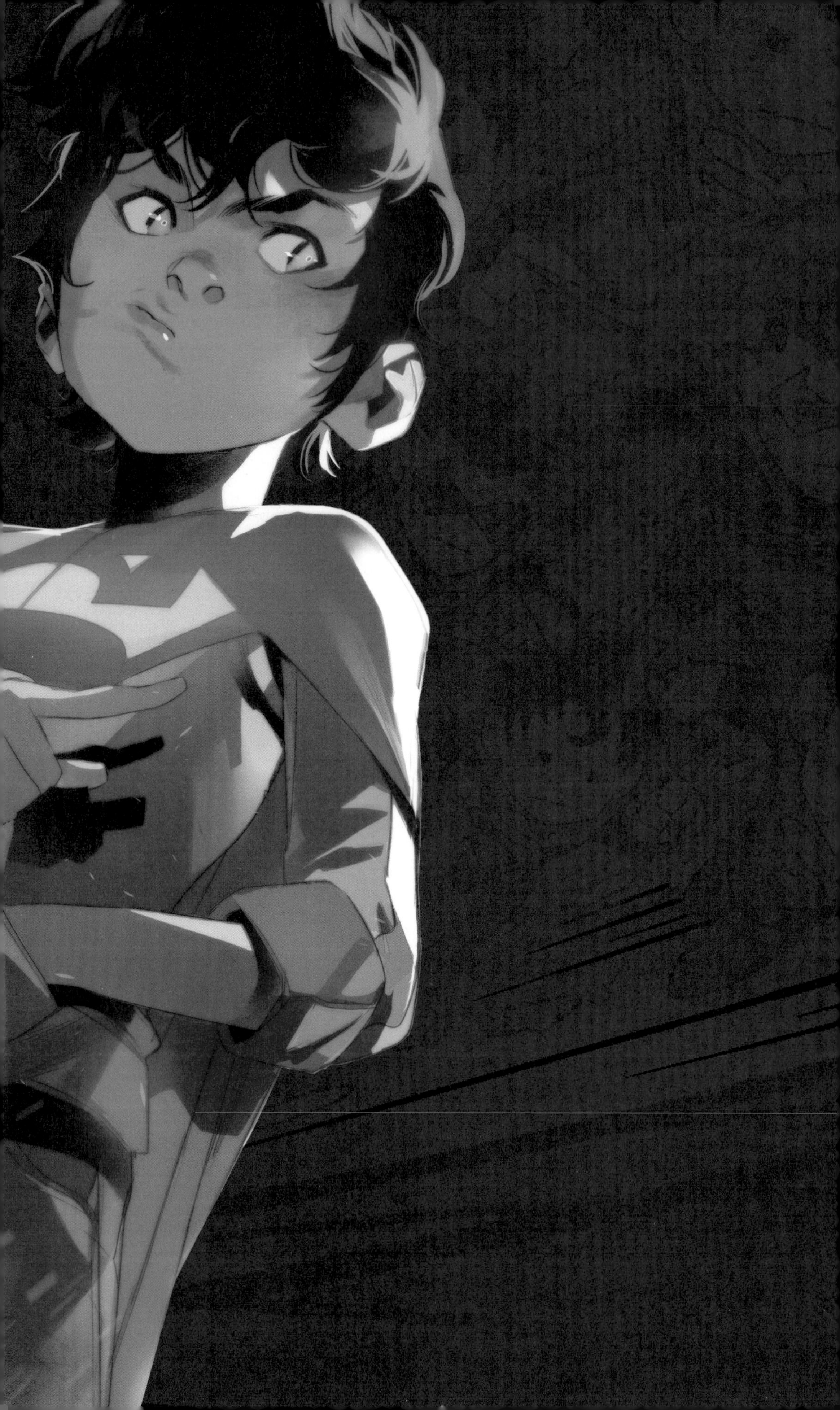

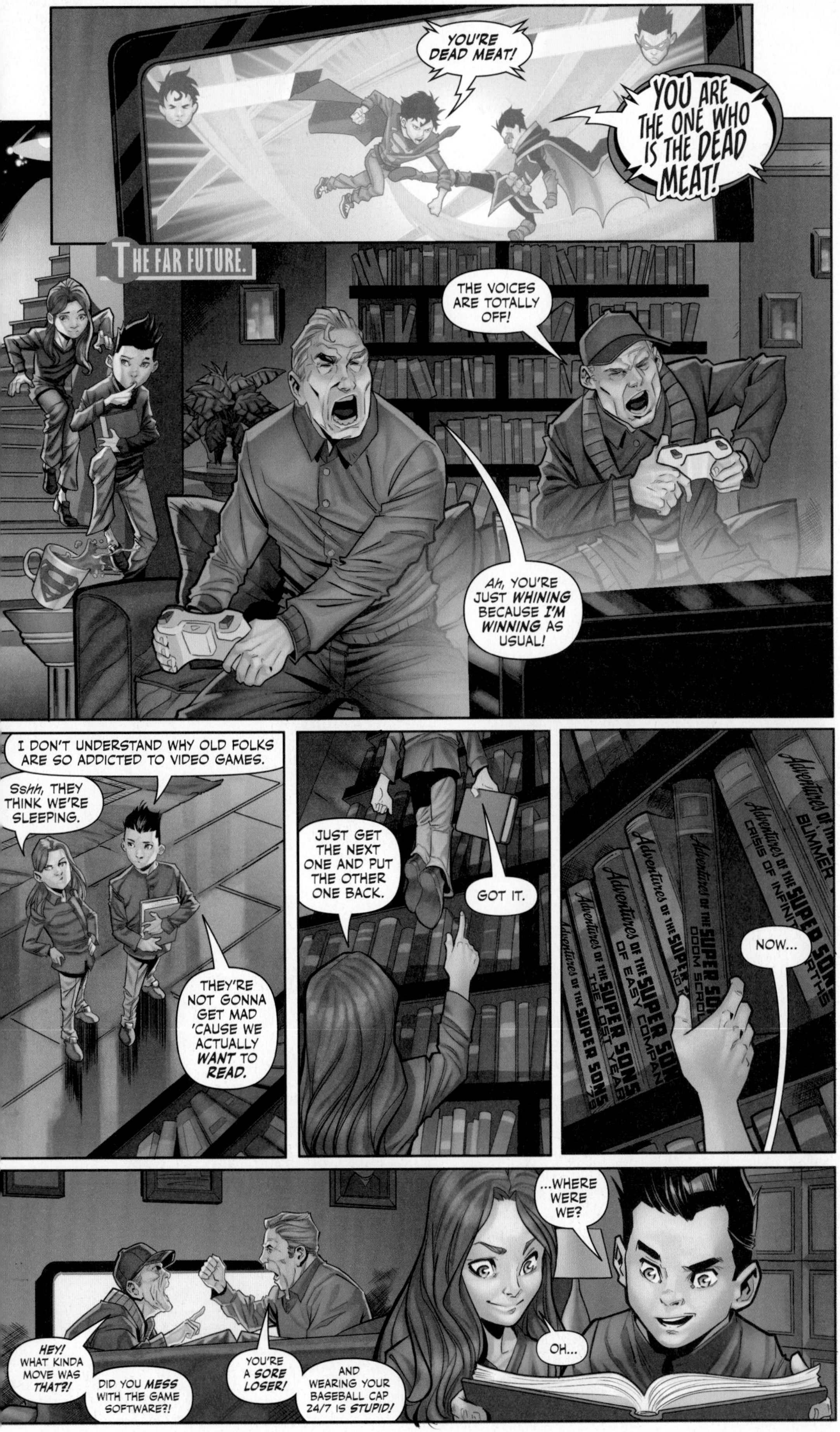
YOU'RE DEAD MEAT!
YOU ARE THE ONE WHO IS THE DEAD MEAT!
THE FAR FUTURE.
THE VOICES ARE TOTALLY OFF!
Ah, YOU'RE JUST WHINING BECAUSE I'M WINNING AS USUAL!
I DON'T UNDERSTAND WHY OLD FOLKS ARE SO ADDICTED TO VIDEO GAMES.
Sshh, THEY THINK WE'RE SLEEPING.
THEY'RE NOT GONNA GET MAD 'CAUSE WE ACTUALLY WANT TO READ.
JUST GET THE NEXT ONE AND PUT THE OTHER ONE BACK.
GOT IT.
NOW...
...WHERE WERE WE?
OH...
HEY! WHAT KINDA MOVE WAS THAT?!
DID YOU MESS WITH THE GAME SOFTWARE?!
YOU'RE A SORE LOSER!
AND WEARING YOUR BASEBALL CAP 24/7 IS STUPID!

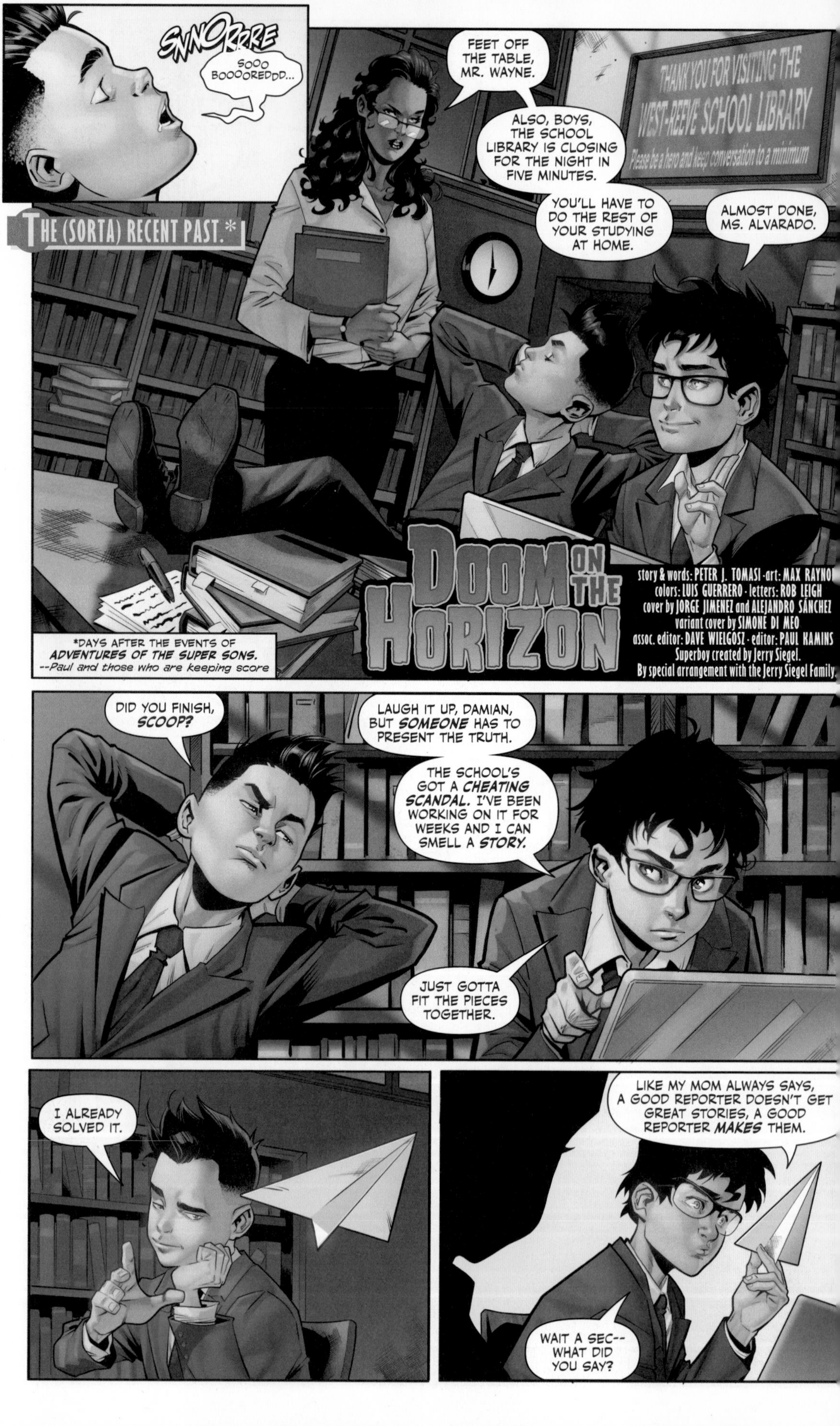
SNNORRRE
SOOO BOOOOREDDD...
FEET OFF THE TABLE, MR. WAYNE.
ALSO, BOYS, THE SCHOOL LIBRARY IS CLOSING FOR THE NIGHT IN FIVE MINUTES.
YOU'LL HAVE TO DO THE REST OF YOUR STUDYING AT HOME.
ALMOST DONE, MS. ALVARADO.
THANK YOU FOR VISITING THE WEST-REEVE SCHOOL LIBRARY
Please be a hero and keep conversation to a minimum
THE (SORTA) RECENT PAST.*
*DAYS AFTER THE EVENTS OF ADVENTURES OF THE SUPER SONS. --Paul and those who are keeping score
DOOM ON THE HORIZON
story & words: PETER J. TOMASI - art: MAX RAYNO
colors: LUIS GUERRERO - letters: ROB LEIGH
cover by JORGE JIMENEZ and ALEJANDRO SÁNCHEZ
variant cover by SIMONE DI MEO
assoc. editor: DAVE WIELGOSZ - editor: PAUL KAMINS
Superboy created by Jerry Siegel.
By special arrangement with the Jerry Siegel Family.
DID YOU FINISH, SCOOP?
LAUGH IT UP, DAMIAN, BUT SOMEONE HAS TO PRESENT THE TRUTH.
THE SCHOOL'S GOT A CHEATING SCANDAL. I'VE BEEN WORKING ON IT FOR WEEKS AND I CAN SMELL A STORY.
JUST GOTTA FIT THE PIECES TOGETHER.
I ALREADY SOLVED IT.
LIKE MY MOM ALWAYS SAYS, A GOOD REPORTER DOESN'T GET GREAT STORIES, A GOOD REPORTER MAKES THEM.
WAIT A SEC-- WHAT DID YOU SAY?

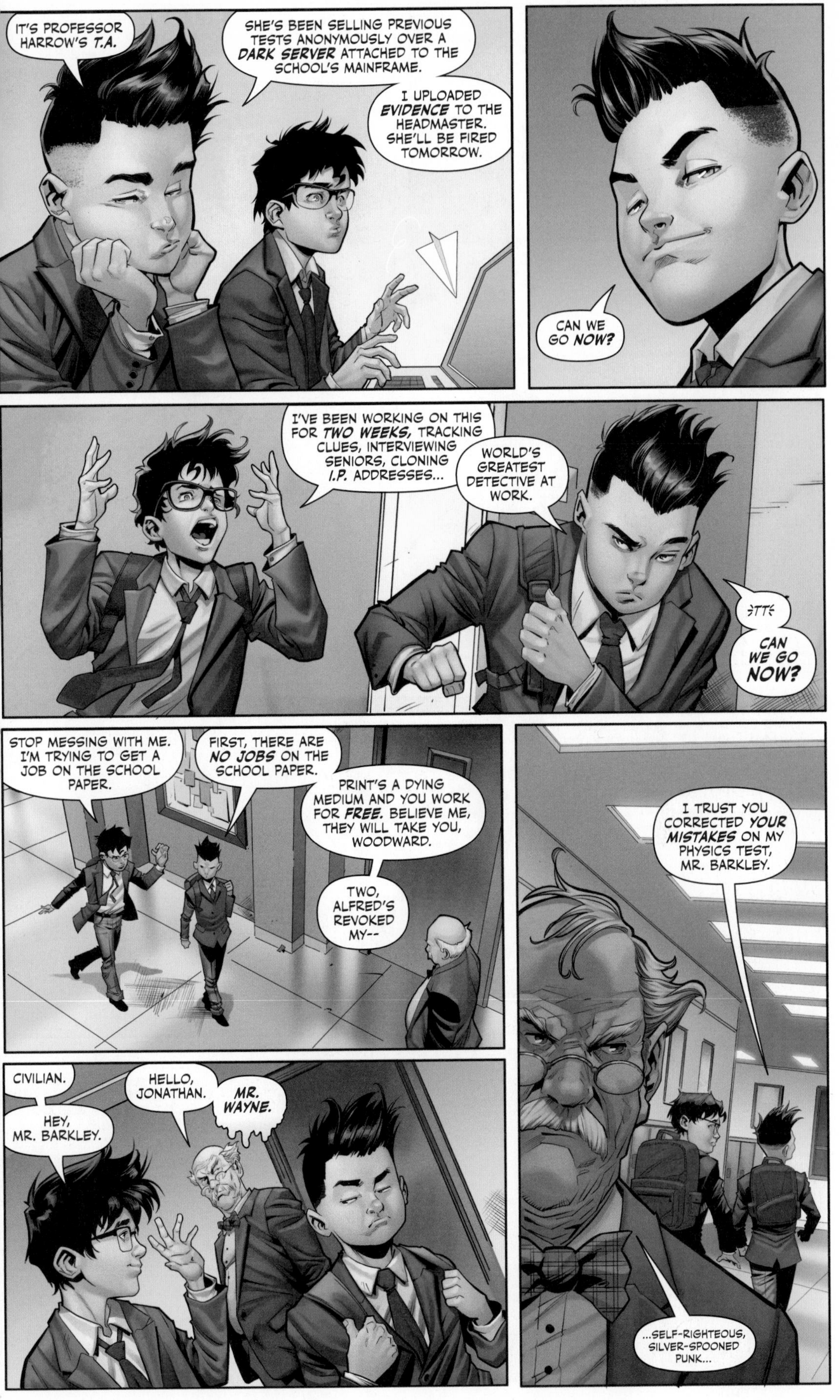
IT'S PROFESSOR HARROW'S *T.A.*
SHE'S BEEN SELLING PREVIOUS TESTS ANONYMOUSLY OVER A *DARK SERVER* ATTACHED TO THE SCHOOL'S MAINFRAME.
I UPLOADED *EVIDENCE* TO THE HEADMASTER. SHE'LL BE FIRED TOMORROW.
CAN WE GO *NOW?*
I'VE BEEN WORKING ON THIS FOR *TWO WEEKS,* TRACKING CLUES, INTERVIEWING SENIORS, CLONING *I.P.* ADDRESSES...
WORLD'S GREATEST DETECTIVE AT WORK.
TT
CAN WE GO NOW?
STOP MESSING WITH ME. I'M TRYING TO GET A JOB ON THE SCHOOL PAPER.
FIRST, THERE ARE *NO JOBS* ON THE SCHOOL PAPER.
PRINT'S A DYING MEDIUM AND YOU WORK FOR *FREE.* BELIEVE ME, THEY WILL TAKE YOU, WOODWARD.
TWO, ALFRED'S REVOKED MY--
CIVILIAN.
HEY, MR. BARKLEY.
HELLO, JONATHAN.
MR. WAYNE.
I TRUST YOU CORRECTED *YOUR MISTAKES* ON MY PHYSICS TEST, MR. BARKLEY.
...SELF-RIGHTEOUS, SILVER-SPOONED PUNK...

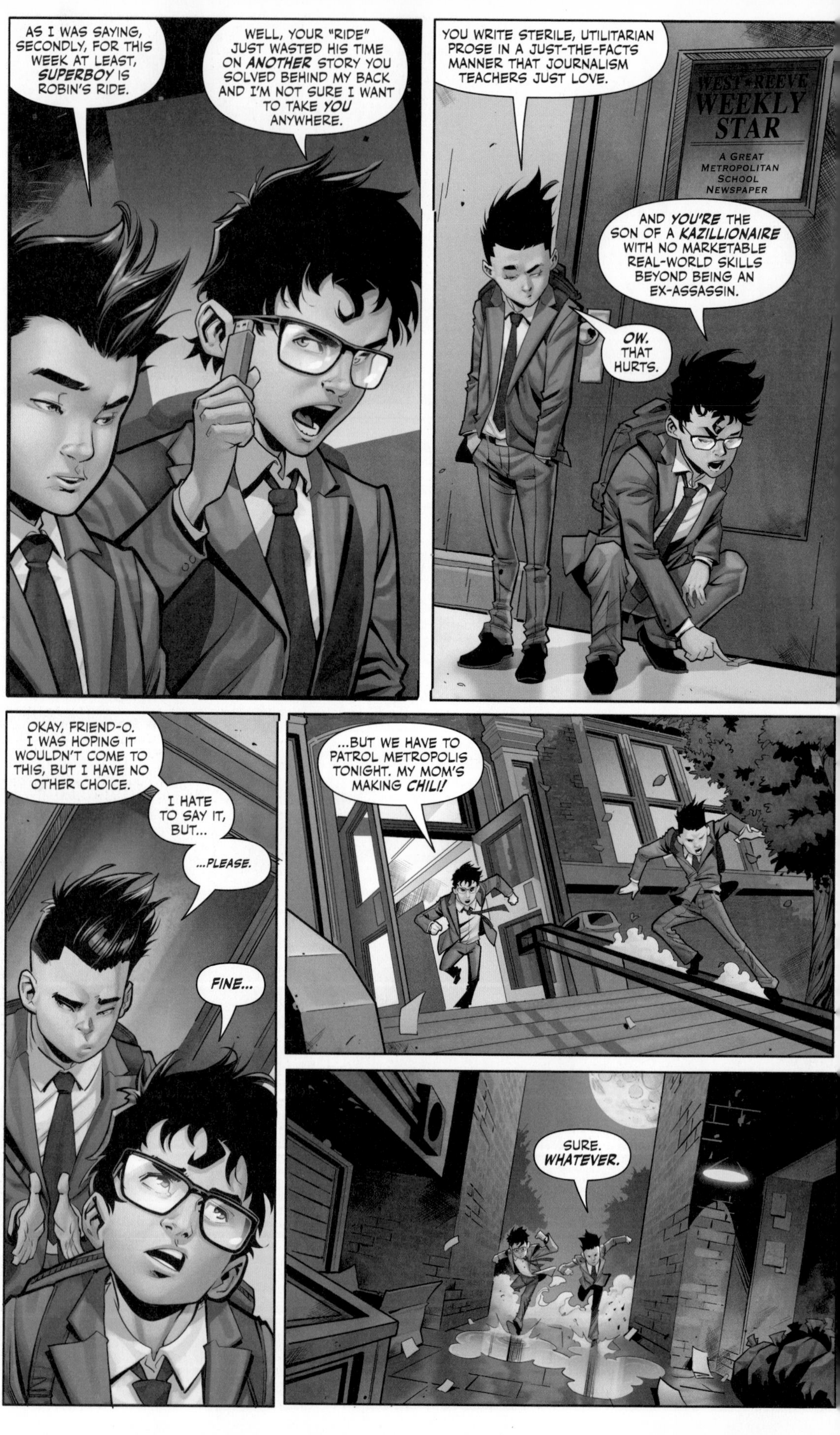
AS I WAS SAYING, SECONDLY, FOR THIS WEEK AT LEAST, SUPERBOY IS ROBIN'S RIDE.
WELL, YOUR "RIDE" JUST WASTED HIS TIME ON ANOTHER STORY YOU SOLVED BEHIND MY BACK AND I'M NOT SURE I WANT TO TAKE YOU ANYWHERE.
YOU WRITE STERILE, UTILITARIAN PROSE IN A JUST-THE-FACTS MANNER THAT JOURNALISM TEACHERS JUST LOVE.
WEST★REEVE WEEKLY STAR
A GREAT METROPOLITAN SCHOOL NEWSPAPER
AND YOU'RE THE SON OF A KAZILLIONAIRE WITH NO MARKETABLE REAL-WORLD SKILLS BEYOND BEING AN EX-ASSASSIN.
OW. THAT HURTS.
OKAY, FRIEND-O. I WAS HOPING IT WOULDN'T COME TO THIS, BUT I HAVE NO OTHER CHOICE.
I HATE TO SAY IT, BUT...
...PLEASE.
FINE...
...BUT WE HAVE TO PATROL METROPOLIS TONIGHT. MY MOM'S MAKING CHILI!
SURE. WHATEVER.

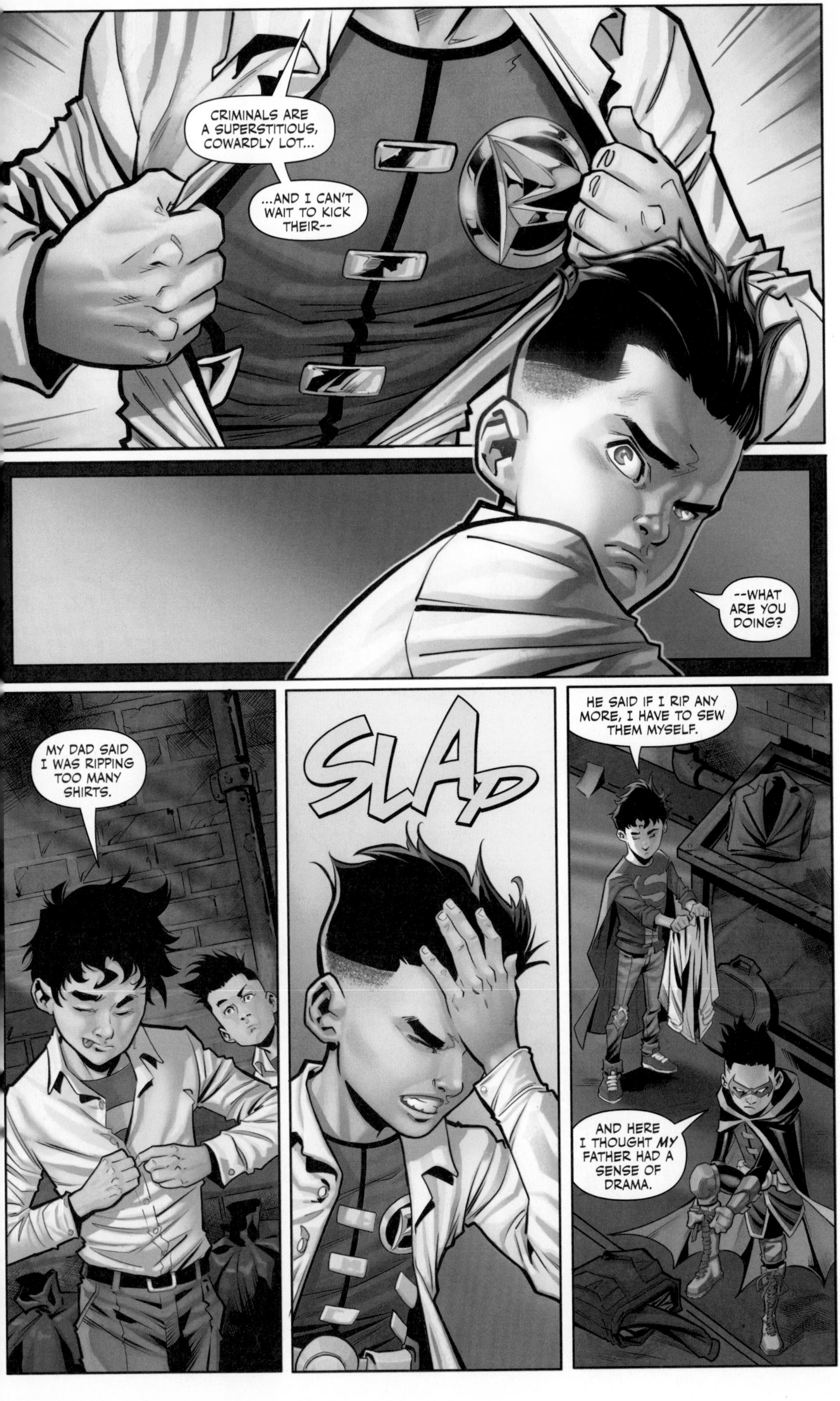
CRIMINALS ARE A SUPERSTITIOUS, COWARDLY LOT...
...AND I CAN'T WAIT TO KICK THEIR--
--WHAT ARE YOU DOING?
MY DAD SAID I WAS RIPPING TOO MANY SHIRTS.
SLAP
HE SAID IF I RIP ANY MORE, I HAVE TO SEW THEM MYSELF.
AND HERE I THOUGHT MY FATHER HAD A SENSE OF DRAMA.

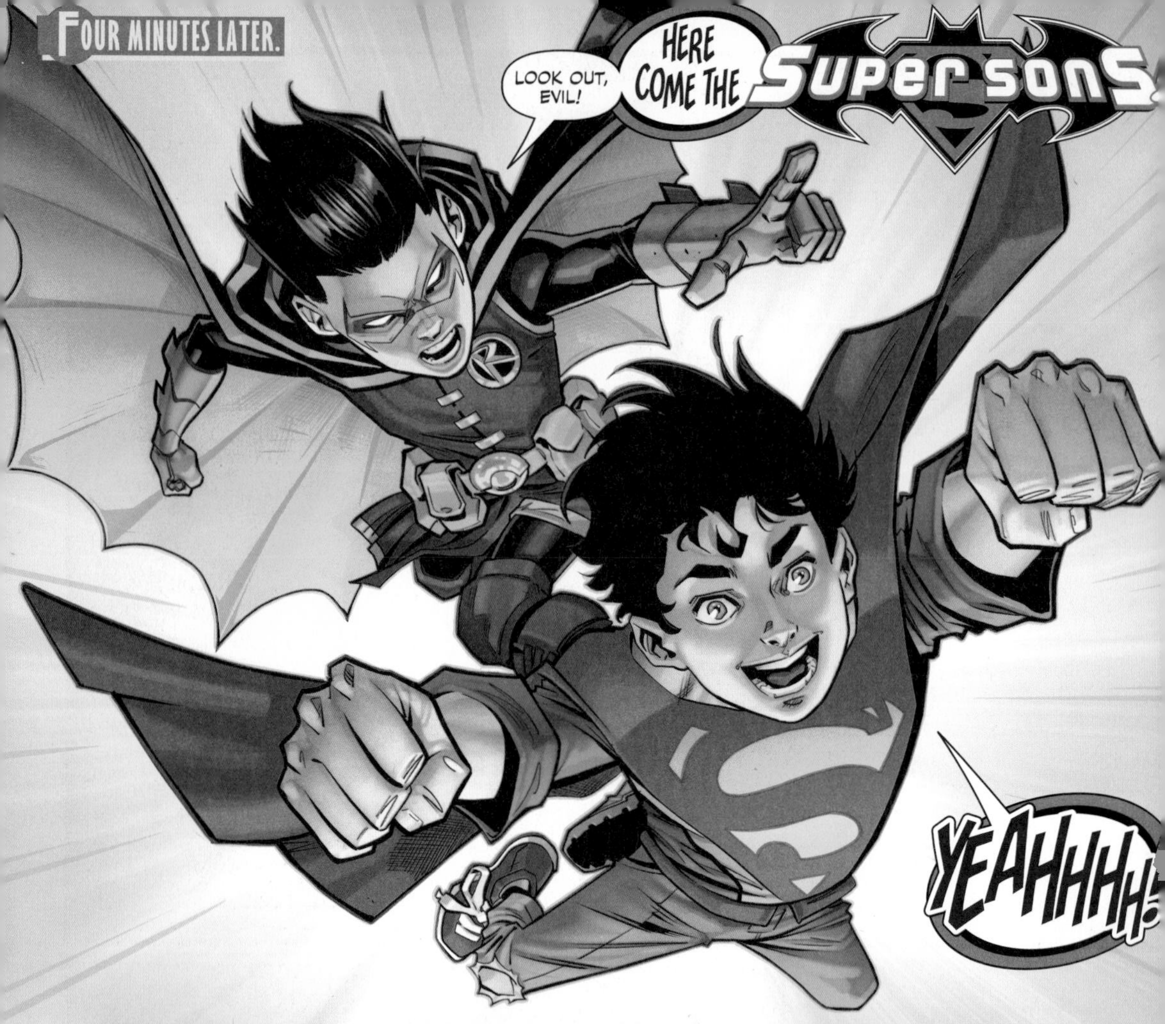
FOUR MINUTES LATER.
LOOK OUT, EVIL!
HERE COME THE
Super sons
YEAHHHH!

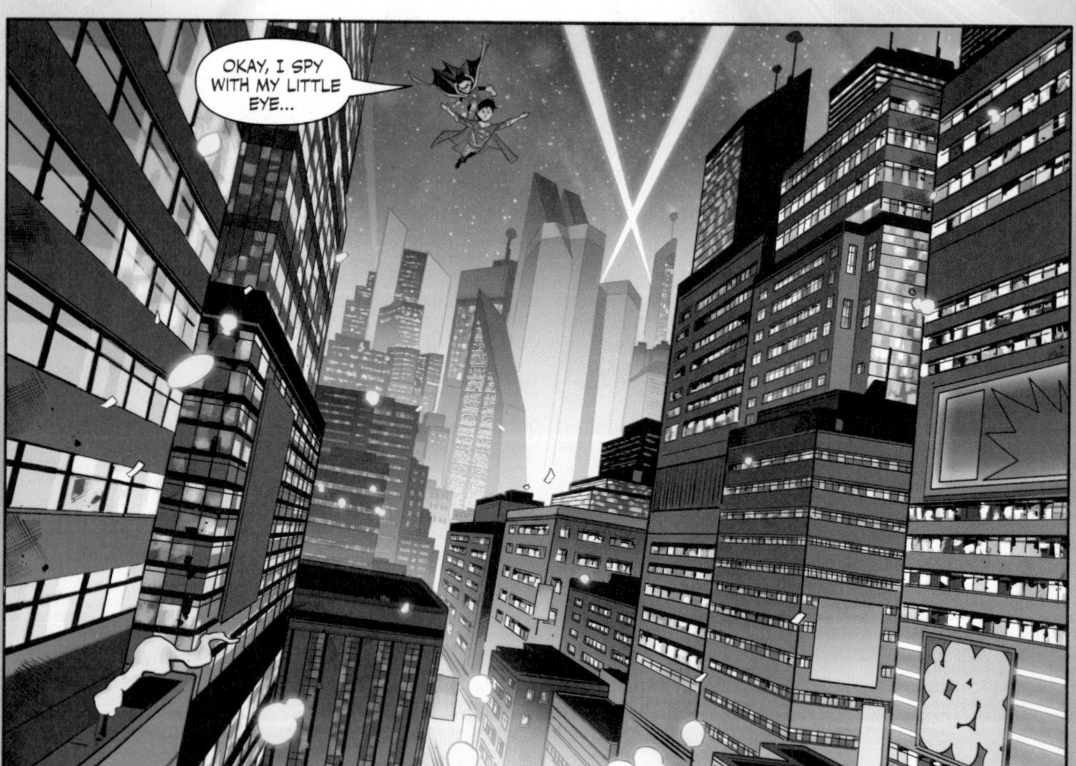
OKAY, I SPY WITH MY LITTLE EYE...

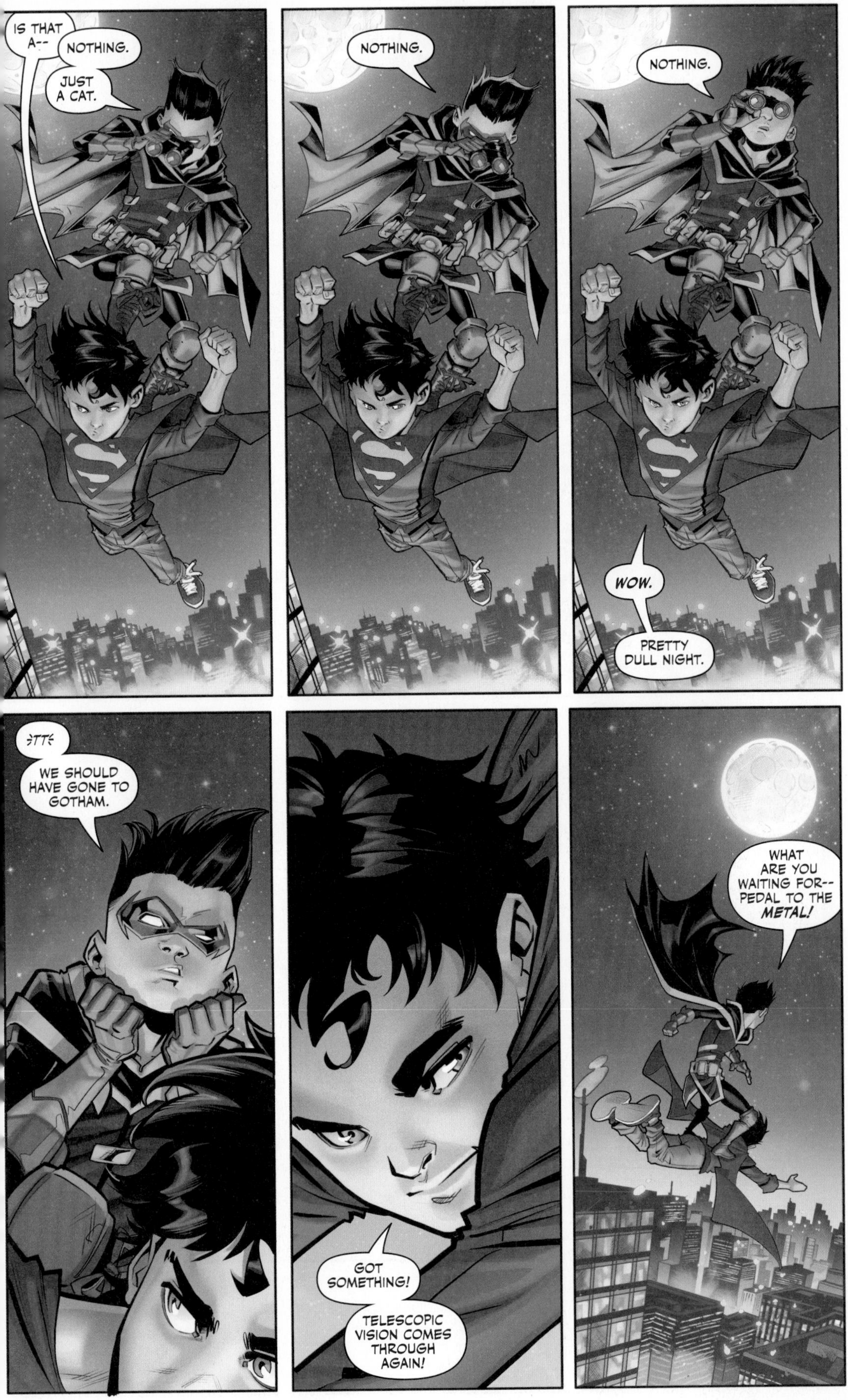
IS THAT A--
NOTHING.
JUST A CAT.
NOTHING.
NOTHING.
WOW.
PRETTY DULL NIGHT.
ᵎTTᵎ
WE SHOULD HAVE GONE TO GOTHAM.
GOT SOMETHING!
TELESCOPIC VISION COMES THROUGH AGAIN!
WHAT ARE YOU WAITING FOR--PEDAL TO THE METAL!

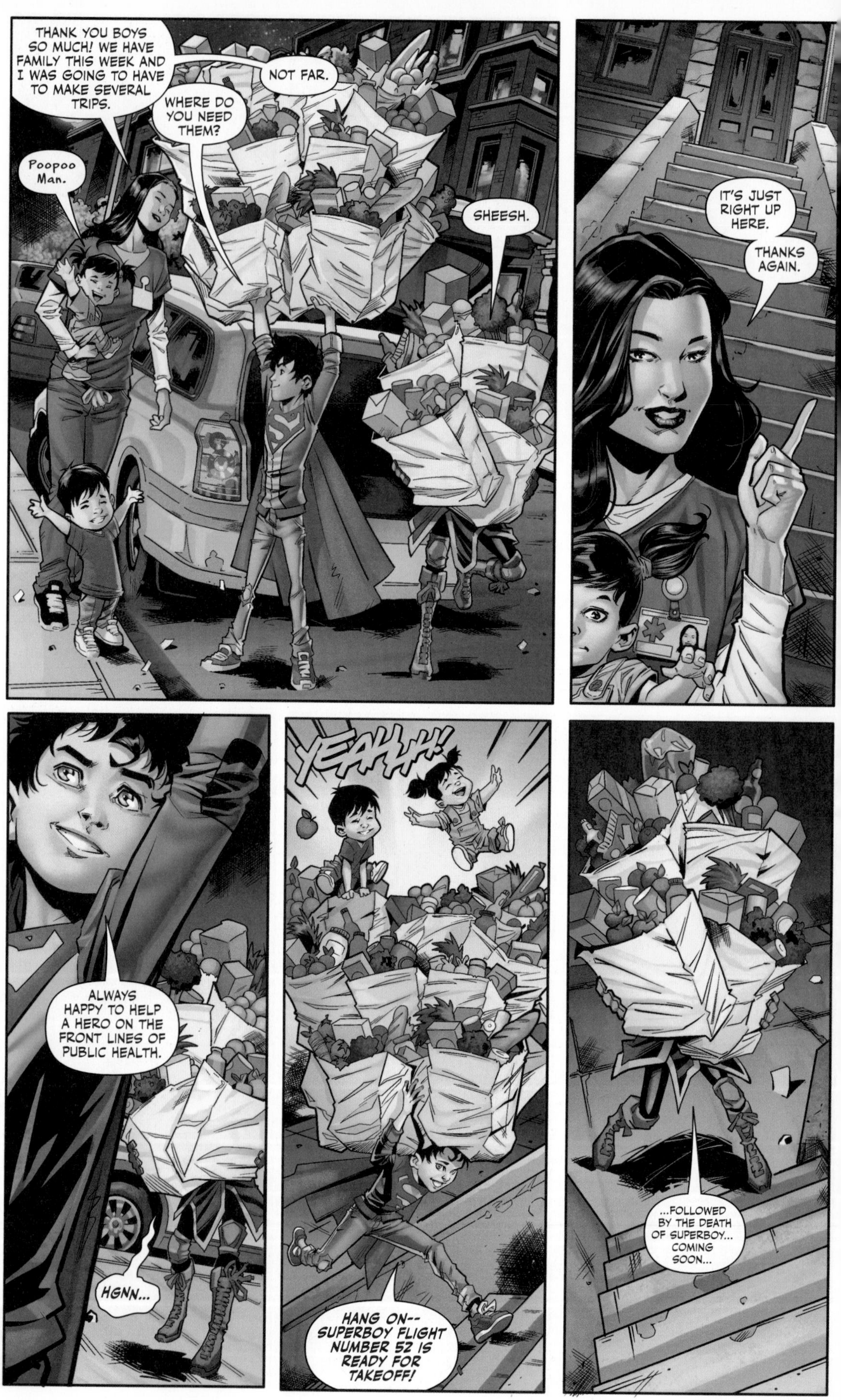

THANK YOU BOYS SO MUCH! WE HAVE FAMILY THIS WEEK AND I WAS GOING TO HAVE TO MAKE SEVERAL TRIPS.
WHERE DO YOU NEED THEM?
NOT FAR.
Poopoo Man.
SHEESH.
IT'S JUST RIGHT UP HERE.
THANKS AGAIN.
ALWAYS HAPPY TO HELP A HERO ON THE FRONT LINES OF PUBLIC HEALTH.
HGNN...
YEAHHH!
HANG ON-- SUPERBOY FLIGHT NUMBER 52 IS READY FOR TAKEOFF!
...FOLLOWED BY THE DEATH OF SUPERBOY... COMING SOON...

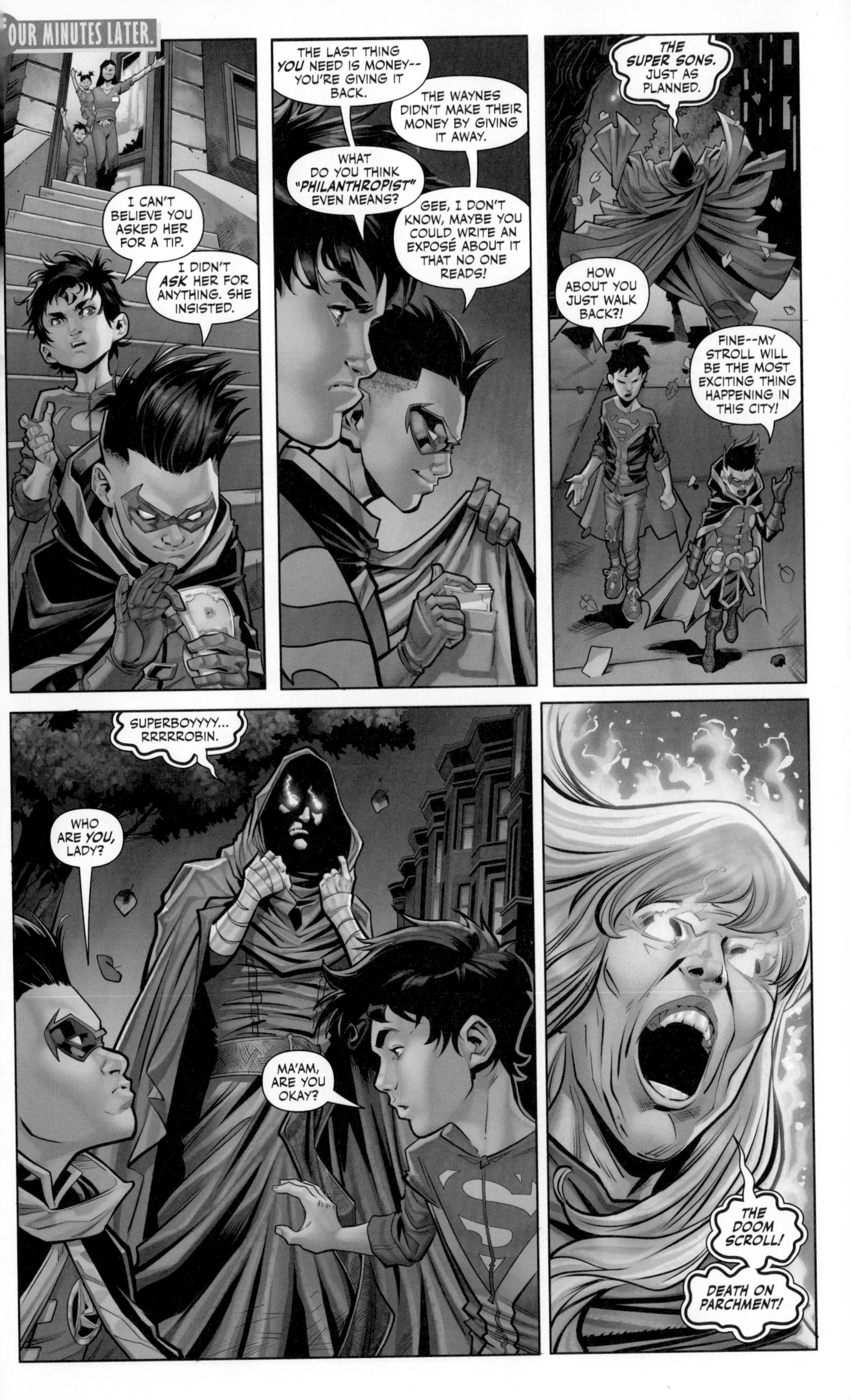
OUR MINUTES LATER.
I CAN'T BELIEVE YOU ASKED HER FOR A TIP.
I DIDN'T ASK HER FOR ANYTHING. SHE INSISTED.
THE LAST THING YOU NEED IS MONEY-- YOU'RE GIVING IT BACK.
THE WAYNES DIDN'T MAKE THEIR MONEY BY GIVING IT AWAY.
WHAT DO YOU THINK "PHILANTHROPIST" EVEN MEANS?
GEE, I DON'T KNOW, MAYBE YOU COULD WRITE AN EXPOSÉ ABOUT IT THAT NO ONE READS!
THE SUPER SONS. JUST AS PLANNED.
HOW ABOUT YOU JUST WALK BACK?!
FINE--MY STROLL WILL BE THE MOST EXCITING THING HAPPENING IN THIS CITY!
SUPERBOYYYY... RRRRROBIN.
WHO ARE YOU, LADY?
MA'AM, ARE YOU OKAY?
THE DOOM SCROLL!
DEATH ON PARCHMENT!

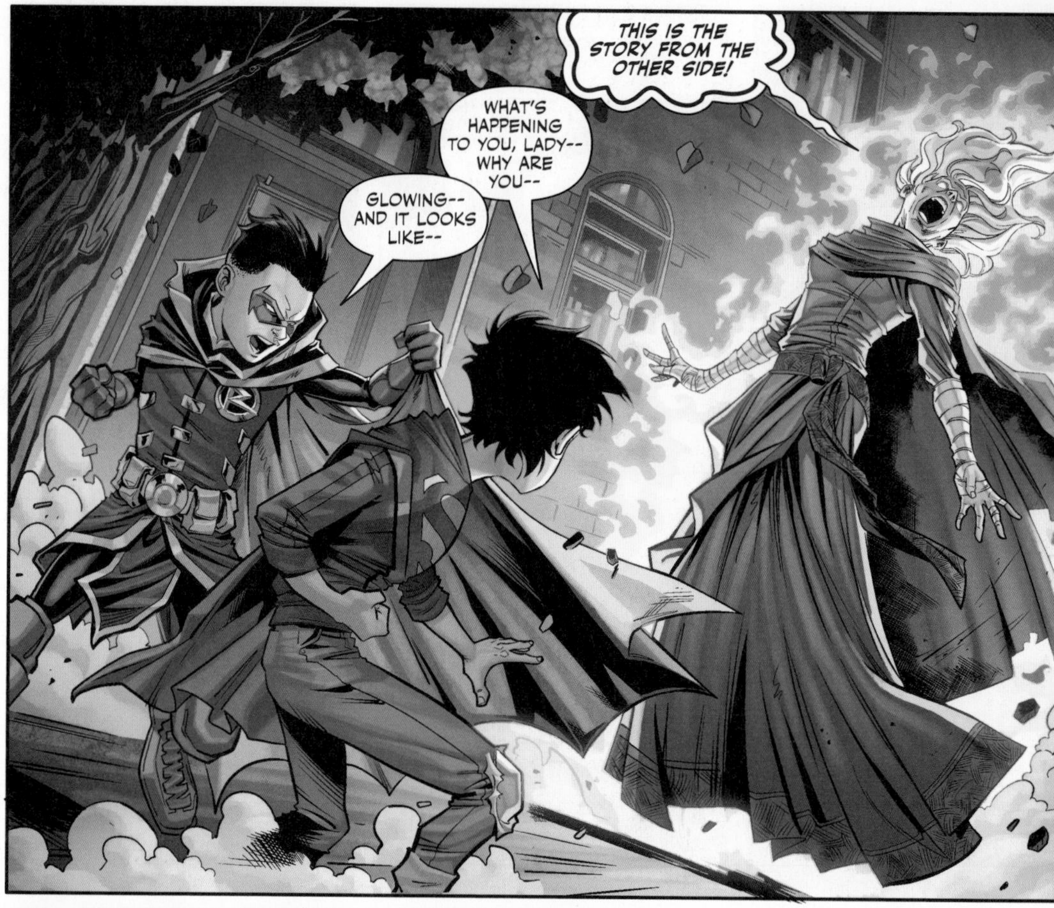
THIS IS THE STORY FROM THE OTHER SIDE!
WHAT'S HAPPENING TO YOU, LADY-- WHY ARE YOU--
GLOWING-- AND IT LOOKS LIKE--

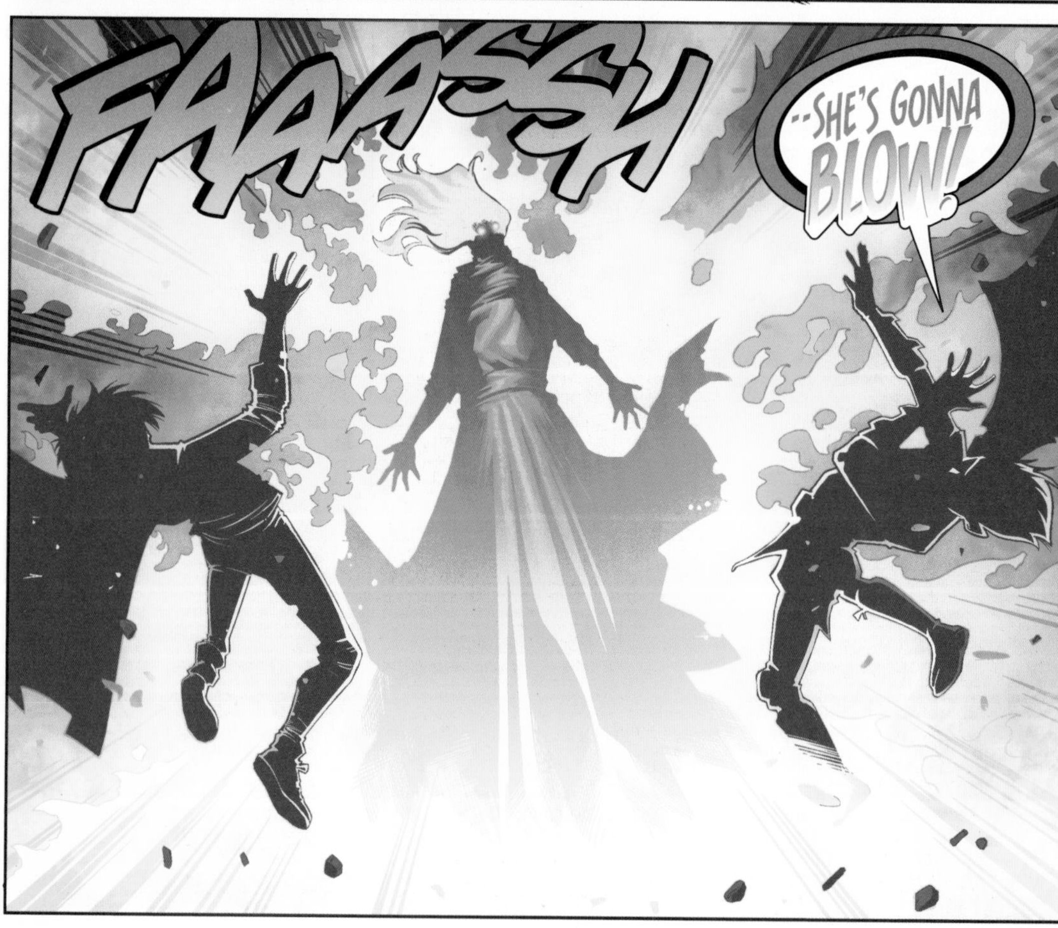
FAAASSH
--SHE'S GONNA BLOW!

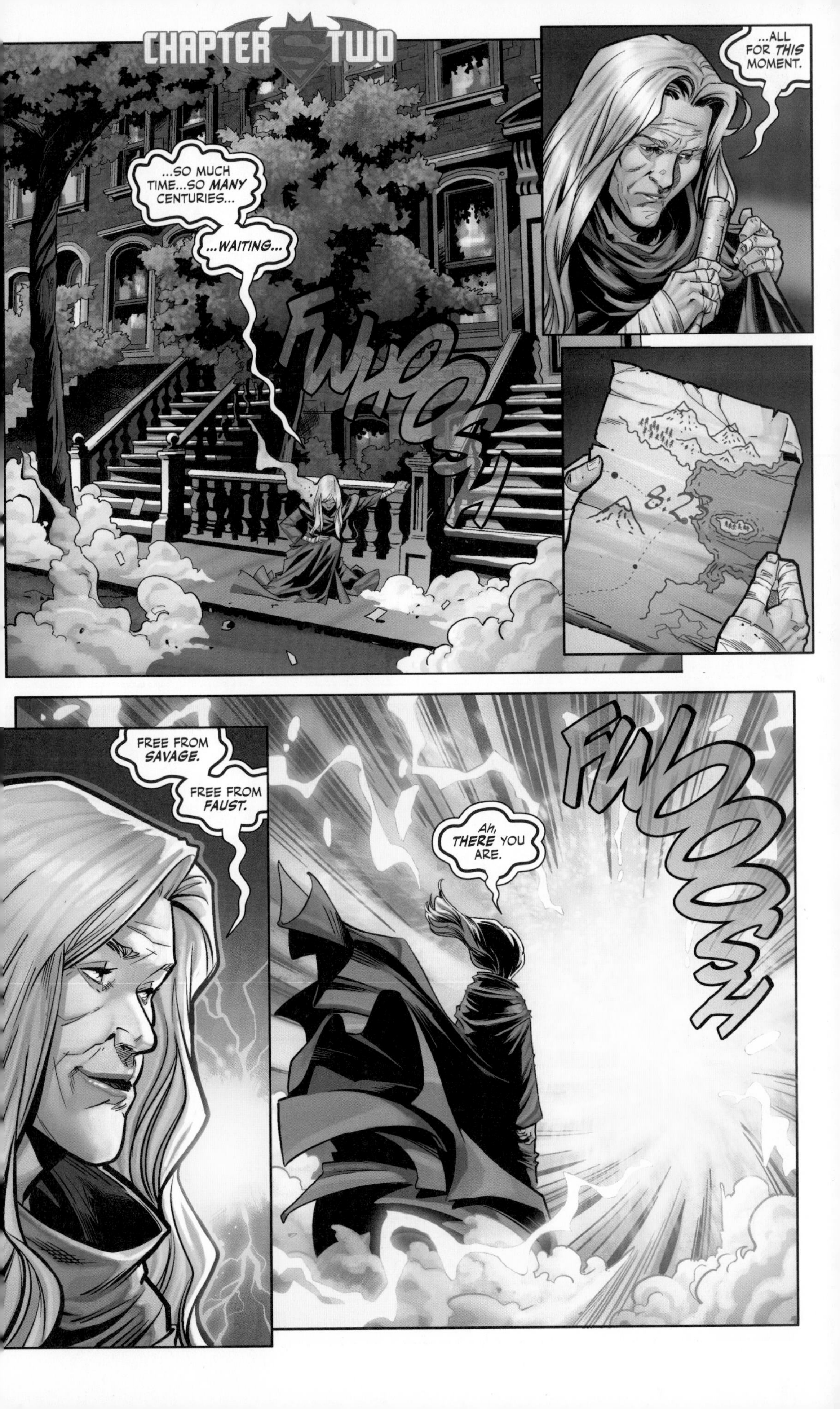
CHAPTER TWO
...SO MUCH TIME...SO MANY CENTURIES...
...WAITING...
FWHOOSH
...ALL FOR THIS MOMENT.
8:23
FREE FROM SAVAGE.
FREE FROM FAUST.
Ah, THERE YOU ARE.
FWOOOOSH

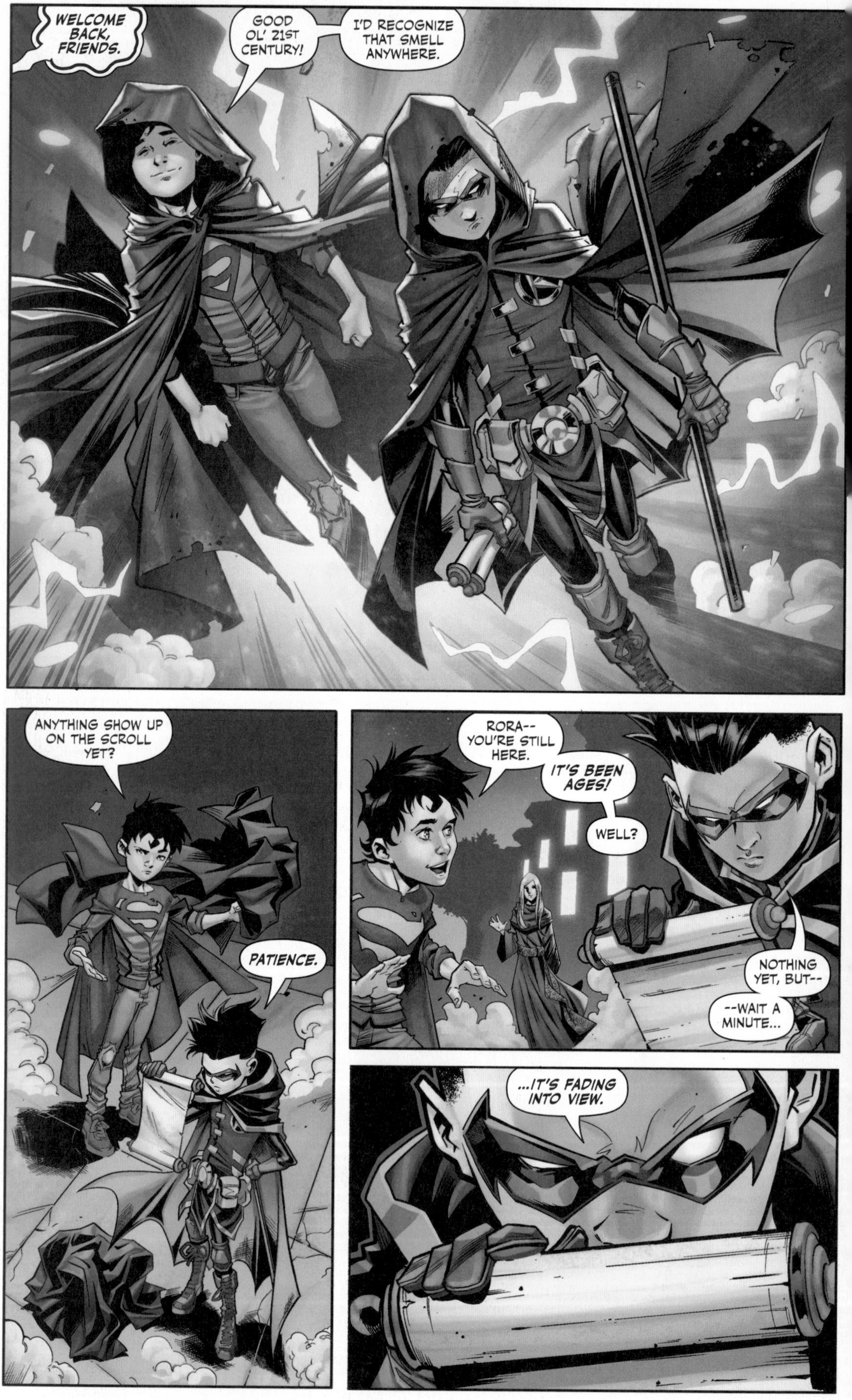
WELCOME BACK, FRIENDS.
GOOD OL' 21ST CENTURY!
I'D RECOGNIZE THAT SMELL ANYWHERE.
ANYTHING SHOW UP ON THE SCROLL YET?
PATIENCE.
RORA-- YOU'RE STILL HERE.
IT'S BEEN AGES!
WELL?
NOTHING YET, BUT--
--WAIT A MINUTE...
...IT'S FADING INTO VIEW.

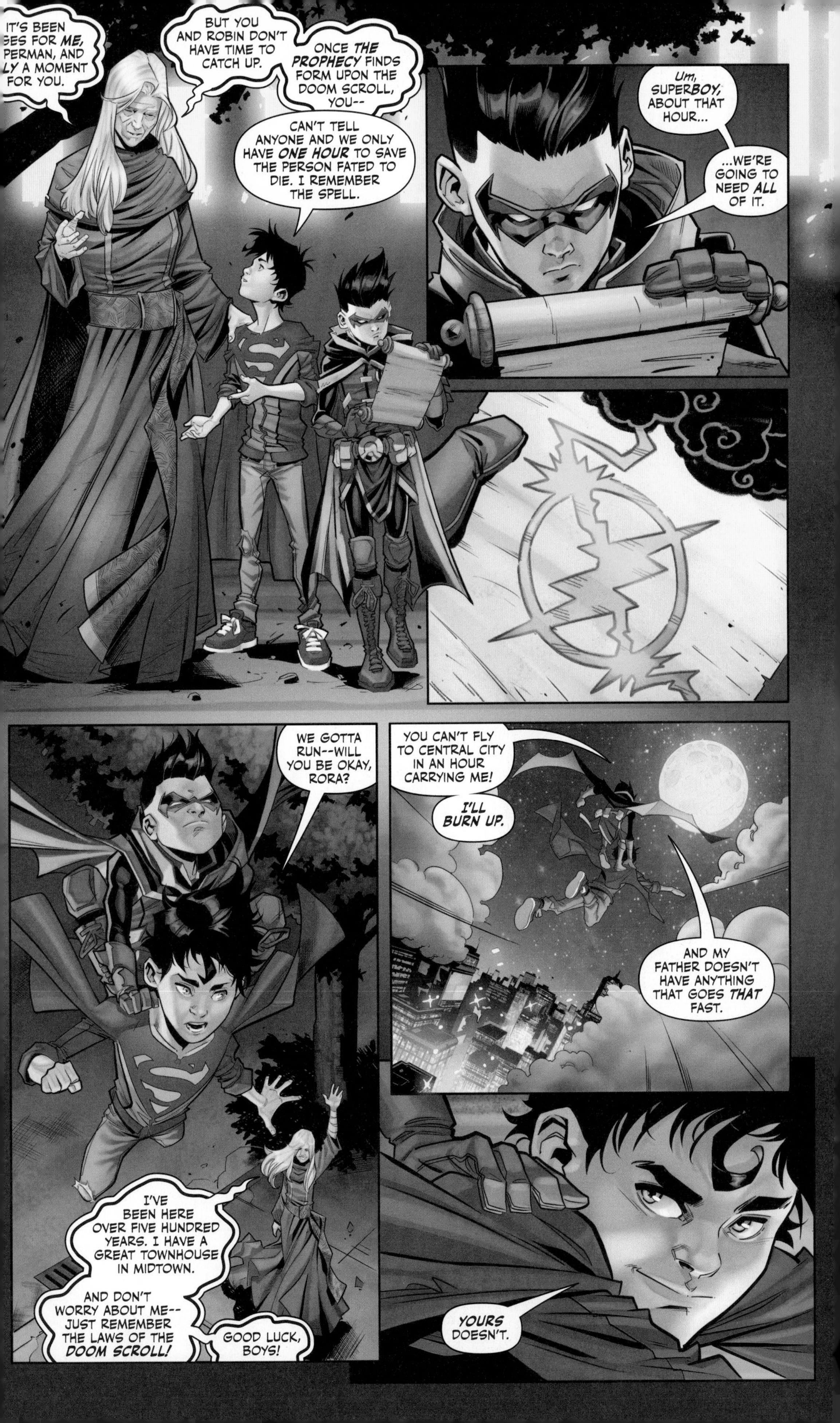
IT'S BEEN
GES FOR ME,
PERMAN, AND
LY A MOMENT
FOR YOU.
BUT YOU AND ROBIN DON'T HAVE TIME TO CATCH UP.
ONCE THE PROPHECY FINDS FORM UPON THE DOOM SCROLL, YOU--
CAN'T TELL ANYONE AND WE ONLY HAVE ONE HOUR TO SAVE THE PERSON FATED TO DIE. I REMEMBER THE SPELL.
Um, SUPERBOY, ABOUT THAT HOUR...
...WE'RE GOING TO NEED ALL OF IT.
WE GOTTA RUN--WILL YOU BE OKAY, RORA?
I'VE BEEN HERE OVER FIVE HUNDRED YEARS. I HAVE A GREAT TOWNHOUSE IN MIDTOWN.
AND DON'T WORRY ABOUT ME--JUST REMEMBER THE LAWS OF THE DOOM SCROLL!
GOOD LUCK, BOYS!
YOU CAN'T FLY TO CENTRAL CITY IN AN HOUR CARRYING ME!
I'LL BURN UP.
AND MY FATHER DOESN'T HAVE ANYTHING THAT GOES THAT FAST.
YOURS DOESN'T.

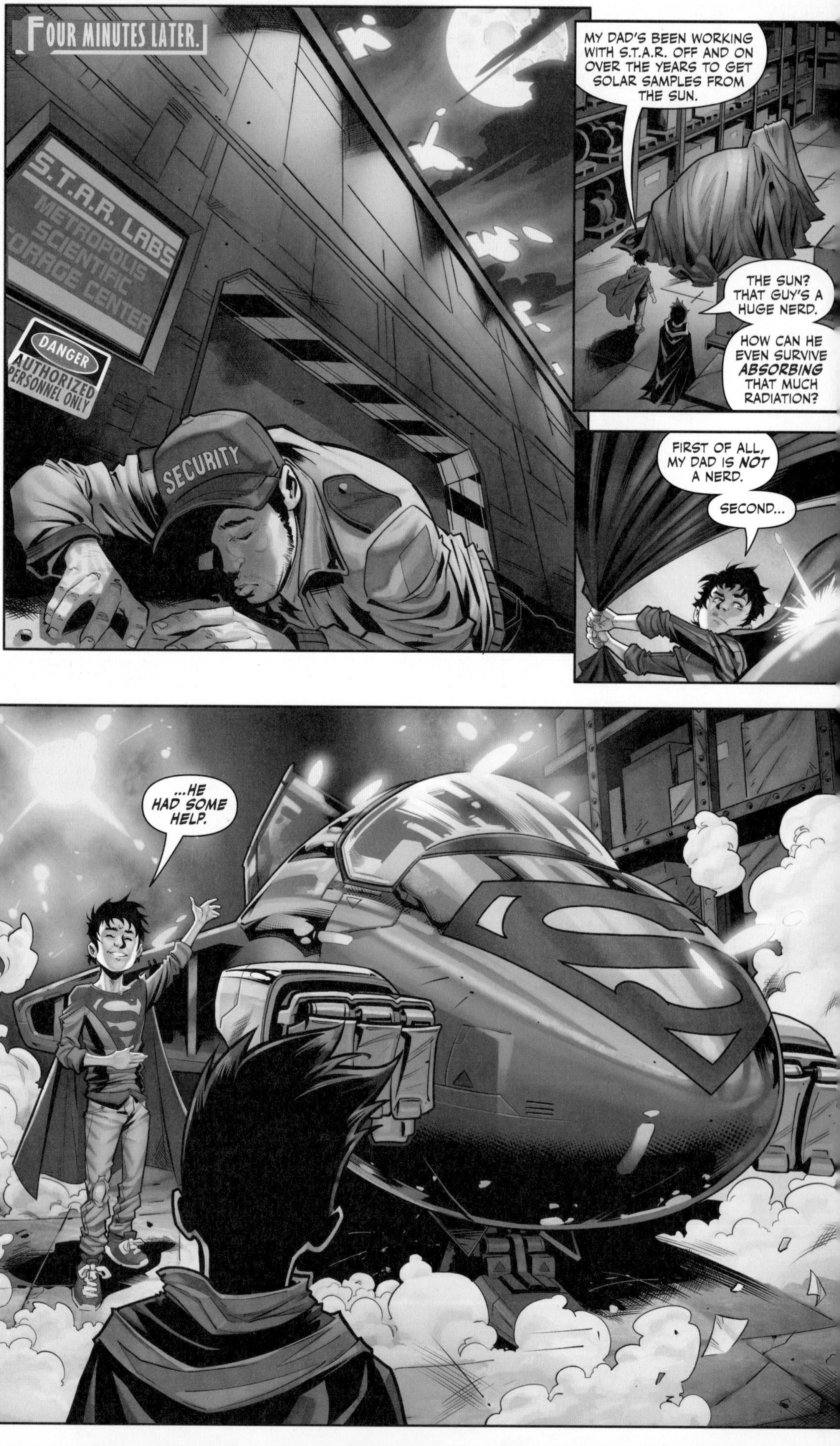
FOUR MINUTES LATER.
S.T.A.R. LABS
METROPOLIS SCIENTIFIC STORAGE CENTER
DANGER
AUTHORIZED PERSONNEL ONLY
SECURITY
MY DAD'S BEEN WORKING WITH S.T.A.R. OFF AND ON OVER THE YEARS TO GET SOLAR SAMPLES FROM THE SUN.
THE SUN? THAT GUY'S A HUGE NERD.
HOW CAN HE EVEN SURVIVE ABSORBING THAT MUCH RADIATION?
FIRST OF ALL, MY DAD IS NOT A NERD.
SECOND...
...HE HAD SOME HELP.

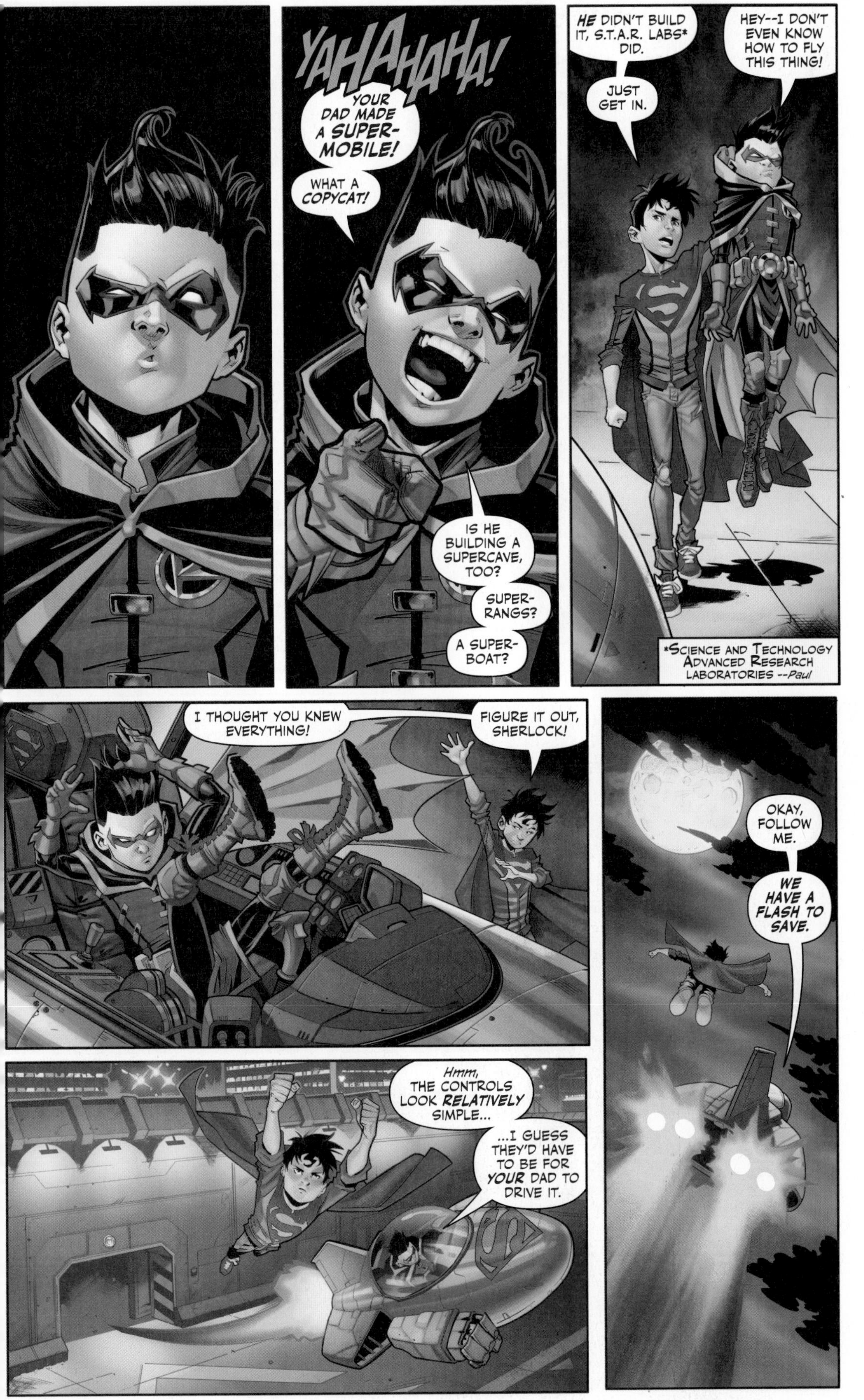
YAHAHAHAHA!
YOUR DAD MADE A SUPER-MOBILE!
WHAT A COPYCAT!
IS HE BUILDING A SUPERCAVE, TOO?
SUPER-RANGS?
A SUPER-BOAT?
HE DIDN'T BUILD IT, S.T.A.R. LABS* DID.
JUST GET IN.
HEY--I DON'T EVEN KNOW HOW TO FLY THIS THING!
*SCIENCE AND TECHNOLOGY ADVANCED RESEARCH LABORATORIES --Paul
I THOUGHT YOU KNEW EVERYTHING!
FIGURE IT OUT, SHERLOCK!
Hmm, THE CONTROLS LOOK RELATIVELY SIMPLE...
...I GUESS THEY'D HAVE TO BE FOR YOUR DAD TO DRIVE IT.
OKAY, FOLLOW ME.
WE HAVE A FLASH TO SAVE.

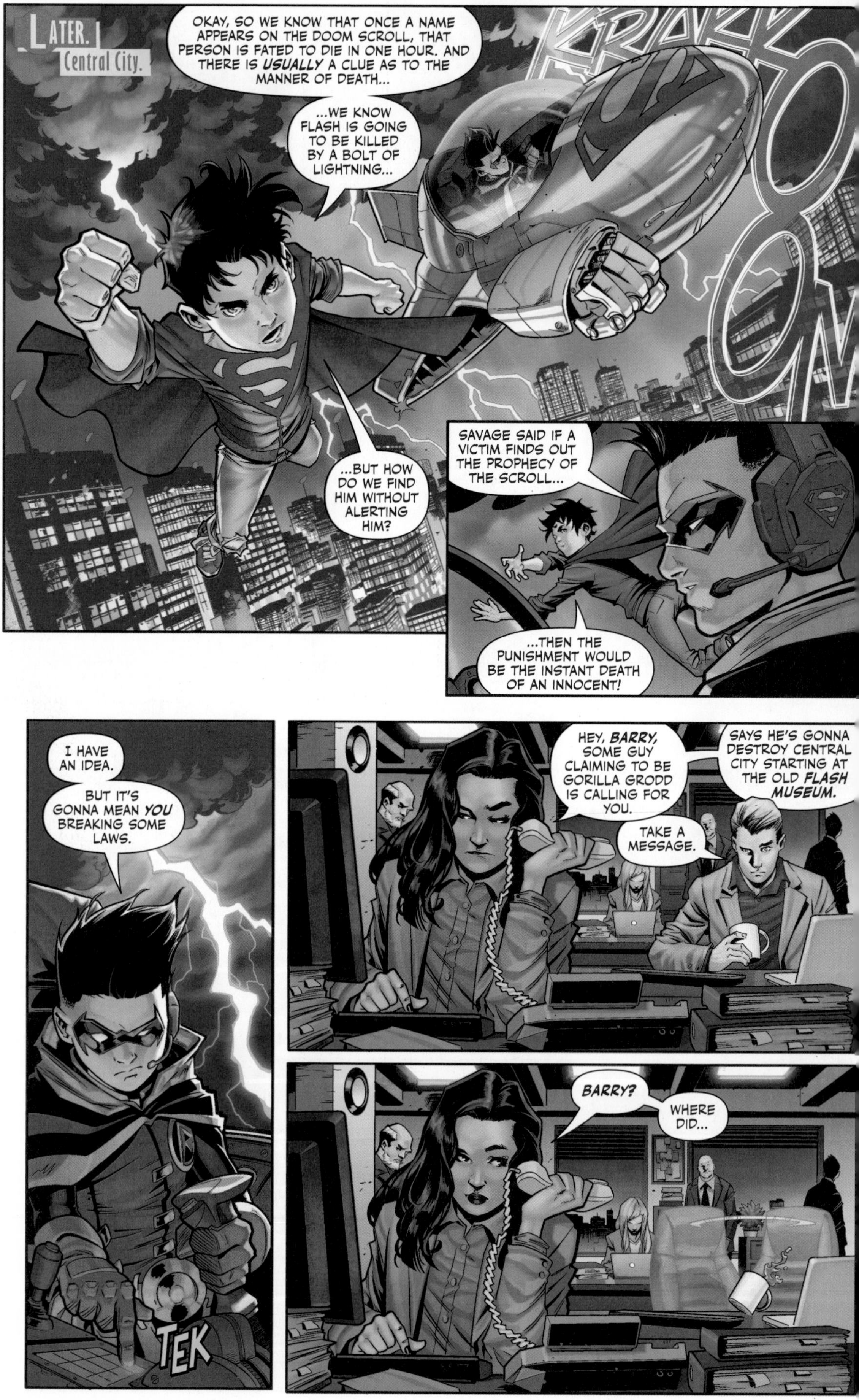
LATER. Central City.
OKAY, SO WE KNOW THAT ONCE A NAME APPEARS ON THE DOOM SCROLL, THAT PERSON IS FATED TO DIE IN ONE HOUR. AND THERE IS USUALLY A CLUE AS TO THE MANNER OF DEATH...
...WE KNOW FLASH IS GOING TO BE KILLED BY A BOLT OF LIGHTNING...
...BUT HOW DO WE FIND HIM WITHOUT ALERTING HIM?
SAVAGE SAID IF A VICTIM FINDS OUT THE PROPHECY OF THE SCROLL...
...THEN THE PUNISHMENT WOULD BE THE INSTANT DEATH OF AN INNOCENT!
I HAVE AN IDEA.
BUT IT'S GONNA MEAN YOU BREAKING SOME LAWS.
TEK
HEY, BARRY, SOME GUY CLAIMING TO BE GORILLA GRODD IS CALLING FOR YOU.
SAYS HE'S GONNA DESTROY CENTRAL CITY STARTING AT THE OLD FLASH MUSEUM.
TAKE A MESSAGE.
BARRY?
WHERE DID...

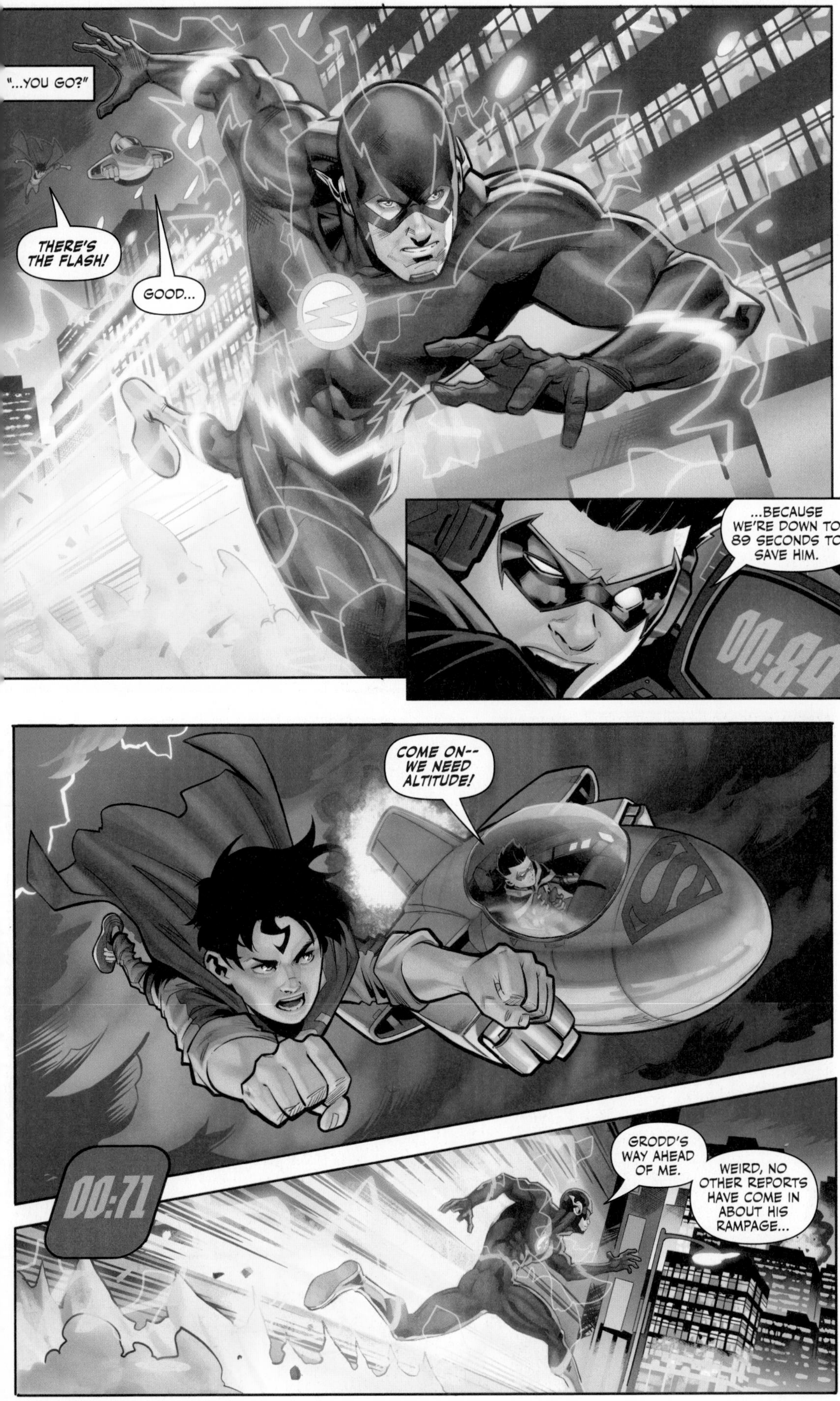
"...YOU GO?"
THERE'S THE FLASH!
GOOD...
...BECAUSE WE'RE DOWN TO 89 SECONDS TO SAVE HIM.
00:89
COME ON-- WE NEED ALTITUDE!
00:71
GRODD'S WAY AHEAD OF ME.
WEIRD, NO OTHER REPORTS HAVE COME IN ABOUT HIS RAMPAGE...

...BUT IT DOESN'T TAKE *BATMAN* TO FOLLOW THESE *CLUES*.

LIGHTNING IS STARTING TO STRIKE ACROSS THE CITY, WE'RE RUNNING OUT OF TIME!

FOLLOW FROM ABOVE WHILE I CALCULATE ATMOSPHERIC CONVECTION AND FIGURE OUT HOW TO CATCH THE HYDROMETEOR COLLISION LOCATION.

HUH?

00:19

I'M TRYING TO PREDICT LIGHTNING, KNUCKLEHEAD!

JUST GO!

DAMMIT--THERE'S NO LIGHTNING STRIKING CLOSE IN THE AREA THAT I CAN TRACK-- IT'S COMPLETELY RANDOM.

THERE'S NO WAY I CAN PREDICT THE EXACT PATH-- *WAIT!*

00:05

JON!

FLY LOW AND HOLD THIS!

00:02

00:00

GOTTA SAY, THAT LITTLE *NUT DOES* HAVE GOOD IDEAS.

HOPE THIS DOESN'T HURT TOO--

KRA KA

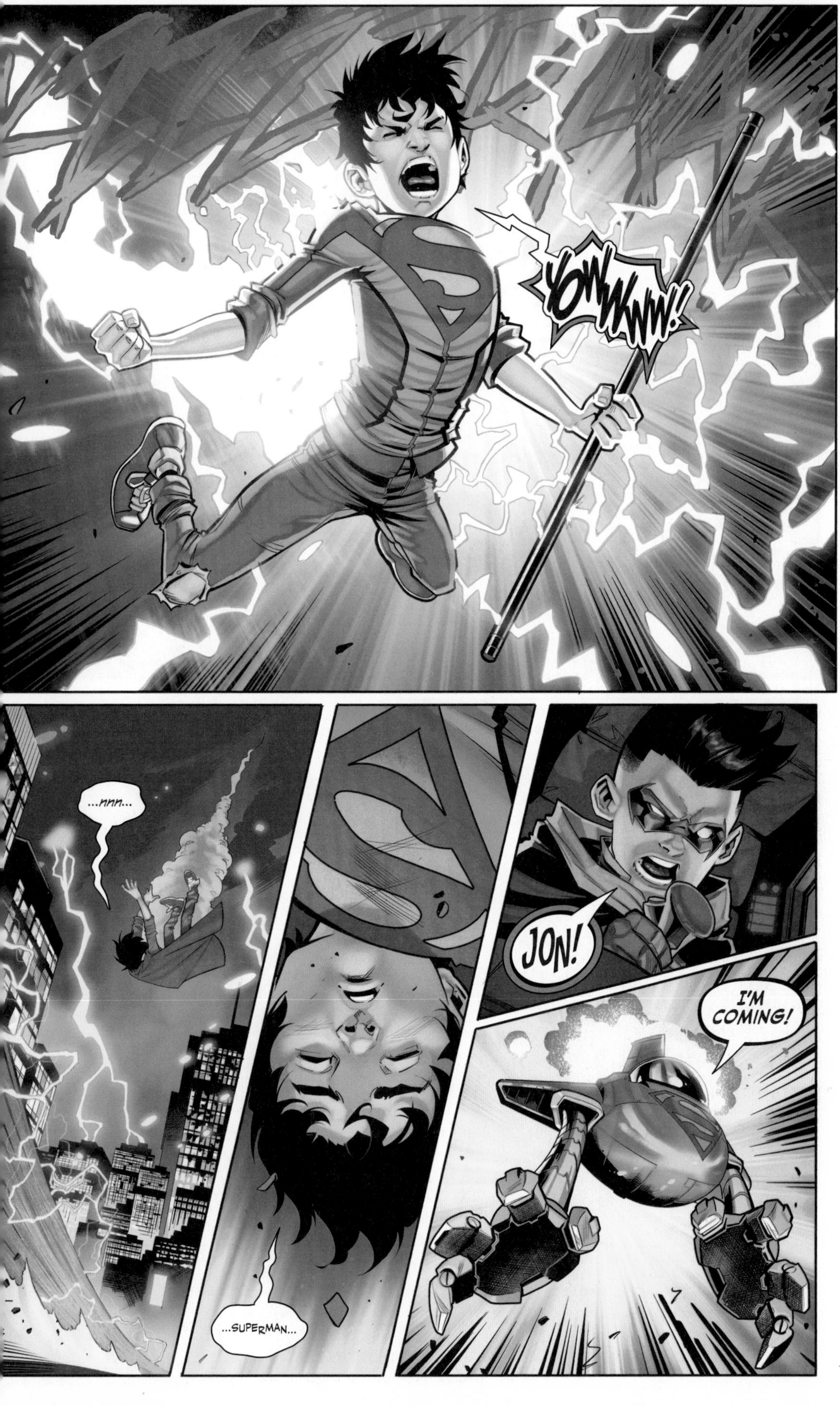

YOWWWW!
...nnn...
...SUPERMAN...
JON!
I'M COMING!

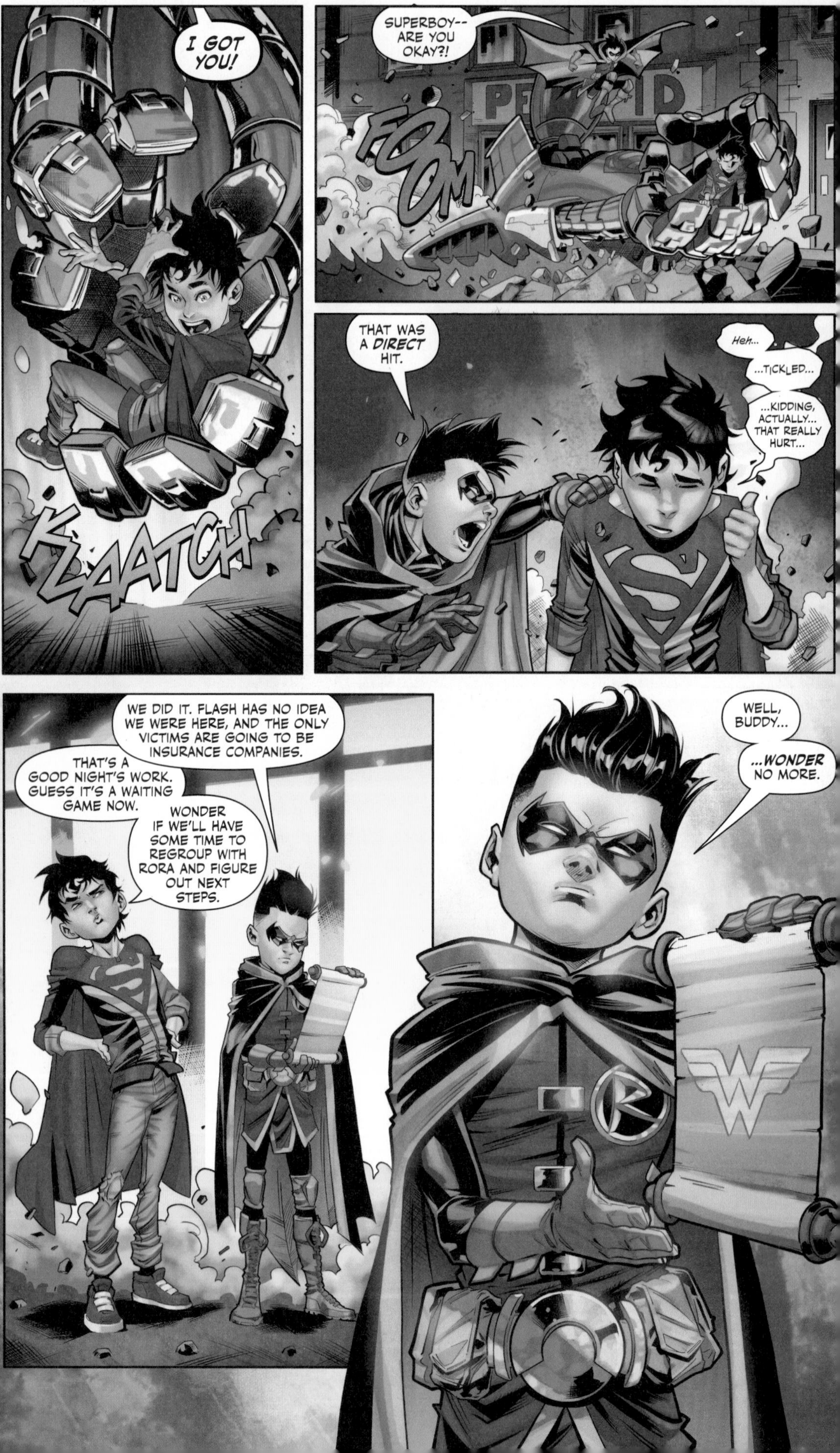
I GOT YOU!
KLAATCH
SUPERBOY-- ARE YOU OKAY?!
FOOM
THAT WAS A *DIRECT* HIT.
Heh...
...TICKLED...
...KIDDING, ACTUALLY... THAT REALLY HURT...
WE DID IT. FLASH HAS NO IDEA WE WERE HERE, AND THE ONLY VICTIMS ARE GOING TO BE INSURANCE COMPANIES.
THAT'S A GOOD NIGHT'S WORK. GUESS IT'S A WAITING GAME NOW.
WONDER IF WE'LL HAVE SOME TIME TO REGROUP WITH RORA AND FIGURE OUT NEXT STEPS.
WELL, BUDDY...
...WONDER NO MORE.

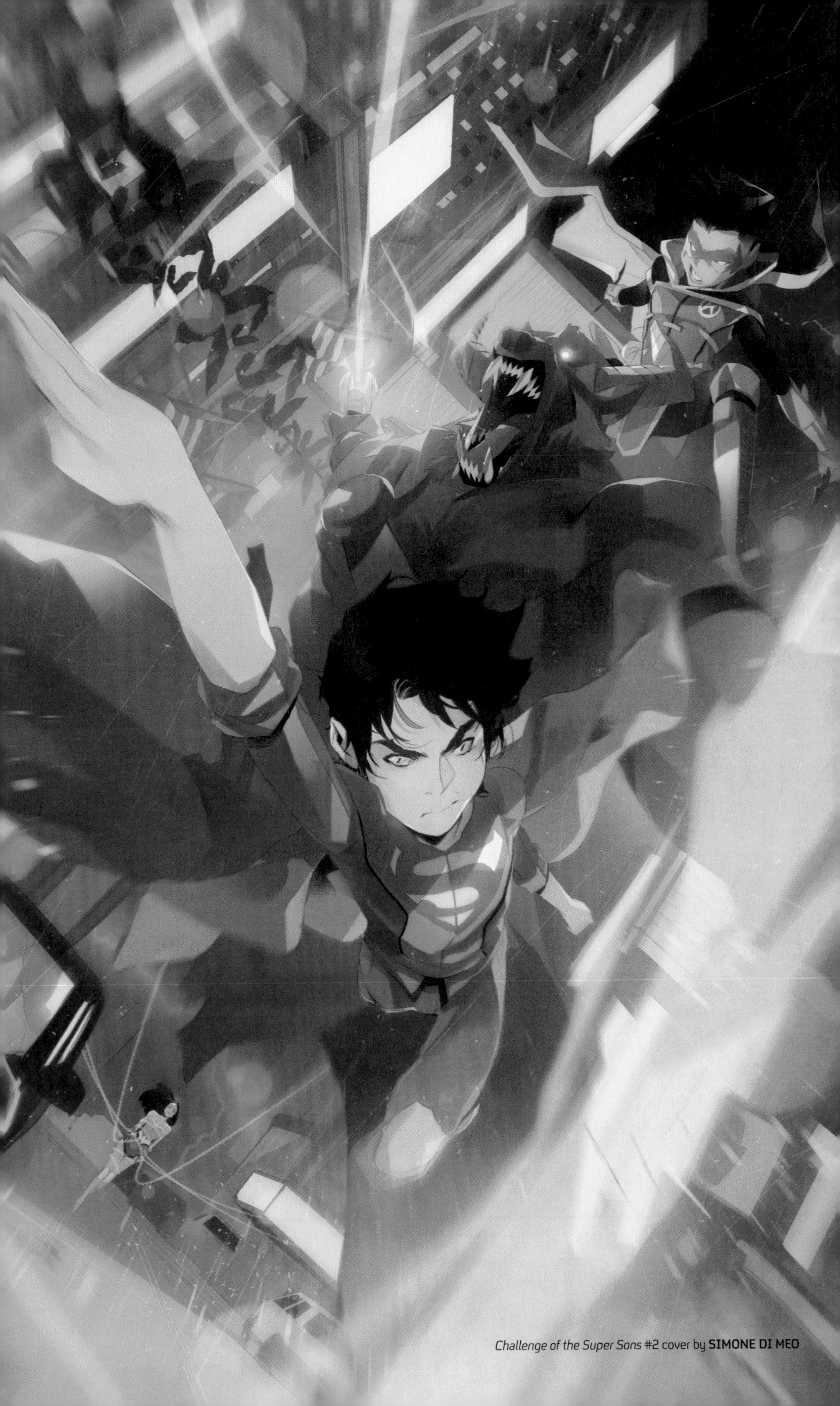

Challenge of the Super Sons #2 cover by **SIMONE DI MEO**

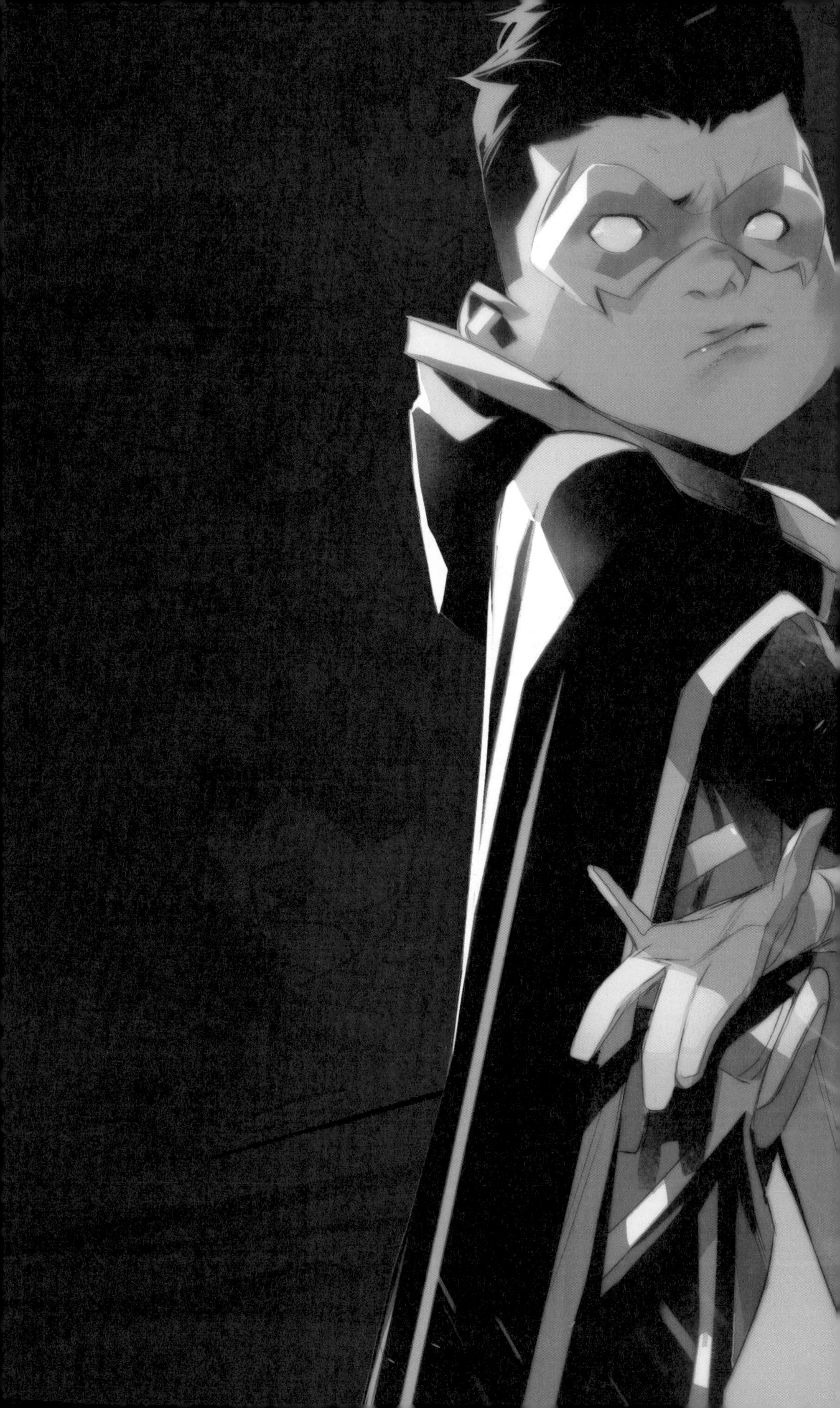

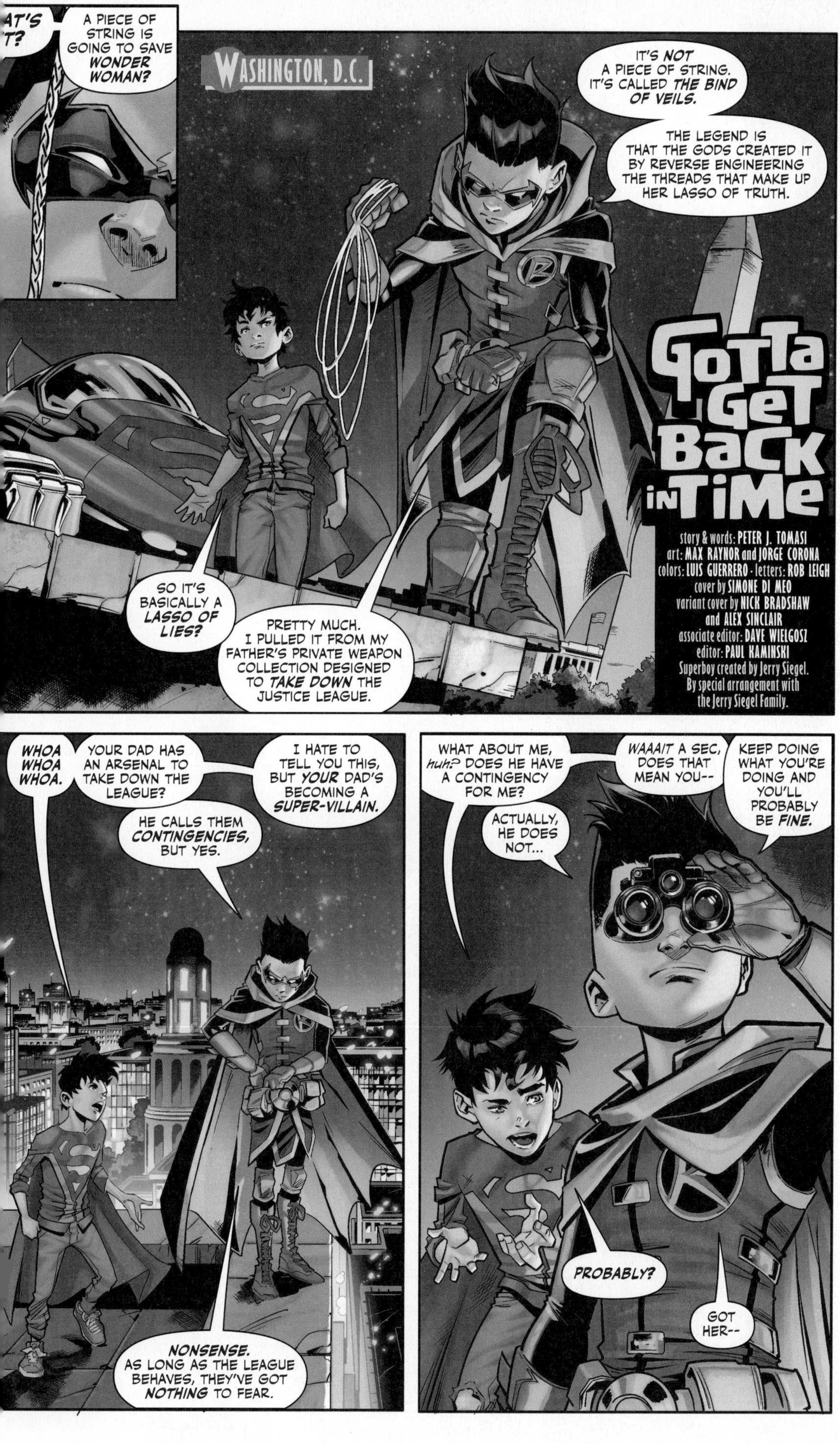
A PIECE OF STRING IS GOING TO SAVE *WONDER WOMAN?*
WASHINGTON, D.C.
IT'S *NOT* A PIECE OF STRING. IT'S CALLED *THE BIND OF VEILS.*
THE LEGEND IS THAT THE GODS CREATED IT BY REVERSE ENGINEERING THE THREADS THAT MAKE UP HER LASSO OF TRUTH.
SO IT'S BASICALLY A *LASSO OF LIES?*
PRETTY MUCH. I PULLED IT FROM MY FATHER'S PRIVATE WEAPON COLLECTION DESIGNED TO *TAKE DOWN* THE JUSTICE LEAGUE.
GOTTA GET BACK IN TIME
story & words: PETER J. TOMASI
art: MAX RAYNOR and JORGE CORONA
colors: LUIS GUERRERO · letters: ROB LEIGH
cover by SIMONE DI MEO
variant cover by NICK BRADSHAW and ALEX SINCLAIR
associate editor: DAVE WIELGOSZ
editor: PAUL KAMINSKI
Superboy created by Jerry Siegel. By special arrangement with the Jerry Siegel Family.
WHOA WHOA WHOA.
YOUR DAD HAS AN ARSENAL TO TAKE DOWN THE LEAGUE?
HE CALLS THEM *CONTINGENCIES,* BUT YES.
I HATE TO TELL YOU THIS, BUT *YOUR* DAD'S BECOMING A *SUPER-VILLAIN.*
NONSENSE. AS LONG AS THE LEAGUE BEHAVES, THEY'VE GOT *NOTHING* TO FEAR.
WHAT ABOUT ME, *huh?* DOES HE HAVE A CONTINGENCY FOR ME?
ACTUALLY, HE DOES NOT...
WAAAIT A SEC, DOES THAT MEAN YOU--
KEEP DOING WHAT YOU'RE DOING AND YOU'LL PROBABLY BE *FINE.*
PROBABLY?
GOT HER--

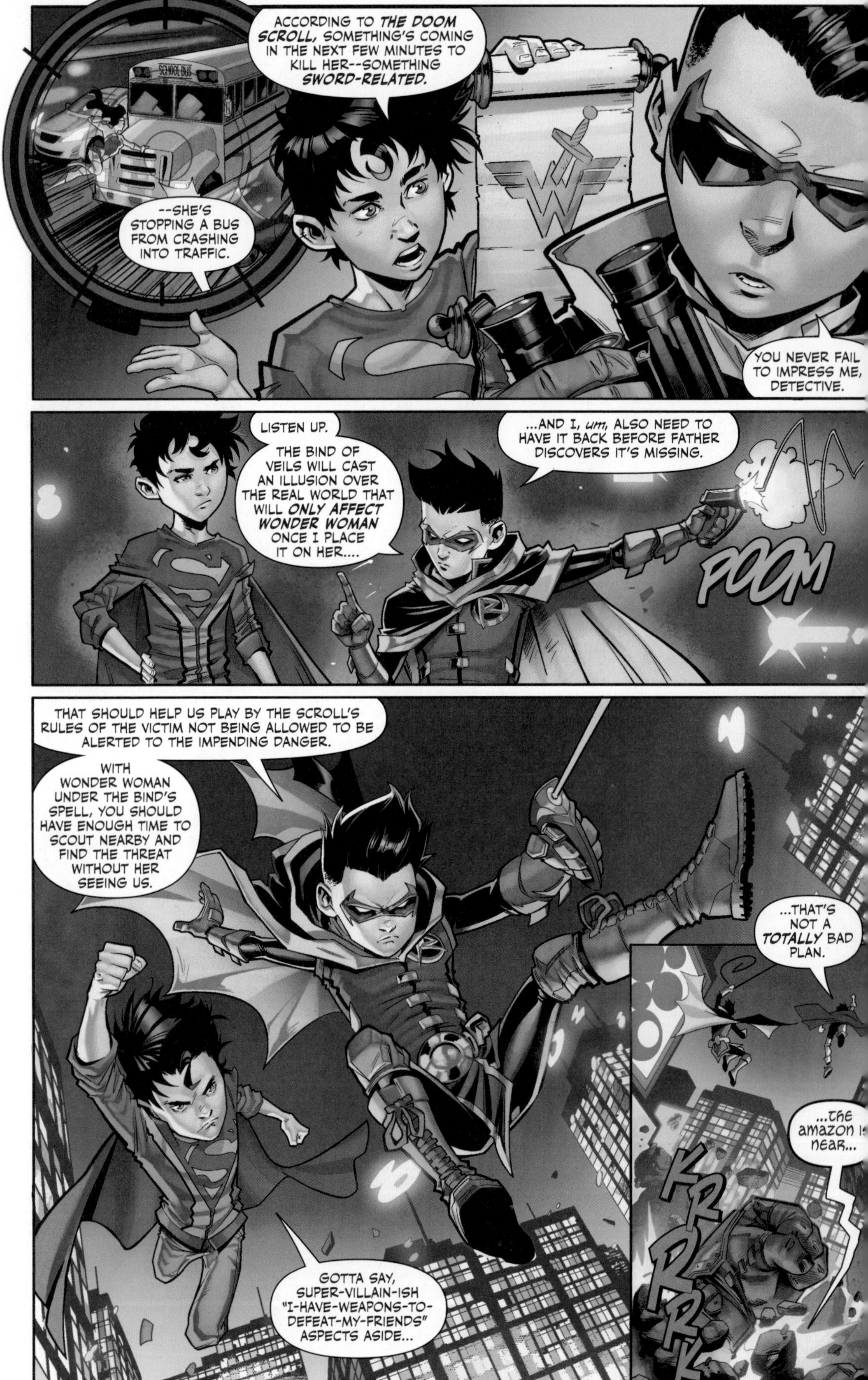

SCHOOL BUS
ACCORDING TO THE DOOM SCROLL, SOMETHING'S COMING IN THE NEXT FEW MINUTES TO KILL HER--SOMETHING SWORD-RELATED.
--SHE'S STOPPING A BUS FROM CRASHING INTO TRAFFIC.
YOU NEVER FAIL TO IMPRESS ME, DETECTIVE.
LISTEN UP.
THE BIND OF VEILS WILL CAST AN ILLUSION OVER THE REAL WORLD THAT WILL ONLY AFFECT WONDER WOMAN ONCE I PLACE IT ON HER....
...AND I, um, ALSO NEED TO HAVE IT BACK BEFORE FATHER DISCOVERS IT'S MISSING.
POOM
THAT SHOULD HELP US PLAY BY THE SCROLL'S RULES OF THE VICTIM NOT BEING ALLOWED TO BE ALERTED TO THE IMPENDING DANGER.
WITH WONDER WOMAN UNDER THE BIND'S SPELL, YOU SHOULD HAVE ENOUGH TIME TO SCOUT NEARBY AND FIND THE THREAT WITHOUT HER SEEING US.
GOTTA SAY, SUPER-VILLAIN-ISH "I-HAVE-WEAPONS-TO-DEFEAT-MY-FRIENDS" ASPECTS ASIDE...
...THAT'S NOT A TOTALLY BAD PLAN.
...the amazon is near...
KRRRK

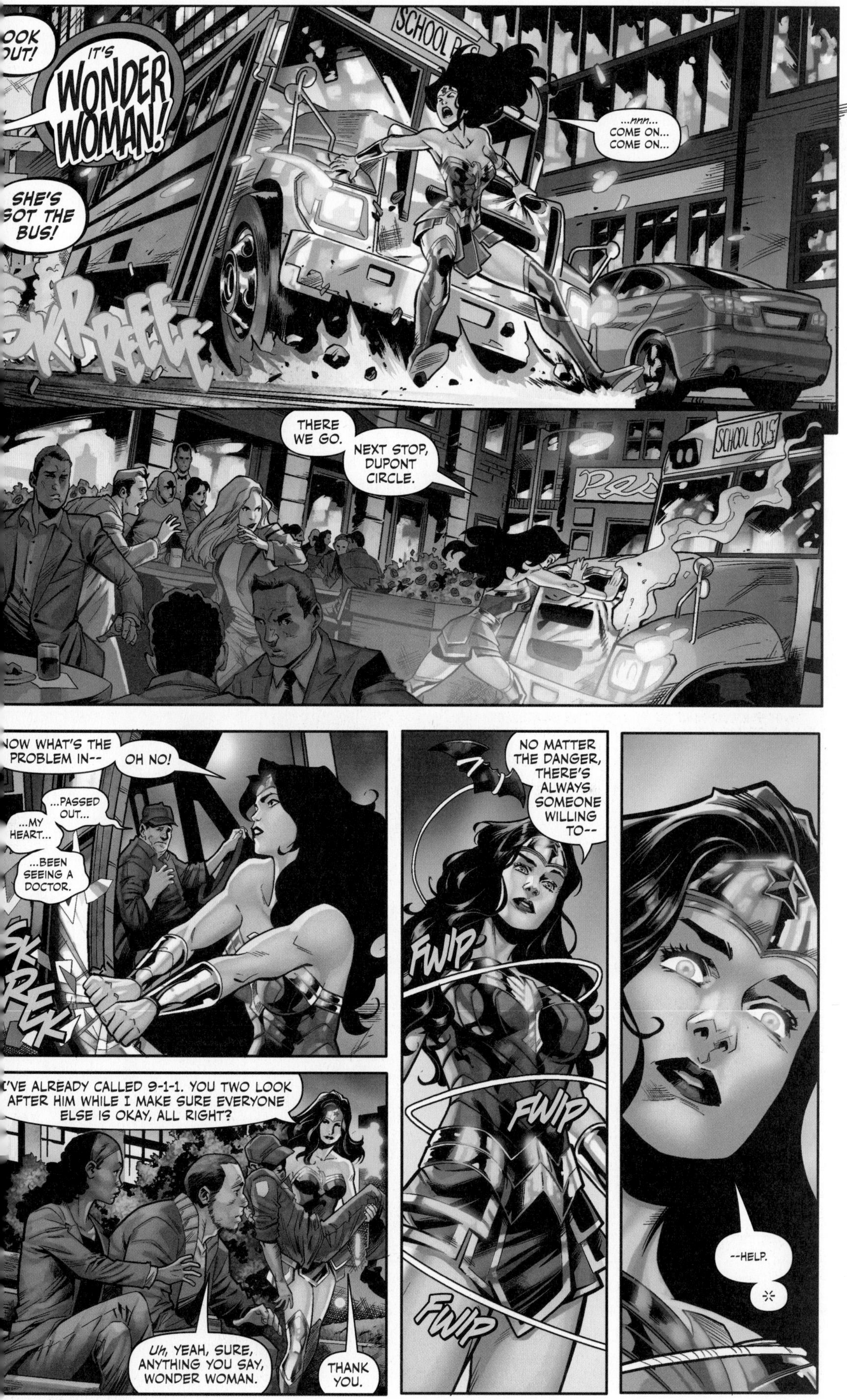

OOK OUT!
IT'S WONDER WOMAN!
SHE'S GOT THE BUS!
...nnn... COME ON... COME ON...
SKRREEE
THERE WE GO.
NEXT STOP, DUPONT CIRCLE.
SCHOOL BUS
NOW WHAT'S THE PROBLEM IN--
OH NO!
...PASSED OUT...
...MY HEART...
...BEEN SEEING A DOCTOR.
SKREEK
I'VE ALREADY CALLED 9-1-1. YOU TWO LOOK AFTER HIM WHILE I MAKE SURE EVERYONE ELSE IS OKAY, ALL RIGHT?
Uh, YEAH, SURE, ANYTHING YOU SAY, WONDER WOMAN.
THANK YOU.
NO MATTER THE DANGER, THERE'S ALWAYS SOMEONE WILLING TO--
FWIP
FWIP
FWIP
--HELP.

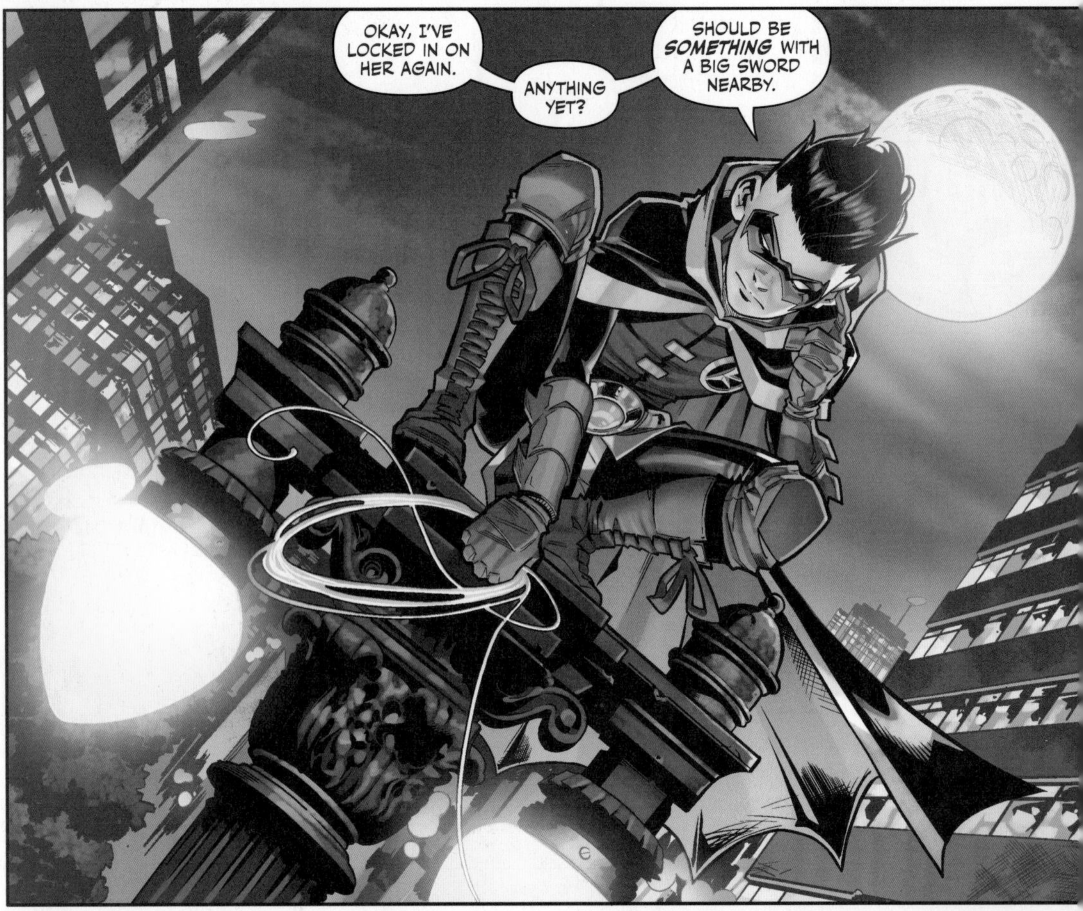
OKAY, I'VE LOCKED IN ON HER AGAIN.
ANYTHING YET?
SHOULD BE *SOMETHING* WITH A BIG SWORD NEARBY.

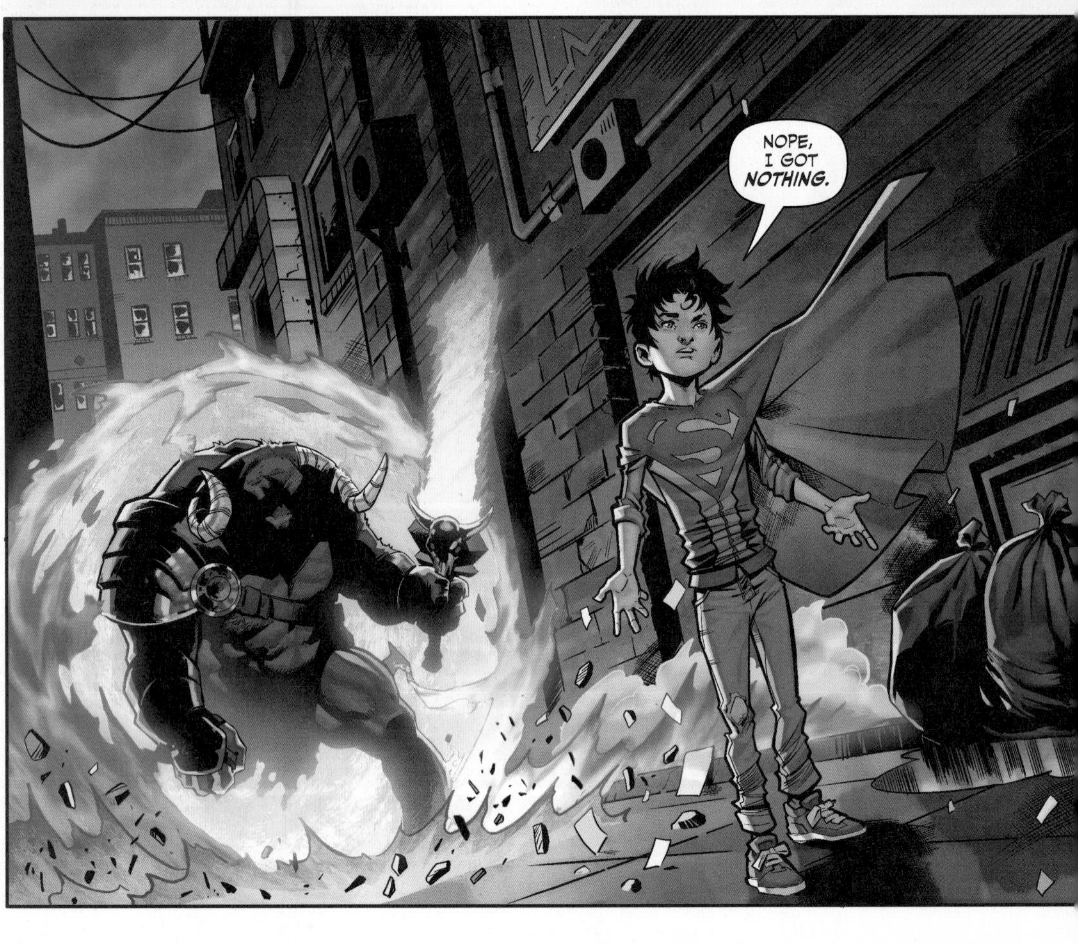
NOPE, I GOT *NOTHING.*

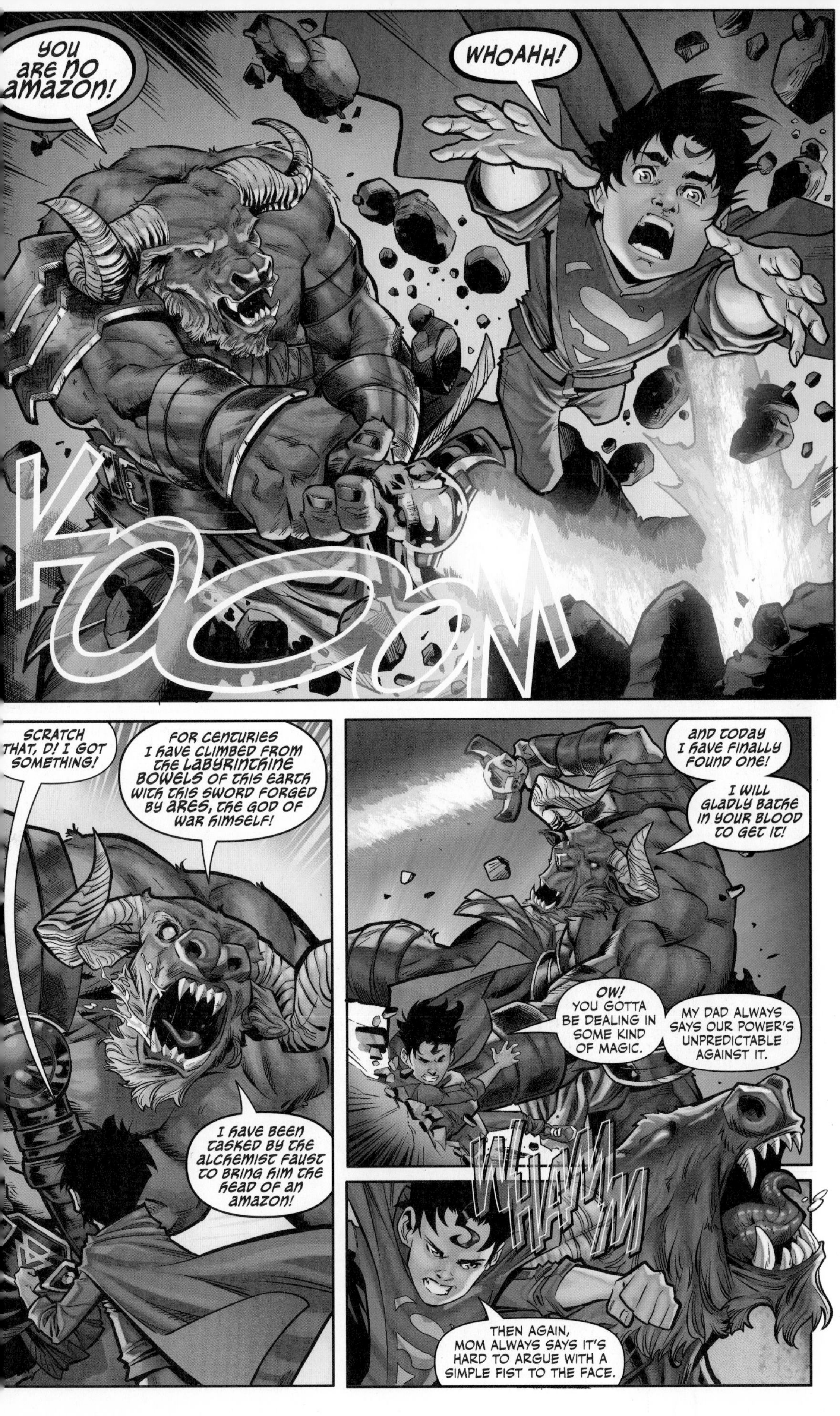
YOU ARE NO AMAZON!
WHOAHH!
KOOOOM
SCRATCH THAT, D! I GOT SOMETHING!
FOR CENTURIES I HAVE CLIMBED FROM THE LABYRINTHINE BOWELS OF THIS EARTH WITH THIS SWORD FORGED BY ARES, THE GOD OF WAR HIMSELF!
I HAVE BEEN TASKED BY THE ALCHEMIST FAUST TO BRING HIM THE HEAD OF AN AMAZON!
AND TODAY I HAVE FINALLY FOUND ONE!
I WILL GLADLY BATHE IN YOUR BLOOD TO GET IT!
OW! YOU GOTTA BE DEALING IN SOME KIND OF MAGIC.
MY DAD ALWAYS SAYS OUR POWER'S UNPREDICTABLE AGAINST IT.
WHAM
THEN AGAIN, MOM ALWAYS SAYS IT'S HARD TO ARGUE WITH A SIMPLE FIST TO THE FACE.

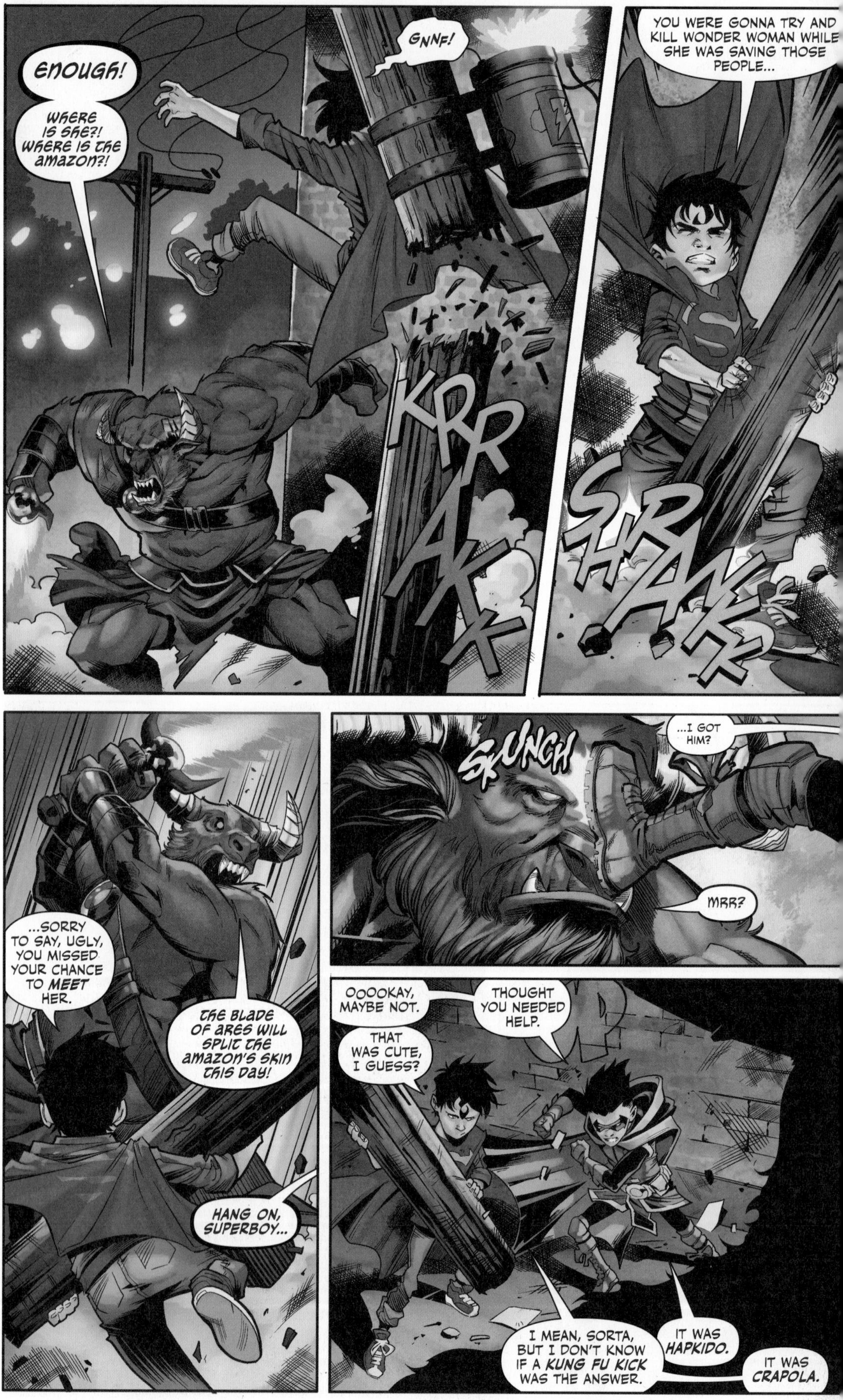
ENOUGH!
WHERE IS SHE?! WHERE IS THE AMAZON?!
GNNF!
KRRAKK
YOU WERE GONNA TRY AND KILL WONDER WOMAN WHILE SHE WAS SAVING THOSE PEOPLE...
SHRAKK
...SORRY TO SAY, UGLY, YOU MISSED YOUR CHANCE TO MEET HER.
THE BLADE OF ARES WILL SPLIT THE AMAZON'S SKIN THIS DAY!
HANG ON, SUPERBOY...
SKUNCH
...I GOT HIM?
MRR?
OOOOKAY, MAYBE NOT.
THOUGHT YOU NEEDED HELP.
THAT WAS CUTE, I GUESS?
I MEAN, SORTA, BUT I DON'T KNOW IF A KUNG FU KICK WAS THE ANSWER.
IT WAS HAPKIDO.
IT WAS CRAPOLA.

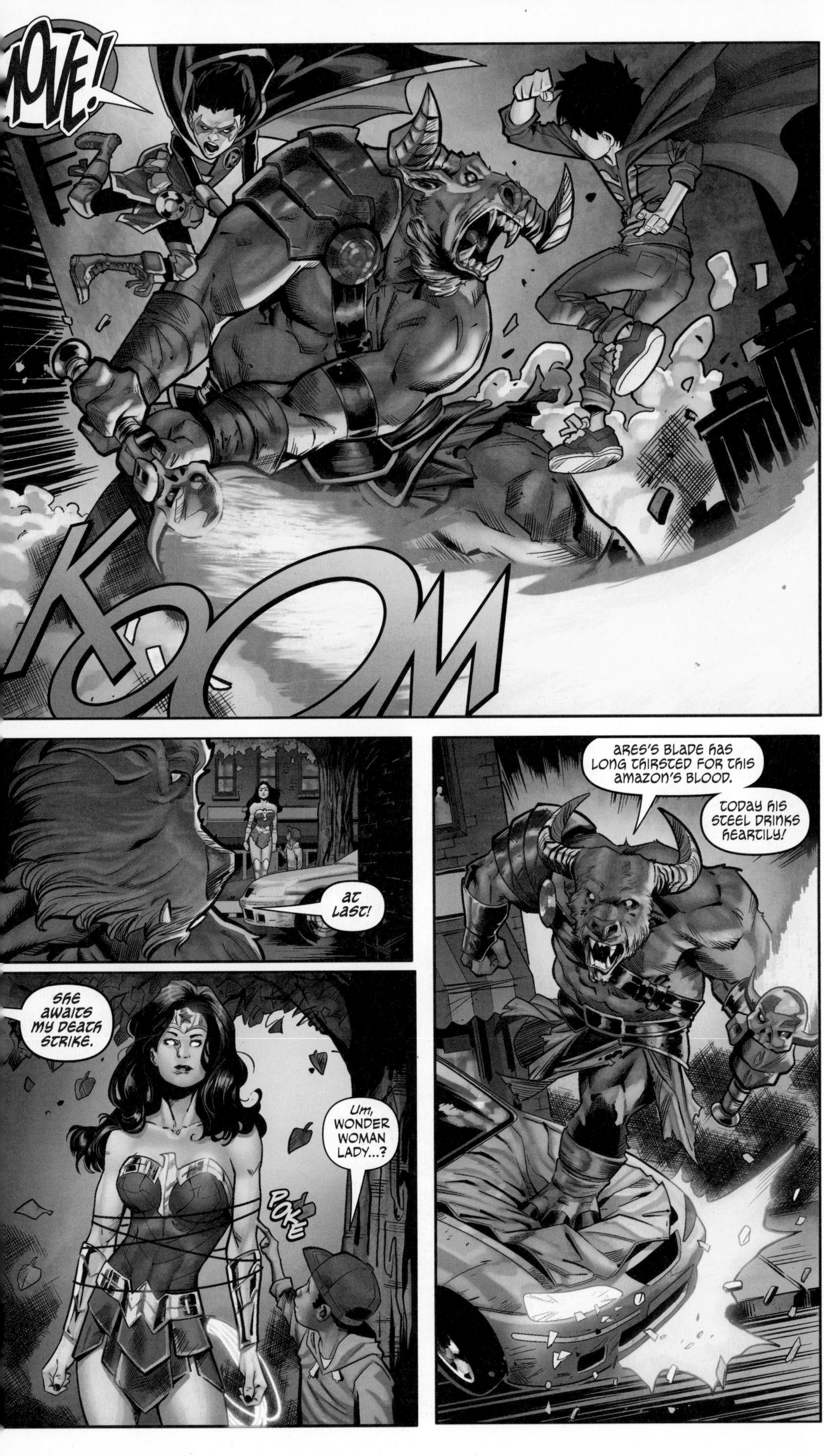
MOVE!
KOOM
AT LAST!
ARES'S BLADE HAS LONG THIRSTED FOR THIS AMAZON'S BLOOD.
TODAY HIS STEEL DRINKS HEARTILY!
SHE AWAITS MY DEATH STRIKE.
UM, WONDER WOMAN LADY...?
POKE

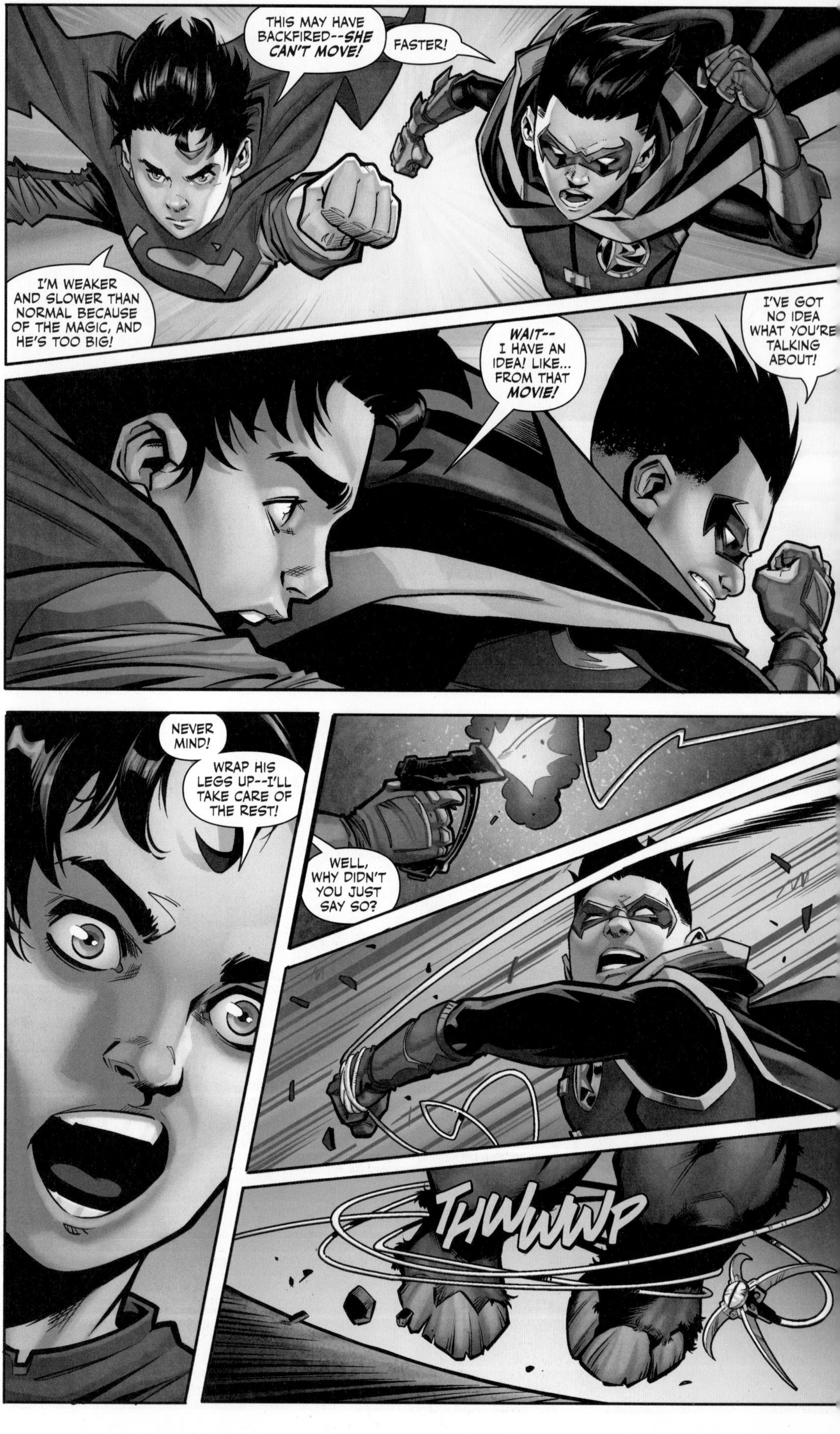

THIS MAY HAVE BACKFIRED--*SHE CAN'T MOVE!*
FASTER!
I'M WEAKER AND SLOWER THAN NORMAL BECAUSE OF THE MAGIC, AND HE'S TOO BIG!
WAIT-- I HAVE AN IDEA! LIKE... FROM THAT *MOVIE!*
I'VE GOT NO IDEA WHAT YOU'RE TALKING ABOUT!
NEVER MIND!
WRAP HIS LEGS UP--I'LL TAKE CARE OF THE REST!
WELL, WHY DIDN'T YOU JUST SAY SO?
THWWWP

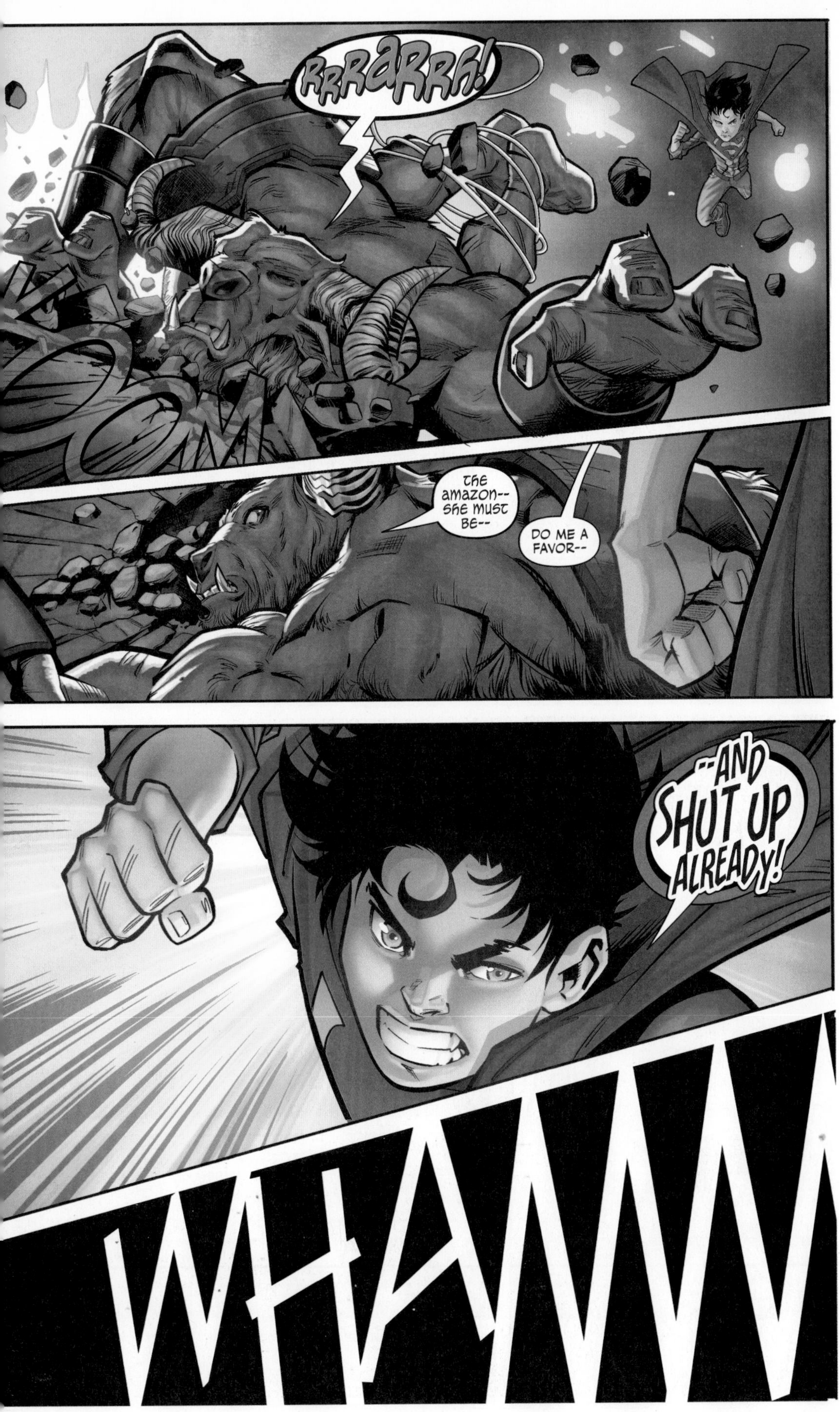
RRRARRRH!
THE AMAZON-- SHE MUST BE--
DO ME A FAVOR--
--AND SHUT UP ALREADY!
WHAMM

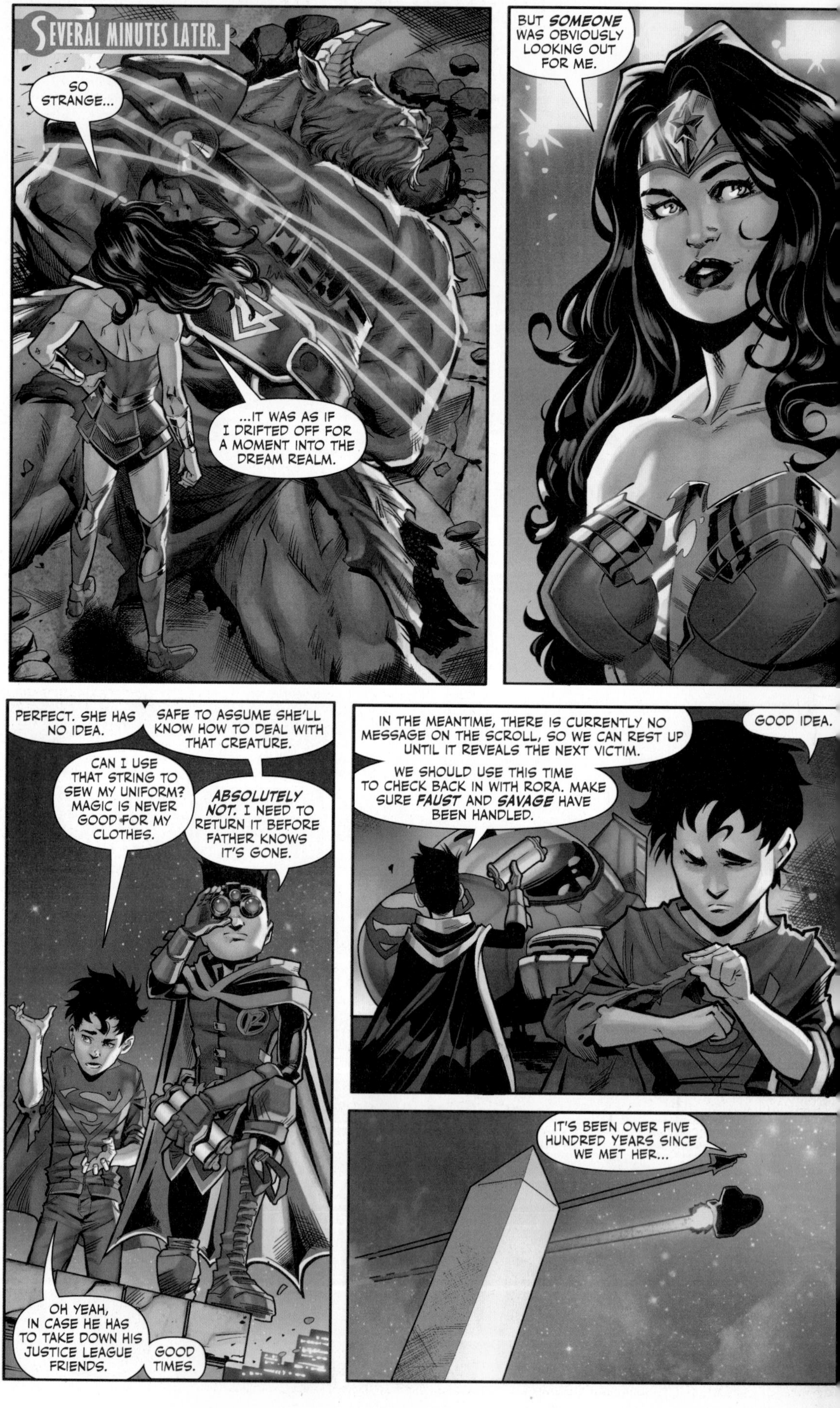
SEVERAL MINUTES LATER.
SO STRANGE...
...IT WAS AS IF I DRIFTED OFF FOR A MOMENT INTO THE DREAM REALM.
BUT SOMEONE WAS OBVIOUSLY LOOKING OUT FOR ME.
PERFECT. SHE HAS NO IDEA.
SAFE TO ASSUME SHE'LL KNOW HOW TO DEAL WITH THAT CREATURE.
CAN I USE THAT STRING TO SEW MY UNIFORM? MAGIC IS NEVER GOOD FOR MY CLOTHES.
ABSOLUTELY NOT. I NEED TO RETURN IT BEFORE FATHER KNOWS IT'S GONE.
OH YEAH, IN CASE HE HAS TO TAKE DOWN HIS JUSTICE LEAGUE FRIENDS.
GOOD TIMES.
IN THE MEANTIME, THERE IS CURRENTLY NO MESSAGE ON THE SCROLL, SO WE CAN REST UP UNTIL IT REVEALS THE NEXT VICTIM.
WE SHOULD USE THIS TIME TO CHECK BACK IN WITH RORA. MAKE SURE FAUST AND SAVAGE HAVE BEEN HANDLED.
GOOD IDEA.
IT'S BEEN OVER FIVE HUNDRED YEARS SINCE WE MET HER...

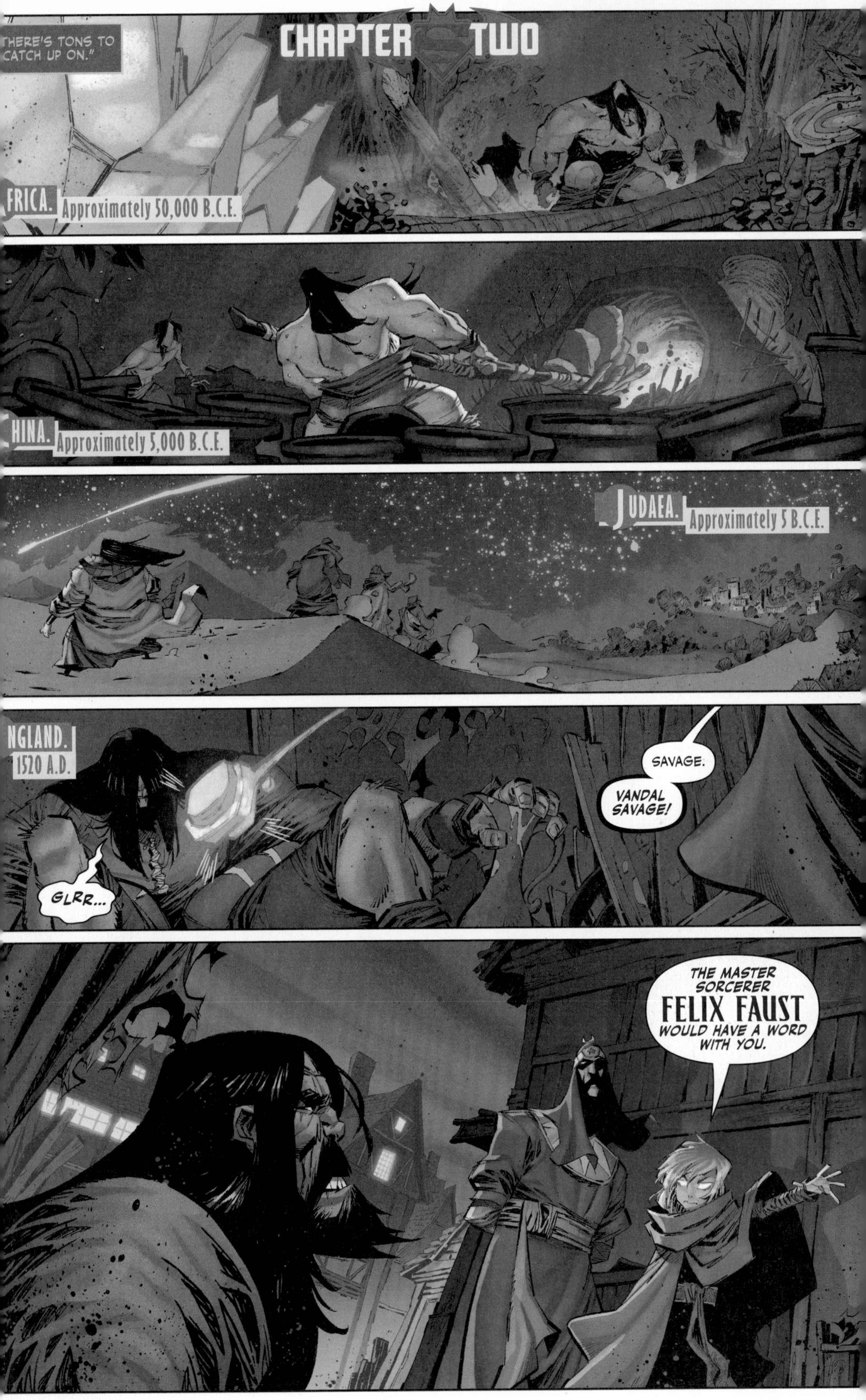

"THERE'S TONS TO CATCH UP ON."
CHAPTER TWO
FRICA. Approximately 50,000 B.C.E.
HINA. Approximately 5,000 B.C.E.
JUDAEA. Approximately 5 B.C.E.
NGLAND. 1520 A.D.
SAVAGE.
VANDAL SAVAGE!
GLRR...
THE MASTER SORCERER FELIX FAUST WOULD HAVE A WORD WITH YOU.

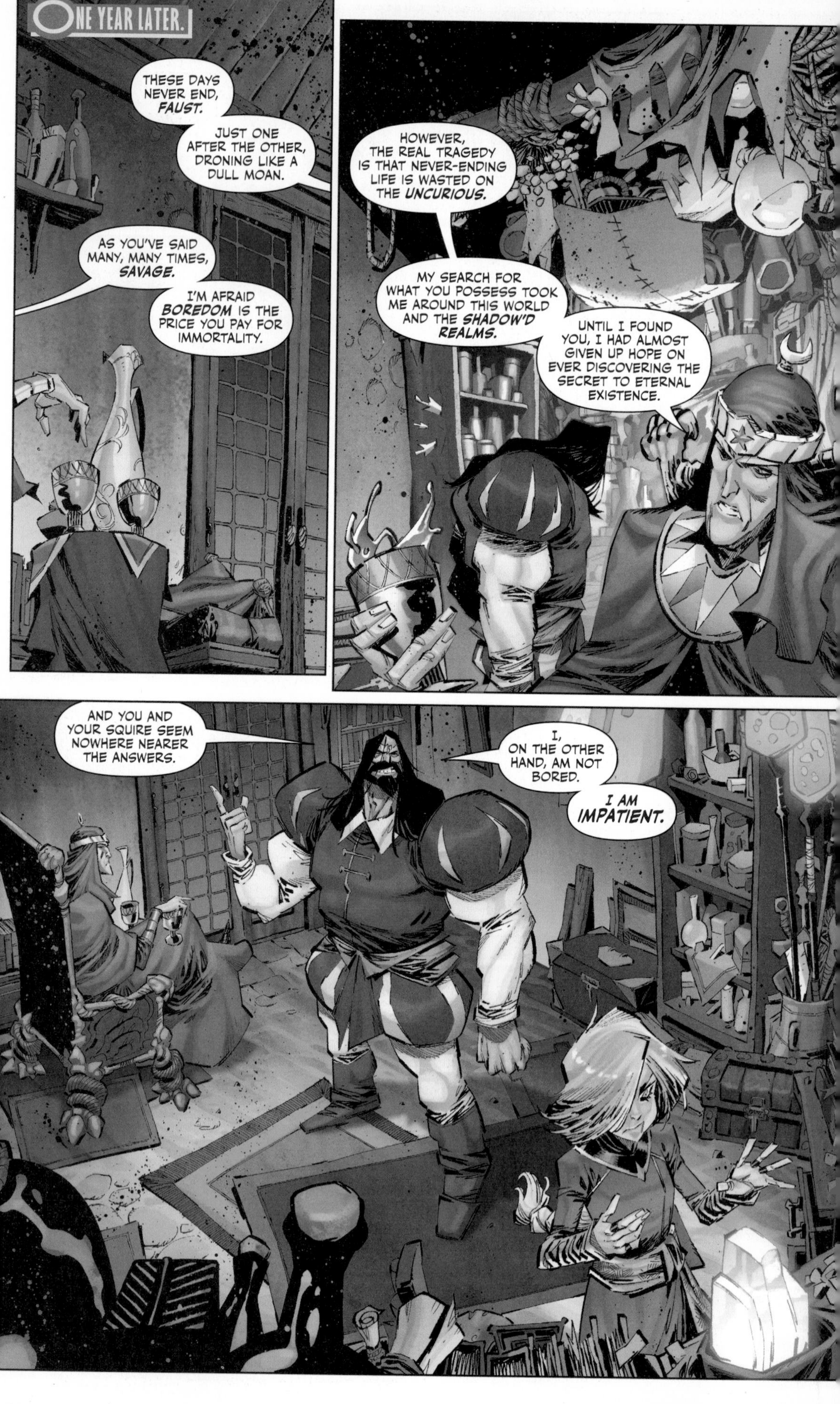
ONE YEAR LATER.
THESE DAYS NEVER END, FAUST.
JUST ONE AFTER THE OTHER, DRONING LIKE A DULL MOAN.
AS YOU'VE SAID MANY, MANY TIMES, SAVAGE.
I'M AFRAID BOREDOM IS THE PRICE YOU PAY FOR IMMORTALITY.
HOWEVER, THE REAL TRAGEDY IS THAT NEVER-ENDING LIFE IS WASTED ON THE UNCURIOUS.
MY SEARCH FOR WHAT YOU POSSESS TOOK ME AROUND THIS WORLD AND THE SHADOW'D REALMS.
UNTIL I FOUND YOU, I HAD ALMOST GIVEN UP HOPE ON EVER DISCOVERING THE SECRET TO ETERNAL EXISTENCE.
AND YOU AND YOUR SQUIRE SEEM NOWHERE NEARER THE ANSWERS.
I, ON THE OTHER HAND, AM NOT BORED.
I AM IMPATIENT.

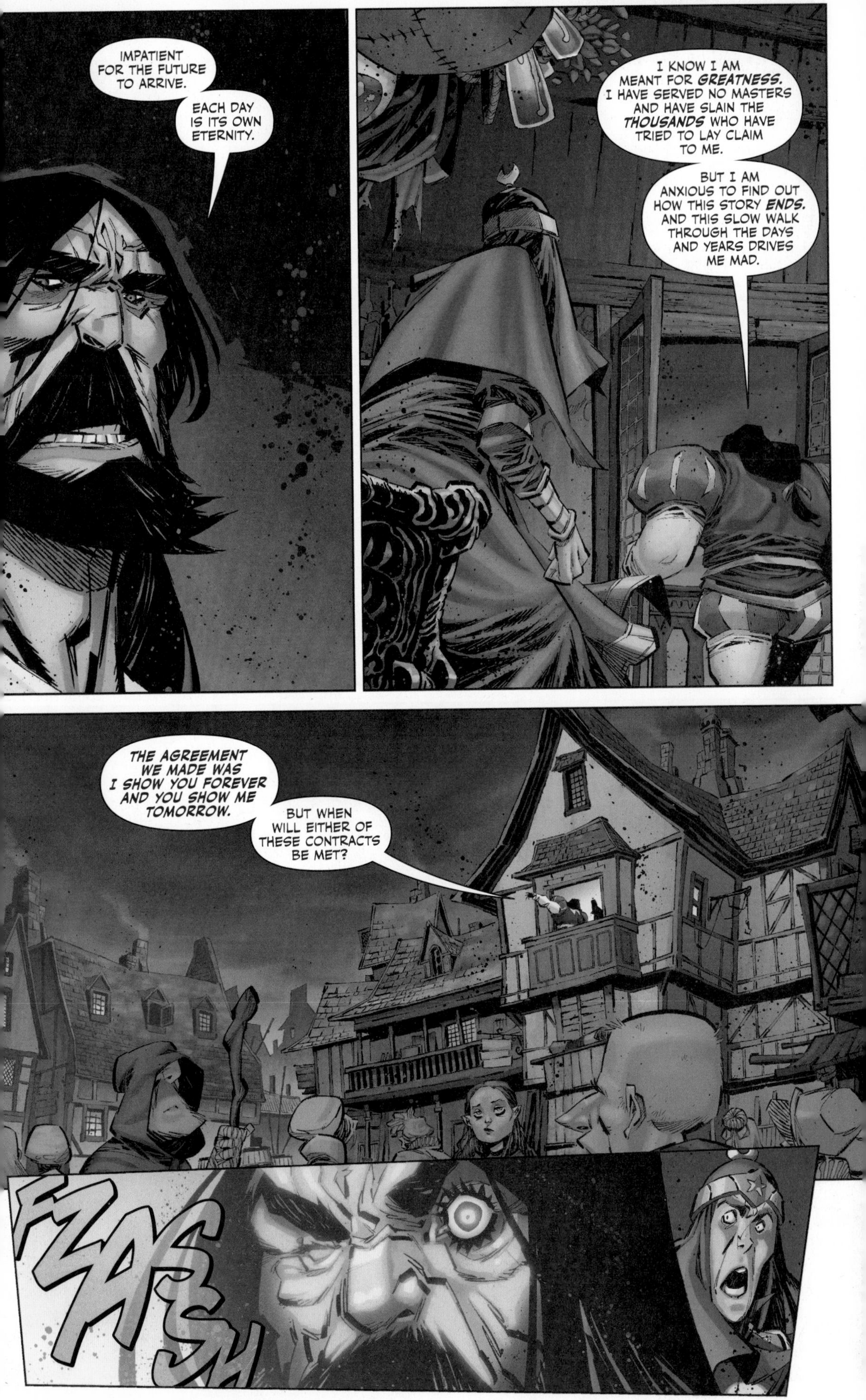
IMPATIENT FOR THE FUTURE TO ARRIVE.
EACH DAY IS ITS OWN ETERNITY.
I KNOW I AM MEANT FOR GREATNESS. I HAVE SERVED NO MASTERS AND HAVE SLAIN THE THOUSANDS WHO HAVE TRIED TO LAY CLAIM TO ME.
BUT I AM ANXIOUS TO FIND OUT HOW THIS STORY ENDS. AND THIS SLOW WALK THROUGH THE DAYS AND YEARS DRIVES ME MAD.
THE AGREEMENT WE MADE WAS I SHOW YOU FOREVER AND YOU SHOW ME TOMORROW.
BUT WHEN WILL EITHER OF THESE CONTRACTS BE MET?
FZZASH

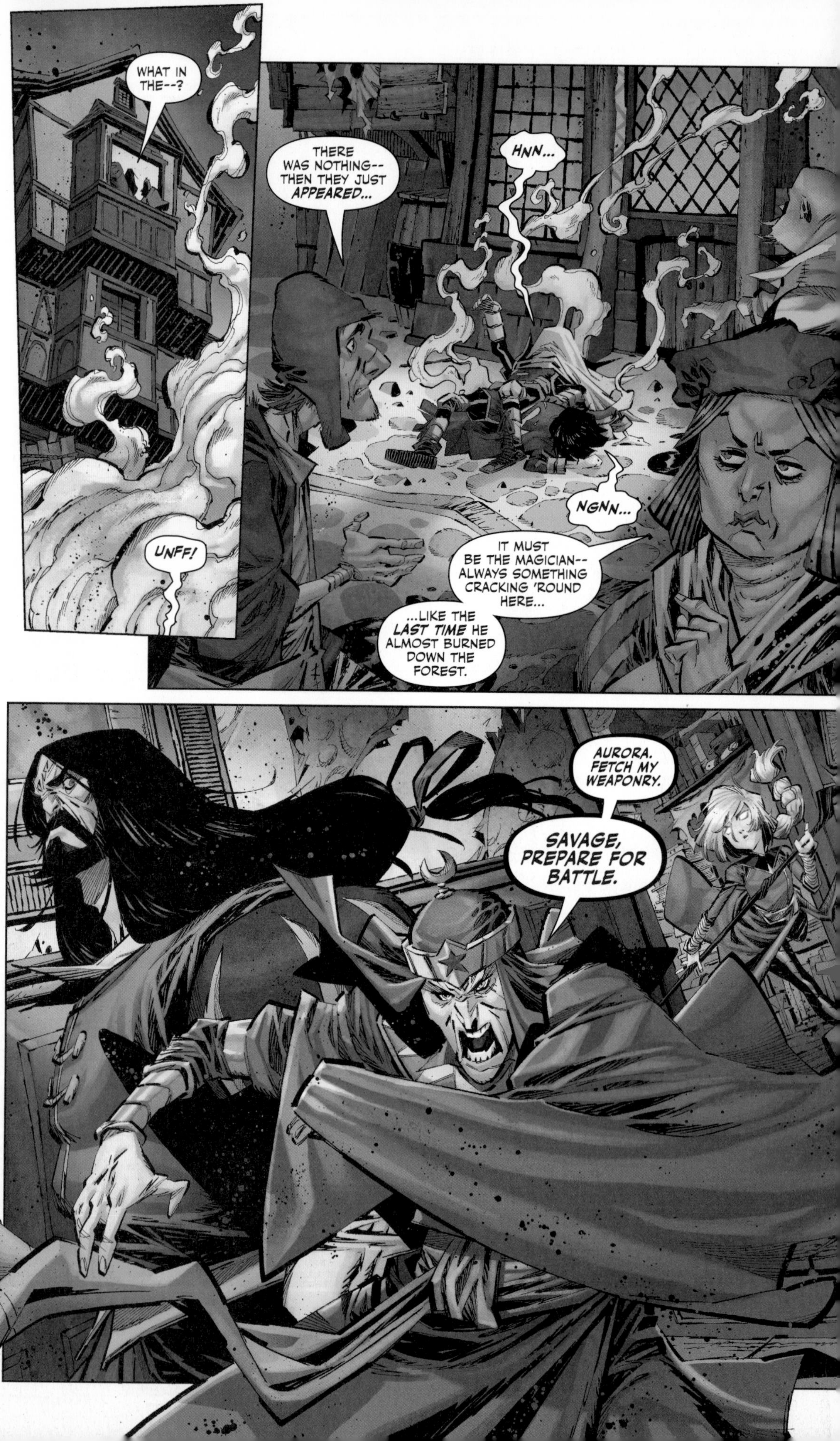

WHAT IN THE--?
UNFF!
THERE WAS NOTHING-- THEN THEY JUST APPEARED...
HNN...
NGNN...
IT MUST BE THE MAGICIAN-- ALWAYS SOMETHING CRACKING 'ROUND HERE...
...LIKE THE LAST TIME HE ALMOST BURNED DOWN THE FOREST.
AURORA. FETCH MY WEAPONRY.
SAVAGE, PREPARE FOR BATTLE.

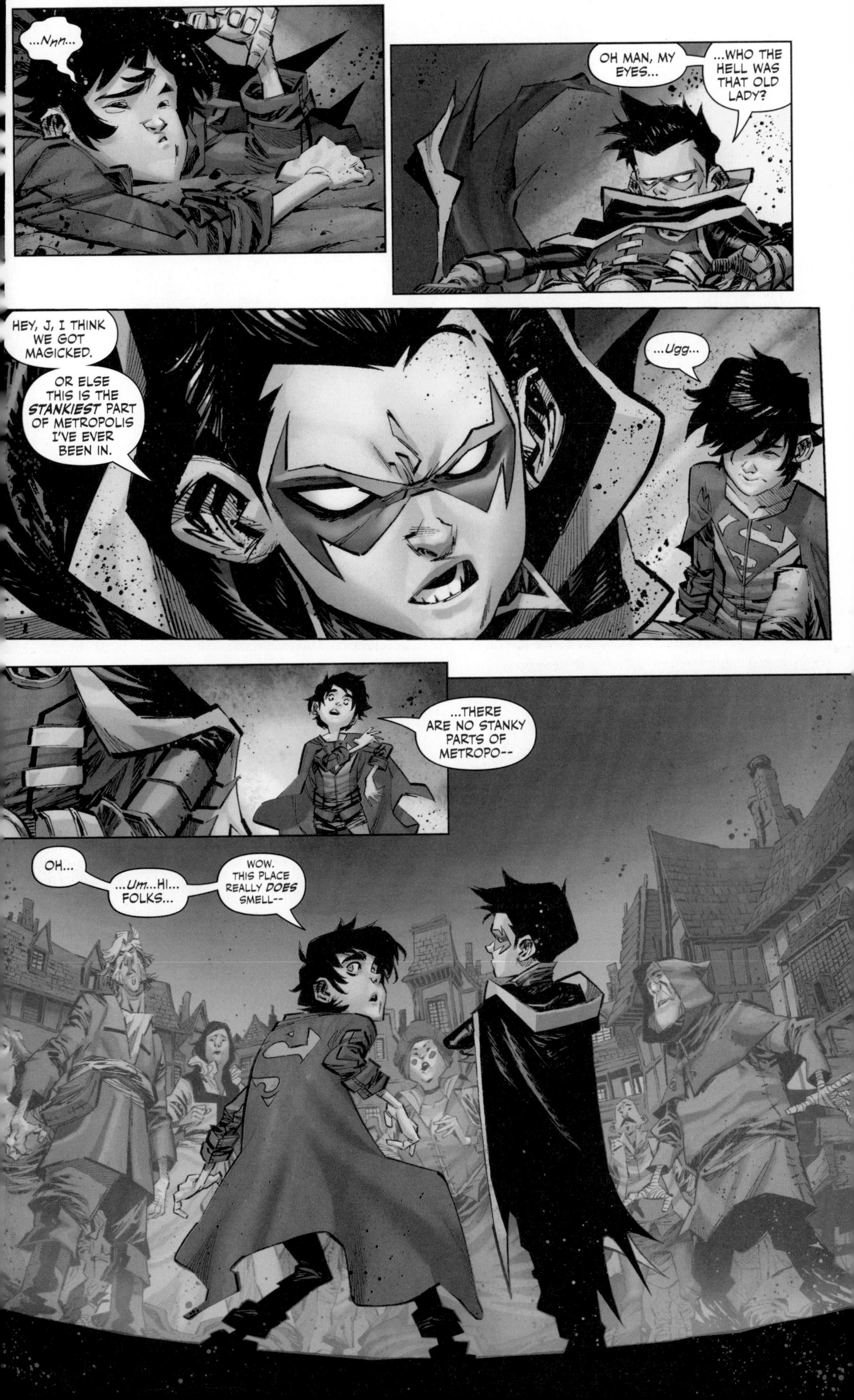
...Nnn...
OH MAN, MY EYES...
...WHO THE HELL WAS THAT OLD LADY?
HEY, J, I THINK WE GOT MAGICKED.
OR ELSE THIS IS THE STANKIEST PART OF METROPOLIS I'VE EVER BEEN IN.
...Ugg...
...THERE ARE NO STANKY PARTS OF METROPO--
OH...
...Um...HI... FOLKS...
WOW. THIS PLACE REALLY DOES SMELL--

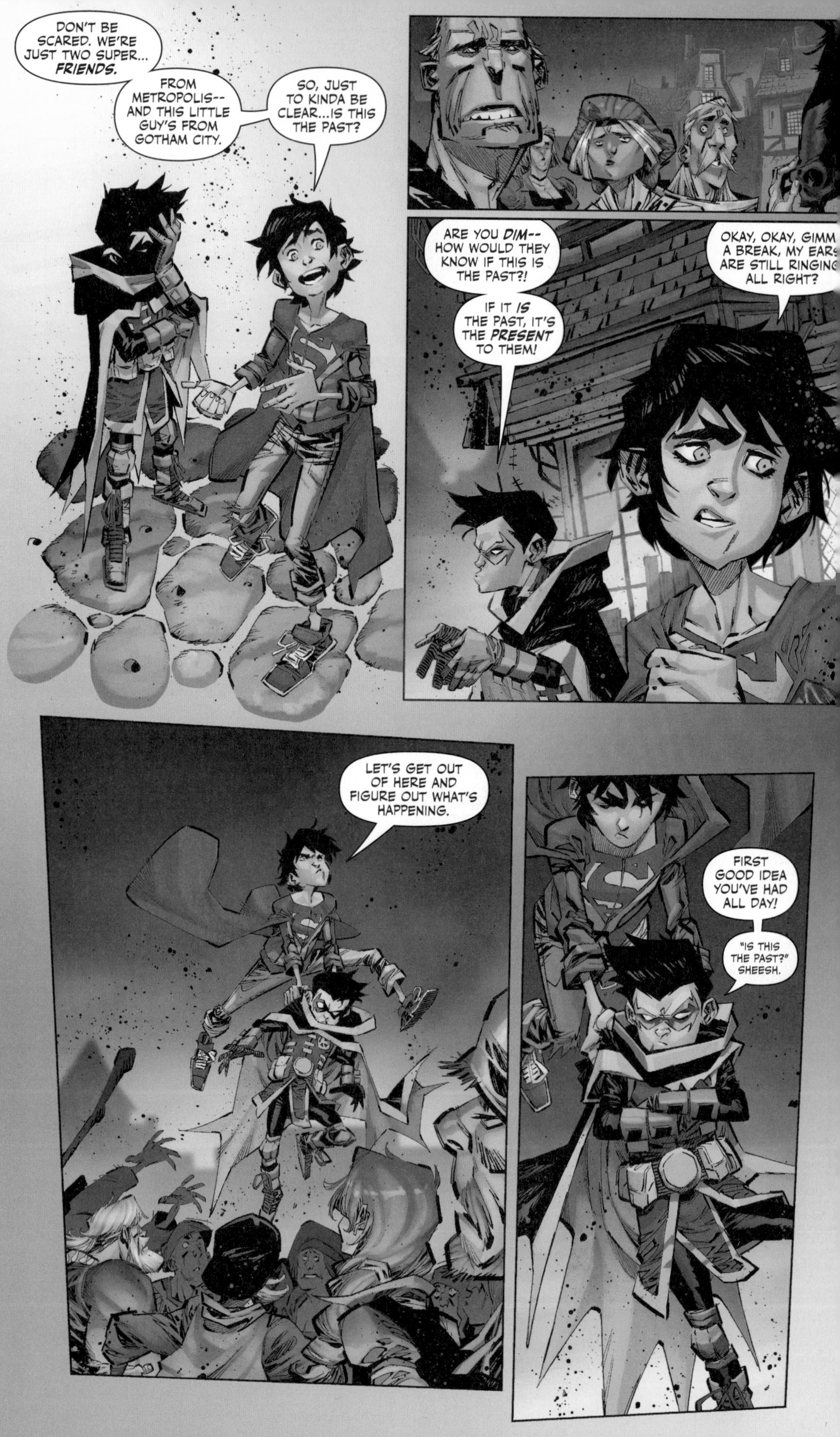

DON'T BE SCARED. WE'RE JUST TWO SUPER... FRIENDS.
FROM METROPOLIS-- AND THIS LITTLE GUY'S FROM GOTHAM CITY.
SO, JUST TO KINDA BE CLEAR...IS THIS THE PAST?
ARE YOU DIM-- HOW WOULD THEY KNOW IF THIS IS THE PAST?!
IF IT IS THE PAST, IT'S THE PRESENT TO THEM!
OKAY, OKAY, GIMM A BREAK, MY EARS ARE STILL RINGING ALL RIGHT?
LET'S GET OUT OF HERE AND FIGURE OUT WHAT'S HAPPENING.
FIRST GOOD IDEA YOU'VE HAD ALL DAY!
"IS THIS THE PAST?" SHEESH.

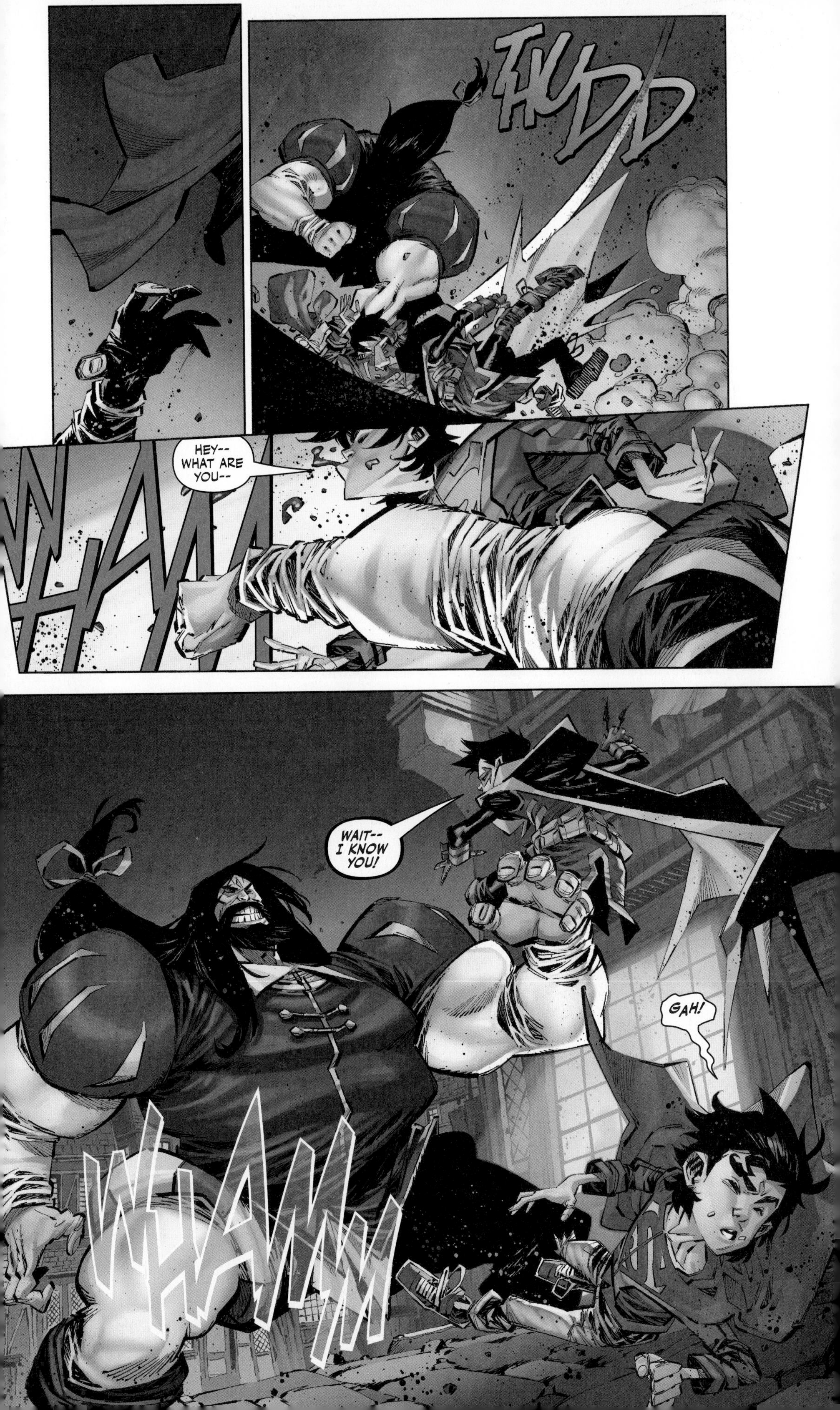
THUDD
HEY-- WHAT ARE YOU--
WHAM
WAIT-- I KNOW YOU!
GAH!
WHAMM

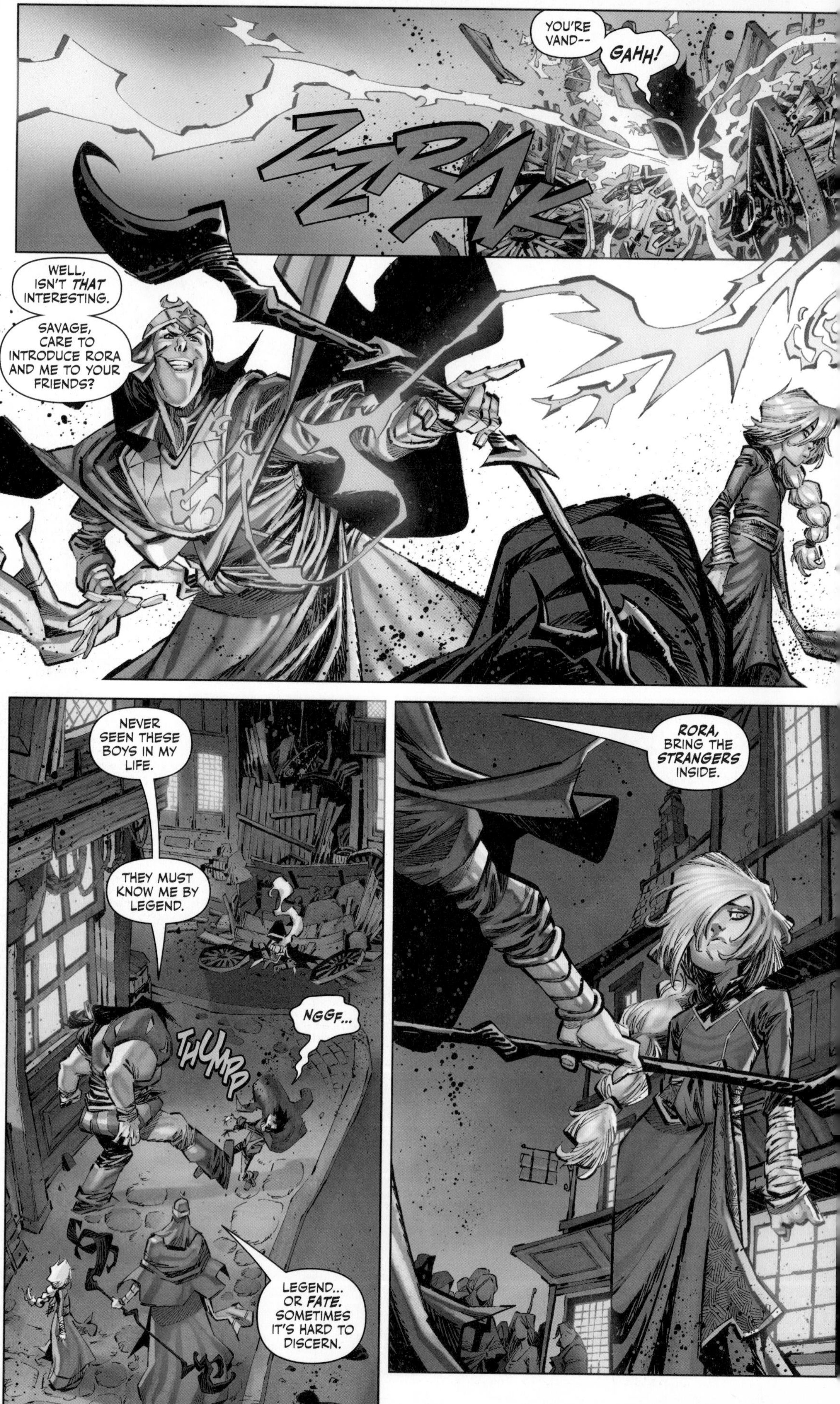
YOU'RE VAND--
GAHH!
ZZRAK
WELL, ISN'T *THAT* INTERESTING.
SAVAGE, CARE TO INTRODUCE RORA AND ME TO YOUR FRIENDS?
NEVER SEEN THESE BOYS IN MY LIFE.
THEY MUST KNOW ME BY LEGEND.
NGGF...
THUMPP
LEGEND... OR *FATE.* SOMETIMES IT'S HARD TO DISCERN.
RORA, BRING THE *STRANGERS* INSIDE.

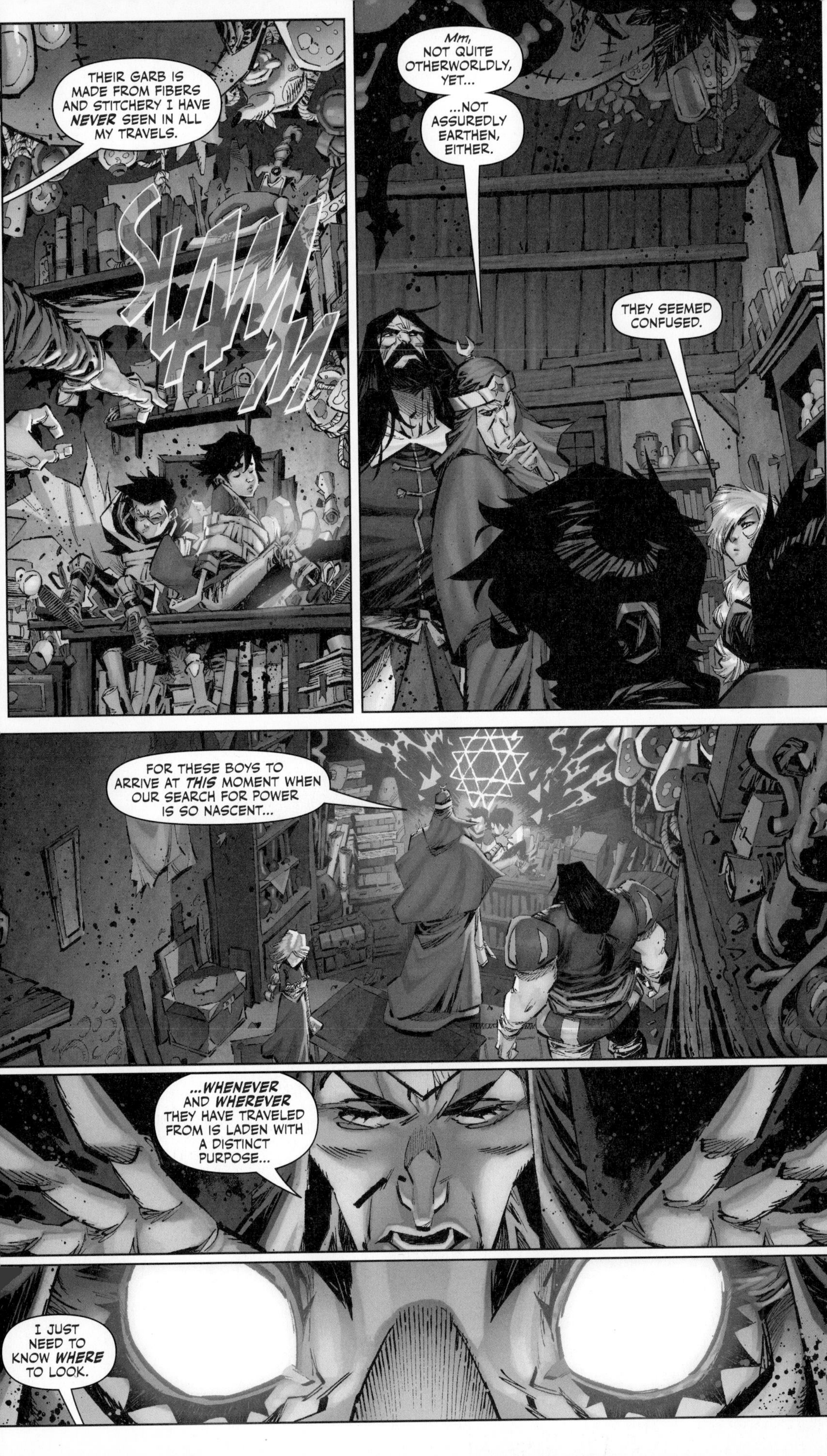
THEIR GARB IS MADE FROM FIBERS AND STITCHERY I HAVE **NEVER** SEEN IN ALL MY TRAVELS.
SLAM
Mm, NOT QUITE OTHERWORLDLY, YET...
...NOT ASSUREDLY EARTHEN, EITHER.
THEY SEEMED CONFUSED.
FOR THESE BOYS TO ARRIVE AT **THIS** MOMENT WHEN OUR SEARCH FOR POWER IS SO NASCENT...
...**WHENEVER** AND **WHEREVER** THEY HAVE TRAVELED FROM IS LADEN WITH A DISTINCT PURPOSE...
I JUST NEED TO KNOW **WHERE** TO LOOK.

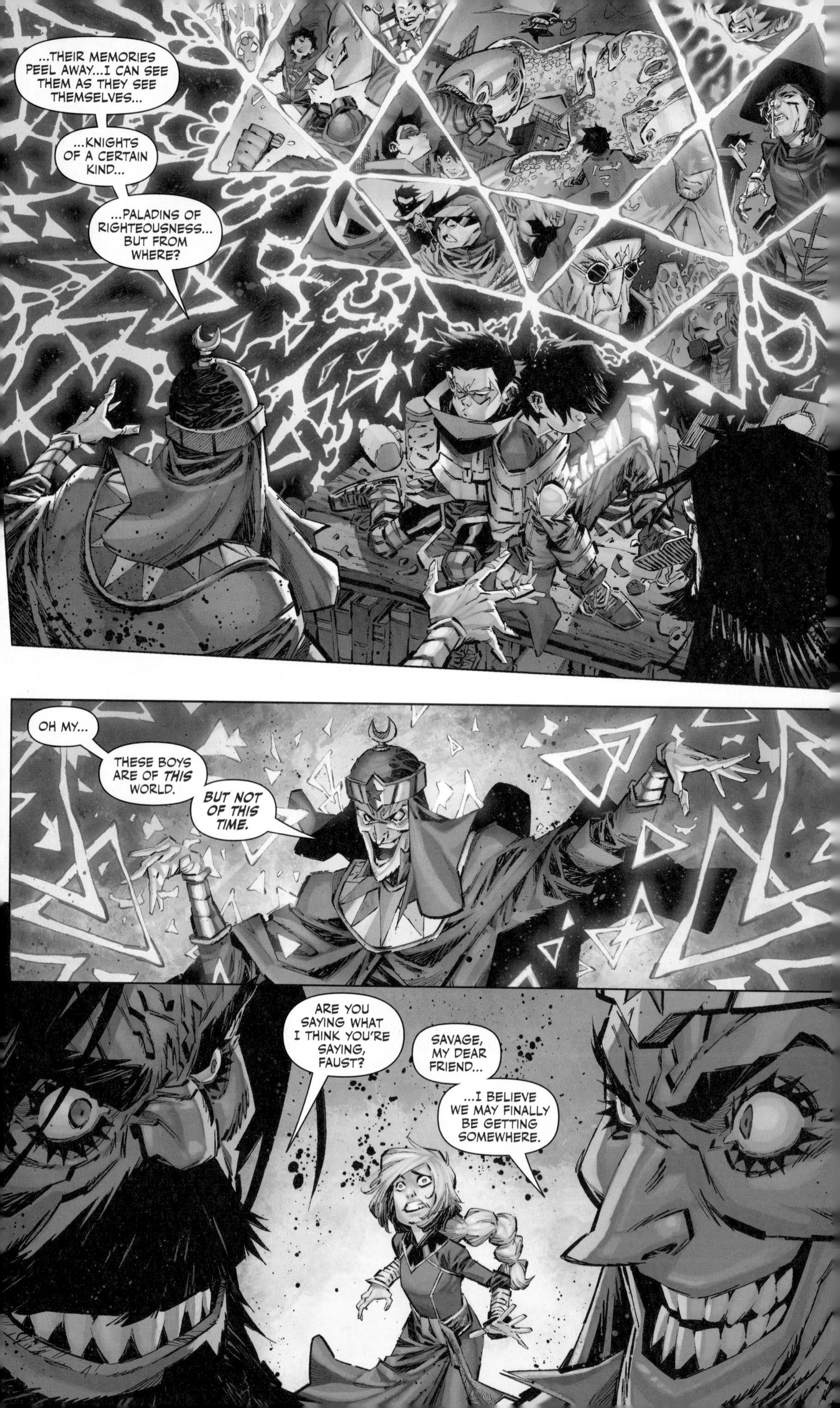

...THEIR MEMORIES PEEL AWAY...I CAN SEE THEM AS THEY SEE THEMSELVES...
...KNIGHTS OF A CERTAIN KIND...
...PALADINS OF RIGHTEOUSNESS... BUT FROM WHERE?
OH MY...
THESE BOYS ARE OF *THIS* WORLD.
BUT NOT OF THIS TIME.
ARE YOU SAYING WHAT I THINK YOU'RE SAYING, FAUST?
SAVAGE, MY DEAR FRIEND...
...I BELIEVE WE MAY FINALLY BE GETTING SOMEWHERE.

Challenge of the Super Sons #3 cover by **SIMONE DI MEO**

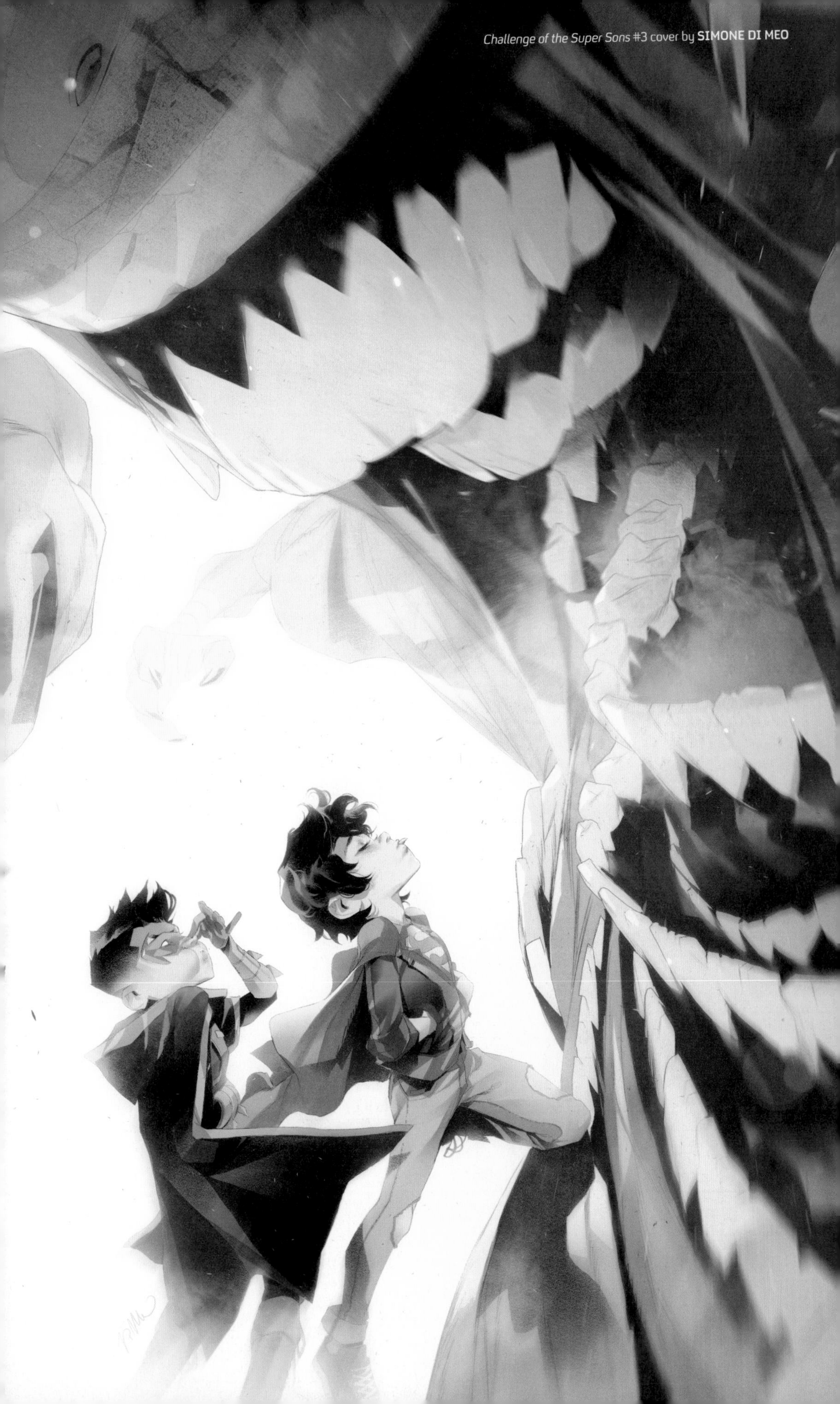

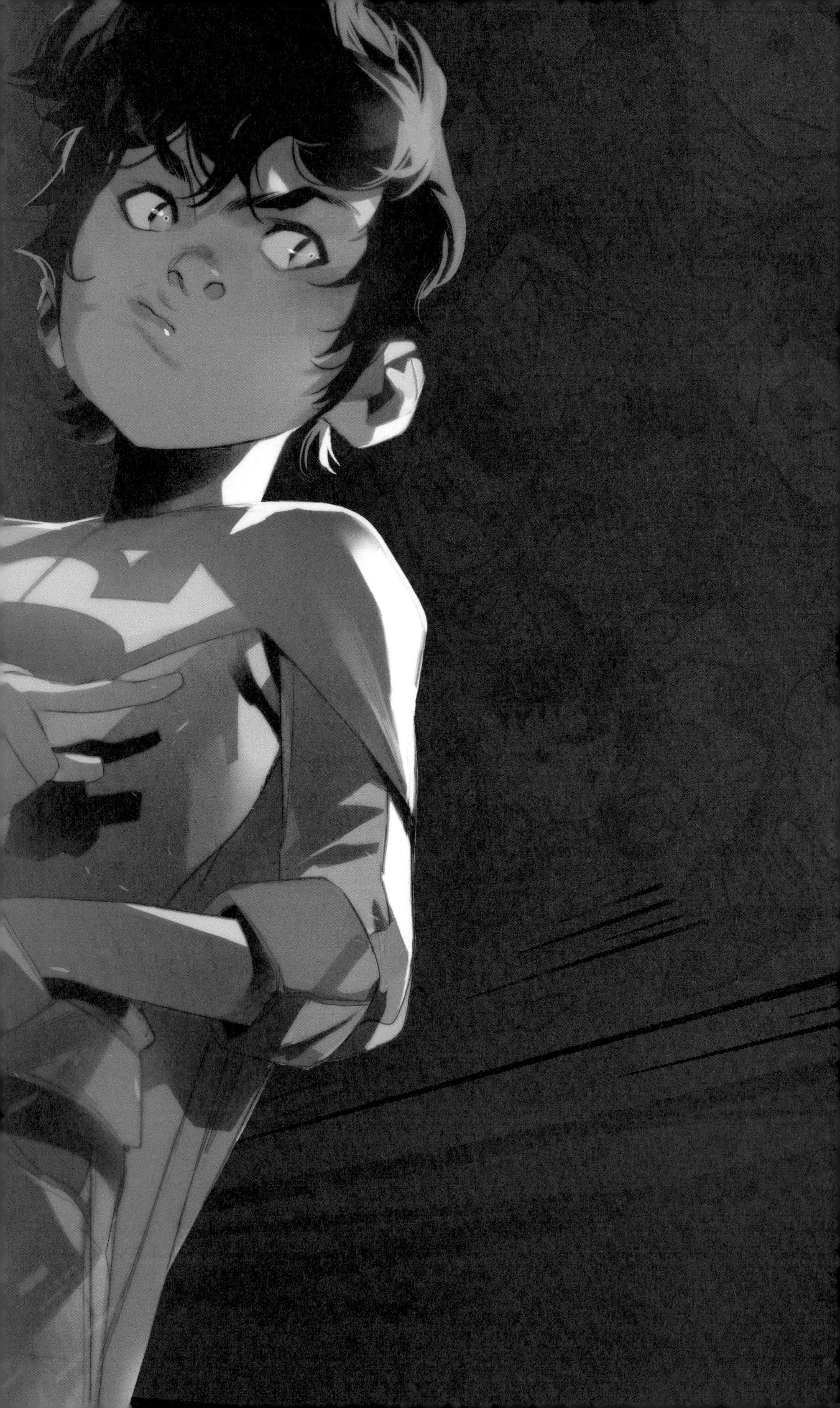

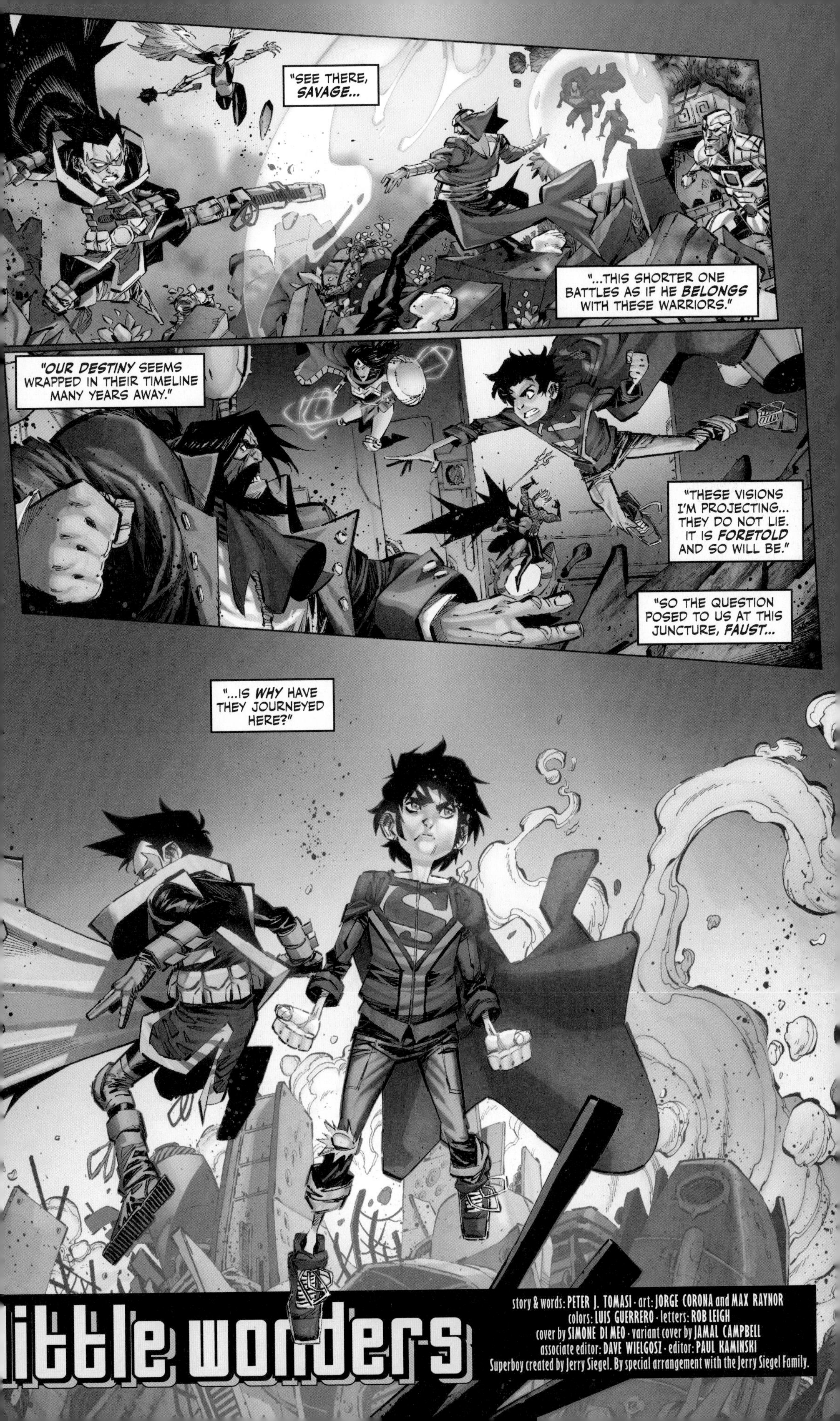
"SEE THERE, SAVAGE...
"...THIS SHORTER ONE BATTLES AS IF HE BELONGS WITH THESE WARRIORS."
"OUR DESTINY SEEMS WRAPPED IN THEIR TIMELINE MANY YEARS AWAY."
"THESE VISIONS I'M PROJECTING... THEY DO NOT LIE. IT IS FORETOLD AND SO WILL BE."
"SO THE QUESTION POSED TO US AT THIS JUNCTURE, FAUST...
"...IS WHY HAVE THEY JOURNEYED HERE?"
little wonders
story & words: PETER J. TOMASI · art: JORGE CORONA and MAX RAYNOR
colors: LUIS GUERRERO · letters: ROB LEIGH
cover by SIMONE DI MEO · variant cover by JAMAL CAMPBELL
associate editor: DAVE WIELGOSZ · editor: PAUL KAMINSKI
Superboy created by Jerry Siegel. By special arrangement with the Jerry Siegel Family.

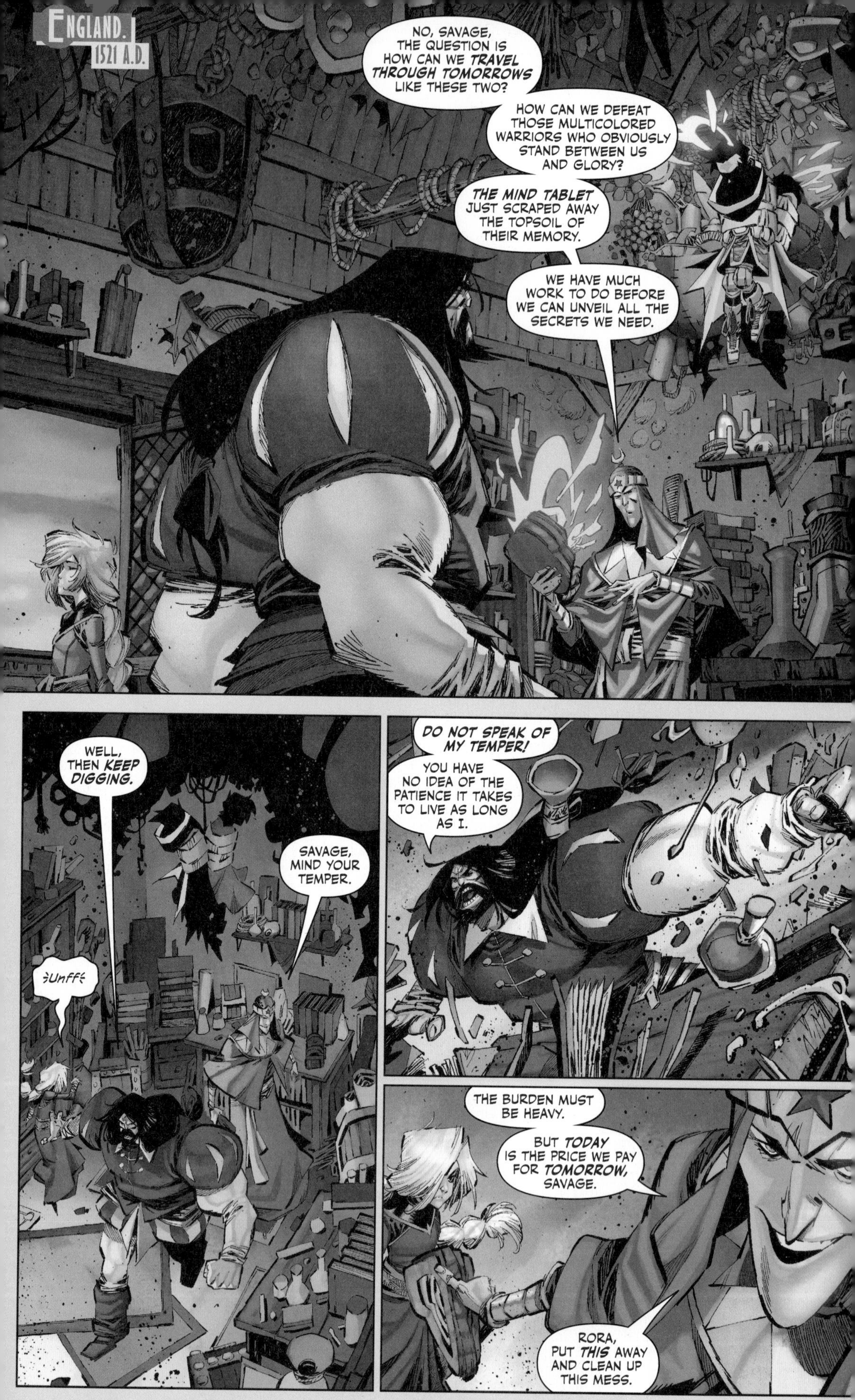
ENGLAND. 1521 A.D.
NO, SAVAGE, THE QUESTION IS HOW CAN WE *TRAVEL THROUGH TOMORROWS* LIKE THESE TWO?
HOW CAN WE DEFEAT THOSE MULTICOLORED WARRIORS WHO OBVIOUSLY STAND BETWEEN US AND GLORY?
THE MIND TABLET JUST SCRAPED AWAY THE TOPSOIL OF THEIR MEMORY.
WE HAVE MUCH WORK TO DO BEFORE WE CAN UNVEIL ALL THE SECRETS WE NEED.
WELL, THEN *KEEP DIGGING.*
SAVAGE, MIND YOUR TEMPER.
UNFF
DO NOT SPEAK OF MY TEMPER!
YOU HAVE NO IDEA OF THE PATIENCE IT TAKES TO LIVE AS LONG AS I.
THE BURDEN MUST BE HEAVY.
BUT *TODAY* IS THE PRICE WE PAY FOR *TOMORROW,* SAVAGE.
RORA, PUT *THIS* AWAY AND CLEAN UP THIS MESS.

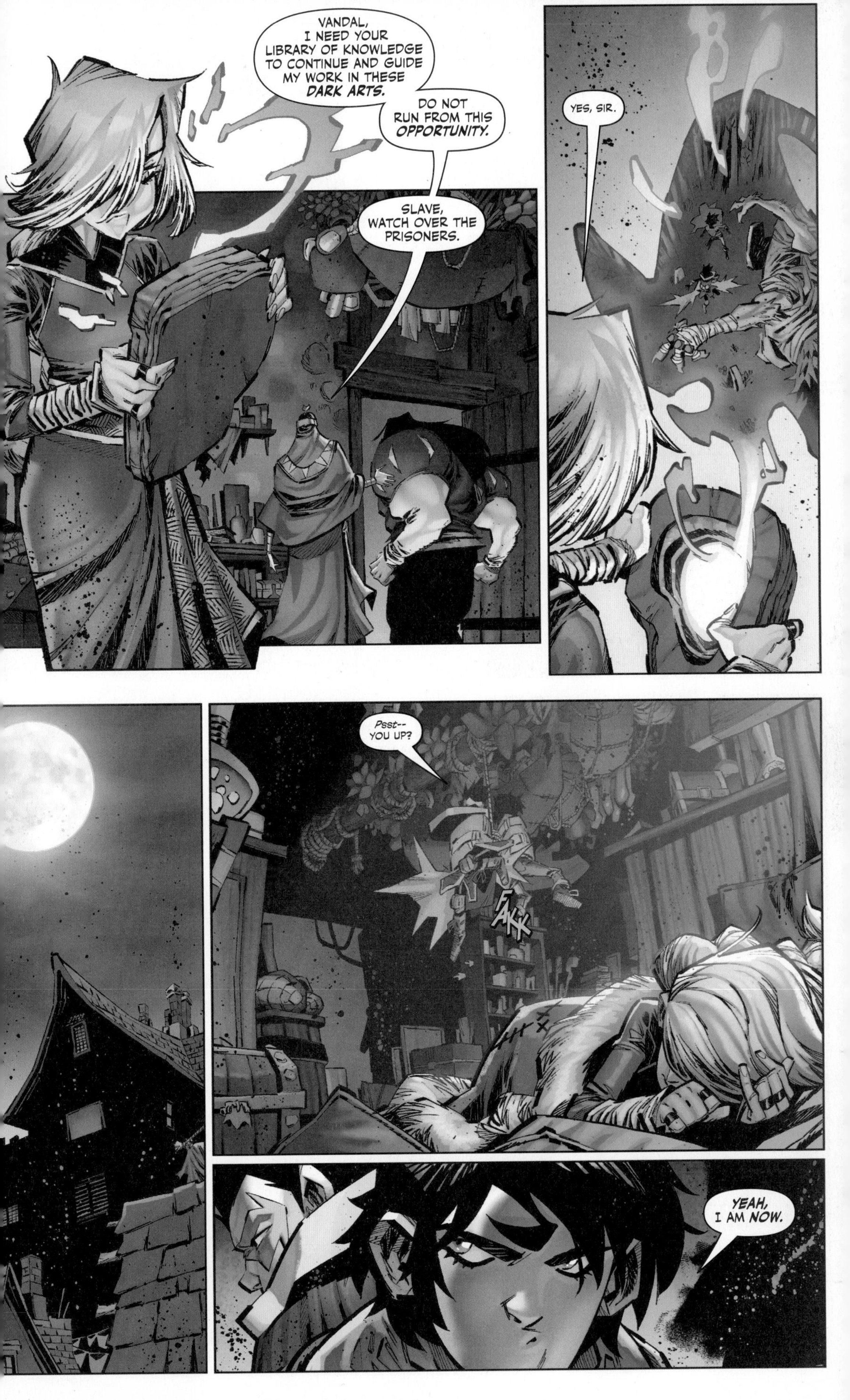
VANDAL, I NEED YOUR LIBRARY OF KNOWLEDGE TO CONTINUE AND GUIDE MY WORK IN THESE DARK ARTS.
DO NOT RUN FROM THIS OPPORTUNITY.
SLAVE, WATCH OVER THE PRISONERS.
YES, SIR.
Psst-- YOU UP?
FAKK
YEAH, I AM NOW.

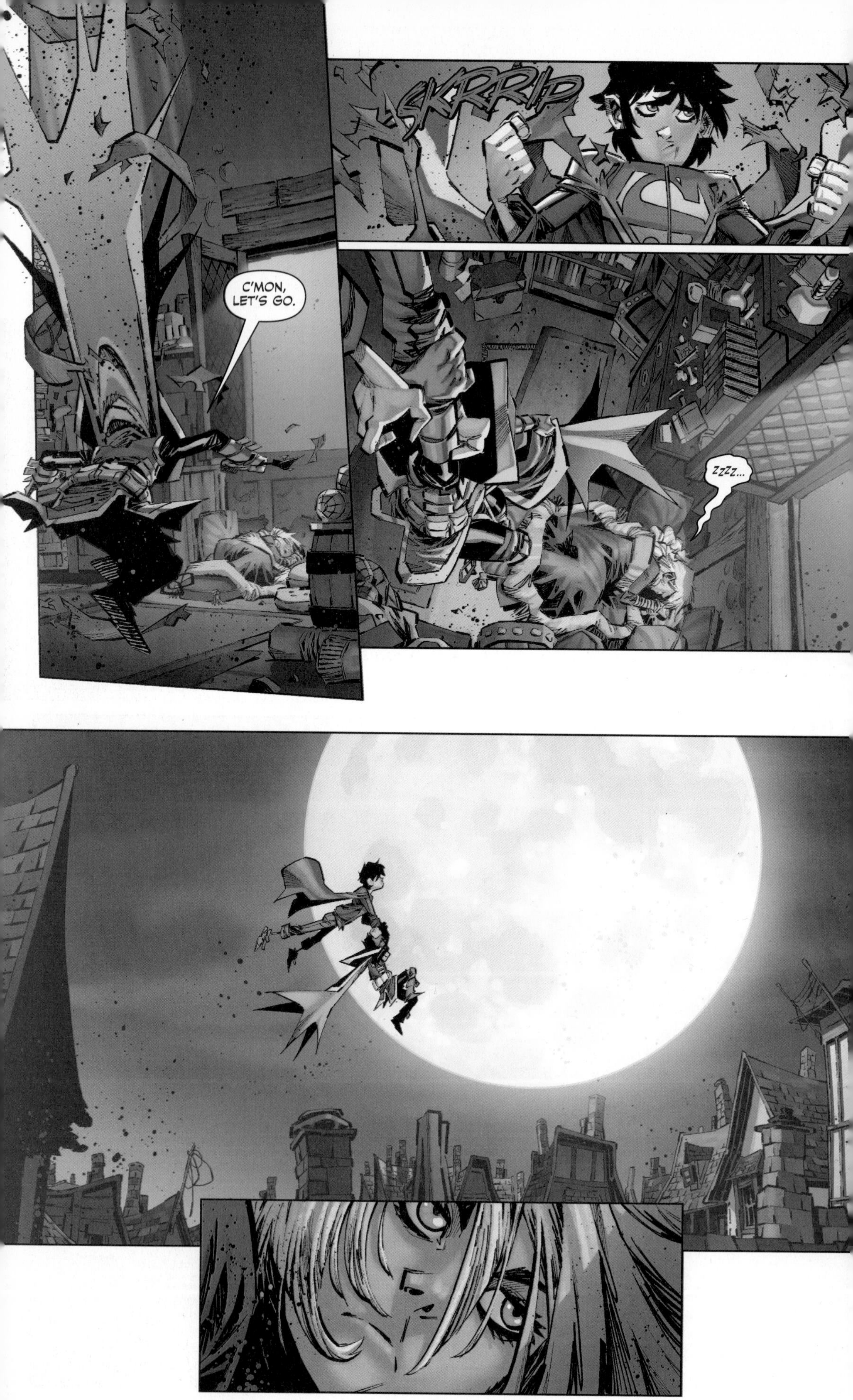
SKRRIP
C'MON, LET'S GO.
ZZZZ...

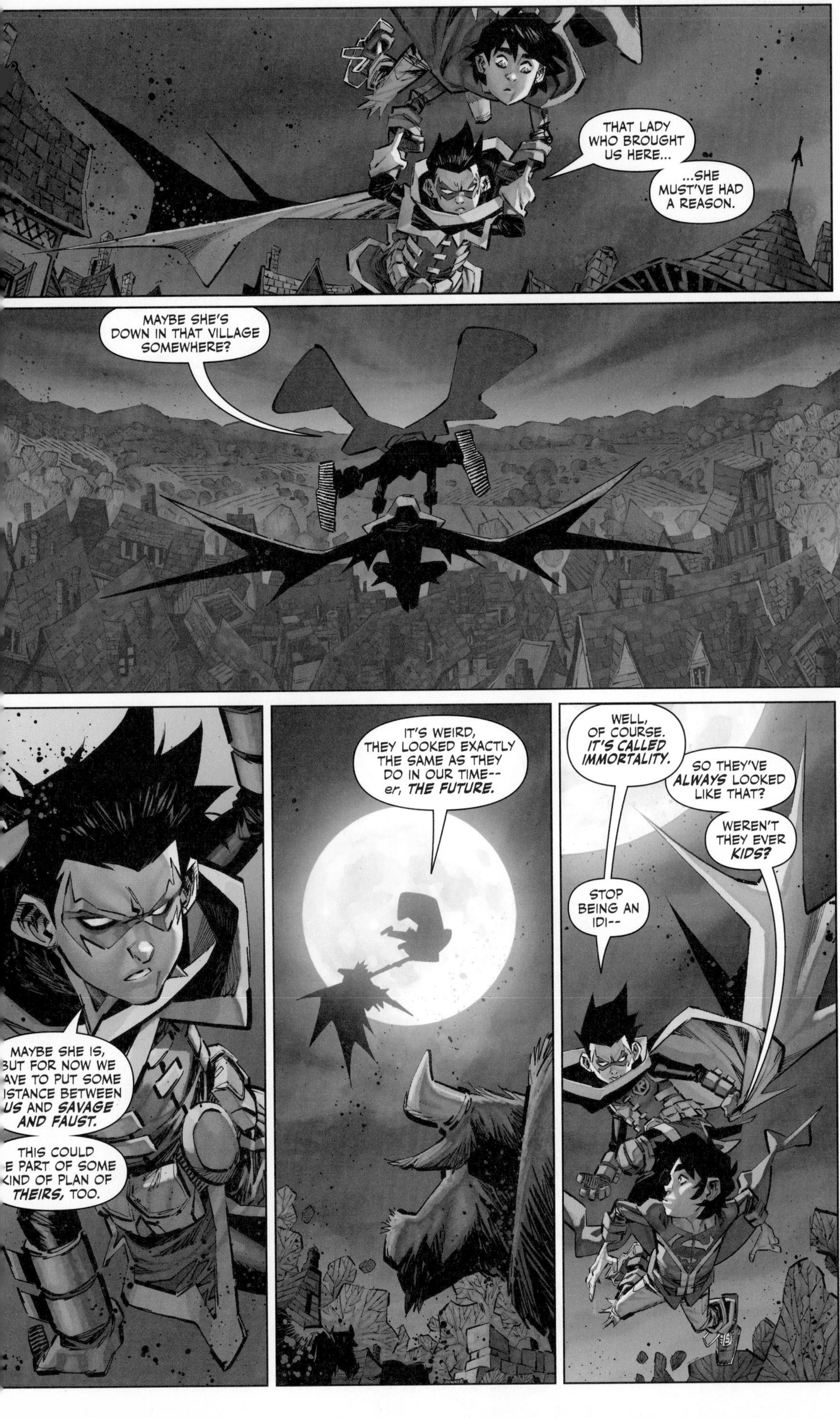

THAT LADY WHO BROUGHT US HERE...
...SHE MUST'VE HAD A REASON.
MAYBE SHE'S DOWN IN THAT VILLAGE SOMEWHERE?
MAYBE SHE IS, UT FOR NOW WE AVE TO PUT SOME ISTANCE BETWEEN US AND *SAVAGE AND FAUST.*
THIS COULD E PART OF SOME KIND OF PLAN OF *THEIRS,* TOO.
IT'S WEIRD, THEY LOOKED EXACTLY THE SAME AS THEY DO IN OUR TIME-- *er,* ***THE FUTURE.***
WELL, OF COURSE. ***IT'S CALLED IMMORTALITY.***
SO THEY'VE ***ALWAYS*** LOOKED LIKE THAT?
WEREN'T THEY EVER ***KIDS?***
STOP BEING AN IDI--

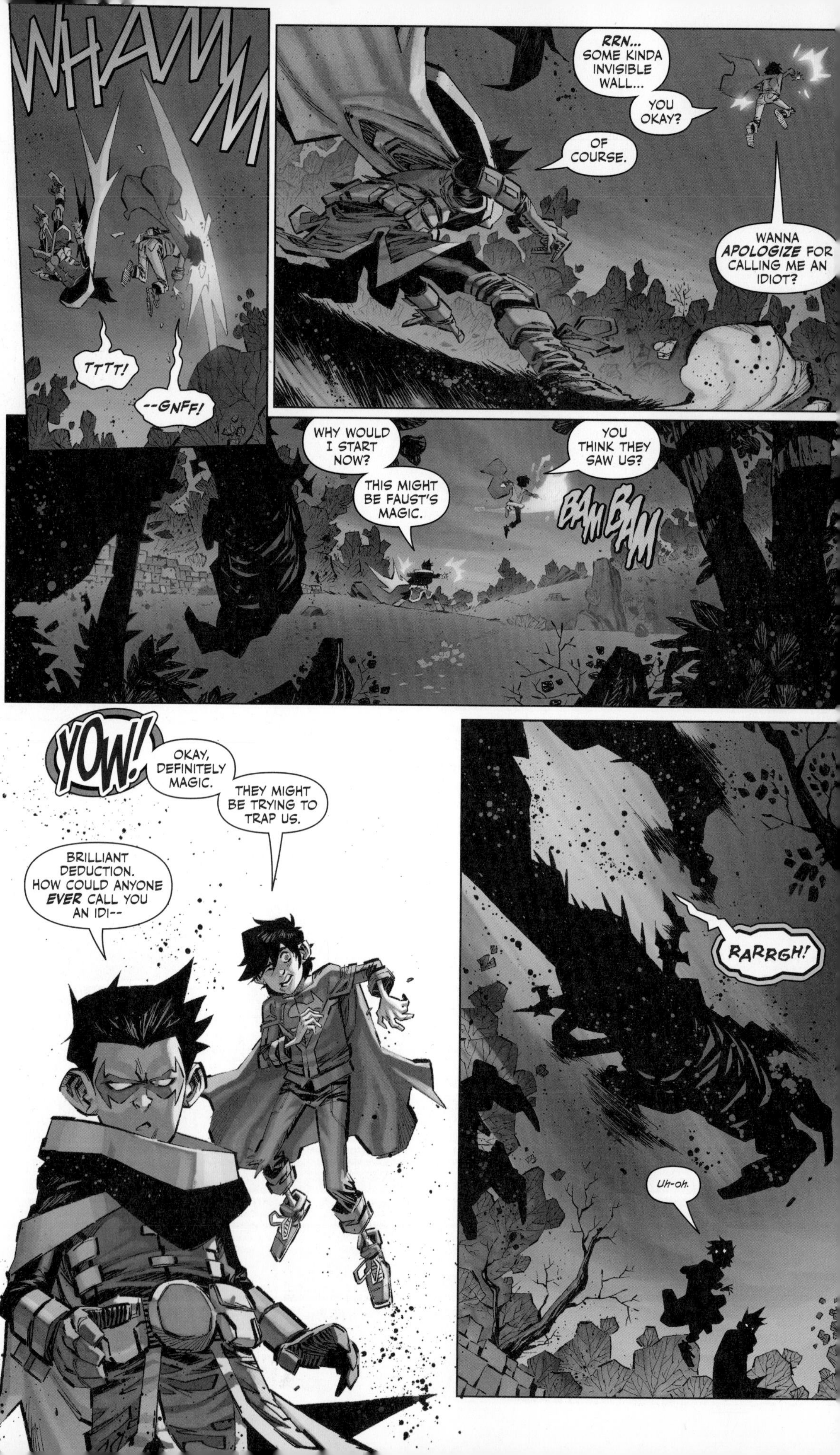

WHAMM
TTTT!
--GNFF!
RRN... SOME KINDA INVISIBLE WALL...
YOU OKAY?
OF COURSE.
WANNA APOLOGIZE FOR CALLING ME AN IDIOT?
WHY WOULD I START NOW?
THIS MIGHT BE FAUST'S MAGIC.
YOU THINK THEY SAW US?
BAM BAM
YOW!
OKAY, DEFINITELY MAGIC.
THEY MIGHT BE TRYING TO TRAP US.
BRILLIANT DEDUCTION. HOW COULD ANYONE EVER CALL YOU AN IDI--
RARRGH!
Uh-oh.

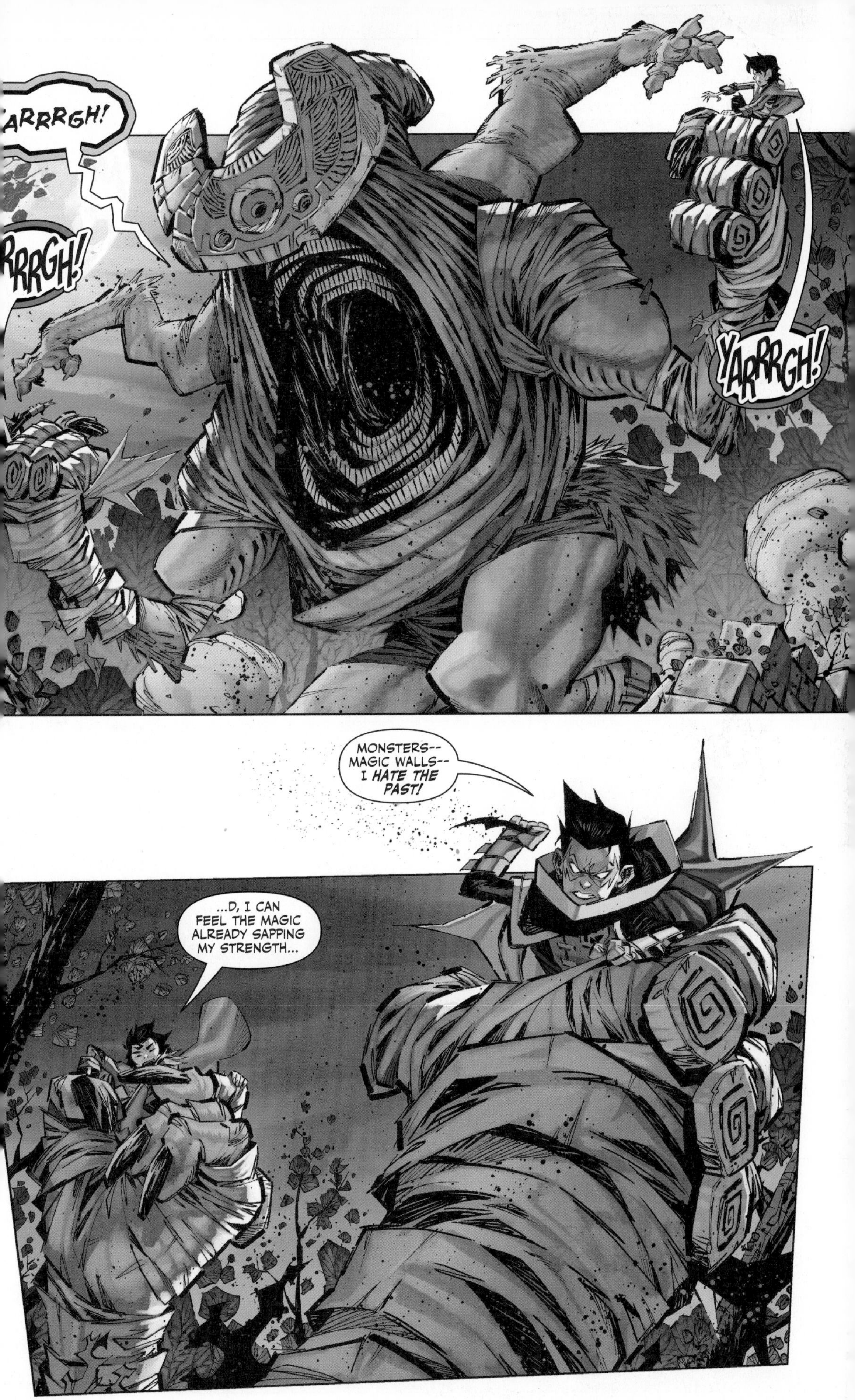
YARRRGH!
RRRGH!
YARRRGH!
MONSTERS-- MAGIC WALLS-- I HATE THE PAST!
...D, I CAN FEEL THE MAGIC ALREADY SAPPING MY STRENGTH...

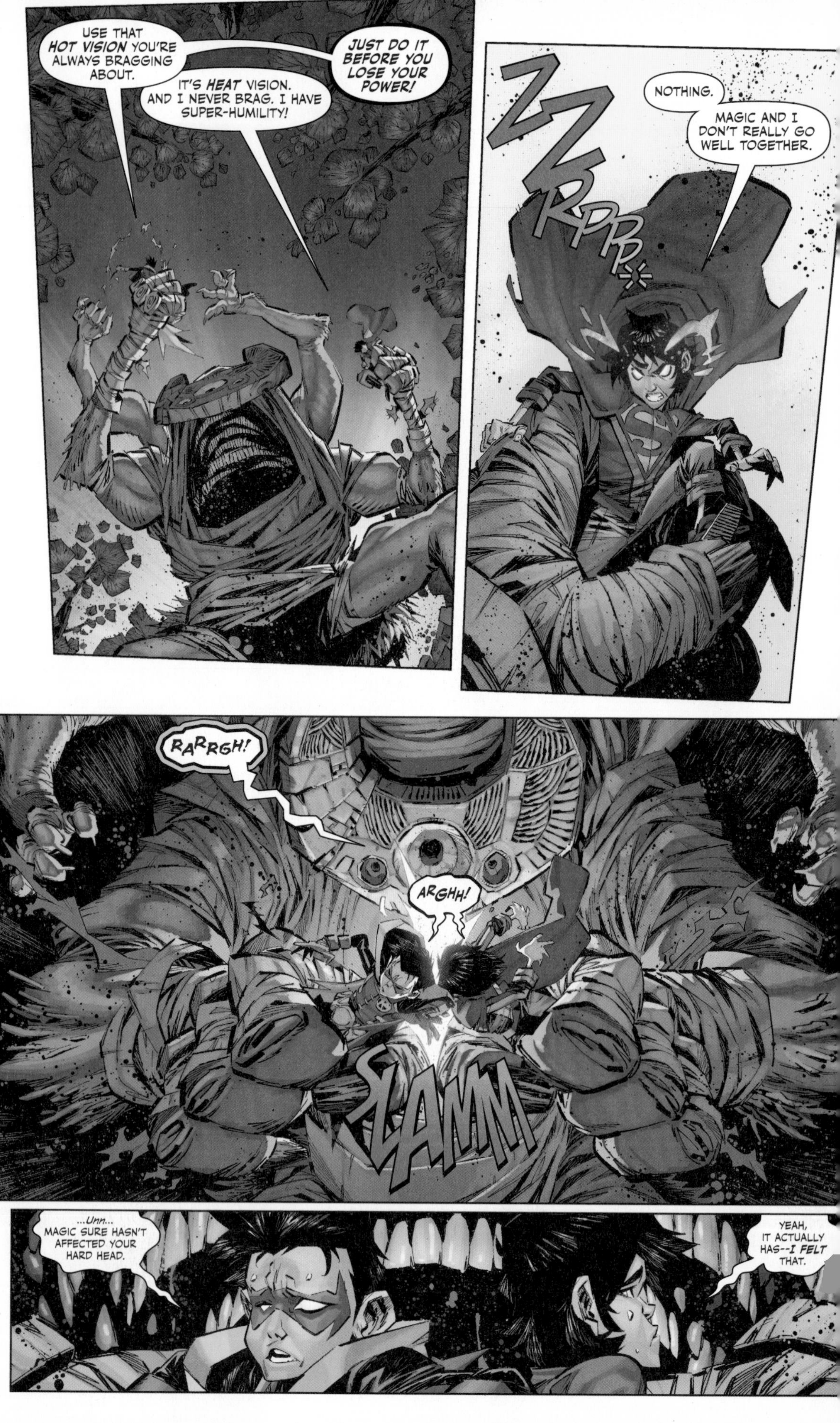

USE THAT HOT VISION YOU'RE ALWAYS BRAGGING ABOUT.
JUST DO IT BEFORE YOU LOSE YOUR POWER!
IT'S HEAT VISION. AND I NEVER BRAG. I HAVE SUPER-HUMILITY!
ZZZRPPP
NOTHING.
MAGIC AND I DON'T REALLY GO WELL TOGETHER.
RARRGH!
ARGHH!
SLAMM
...Unn... MAGIC SURE HASN'T AFFECTED YOUR HARD HEAD.
YEAH, IT ACTUALLY HAS--I FELT THAT.

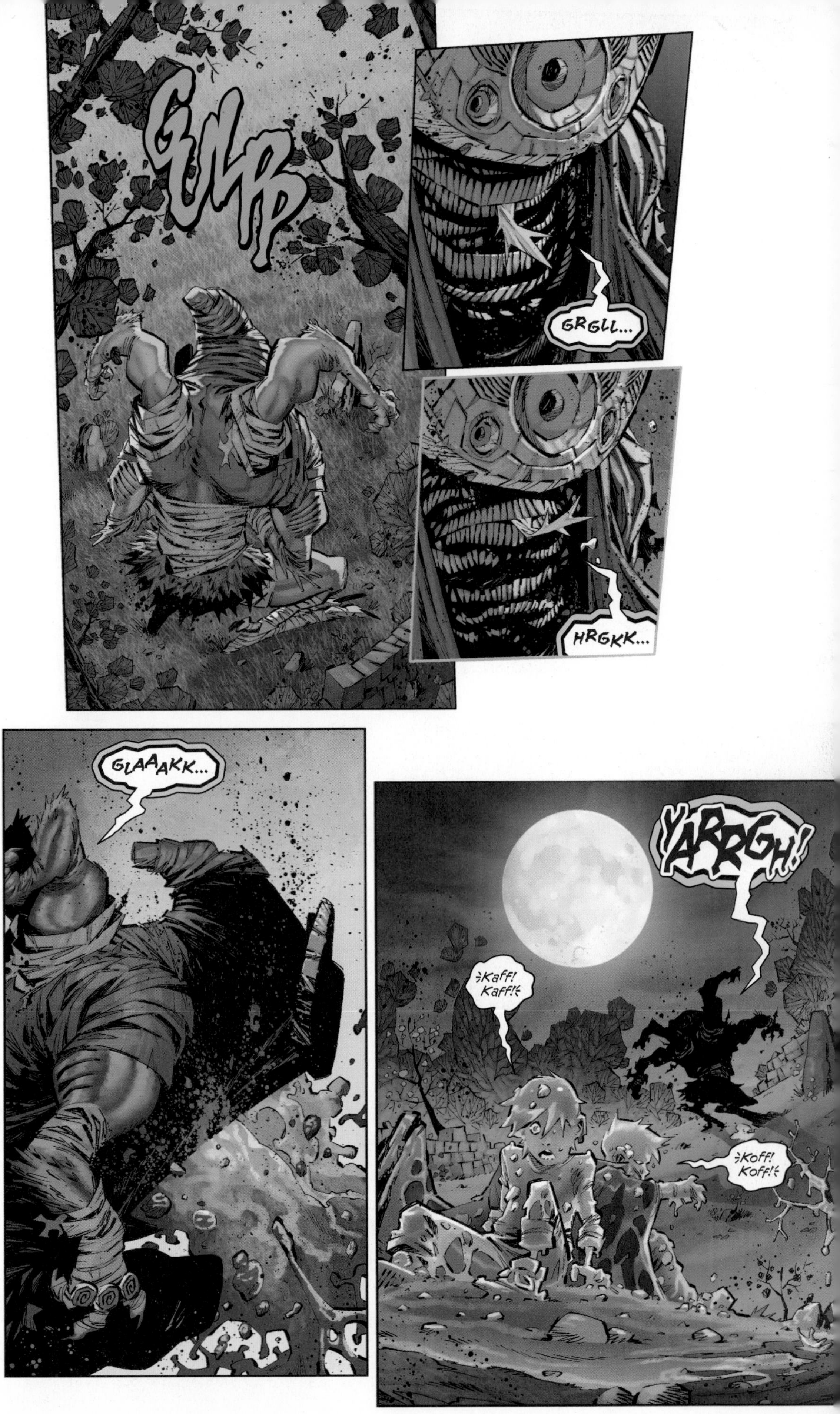
GULP
GRGLL...
HRGKK...
GLAAAKK...
YARRGH!
Kaff! Kaff!
Koff! Koff!

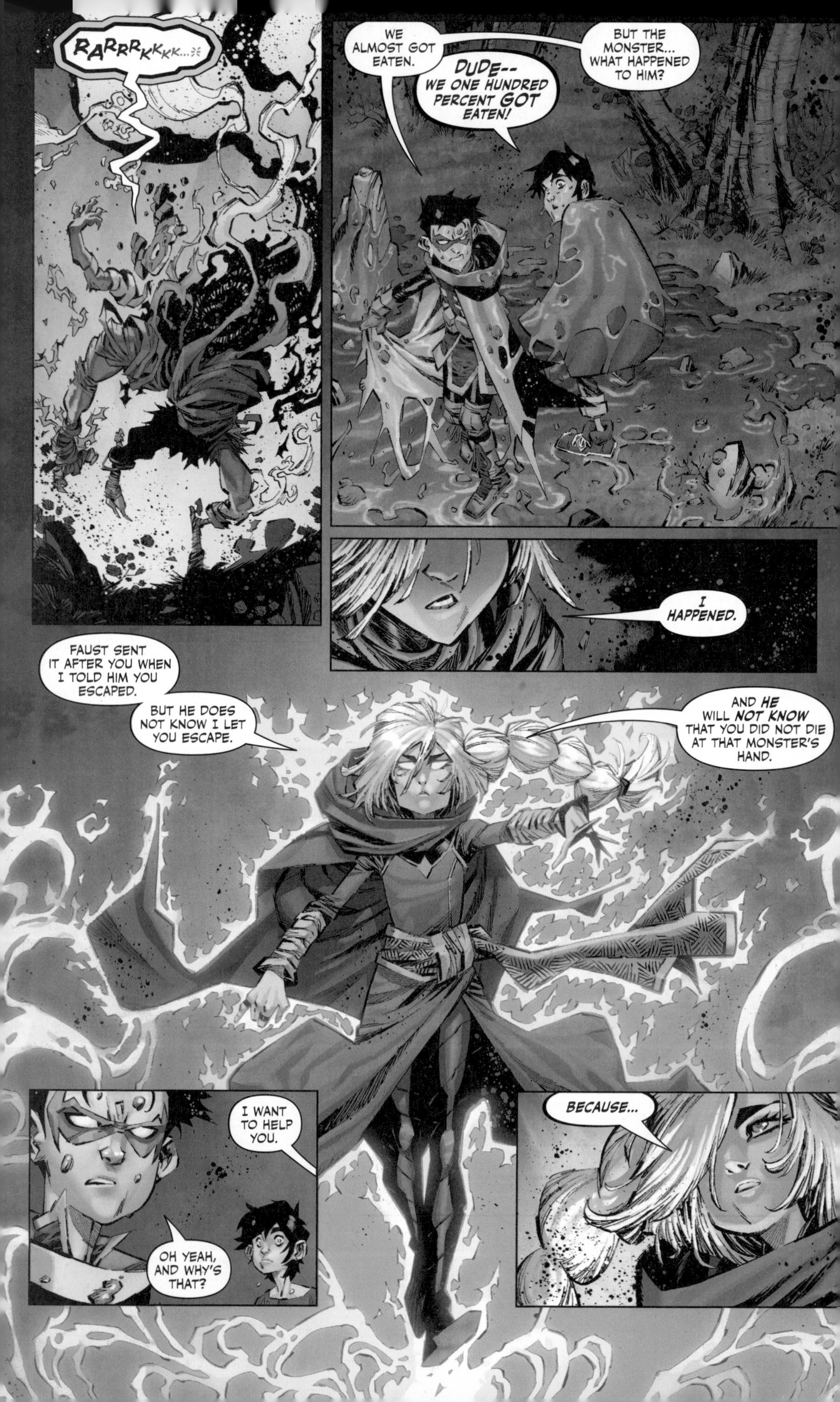
RARRRKKKK...
WE ALMOST GOT EATEN.
DUDE-- WE ONE HUNDRED PERCENT GOT EATEN!
BUT THE MONSTER... WHAT HAPPENED TO HIM?
I HAPPENED.
FAUST SENT IT AFTER YOU WHEN I TOLD HIM YOU ESCAPED.
BUT HE DOES NOT KNOW I LET YOU ESCAPE.
AND HE WILL NOT KNOW THAT YOU DID NOT DIE AT THAT MONSTER'S HAND.
I WANT TO HELP YOU.
OH YEAH, AND WHY'S THAT?
BECAUSE...

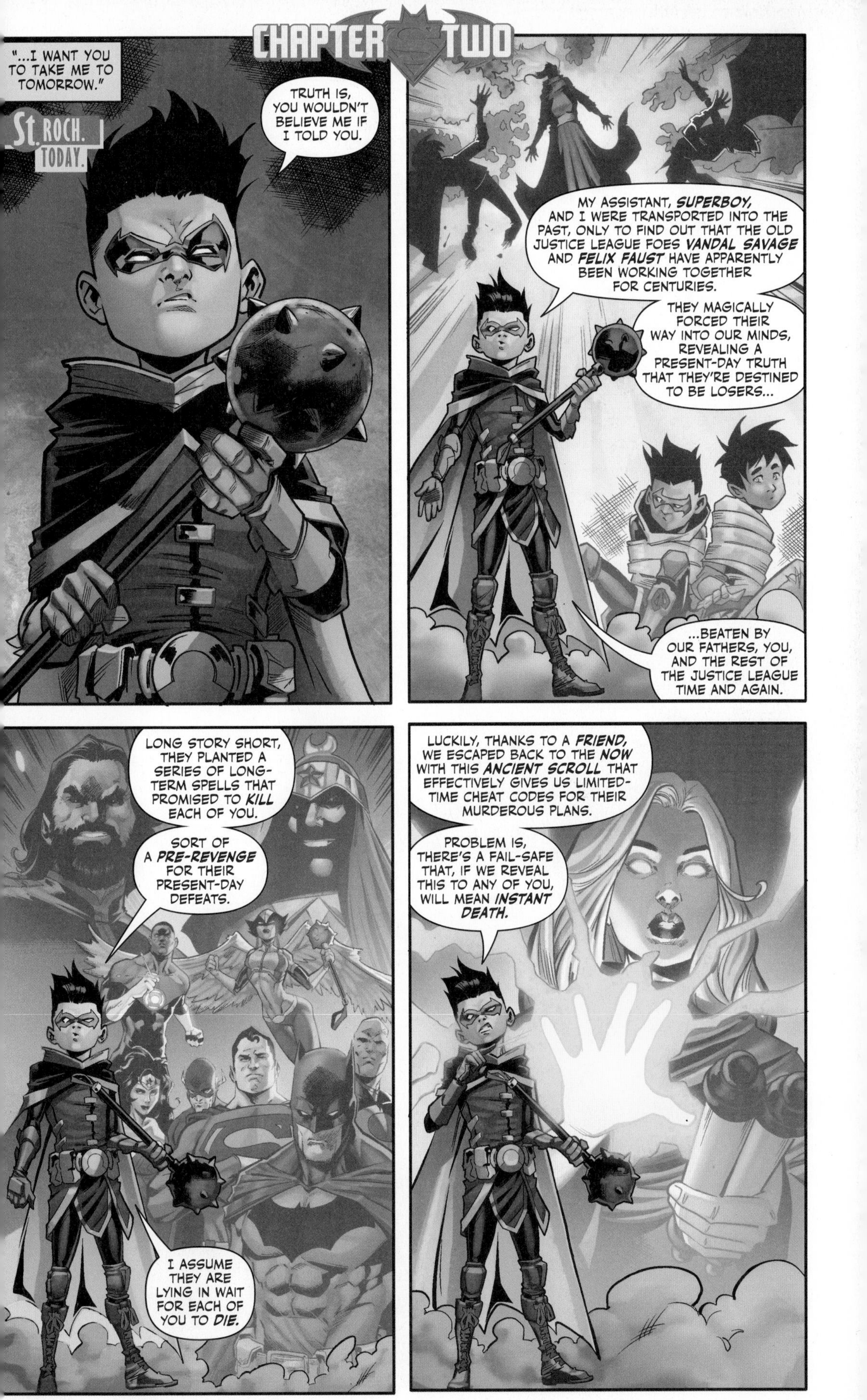
CHAPTER TWO
"...I WANT YOU TO TAKE ME TO TOMORROW."
St. ROCH. TODAY.
TRUTH IS, YOU WOULDN'T BELIEVE ME IF I TOLD YOU.
MY ASSISTANT, SUPERBOY, AND I WERE TRANSPORTED INTO THE PAST, ONLY TO FIND OUT THAT THE OLD JUSTICE LEAGUE FOES VANDAL SAVAGE AND FELIX FAUST HAVE APPARENTLY BEEN WORKING TOGETHER FOR CENTURIES.
THEY MAGICALLY FORCED THEIR WAY INTO OUR MINDS, REVEALING A PRESENT-DAY TRUTH THAT THEY'RE DESTINED TO BE LOSERS...
...BEATEN BY OUR FATHERS, YOU, AND THE REST OF THE JUSTICE LEAGUE TIME AND AGAIN.
LONG STORY SHORT, THEY PLANTED A SERIES OF LONG-TERM SPELLS THAT PROMISED TO KILL EACH OF YOU.
SORT OF A PRE-REVENGE FOR THEIR PRESENT-DAY DEFEATS.
I ASSUME THEY ARE LYING IN WAIT FOR EACH OF YOU TO DIE.
LUCKILY, THANKS TO A FRIEND, WE ESCAPED BACK TO THE NOW WITH THIS ANCIENT SCROLL THAT EFFECTIVELY GIVES US LIMITED-TIME CHEAT CODES FOR THEIR MURDEROUS PLANS.
PROBLEM IS, THERE'S A FAIL-SAFE THAT, IF WE REVEAL THIS TO ANY OF YOU, WILL MEAN INSTANT DEATH.

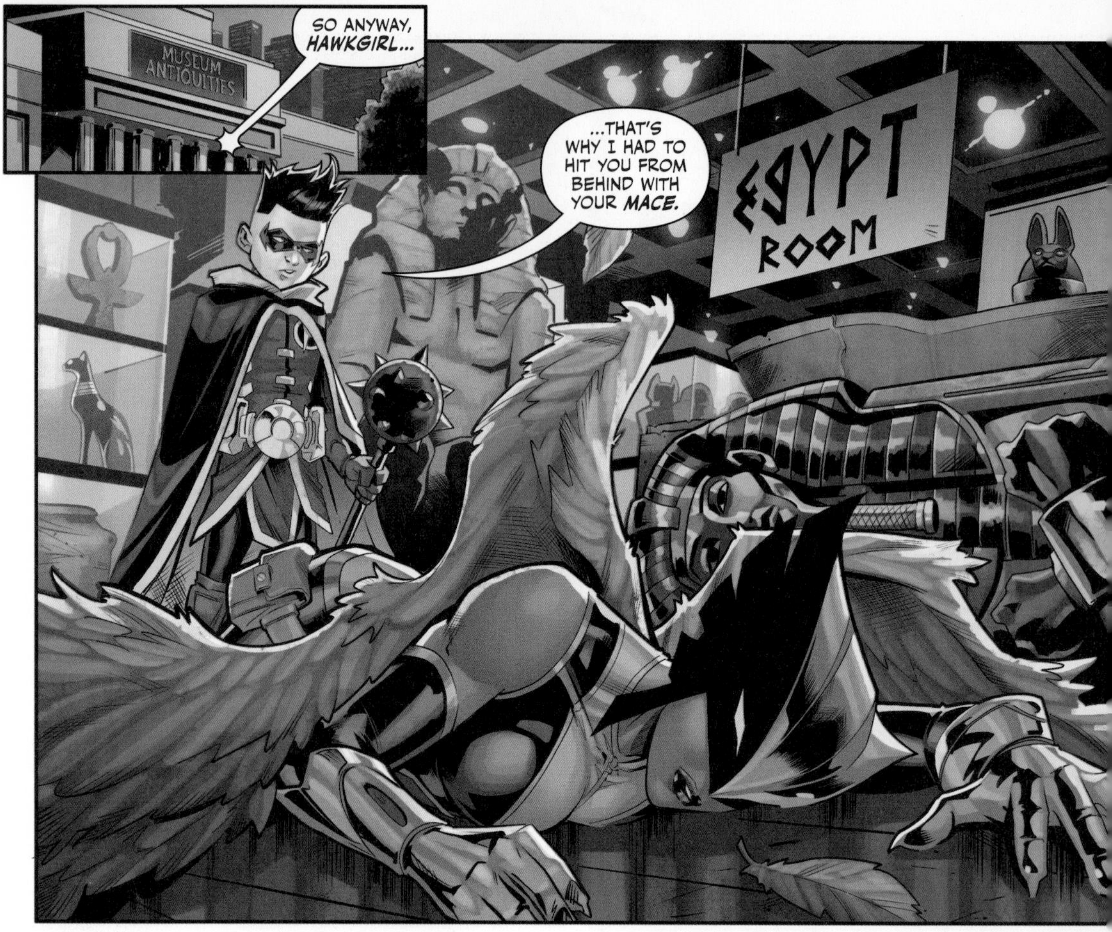
MUSEUM ANTIQUITIES
SO ANYWAY, HAWKGIRL...
...THAT'S WHY I HAD TO HIT YOU FROM BEHIND WITH YOUR MACE.
EGYPT ROOM

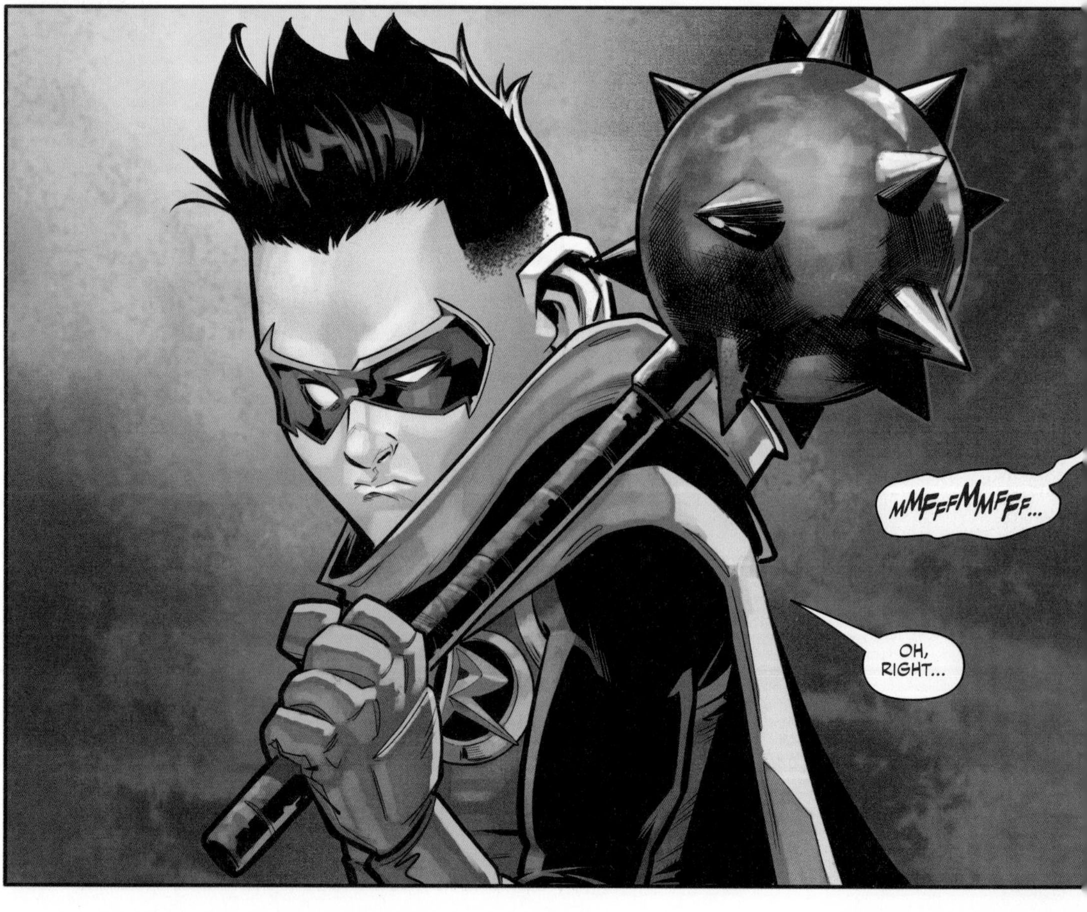
MMFFFMMFFF...
OH, RIGHT...

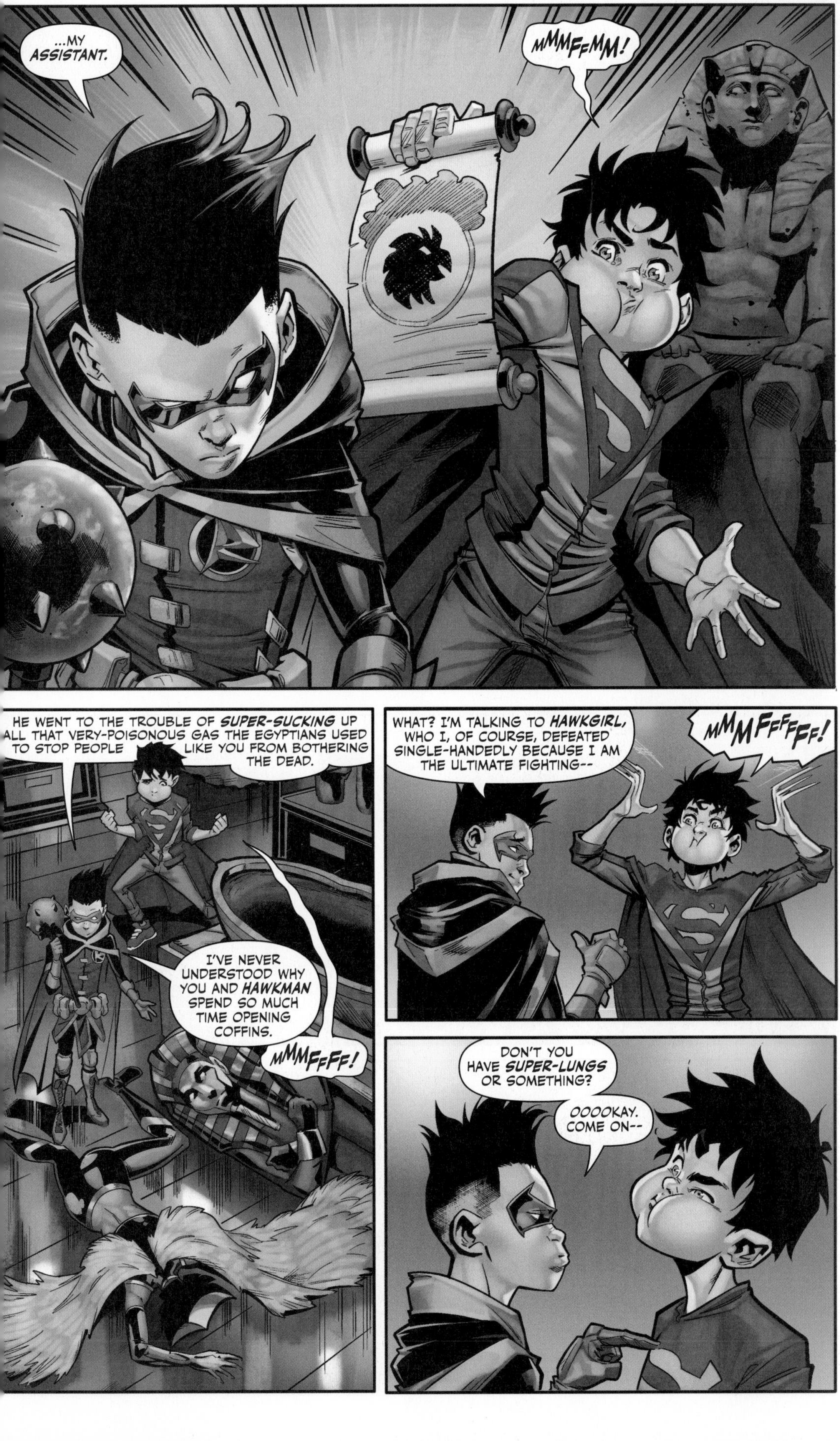

...MY ASSISTANT.
MMMFFMM!
HE WENT TO THE TROUBLE OF SUPER-SUCKING UP ALL THAT VERY-POISONOUS GAS THE EGYPTIANS USED TO STOP PEOPLE LIKE YOU FROM BOTHERING THE DEAD.
I'VE NEVER UNDERSTOOD WHY YOU AND HAWKMAN SPEND SO MUCH TIME OPENING COFFINS.
MMMFFFF!
WHAT? I'M TALKING TO HAWKGIRL, WHO I, OF COURSE, DEFEATED SINGLE-HANDEDLY BECAUSE I AM THE ULTIMATE FIGHTING--
MMMFFFFFF!
DON'T YOU HAVE SUPER-LUNGS OR SOMETHING?
OOOOKAY. COME ON--

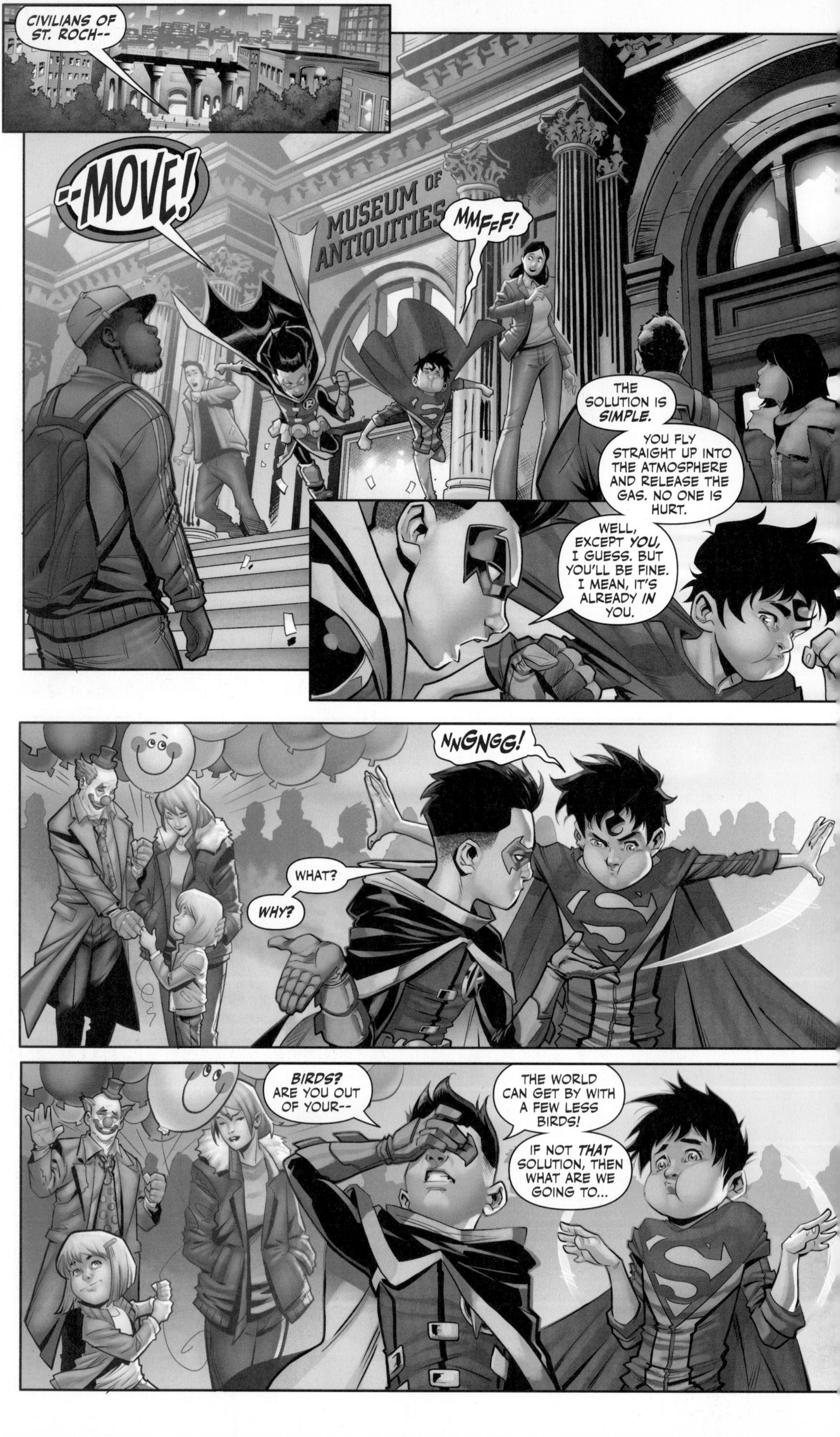
CIVILIANS OF ST. ROCH--
--MOVE!
MUSEUM OF ANTIQUITIES
MMFFF!
THE SOLUTION IS SIMPLE.
YOU FLY STRAIGHT UP INTO THE ATMOSPHERE AND RELEASE THE GAS. NO ONE IS HURT.
WELL, EXCEPT YOU, I GUESS. BUT YOU'LL BE FINE. I MEAN, IT'S ALREADY IN YOU.
NNGNGG!
WHAT?
WHY?
BIRDS? ARE YOU OUT OF YOUR--
THE WORLD CAN GET BY WITH A FEW LESS BIRDS!
IF NOT THAT SOLUTION, THEN WHAT ARE WE GOING TO...

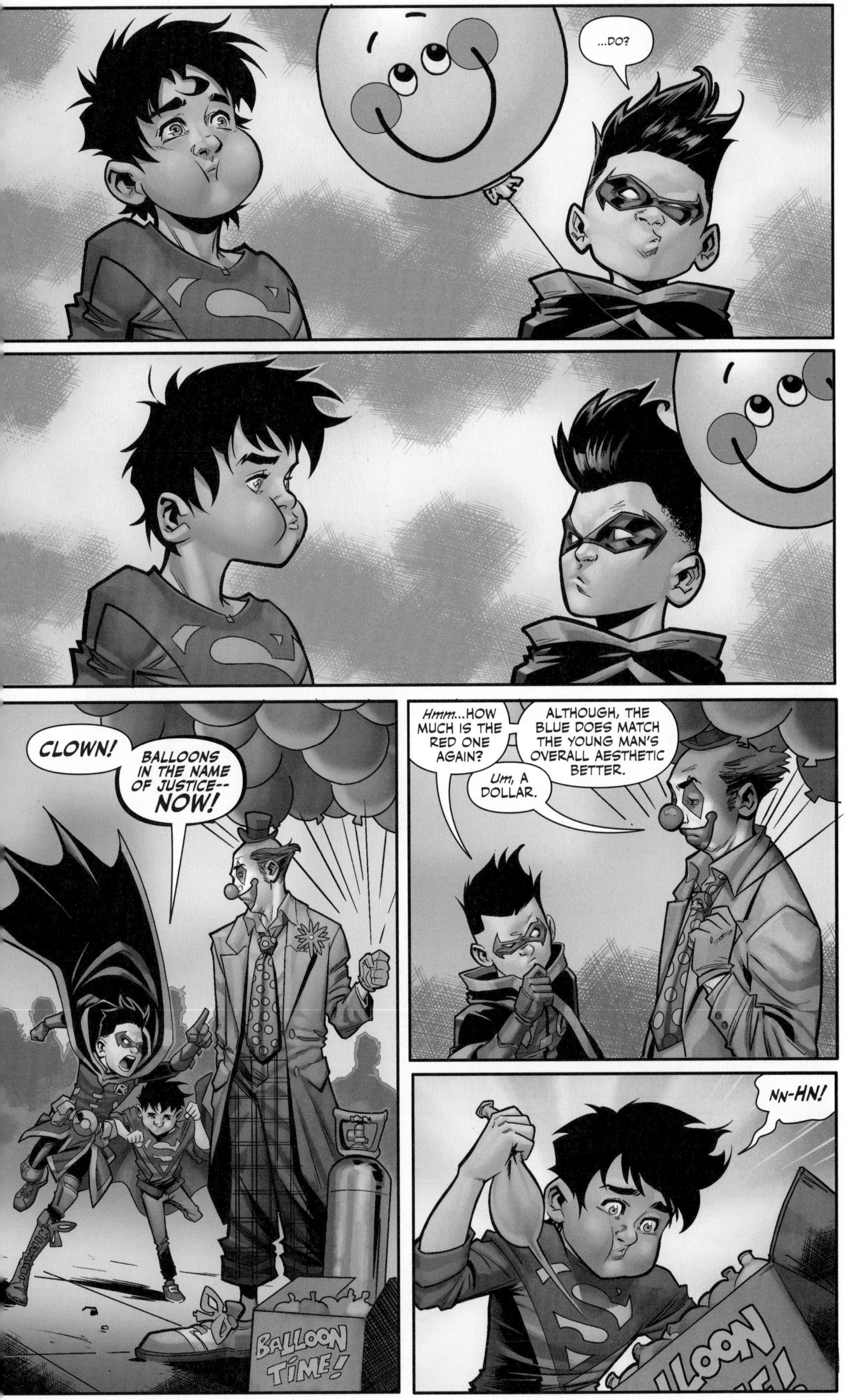
...DO?
CLOWN!
BALLOONS IN THE NAME OF JUSTICE-- NOW!
BALLOON TIME!
Hmm...HOW MUCH IS THE RED ONE AGAIN?
ALTHOUGH, THE BLUE DOES MATCH THE YOUNG MAN'S OVERALL AESTHETIC BETTER.
Um, A DOLLAR.
NN-HN!

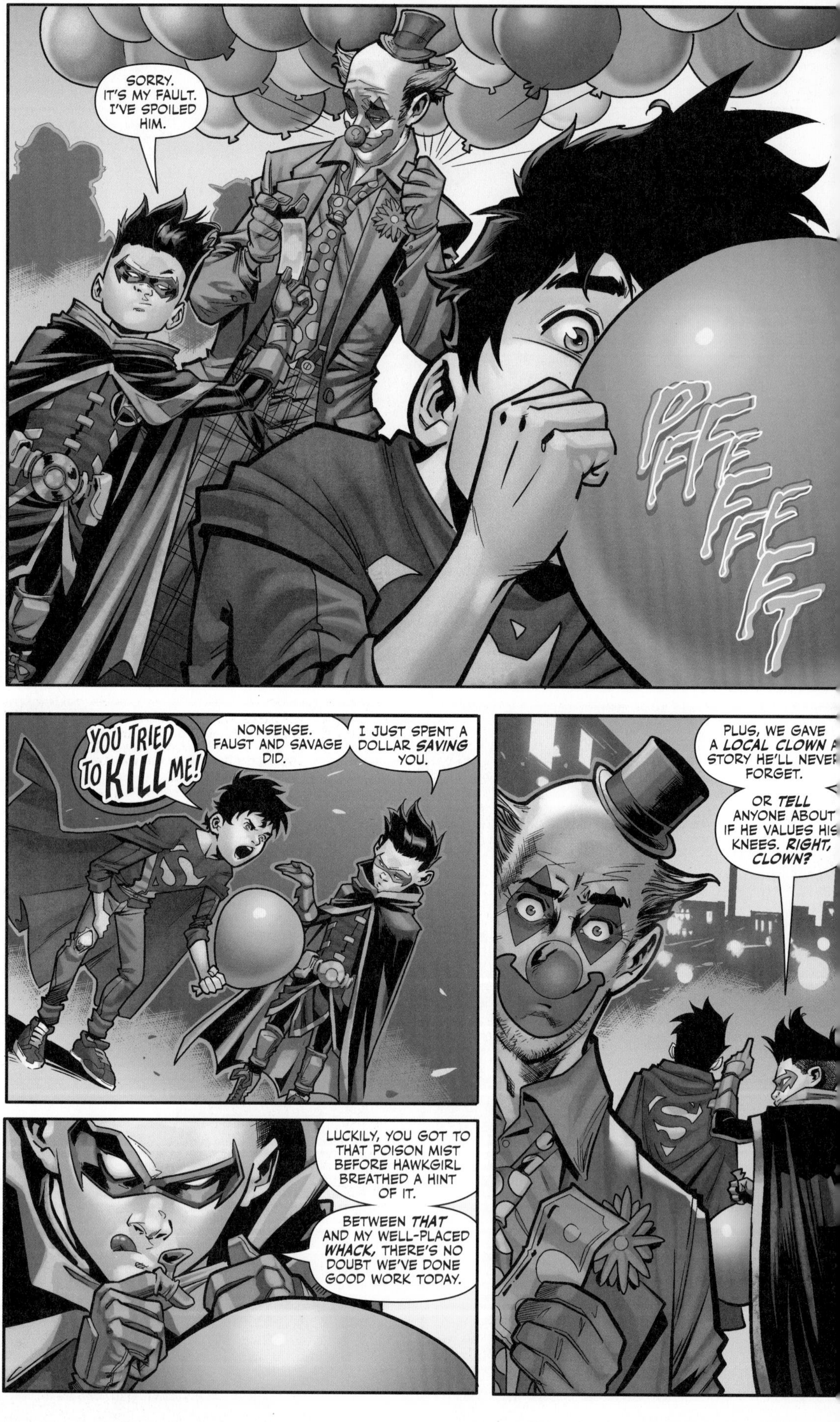
SORRY. IT'S MY FAULT. I'VE SPOILED HIM.
PFFFFFT
YOU TRIED TO KILL ME!
NONSENSE. FAUST AND SAVAGE DID.
I JUST SPENT A DOLLAR *SAVING* YOU.
LUCKILY, YOU GOT TO THAT POISON MIST BEFORE HAWKGIRL BREATHED A HINT OF IT.
BETWEEN *THAT* AND MY WELL-PLACED *WHACK*, THERE'S NO DOUBT WE'VE DONE GOOD WORK TODAY.
PLUS, WE GAVE A *LOCAL CLOWN* STORY HE'LL NEVER FORGET.
OR *TELL* ANYONE ABOUT IF HE VALUES HIS KNEES. *RIGHT, CLOWN?*

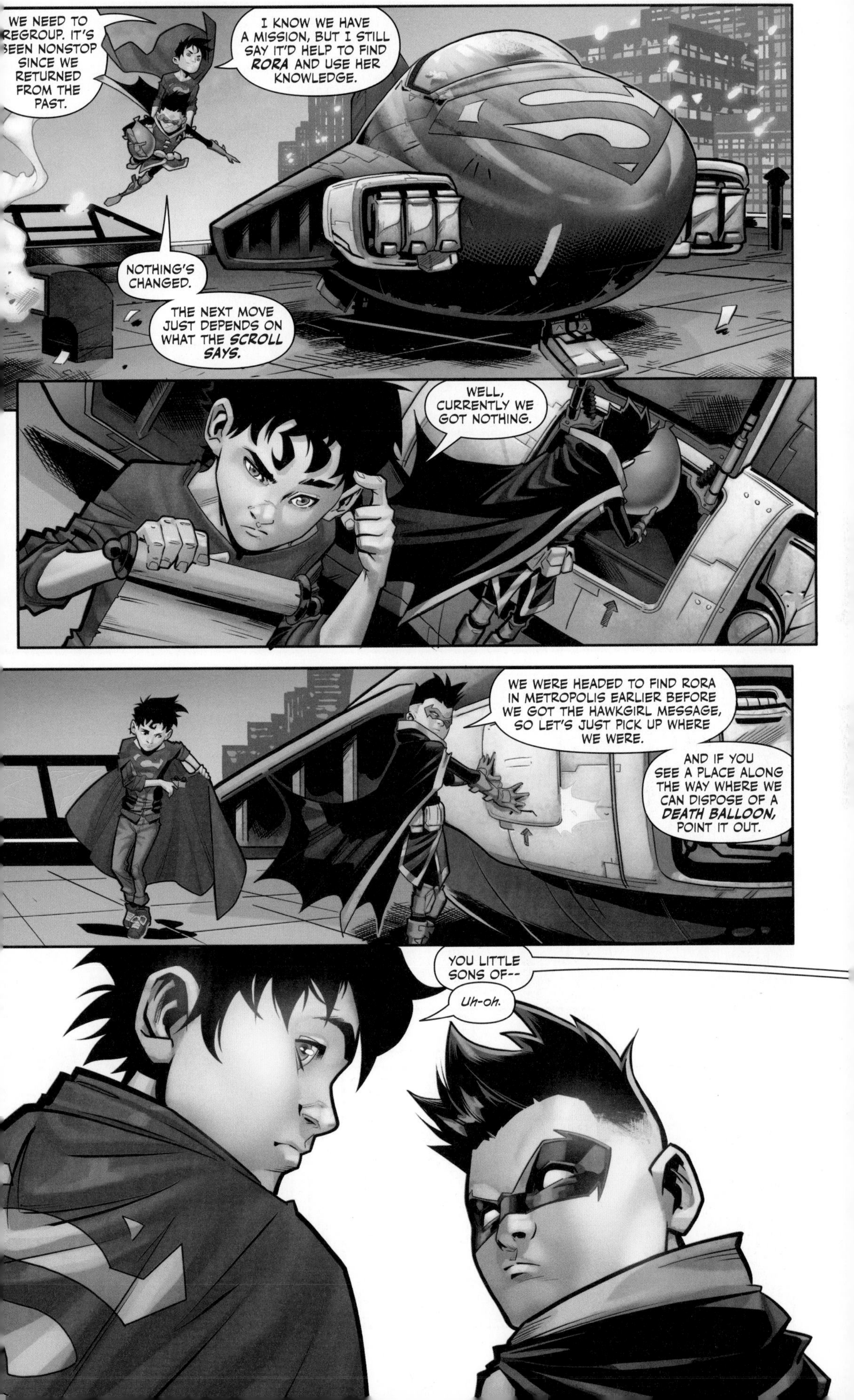
WE NEED TO REGROUP. IT'S BEEN NONSTOP SINCE WE RETURNED FROM THE PAST.
I KNOW WE HAVE A MISSION, BUT I STILL SAY IT'D HELP TO FIND RORA AND USE HER KNOWLEDGE.
NOTHING'S CHANGED.
THE NEXT MOVE JUST DEPENDS ON WHAT THE SCROLL SAYS.
WELL, CURRENTLY WE GOT NOTHING.
WE WERE HEADED TO FIND RORA IN METROPOLIS EARLIER BEFORE WE GOT THE HAWKGIRL MESSAGE, SO LET'S JUST PICK UP WHERE WE WERE.
AND IF YOU SEE A PLACE ALONG THE WAY WHERE WE CAN DISPOSE OF A DEATH BALLOON, POINT IT OUT.
YOU LITTLE SONS OF--
Uh-oh.

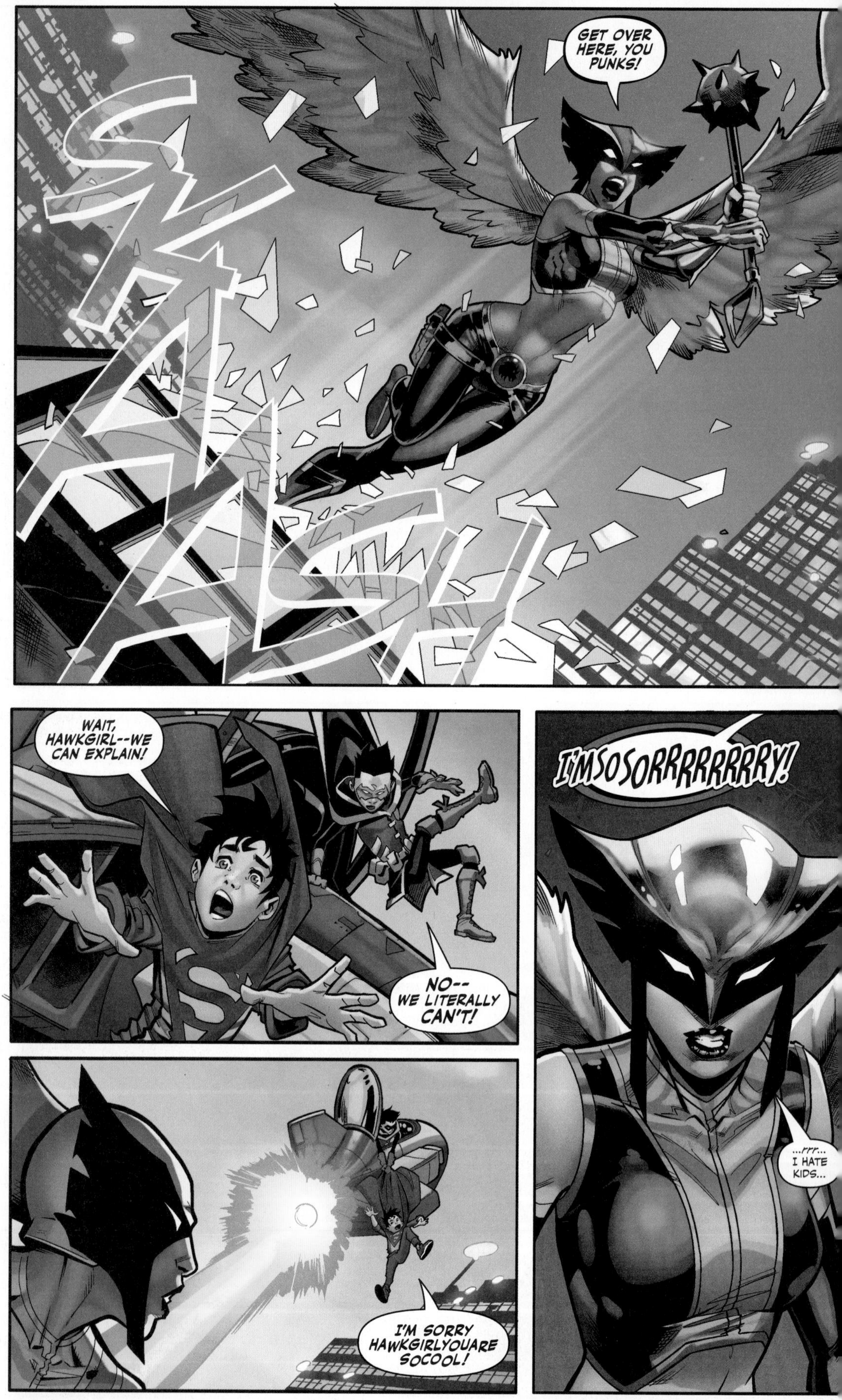
GET OVER HERE, YOU PUNKS!
SMASH
WAIT, HAWKGIRL--WE CAN EXPLAIN!
NO-- WE LITERALLY CAN'T!
I'M SORRY HAWKGIRLYOUARE SOCOOL!
I'MSOSORRRRRRRRY!
...rrr... I HATE KIDS...

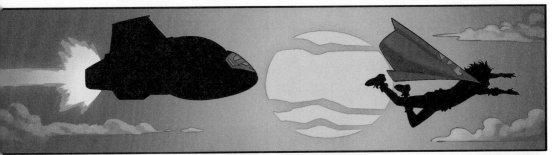

IT WAS RIGHT AROUND HERE.

THAT REMINDS ME, YOU STILL NEED TO GIVE THAT NICE MOM BACK HER MONEY.

I *EARNED* THAT TIP FOR CARRYING THAT METRIC TON OF GROCERIES!

JUST USE YOUR *HYPER-VISION* OR WHATEVER TO SEARCH FOR CLUES AS TO WHERE RORA WENT.

THERE'S *NO* SUCH THING AS HYPER-VISION. *HEAT* VISION AND *TELESCOPIC* VISION ARE ALL I--

--WHAT IS *THAT?*

FROM THERE WE CAN HOPEFULLY RETRACE RORA'S MOVEMENTS AND TRACK HER DOWN.

THEN SHE CAN HELP US SAVE THE REST OF THE JUSTICE LEAGUE.

CHRONO-VISION.

MY FATHER INVENTED IT FOR ONE OF THE CRISES IN THE PAST COUPLE YEARS.

DOESN'T DO MUCH, BUT IT WILL ALERT US TO ANY *LOCALIZED TIME DISPLACEMENTS.*

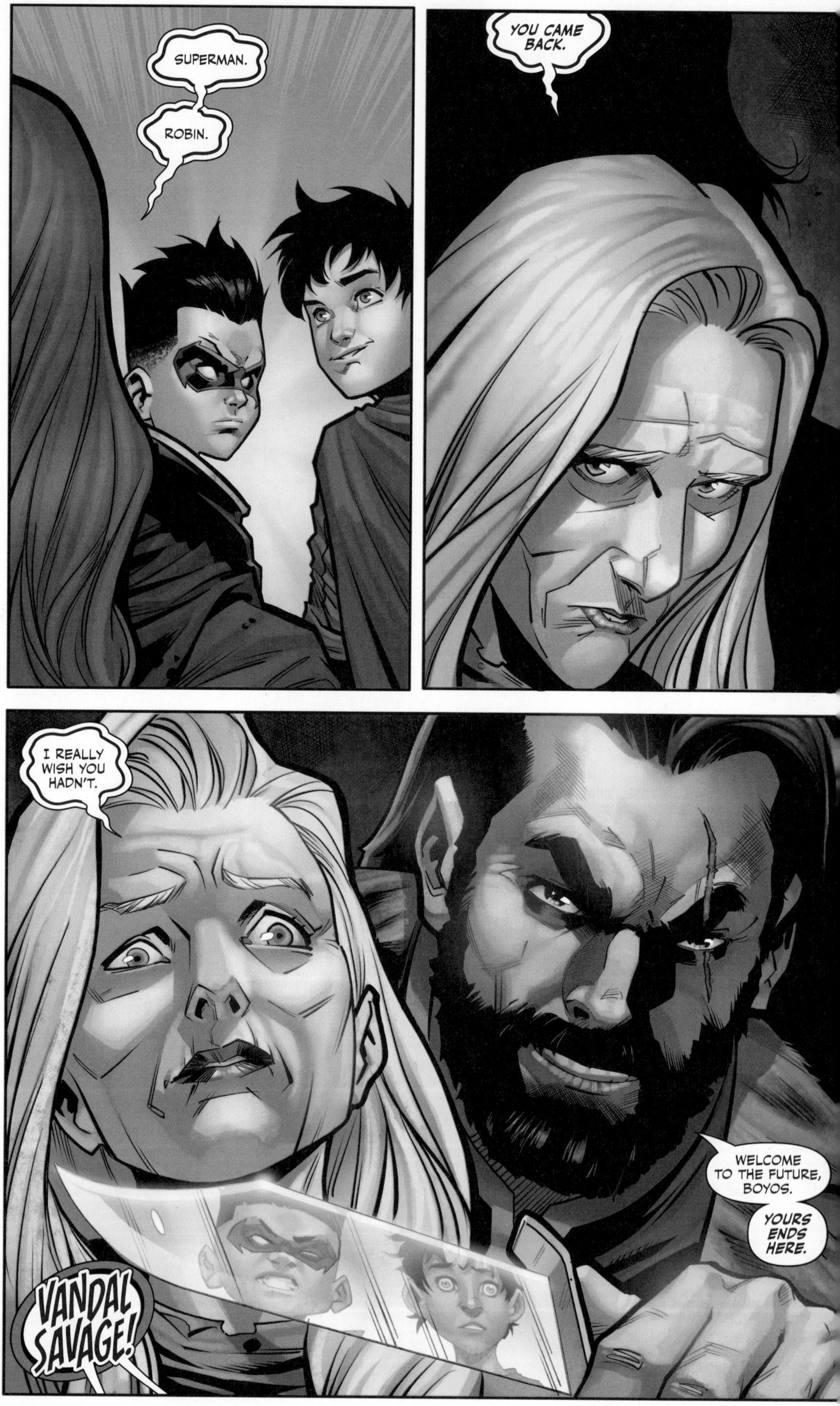
SUPERMAN.
ROBIN.
YOU CAME BACK.
I REALLY WISH YOU HADN'T.
VANDAL SAVAGE!
WELCOME TO THE FUTURE, BOYOS.
YOURS ENDS HERE.

Challenge of the Super Sons #4 cover by **SIMONE DI MEO**

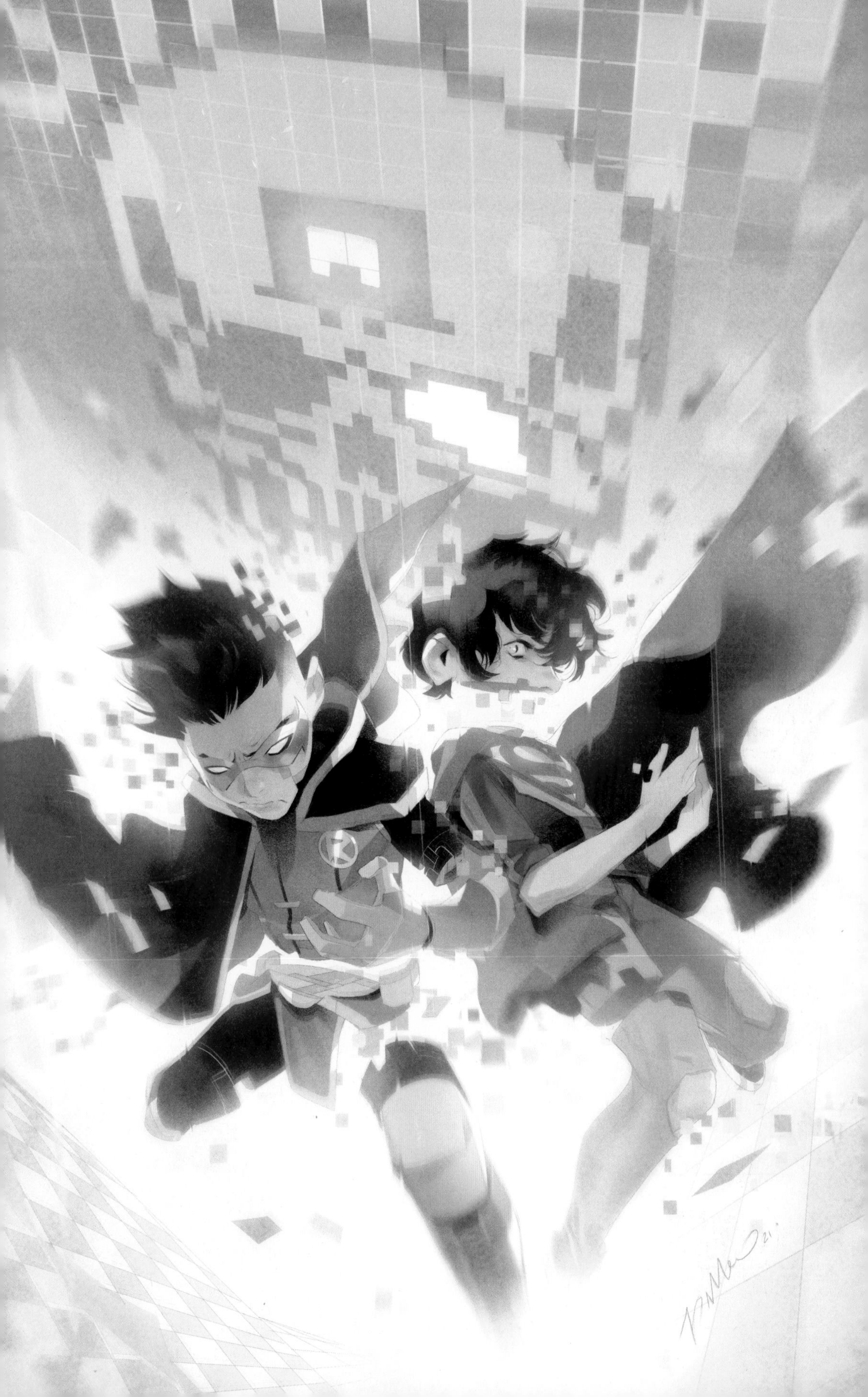

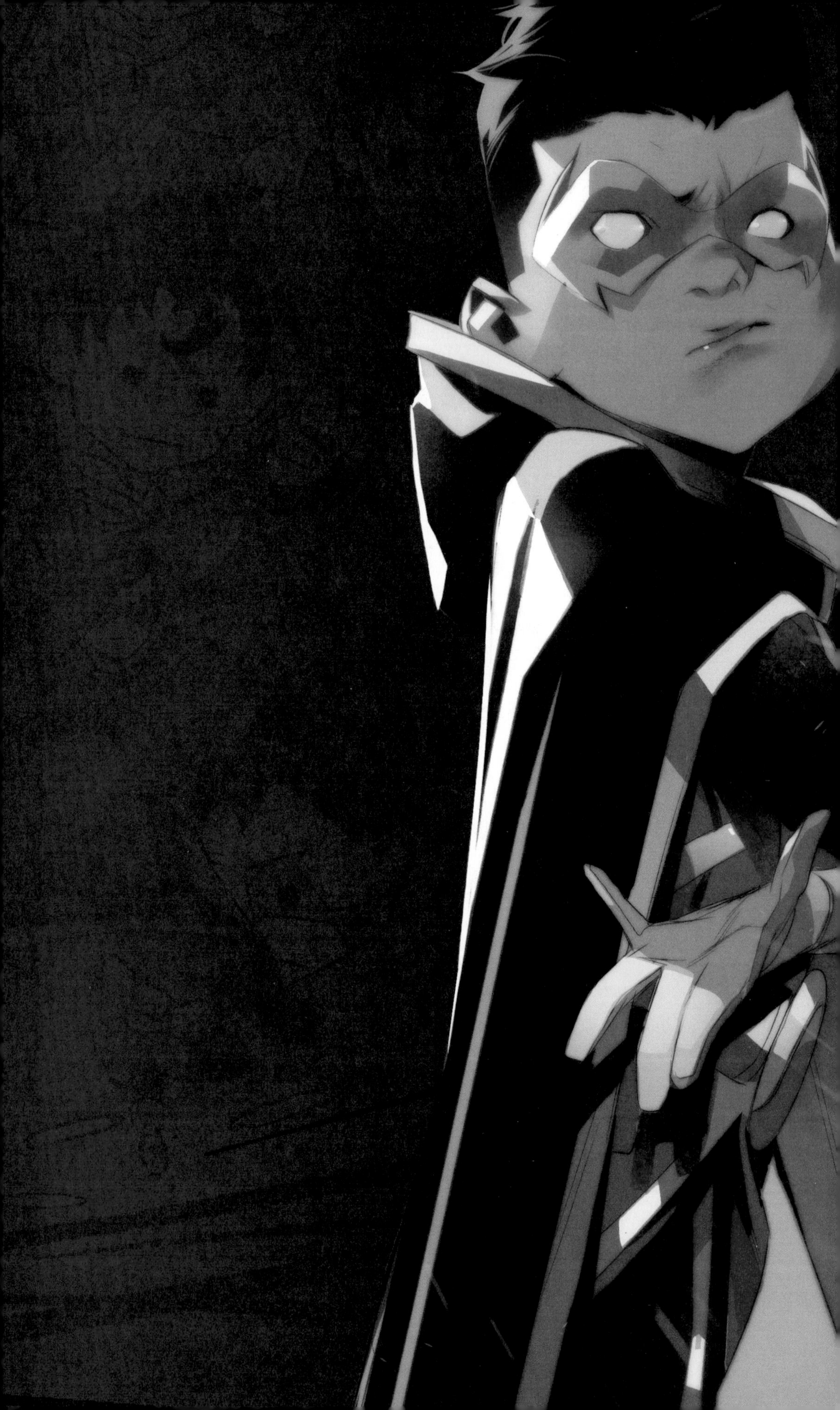

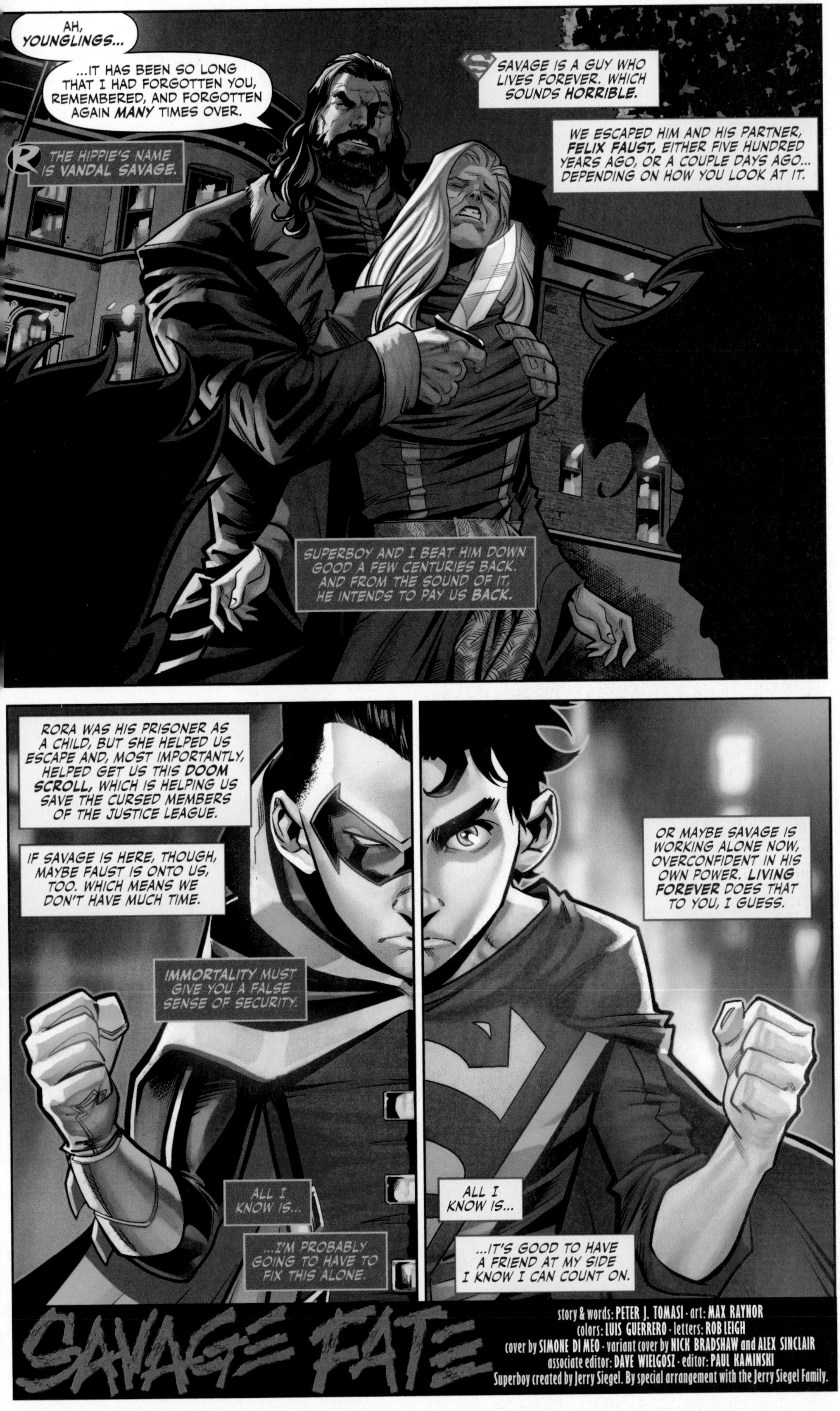
AH, YOUNGLINGS...
...IT HAS BEEN SO LONG THAT I HAD FORGOTTEN YOU, REMEMBERED, AND FORGOTTEN AGAIN MANY TIMES OVER.
THE HIPPIE'S NAME IS VANDAL SAVAGE.
SAVAGE IS A GUY WHO LIVES FOREVER. WHICH SOUNDS HORRIBLE.
WE ESCAPED HIM AND HIS PARTNER, FELIX FAUST, EITHER FIVE HUNDRED YEARS AGO, OR A COUPLE DAYS AGO... DEPENDING ON HOW YOU LOOK AT IT.
SUPERBOY AND I BEAT HIM DOWN GOOD A FEW CENTURIES BACK. AND FROM THE SOUND OF IT, HE INTENDS TO PAY US BACK.
RORA WAS HIS PRISONER AS A CHILD, BUT SHE HELPED US ESCAPE AND, MOST IMPORTANTLY, HELPED GET US THIS DOOM SCROLL, WHICH IS HELPING US SAVE THE CURSED MEMBERS OF THE JUSTICE LEAGUE.
IF SAVAGE IS HERE, THOUGH, MAYBE FAUST IS ONTO US, TOO. WHICH MEANS WE DON'T HAVE MUCH TIME.
IMMORTALITY MUST GIVE YOU A FALSE SENSE OF SECURITY.
ALL I KNOW IS...
...I'M PROBABLY GOING TO HAVE TO FIX THIS ALONE.
OR MAYBE SAVAGE IS WORKING ALONE NOW, OVERCONFIDENT IN HIS OWN POWER. LIVING FOREVER DOES THAT TO YOU, I GUESS.
ALL I KNOW IS...
...IT'S GOOD TO HAVE A FRIEND AT MY SIDE I KNOW I CAN COUNT ON.
SAVAGE FATE
story & words: PETER J. TOMASI · art: MAX RAYNOR
colors: LUIS GUERRERO · letters: ROB LEIGH
cover by SIMONE DI MEO · variant cover by NICK BRADSHAW and ALEX SINCLAIR
associate editor: DAVE WIELGOSZ · editor: PAUL KAMINSKI
Superboy created by Jerry Siegel. By special arrangement with the Jerry Siegel Family.

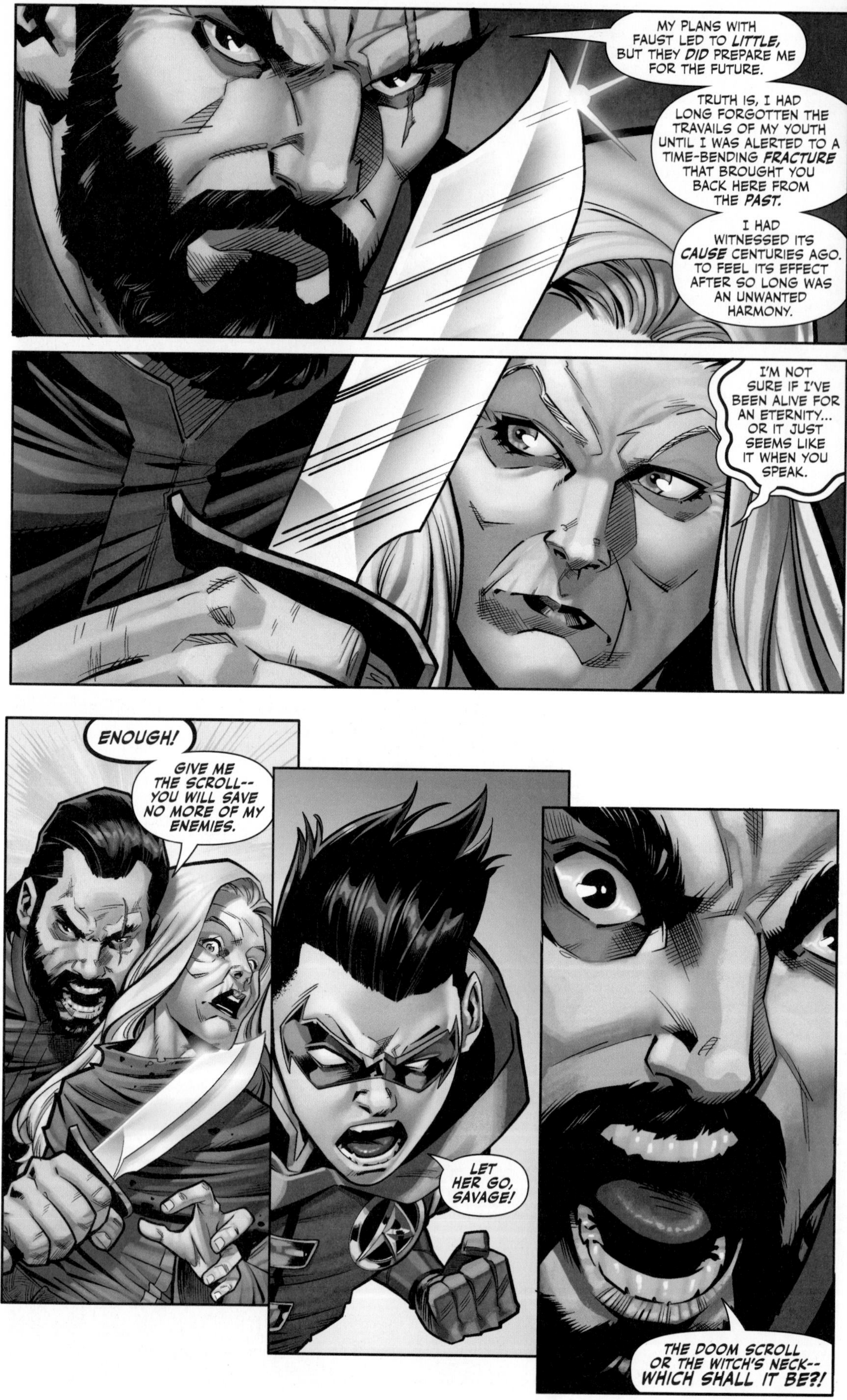
MY PLANS WITH FAUST LED TO *LITTLE,* BUT THEY *DID* PREPARE ME FOR THE FUTURE.
TRUTH IS, I HAD LONG FORGOTTEN THE TRAVAILS OF MY YOUTH UNTIL I WAS ALERTED TO A TIME-BENDING *FRACTURE* THAT BROUGHT YOU BACK HERE FROM THE *PAST.*
I HAD WITNESSED ITS *CAUSE* CENTURIES AGO. TO FEEL ITS EFFECT AFTER SO LONG WAS AN UNWANTED HARMONY.
I'M NOT SURE IF I'VE BEEN ALIVE FOR AN ETERNITY... OR IT JUST SEEMS LIKE IT WHEN YOU SPEAK.
ENOUGH!
GIVE ME THE SCROLL-- YOU WILL SAVE NO MORE OF MY ENEMIES.
LET HER GO, SAVAGE!
THE DOOM SCROLL OR THE WITCH'S NECK-- WHICH SHALL IT BE?!

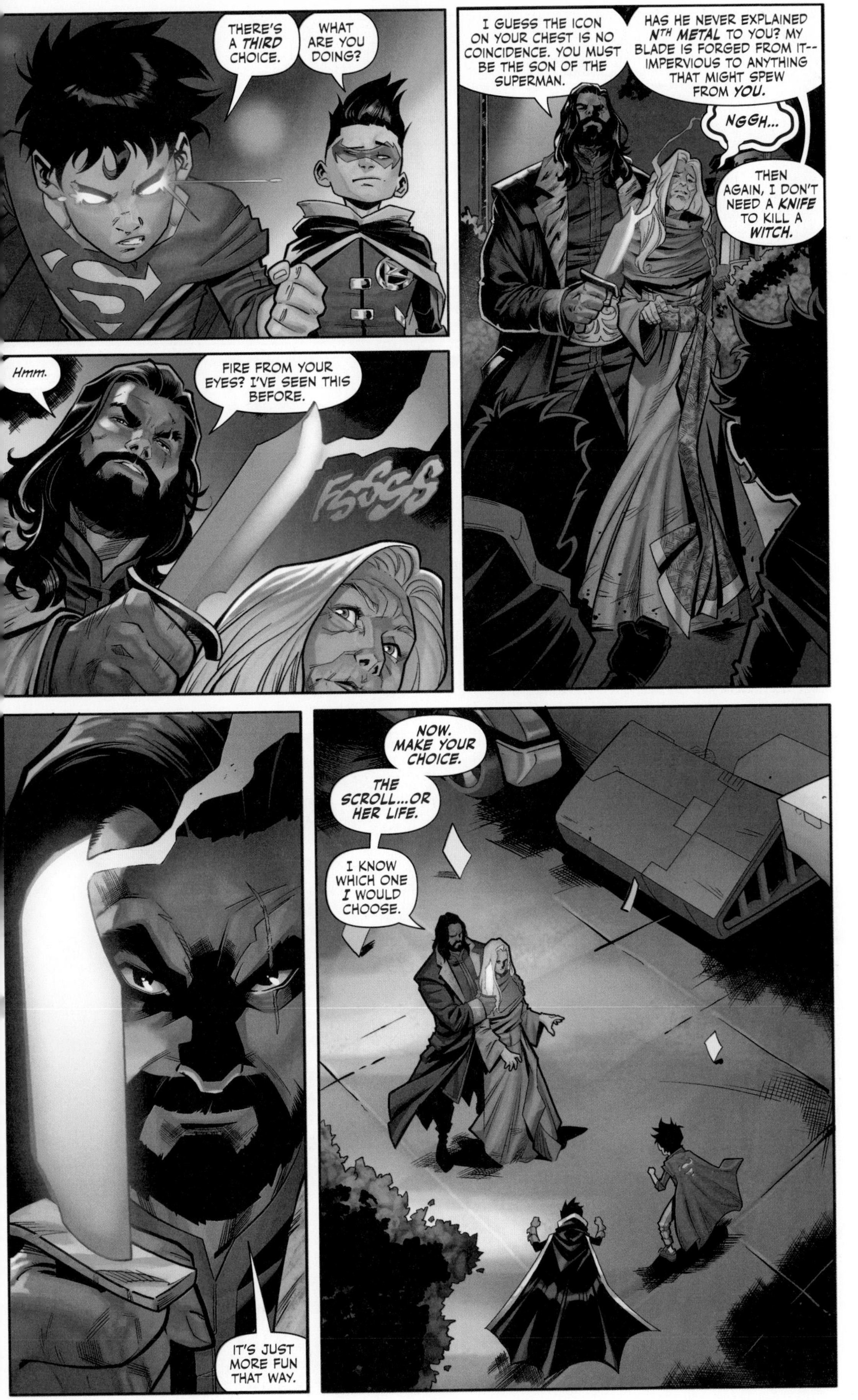
THERE'S A *THIRD* CHOICE.
WHAT ARE YOU DOING?
Hmm.
FIRE FROM YOUR EYES? I'VE SEEN THIS BEFORE.
FSSSS
I GUESS THE ICON ON YOUR CHEST IS NO COINCIDENCE. YOU MUST BE THE SON OF THE SUPERMAN.
HAS HE NEVER EXPLAINED *NTH METAL* TO YOU? MY BLADE IS FORGED FROM IT-- IMPERVIOUS TO ANYTHING THAT MIGHT SPEW FROM *YOU*.
NGGH...
THEN AGAIN, I DON'T NEED A *KNIFE* TO KILL A *WITCH*.
IT'S JUST MORE FUN THAT WAY.
NOW. MAKE YOUR CHOICE.
THE SCROLL...OR HER LIFE.
I KNOW WHICH ONE *I* WOULD CHOOSE.

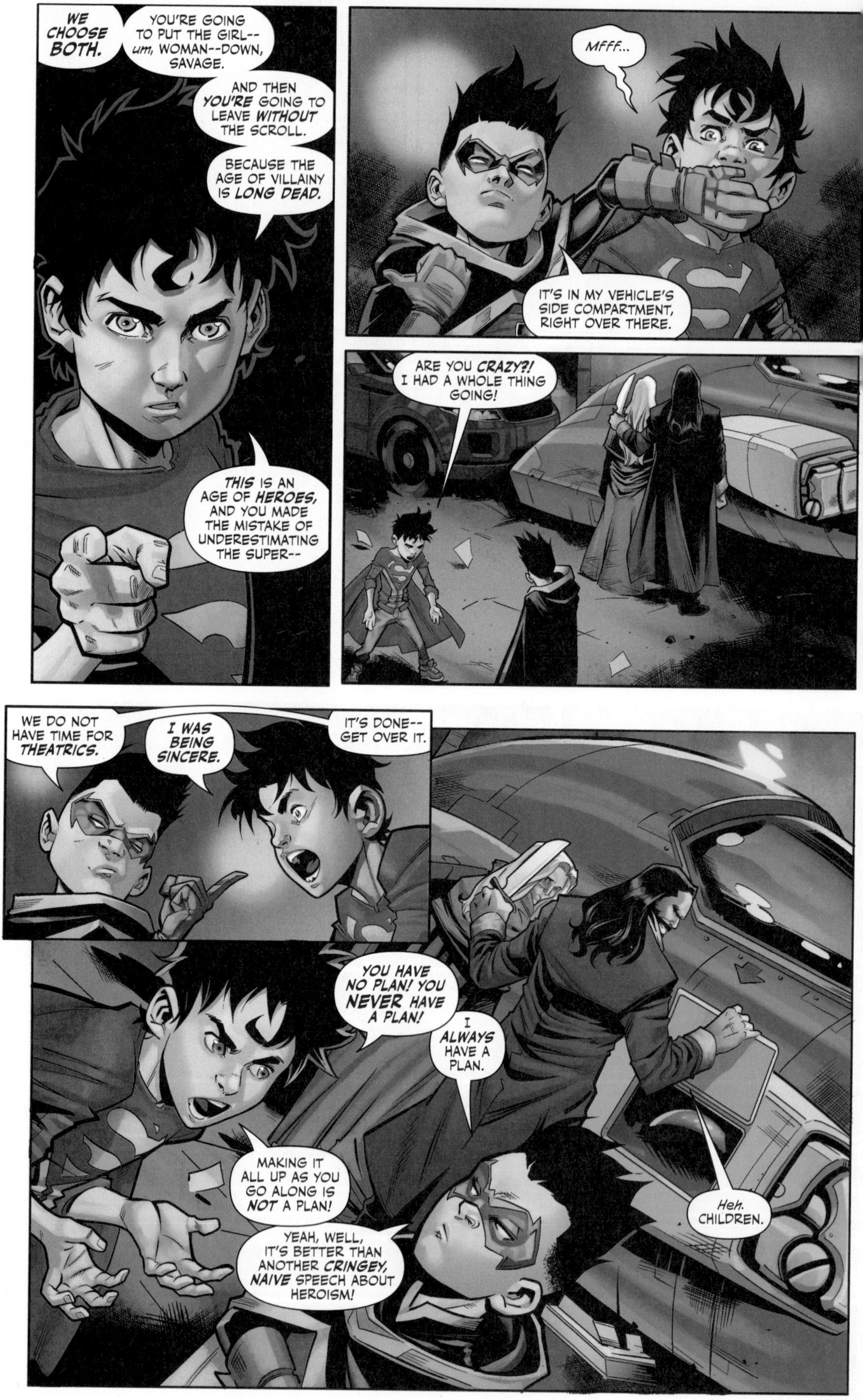

WE CHOOSE BOTH.
YOU'RE GOING TO PUT THE GIRL-- *um,* WOMAN--DOWN, SAVAGE.
AND THEN *YOU'RE* GOING TO LEAVE *WITHOUT* THE SCROLL.
BECAUSE THE AGE OF VILLAINY IS *LONG DEAD.*
THIS IS AN AGE OF *HEROES,* AND YOU MADE THE MISTAKE OF UNDERESTIMATING THE SUPER--
MFFF...
IT'S IN MY VEHICLE'S SIDE COMPARTMENT, RIGHT OVER THERE.
ARE YOU *CRAZY?!* I HAD A WHOLE THING GOING!
WE DO NOT HAVE TIME FOR *THEATRICS.*
I WAS BEING SINCERE.
IT'S DONE-- GET OVER IT.
YOU HAVE NO PLAN! YOU **NEVER** *HAVE A PLAN!*
I *ALWAYS* HAVE A PLAN.
MAKING IT ALL UP AS YOU GO ALONG IS *NOT* A PLAN!
YEAH, WELL, IT'S BETTER THAN ANOTHER *CRINGEY, NAIVE* SPEECH ABOUT HEROISM!
Heh. CHILDREN.

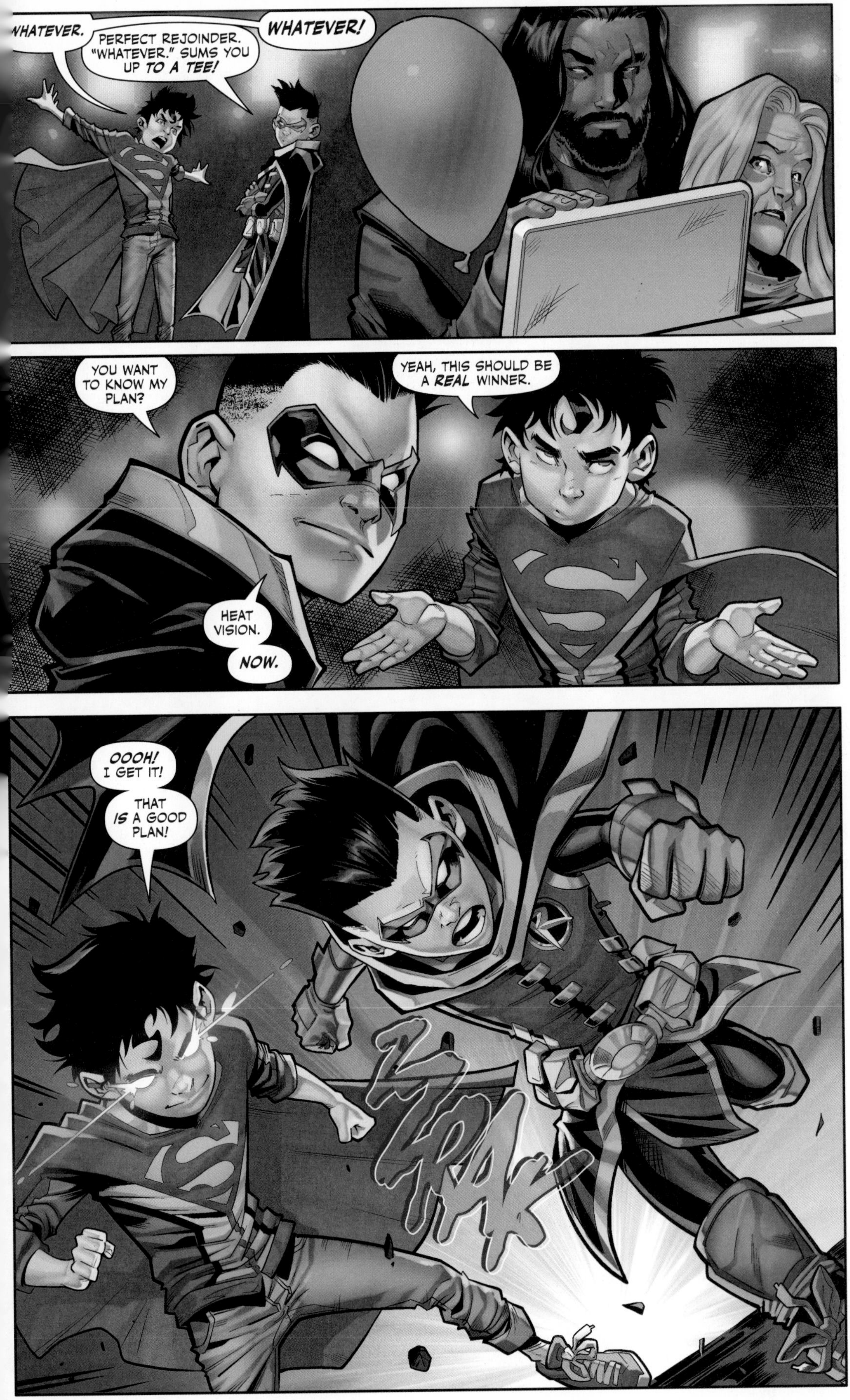
WHATEVER.
PERFECT REJOINDER. "WHATEVER." SUMS YOU UP TO A TEE!
WHATEVER!
YOU WANT TO KNOW MY PLAN?
YEAH, THIS SHOULD BE A REAL WINNER.
HEAT VISION.
NOW.
OOOH! I GET IT!
THAT IS A GOOD PLAN!
KRAK

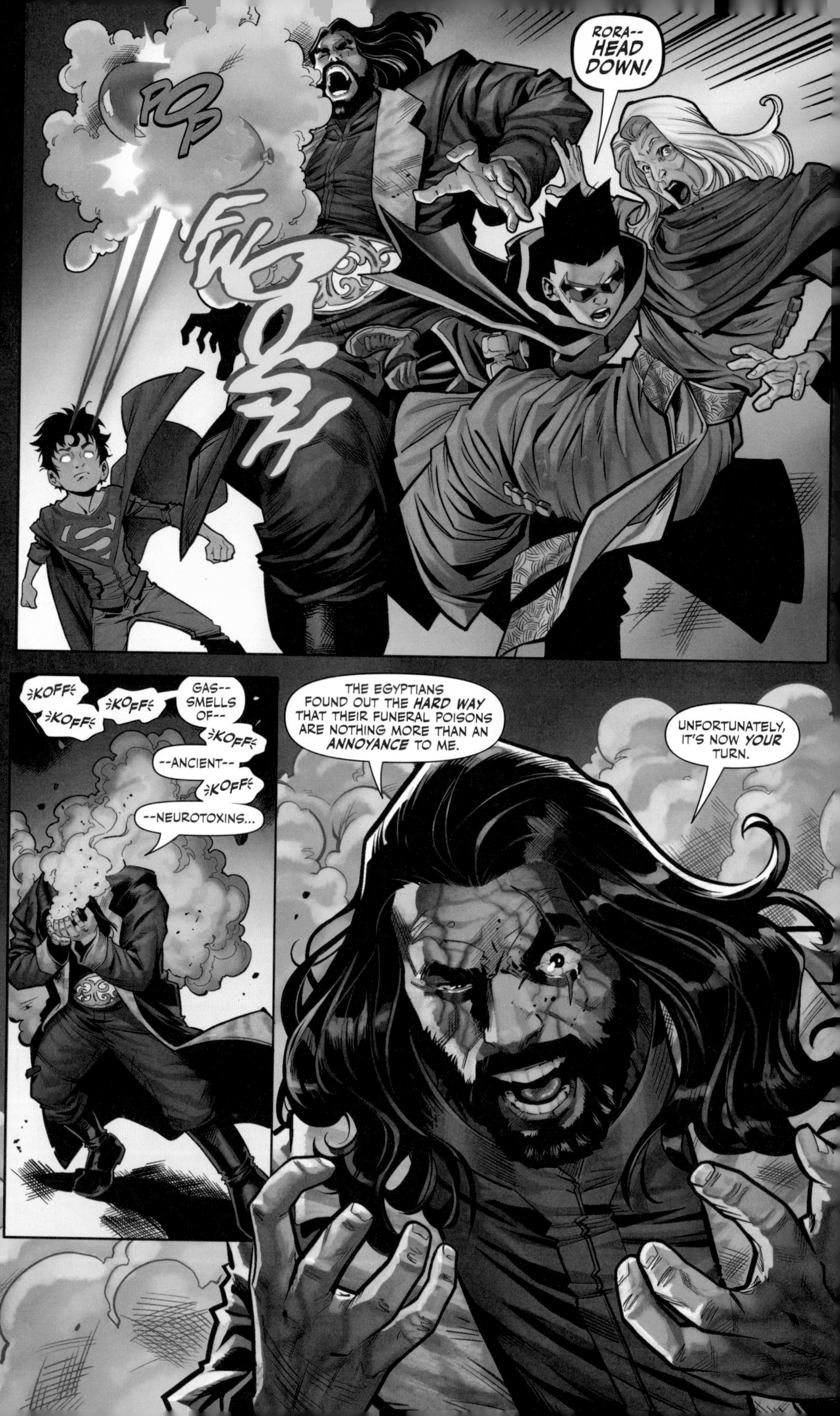
POP
RORA-- HEAD DOWN!
FWOOOM
KOFF
KOFF
KOFF
GAS-- SMELLS OF--
KOFF
--ANCIENT--
KOFF
--NEUROTOXINS...
THE EGYPTIANS FOUND OUT THE HARD WAY THAT THEIR FUNERAL POISONS ARE NOTHING MORE THAN AN ANNOYANCE TO ME.
UNFORTUNATELY, IT'S NOW YOUR TURN.

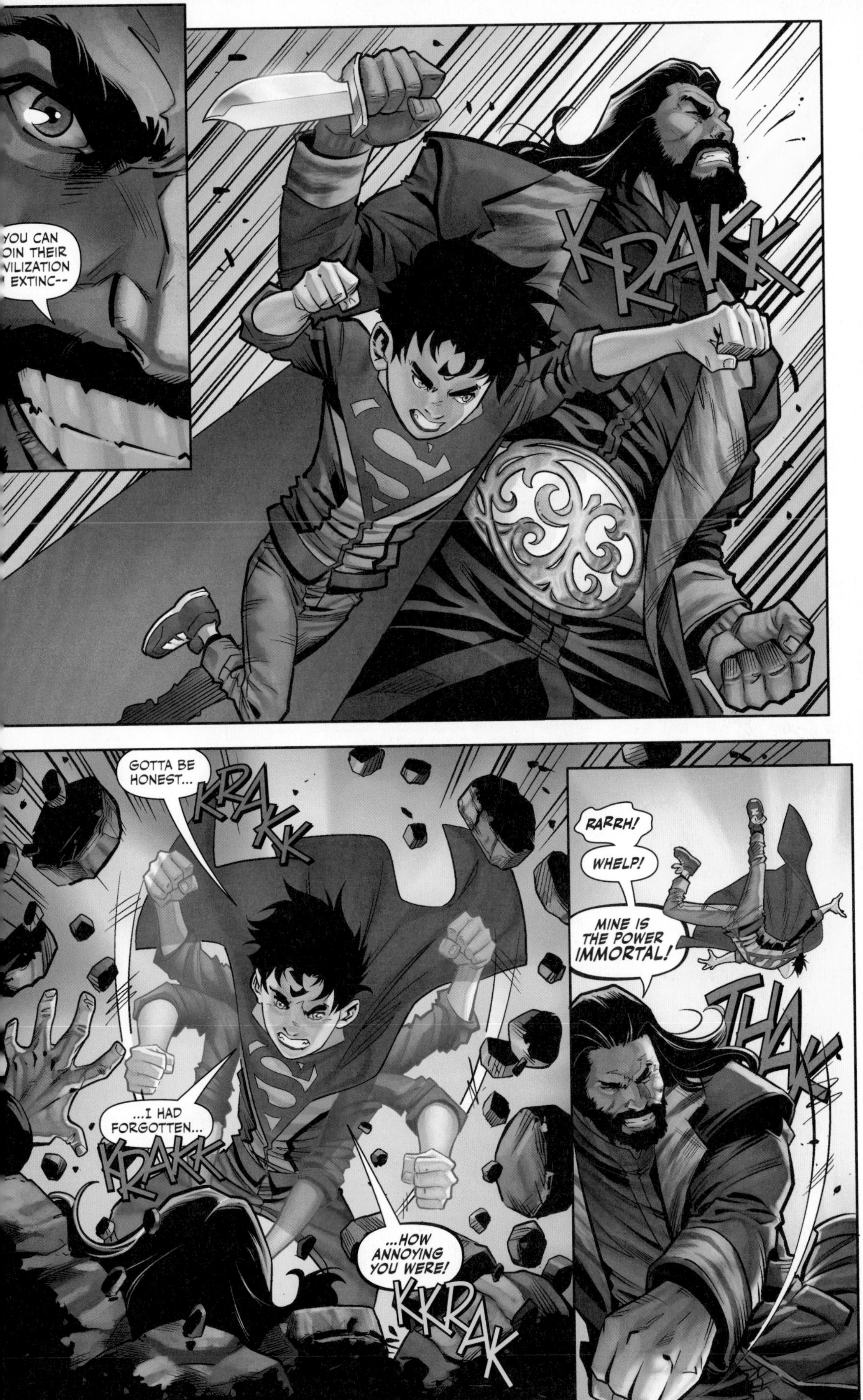

YOU CAN
OIN THEIR
VILIZATION
EXTINC--
KRAKK
GOTTA BE HONEST...
KRAKK
...I HAD FORGOTTEN...
KRAKK
...HOW ANNOYING YOU WERE!
KKRAK
RARRH!
WHELP!
MINE IS THE POWER IMMORTAL!
THAK

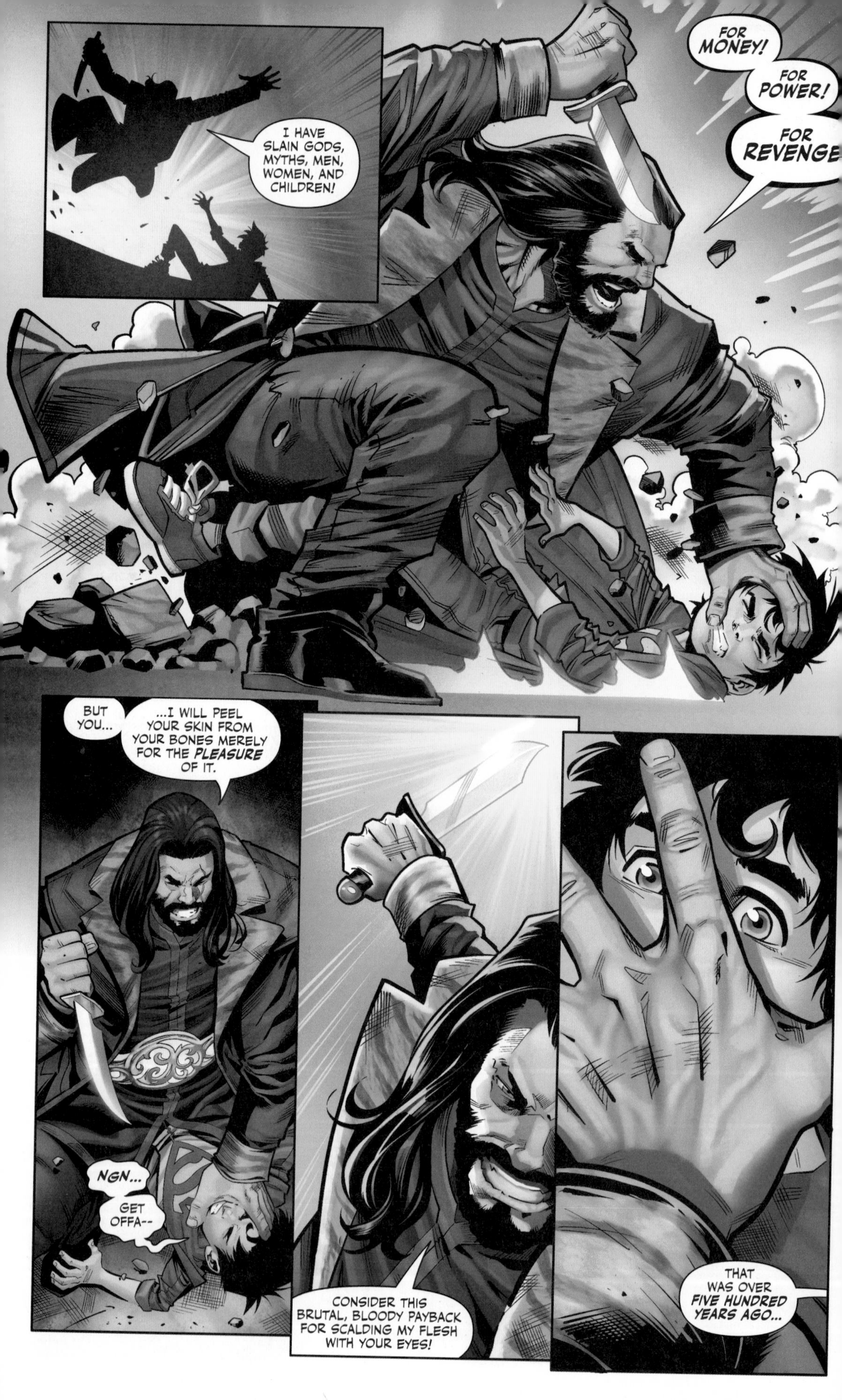
I HAVE SLAIN GODS, MYTHS, MEN, WOMEN, AND CHILDREN!
FOR MONEY!
FOR POWER!
FOR REVENGE
BUT YOU...
...I WILL PEEL YOUR SKIN FROM YOUR BONES MERELY FOR THE PLEASURE OF IT.
NGN...
GET OFFA--
CONSIDER THIS BRUTAL, BLOODY PAYBACK FOR SCALDING MY FLESH WITH YOUR EYES!
THAT WAS OVER FIVE HUNDRED YEARS AGO...

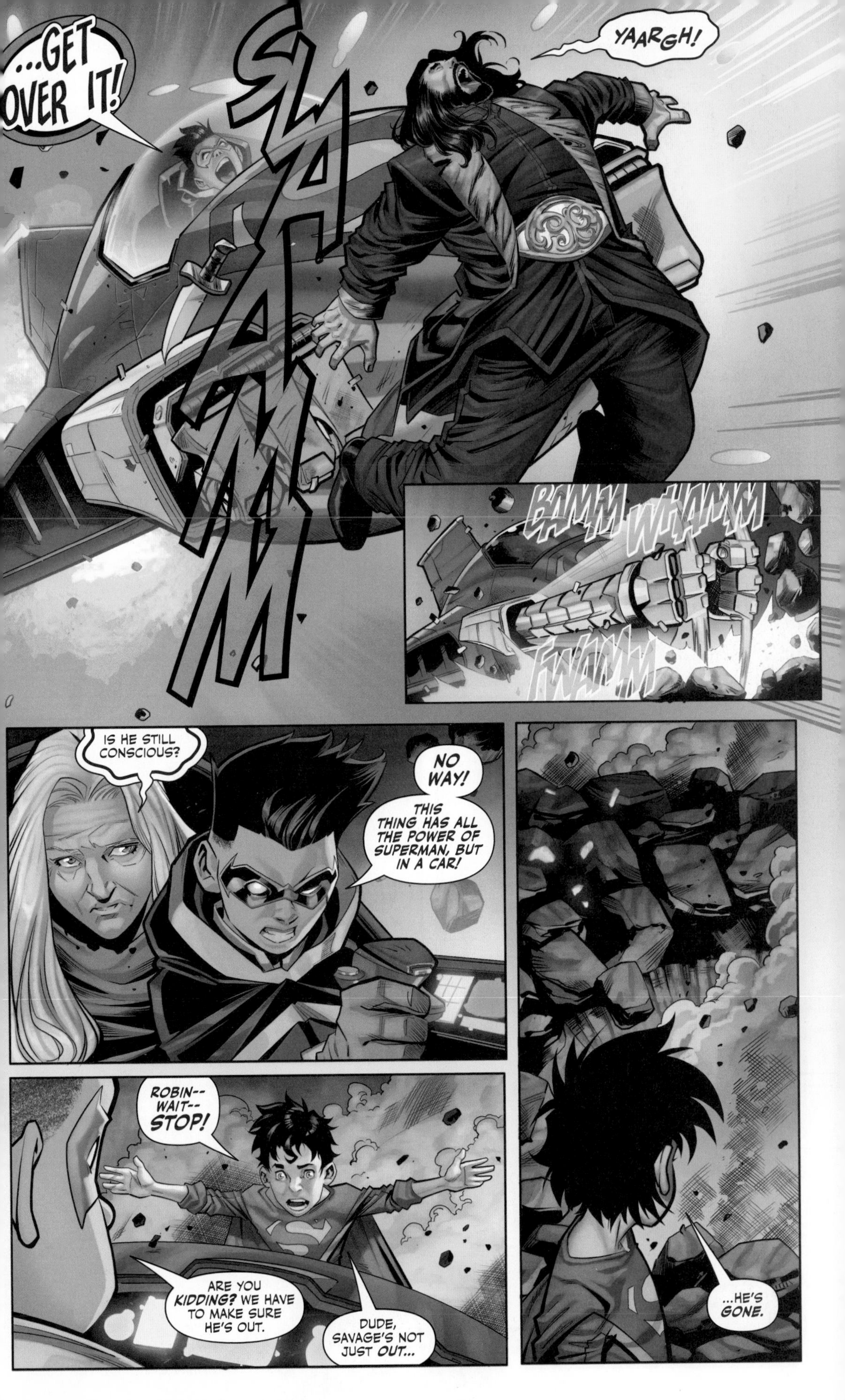
...GET OVER IT!
SLAAAMM
YAARGH!
BAMM WHAMM
FWAMM
IS HE STILL CONSCIOUS?
NO WAY!
THIS THING HAS ALL THE POWER OF SUPERMAN, BUT IN A CAR!
ROBIN-- WAIT-- STOP!
ARE YOU KIDDING? WE HAVE TO MAKE SURE HE'S OUT.
DUDE, SAVAGE'S NOT JUST OUT...
...HE'S GONE.

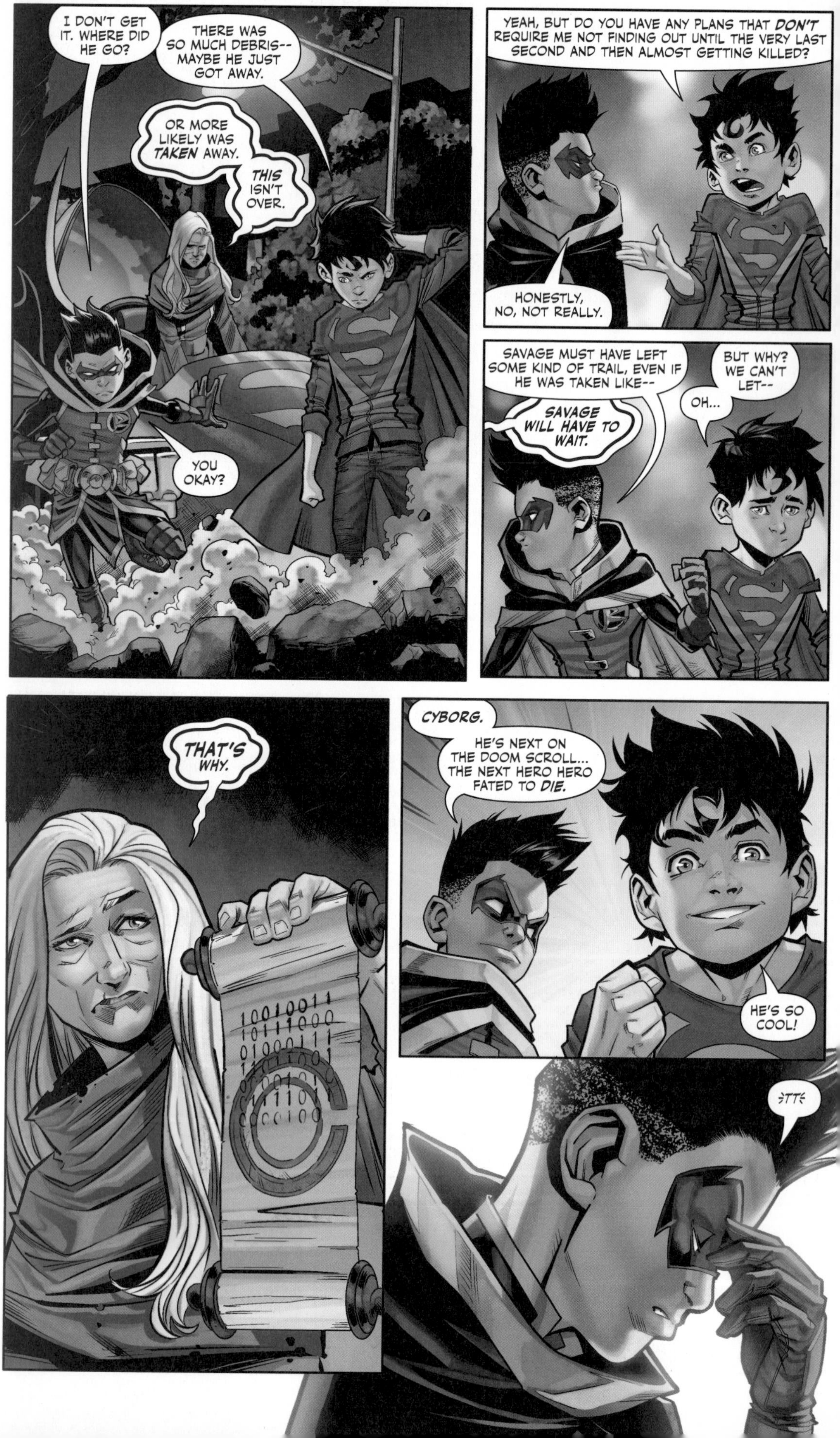
I DON'T GET IT. WHERE DID HE GO?
THERE WAS SO MUCH DEBRIS-- MAYBE HE JUST GOT AWAY.
OR MORE LIKELY WAS *TAKEN* AWAY.
THIS ISN'T OVER.
YOU OKAY?
YEAH, BUT DO YOU HAVE ANY PLANS THAT *DON'T* REQUIRE ME NOT FINDING OUT UNTIL THE VERY LAST SECOND AND THEN ALMOST GETTING KILLED?
HONESTLY, NO, NOT REALLY.
SAVAGE MUST HAVE LEFT SOME KIND OF TRAIL, EVEN IF HE WAS TAKEN LIKE--
SAVAGE WILL HAVE TO WAIT.
BUT WHY? WE CAN'T LET--
OH...
THAT'S WHY.
CYBORG.
HE'S NEXT ON THE DOOM SCROLL... THE NEXT HERO HERO FATED TO *DIE*.
HE'S SO COOL!
TT

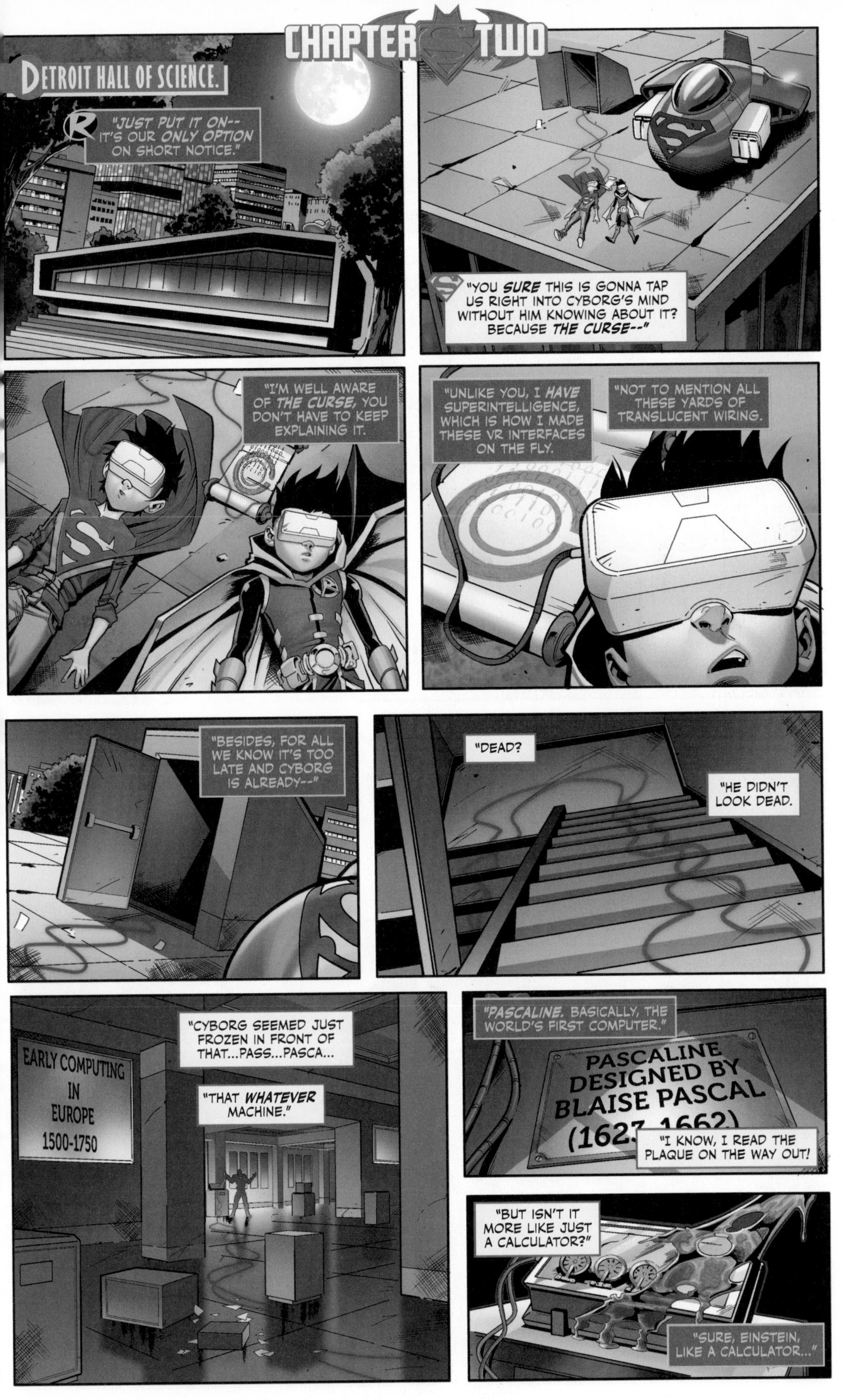

CHAPTER TWO
DETROIT HALL OF SCIENCE.
"JUST PUT IT ON-- IT'S OUR ONLY OPTION ON SHORT NOTICE."
"YOU SURE THIS IS GONNA TAP US RIGHT INTO CYBORG'S MIND WITHOUT HIM KNOWING ABOUT IT? BECAUSE THE CURSE--"
"I'M WELL AWARE OF THE CURSE, YOU DON'T HAVE TO KEEP EXPLAINING IT.
"UNLIKE YOU, I HAVE SUPERINTELLIGENCE, WHICH IS HOW I MADE THESE VR INTERFACES ON THE FLY.
"NOT TO MENTION ALL THESE YARDS OF TRANSLUCENT WIRING.
"BESIDES, FOR ALL WE KNOW IT'S TOO LATE AND CYBORG IS ALREADY--"
"DEAD?
"HE DIDN'T LOOK DEAD.
"CYBORG SEEMED JUST FROZEN IN FRONT OF THAT...PASS...PASCA...
"THAT WHATEVER MACHINE."
EARLY COMPUTING IN EUROPE 1500-1750
"PASCALINE. BASICALLY, THE WORLD'S FIRST COMPUTER."
PASCALINE DESIGNED BY BLAISE PASCAL (1623-1662)
"I KNOW, I READ THE PLAQUE ON THE WAY OUT!
"BUT ISN'T IT MORE LIKE JUST A CALCULATOR?"
"SURE, EINSTEIN, LIKE A CALCULATOR..."

I THINK WE'RE IN, JON.

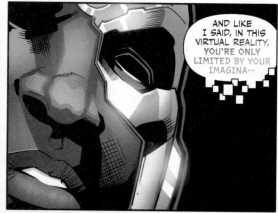

AND LIKE I SAID, IN THIS VIRTUAL REALITY, YOU'RE ONLY LIMITED BY YOUR IMAGINA--

YIPEE-KI-YAY!

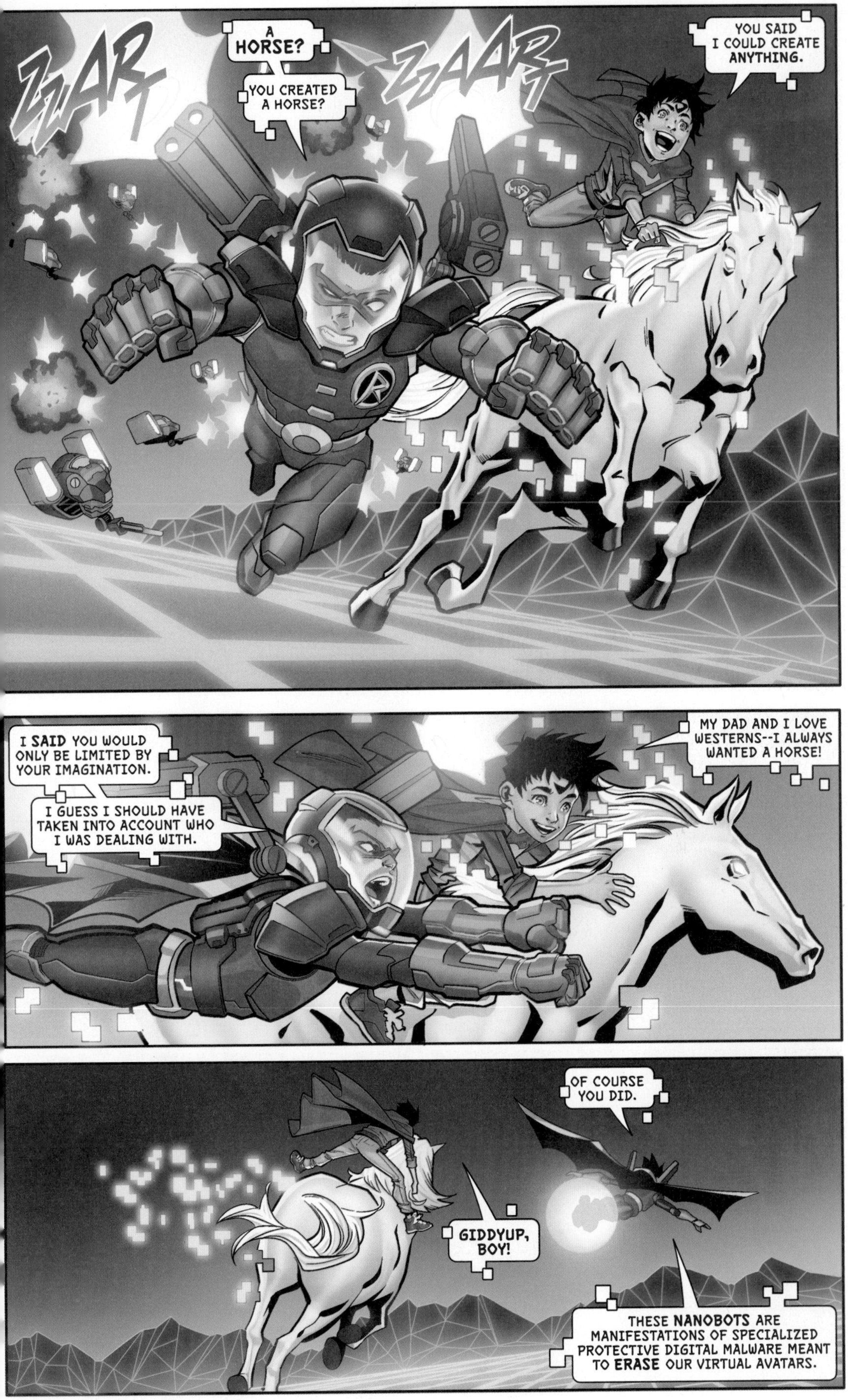
ZZAART
A HORSE?
YOU CREATED A HORSE?
ZZAART
YOU SAID I COULD CREATE ANYTHING.
I SAID YOU WOULD ONLY BE LIMITED BY YOUR IMAGINATION.
I GUESS I SHOULD HAVE TAKEN INTO ACCOUNT WHO I WAS DEALING WITH.
MY DAD AND I LOVE WESTERNS--I ALWAYS WANTED A HORSE!
OF COURSE YOU DID.
GIDDYUP, BOY!
THESE NANOBOTS ARE MANIFESTATIONS OF SPECIALIZED PROTECTIVE DIGITAL MALWARE MEANT TO ERASE OUR VIRTUAL AVATARS.

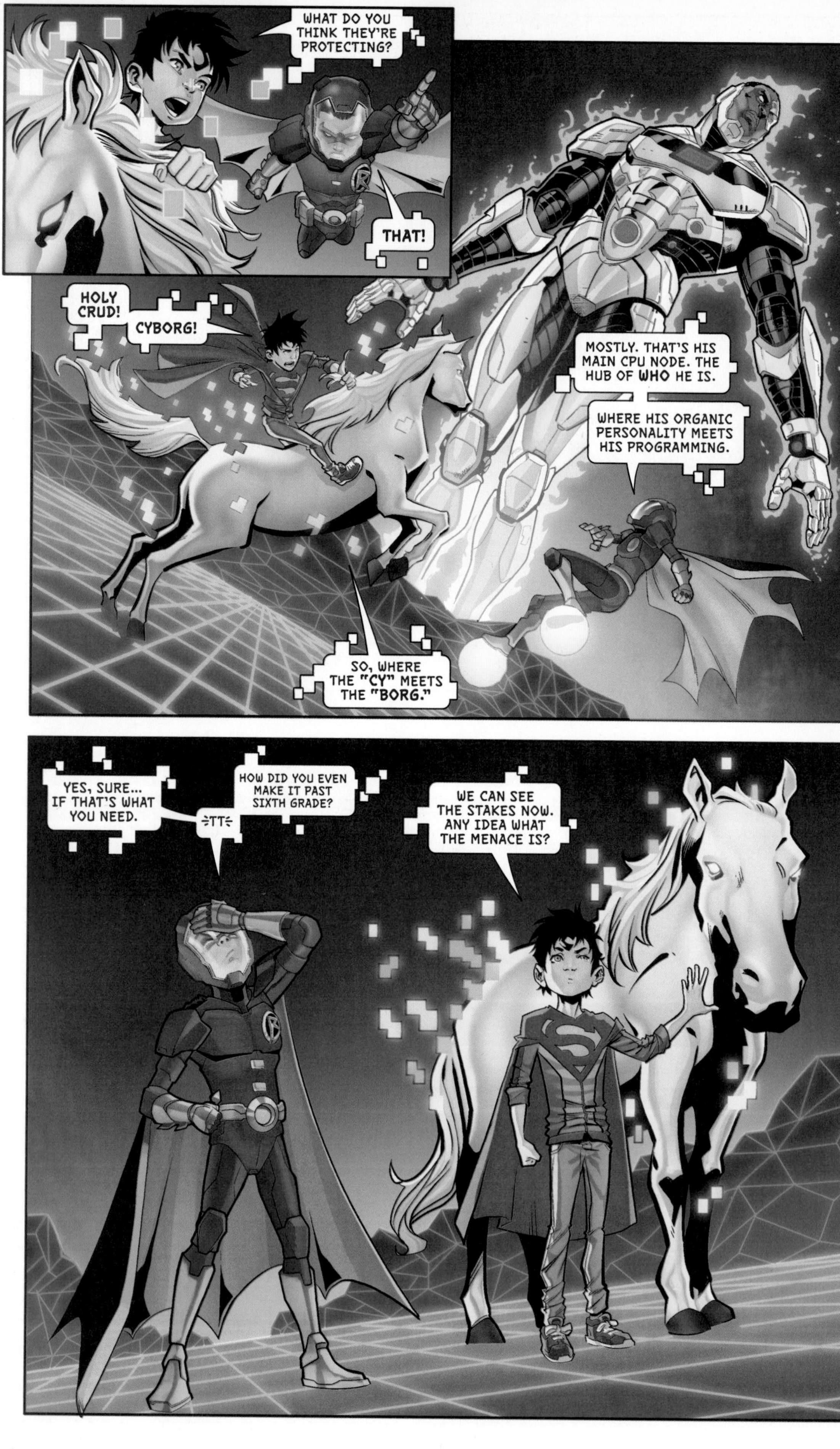
WHAT DO YOU THINK THEY'RE PROTECTING?
THAT!
HOLY CRUD!
CYBORG!
MOSTLY. THAT'S HIS MAIN CPU NODE. THE HUB OF WHO HE IS.
WHERE HIS ORGANIC PERSONALITY MEETS HIS PROGRAMMING.
SO, WHERE THE "CY" MEETS THE "BORG."
YES, SURE... IF THAT'S WHAT YOU NEED.
TT
HOW DID YOU EVEN MAKE IT PAST SIXTH GRADE?
WE CAN SEE THE STAKES NOW. ANY IDEA WHAT THE MENACE IS?

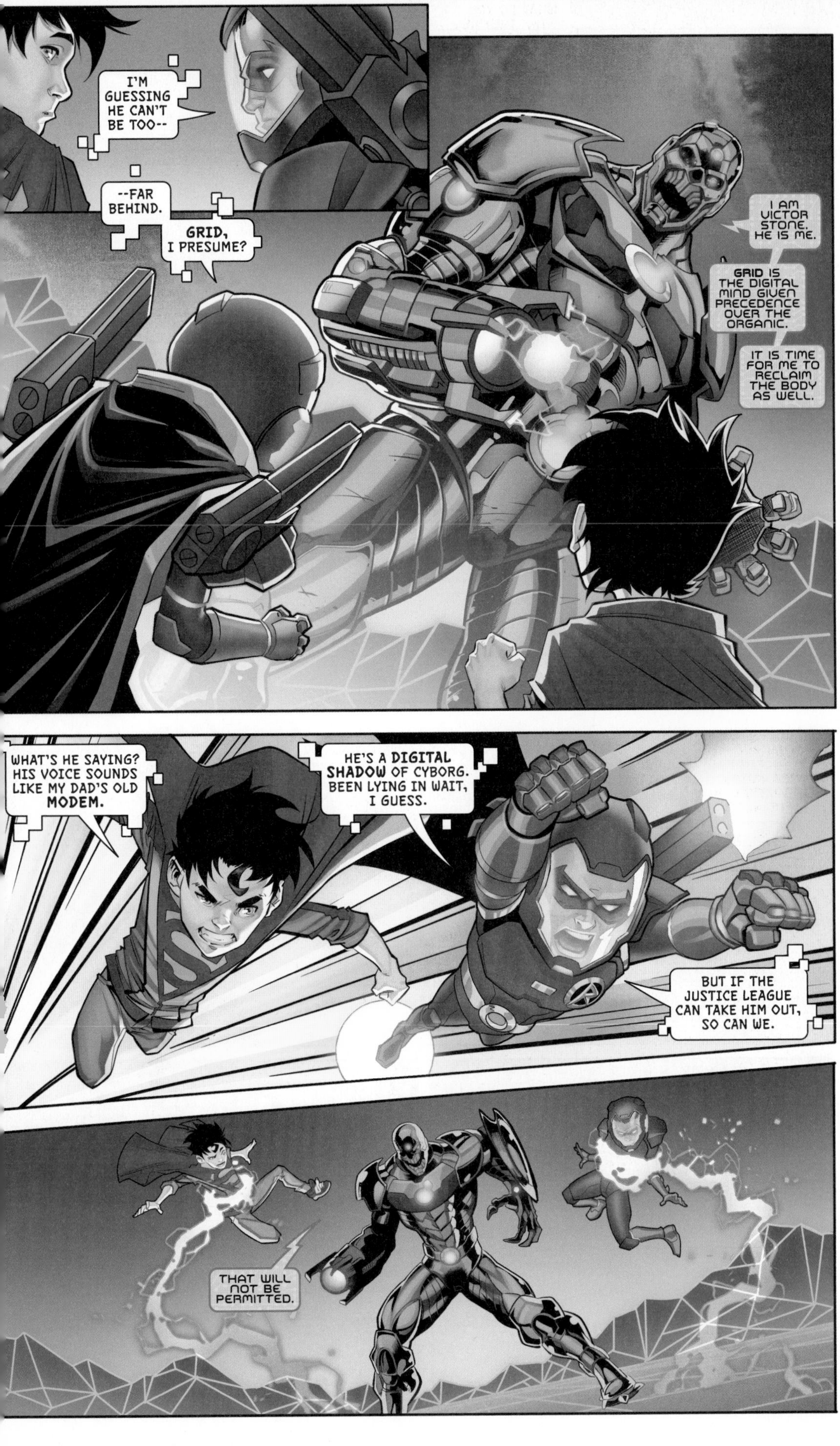
I'M GUESSING HE CAN'T BE TOO--
--FAR BEHIND.
GRID, I PRESUME?
I AM VICTOR STONE. HE IS ME.
GRID IS THE DIGITAL MIND GIVEN PRECEDENCE OVER THE ORGANIC.
IT IS TIME FOR ME TO RECLAIM THE BODY AS WELL.
WHAT'S HE SAYING? HIS VOICE SOUNDS LIKE MY DAD'S OLD MODEM.
HE'S A DIGITAL SHADOW OF CYBORG. BEEN LYING IN WAIT, I GUESS.
BUT IF THE JUSTICE LEAGUE CAN TAKE HIM OUT, SO CAN WE.
THAT WILL NOT BE PERMITTED.

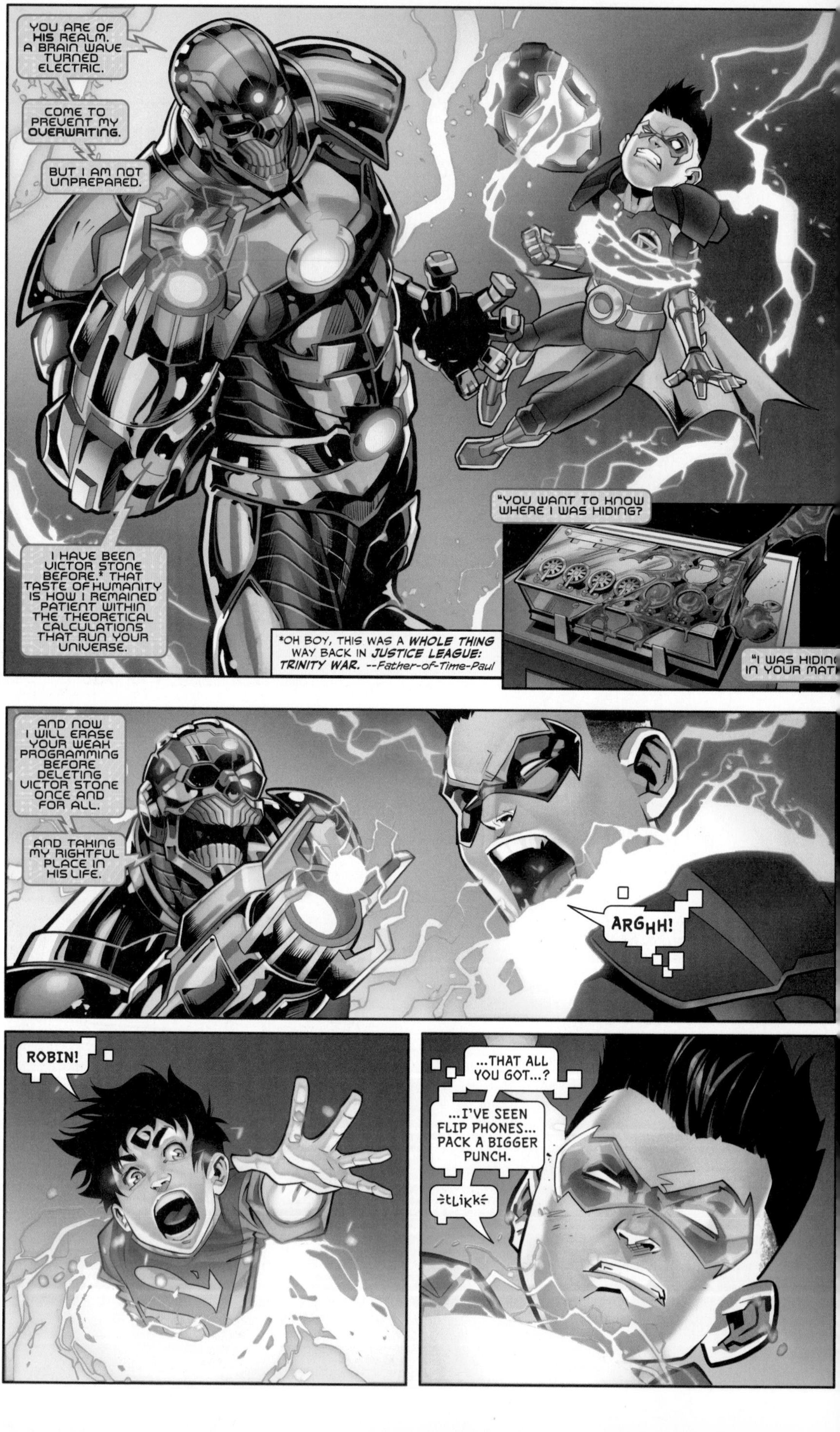

YOU ARE OF HIS REALM. A BRAIN WAVE TURNED ELECTRIC.
COME TO PREVENT MY OVERWRITING.
BUT I AM NOT UNPREPARED.
I HAVE BEEN VICTOR STONE BEFORE.* THAT TASTE OF HUMANITY IS HOW I REMAINED PATIENT WITHIN THE THEORETICAL CALCULATIONS THAT RUN YOUR UNIVERSE.
*OH BOY, THIS WAS A WHOLE THING WAY BACK IN JUSTICE LEAGUE: TRINITY WAR. --Father-of-Time-Paul
"YOU WANT TO KNOW WHERE I WAS HIDING?
"I WAS HIDING IN YOUR MAT
AND NOW I WILL ERASE YOUR WEAK PROGRAMMING BEFORE DELETING VICTOR STONE ONCE AND FOR ALL.
AND TAKING MY RIGHTFUL PLACE IN HIS LIFE.
ARGHH!
ROBIN!
...THAT ALL YOU GOT...?
...I'VE SEEN FLIP PHONES... PACK A BIGGER PUNCH.
tLIKK

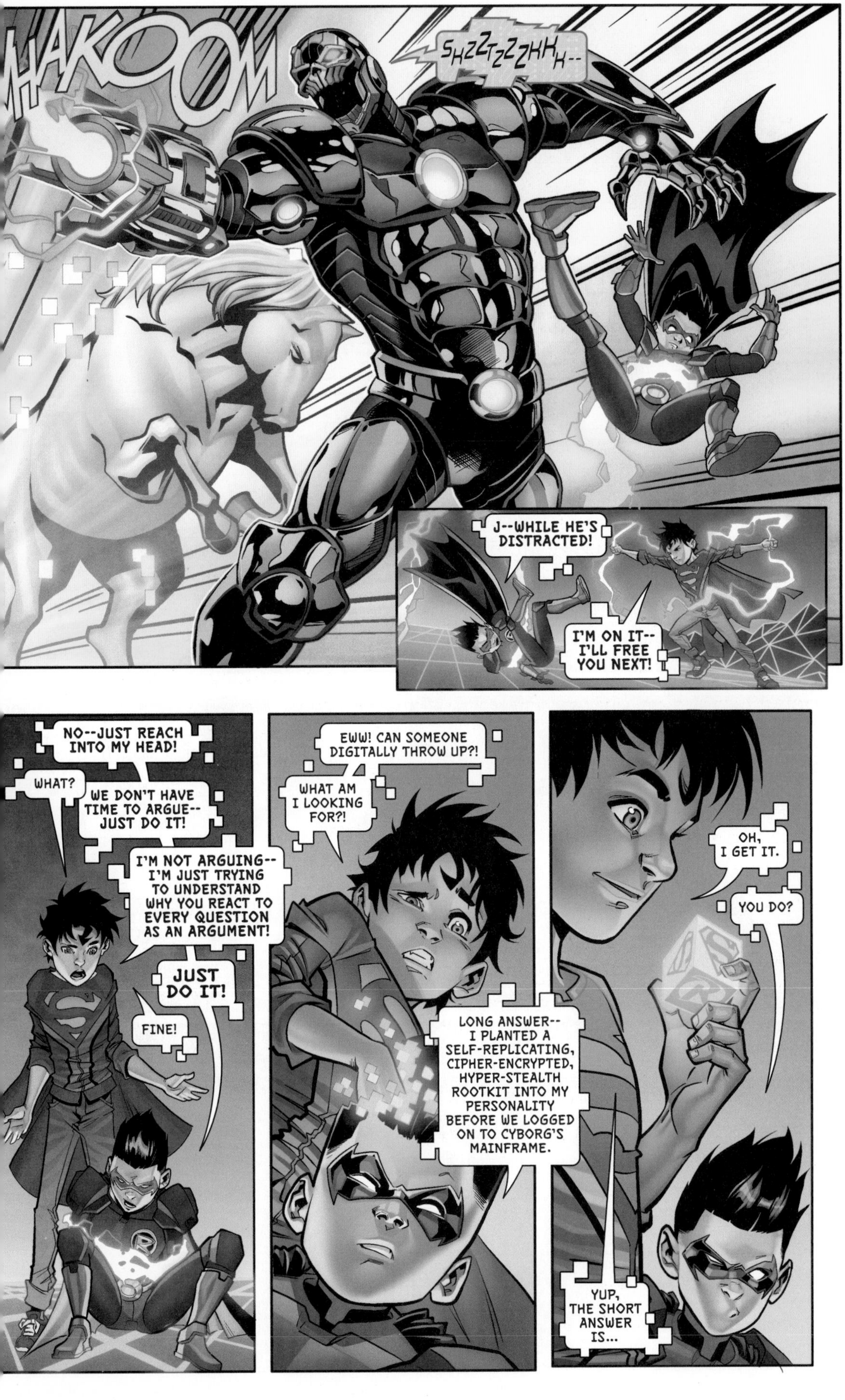

HAKOOM
SHZZTZZZHKH--
J--WHILE HE'S DISTRACTED!
I'M ON IT-- I'LL FREE YOU NEXT!
NO--JUST REACH INTO MY HEAD!
WHAT?
WE DON'T HAVE TIME TO ARGUE-- JUST DO IT!
I'M NOT ARGUING-- I'M JUST TRYING TO UNDERSTAND WHY YOU REACT TO EVERY QUESTION AS AN ARGUMENT!
JUST DO IT!
FINE!
EWW! CAN SOMEONE DIGITALLY THROW UP?!
WHAT AM I LOOKING FOR?!
LONG ANSWER-- I PLANTED A SELF-REPLICATING, CIPHER-ENCRYPTED, HYPER-STEALTH ROOTKIT INTO MY PERSONALITY BEFORE WE LOGGED ON TO CYBORG'S MAINFRAME.
OH, I GET IT.
YOU DO?
YUP, THE SHORT ANSWER IS...

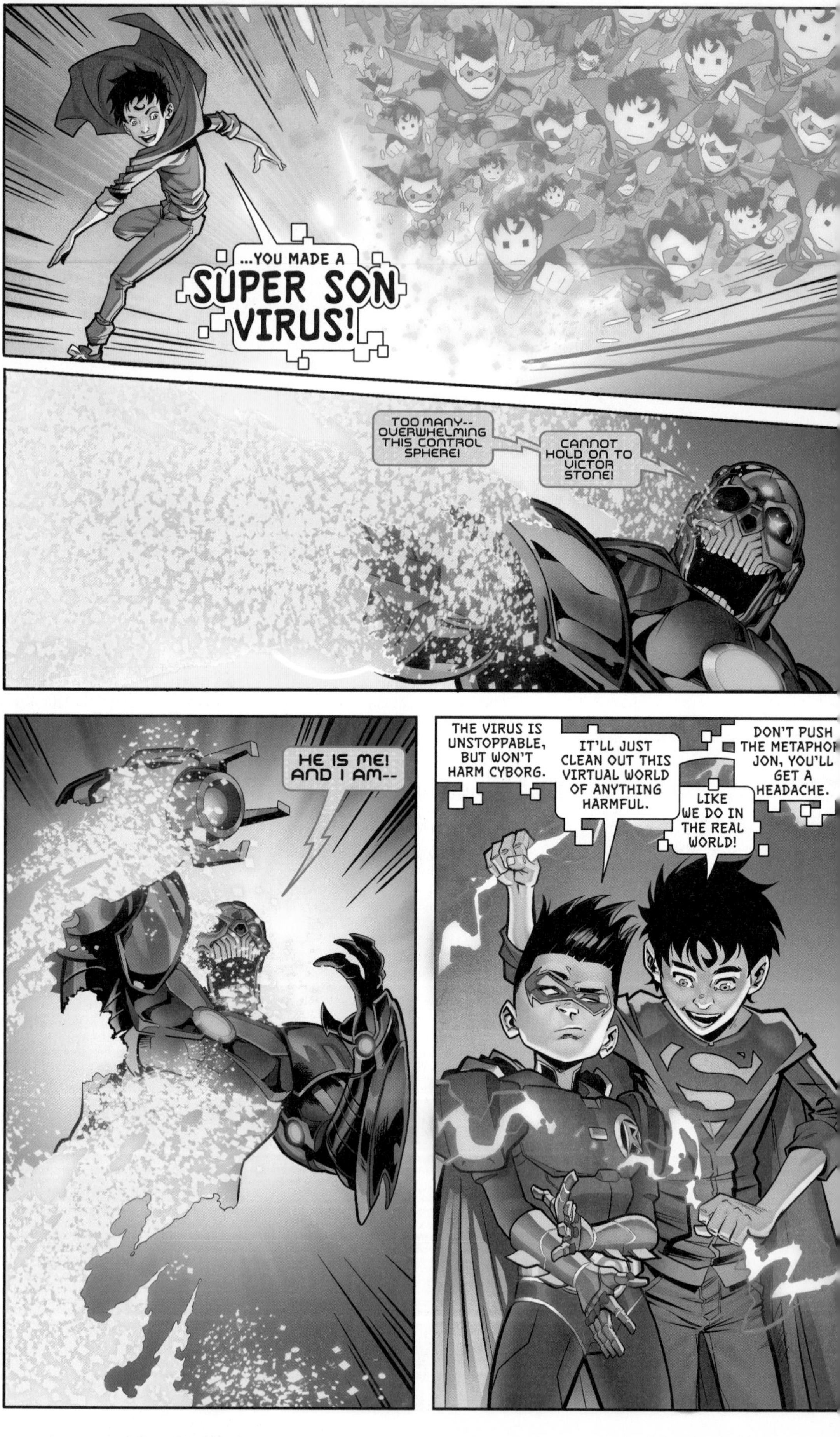
...YOU MADE A
SUPER SON VIRUS!
TOO MANY-- OVERWHELMING THIS CONTROL SPHERE!
CANNOT HOLD ON TO VICTOR STONE!
HE IS ME! AND I AM--
THE VIRUS IS UNSTOPPABLE, BUT WON'T HARM CYBORG.
IT'LL JUST CLEAN OUT THIS VIRTUAL WORLD OF ANYTHING HARMFUL.
LIKE WE DO IN THE REAL WORLD!
DON'T PUSH THE METAPHOR JON, YOU'LL GET A HEADACHE.

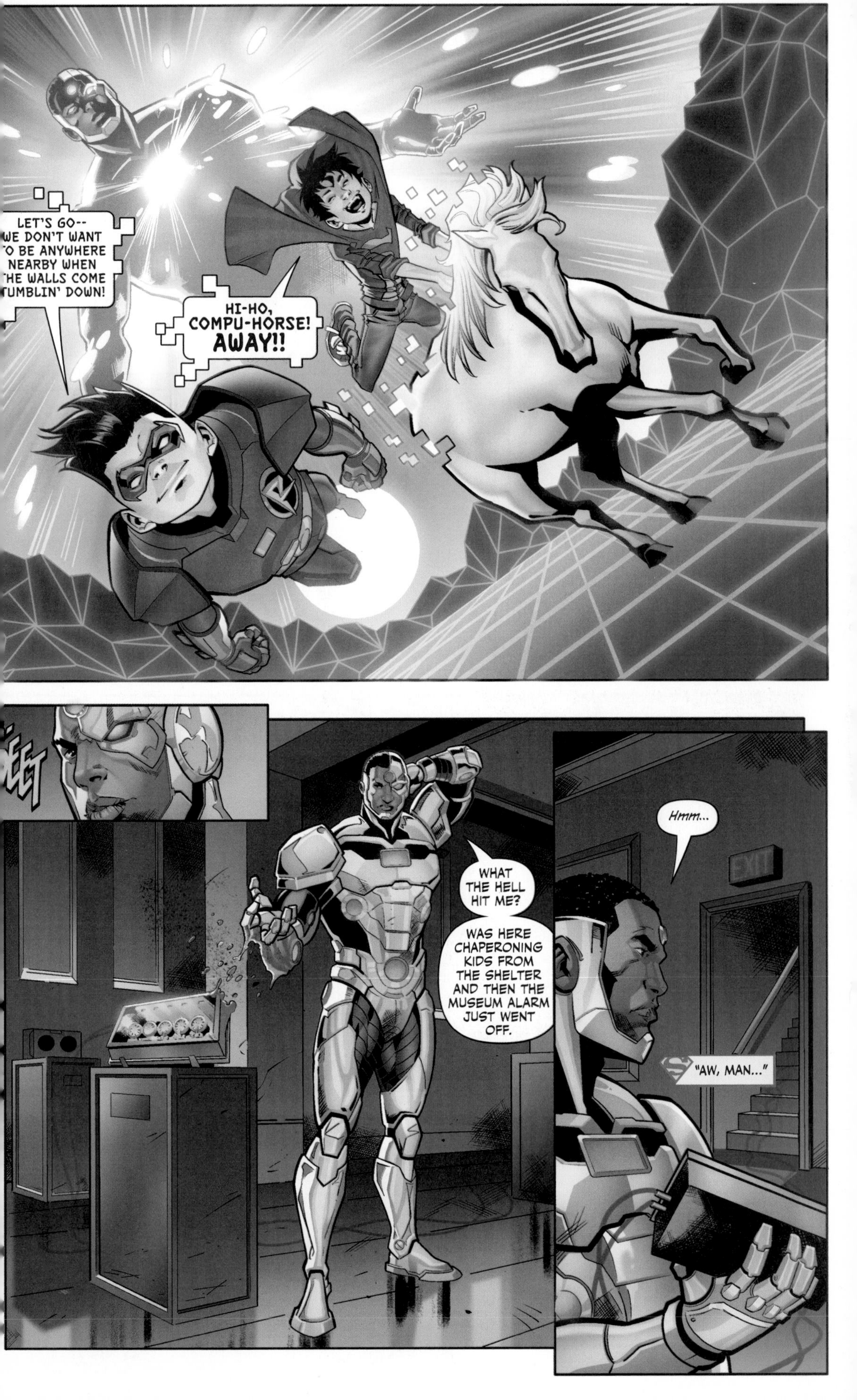
LET'S GO-- WE DON'T WANT TO BE ANYWHERE NEARBY WHEN THE WALLS COME TUMBLIN' DOWN!
HI-HO, COMPU-HORSE! AWAY!!
WHAT THE HELL HIT ME?
WAS HERE CHAPERONING KIDS FROM THE SHELTER AND THEN THE MUSEUM ALARM JUST WENT OFF.
Hmm...
EXIT
"AW, MAN..."

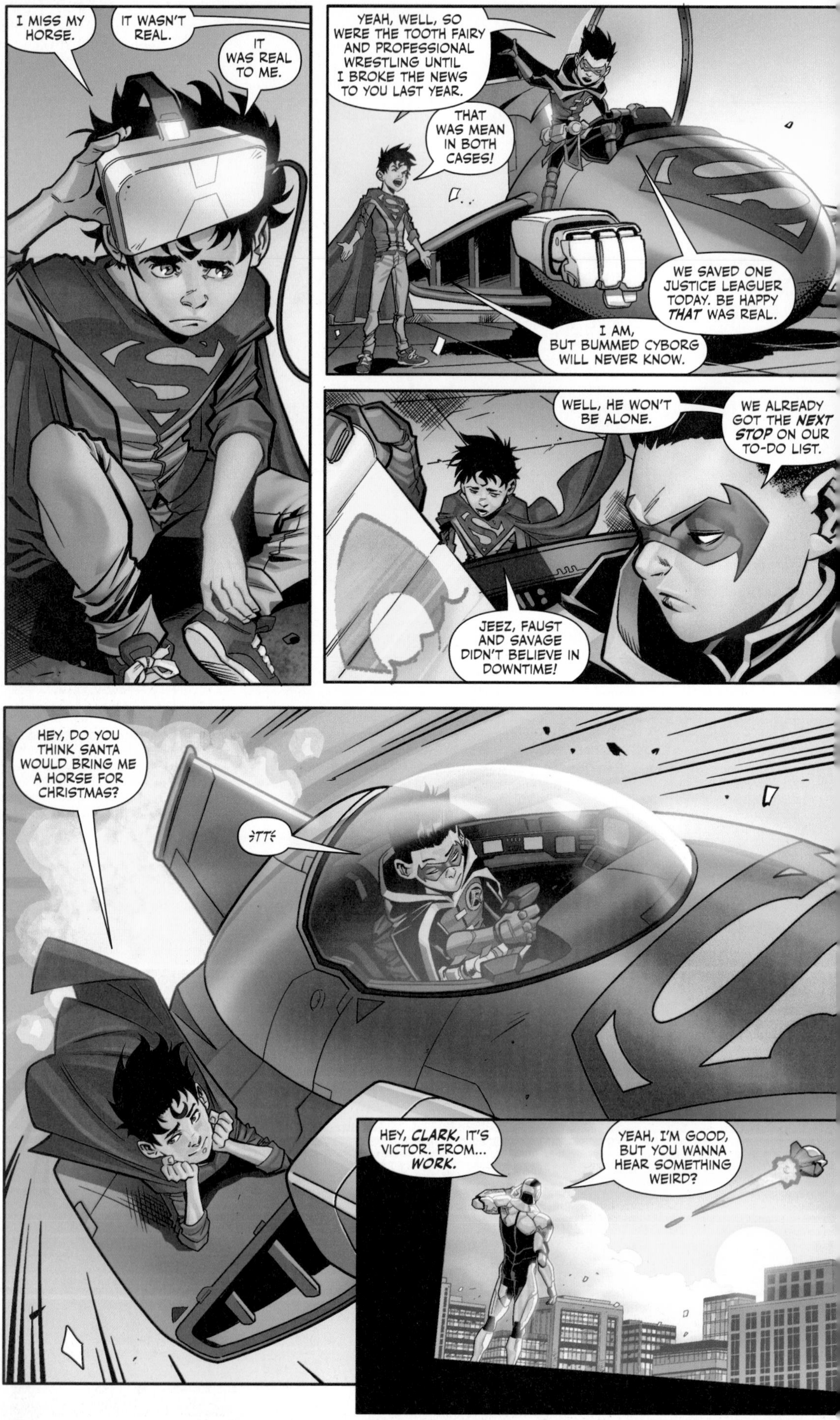
I MISS MY HORSE.
IT WASN'T REAL.
IT WAS REAL TO ME.
YEAH, WELL, SO WERE THE TOOTH FAIRY AND PROFESSIONAL WRESTLING UNTIL I BROKE THE NEWS TO YOU LAST YEAR.
THAT WAS MEAN IN BOTH CASES!
WE SAVED ONE JUSTICE LEAGUER TODAY. BE HAPPY *THAT* WAS REAL.
I AM, BUT BUMMED CYBORG WILL NEVER KNOW.
WELL, HE WON'T BE ALONE.
WE ALREADY GOT THE *NEXT STOP* ON OUR TO-DO LIST.
JEEZ, FAUST AND SAVAGE DIDN'T BELIEVE IN DOWNTIME!
HEY, DO YOU THINK SANTA WOULD BRING ME A HORSE FOR CHRISTMAS?
TT
HEY, *CLARK*, IT'S VICTOR. FROM... *WORK.*
YEAH, I'M GOOD, BUT YOU WANNA HEAR SOMETHING WEIRD?

Challenge of the Super Sons #5 cover by **SIMONE DI MEO**

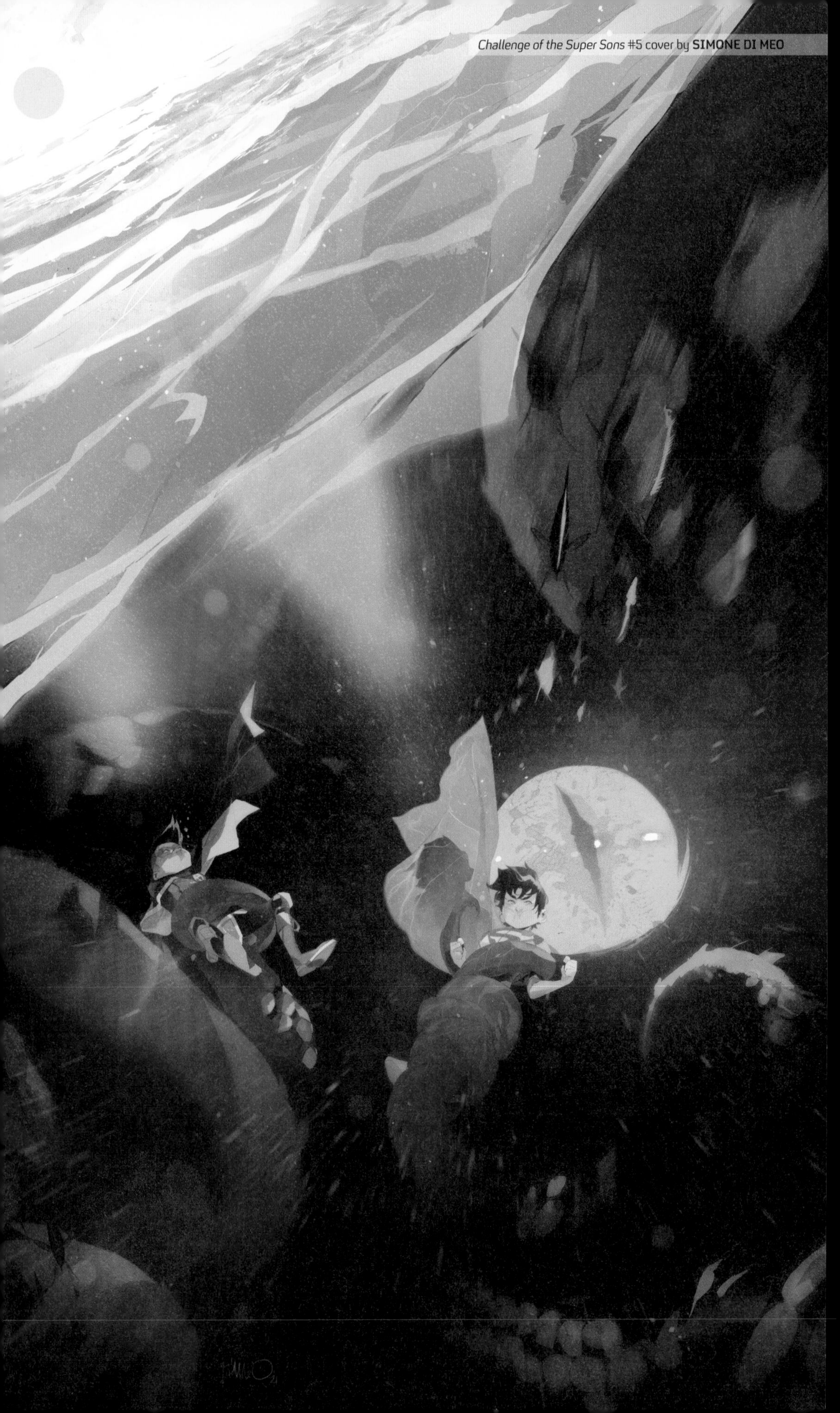

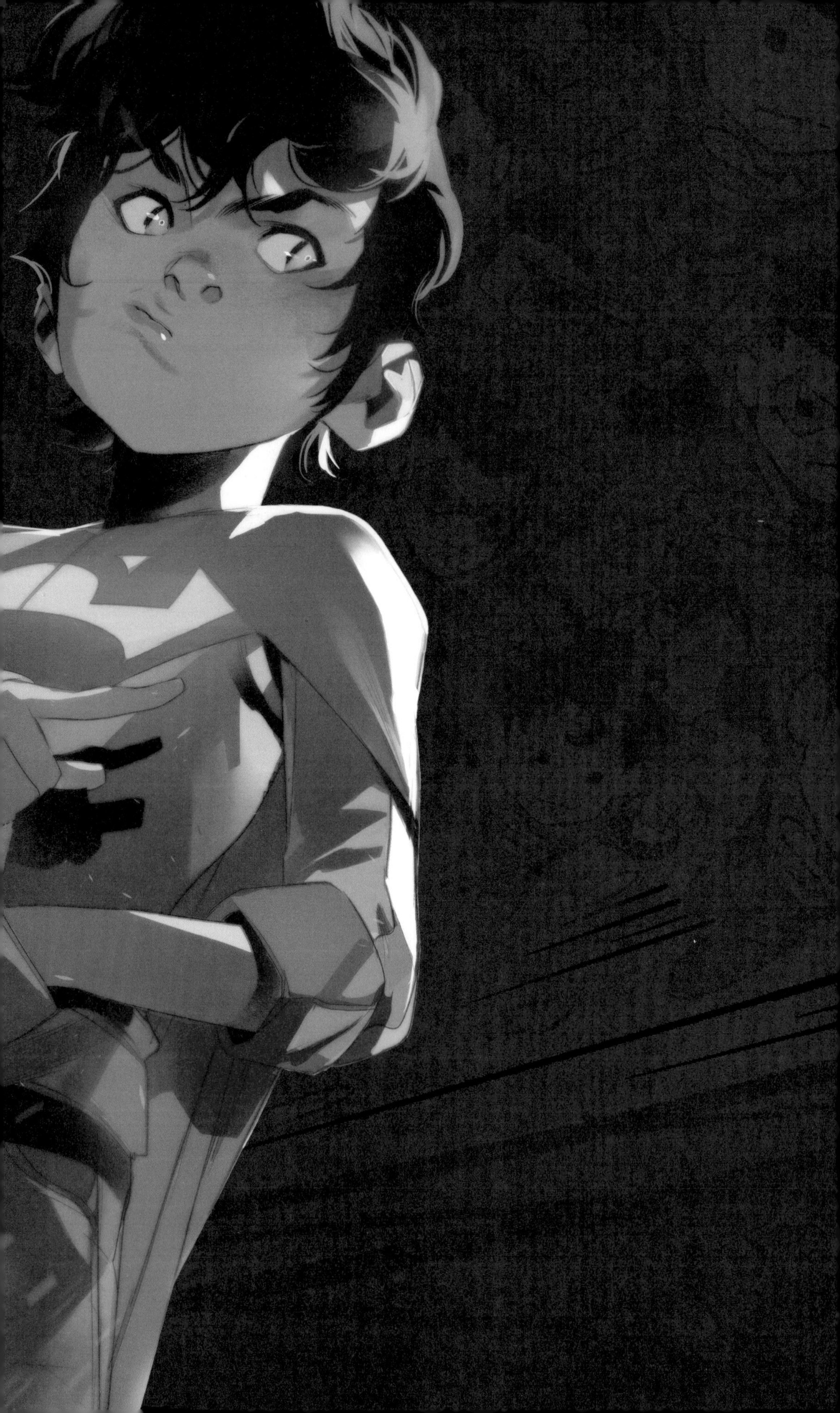

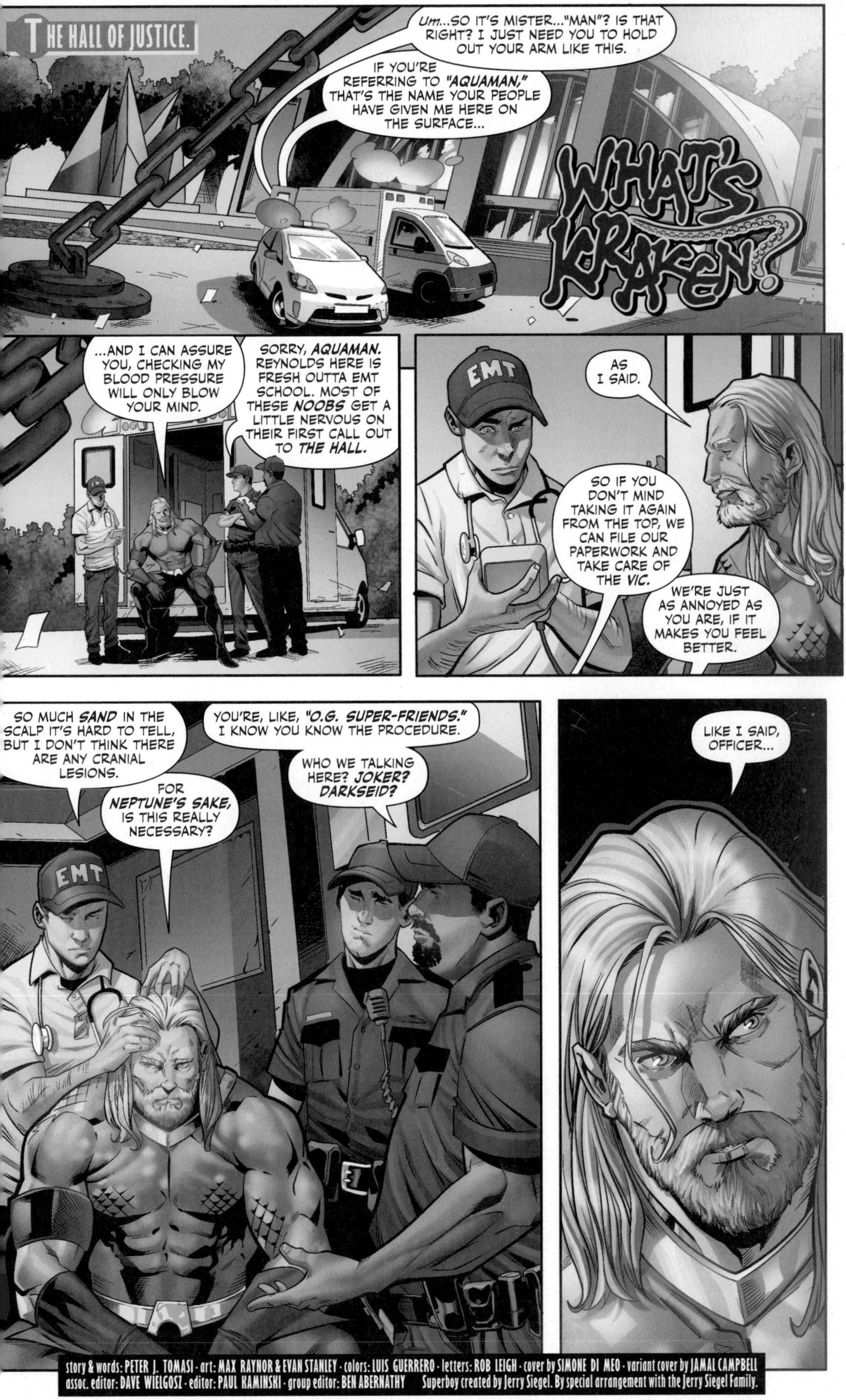
THE HALL OF JUSTICE.
Um...SO IT'S MISTER..."MAN"? IS THAT RIGHT? I JUST NEED YOU TO HOLD OUT YOUR ARM LIKE THIS.
IF YOU'RE REFERRING TO "AQUAMAN," THAT'S THE NAME YOUR PEOPLE HAVE GIVEN ME HERE ON THE SURFACE...
WHAT'S KRAKEN?
...AND I CAN ASSURE YOU, CHECKING MY BLOOD PRESSURE WILL ONLY BLOW YOUR MIND.
SORRY, AQUAMAN. REYNOLDS HERE IS FRESH OUTTA EMT SCHOOL. MOST OF THESE NOOBS GET A LITTLE NERVOUS ON THEIR FIRST CALL OUT TO THE HALL.
AS I SAID.
SO IF YOU DON'T MIND TAKING IT AGAIN FROM THE TOP, WE CAN FILE OUR PAPERWORK AND TAKE CARE OF THE VIC.
WE'RE JUST AS ANNOYED AS YOU ARE, IF IT MAKES YOU FEEL BETTER.
SO MUCH SAND IN THE SCALP IT'S HARD TO TELL, BUT I DON'T THINK THERE ARE ANY CRANIAL LESIONS.
FOR NEPTUNE'S SAKE, IS THIS REALLY NECESSARY?
YOU'RE, LIKE, "O.G. SUPER-FRIENDS." I KNOW YOU KNOW THE PROCEDURE.
WHO WE TALKING HERE? JOKER? DARKSEID?
LIKE I SAID, OFFICER...
story & words: PETER J. TOMASI · art: MAX RAYNOR & EVAN STANLEY · colors: LUIS GUERRERO · letters: ROB LEIGH · cover by SIMONE DI MEO · variant cover by JAMAL CAMPBELL
assoc. editor: DAVE WIELGOSZ · editor: PAUL KAMINSKI · group editor: BEN ABERNATHY Superboy created by Jerry Siegel. By special arrangement with the Jerry Siegel Family.

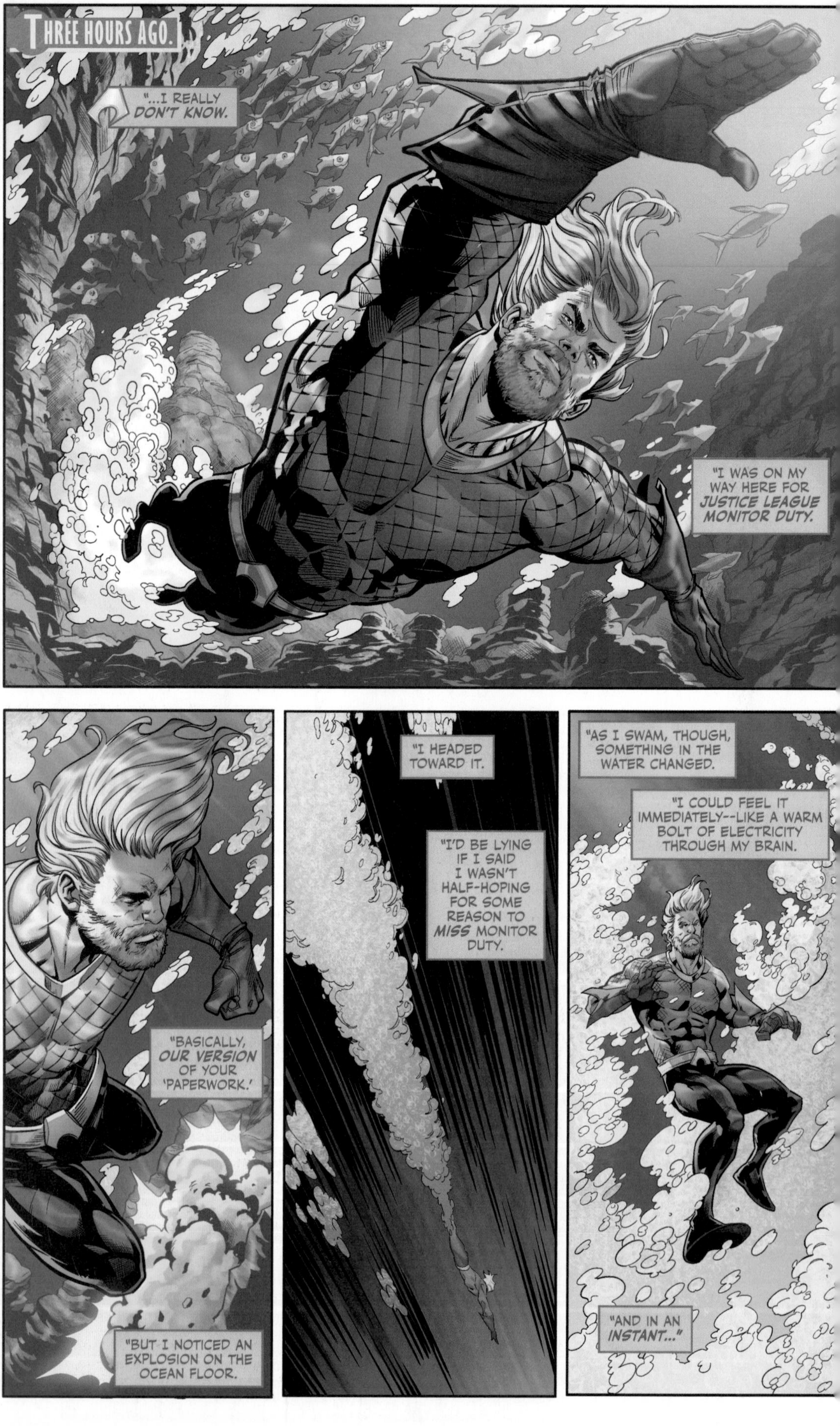
THREE HOURS AGO.
"...I REALLY DON'T KNOW.
"I WAS ON MY WAY HERE FOR JUSTICE LEAGUE MONITOR DUTY.
"BASICALLY, OUR VERSION OF YOUR 'PAPERWORK.'
"BUT I NOTICED AN EXPLOSION ON THE OCEAN FLOOR.
"I HEADED TOWARD IT.
"I'D BE LYING IF I SAID I WASN'T HALF-HOPING FOR SOME REASON TO MISS MONITOR DUTY.
"AS I SWAM, THOUGH, SOMETHING IN THE WATER CHANGED.
"I COULD FEEL IT IMMEDIATELY--LIKE A WARM BOLT OF ELECTRICITY THROUGH MY BRAIN.
"AND IN AN INSTANT..."

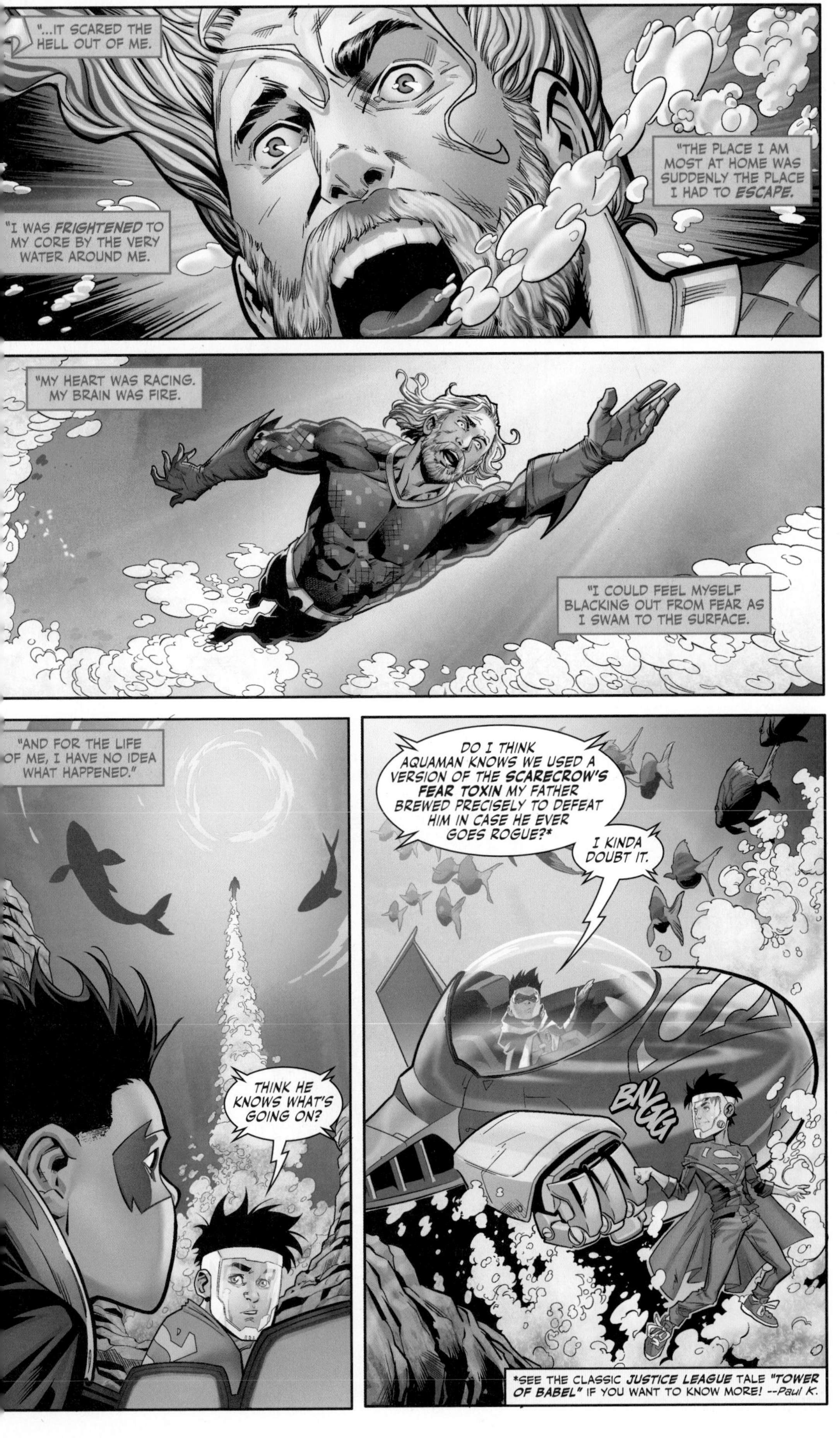
"...IT SCARED THE HELL OUT OF ME.
"I WAS FRIGHTENED TO MY CORE BY THE VERY WATER AROUND ME.
"THE PLACE I AM MOST AT HOME WAS SUDDENLY THE PLACE I HAD TO ESCAPE.
"MY HEART WAS RACING. MY BRAIN WAS FIRE.
"I COULD FEEL MYSELF BLACKING OUT FROM FEAR AS I SWAM TO THE SURFACE.
"AND FOR THE LIFE OF ME, I HAVE NO IDEA WHAT HAPPENED."
THINK HE KNOWS WHAT'S GOING ON?
DO I THINK AQUAMAN KNOWS WE USED A VERSION OF THE SCARECROW'S FEAR TOXIN MY FATHER BREWED PRECISELY TO DEFEAT HIM IN CASE HE EVER GOES ROGUE?*
I KINDA DOUBT IT.
BNGG
*SEE THE CLASSIC JUSTICE LEAGUE TALE "TOWER OF BABEL" IF YOU WANT TO KNOW MORE! --Paul K.

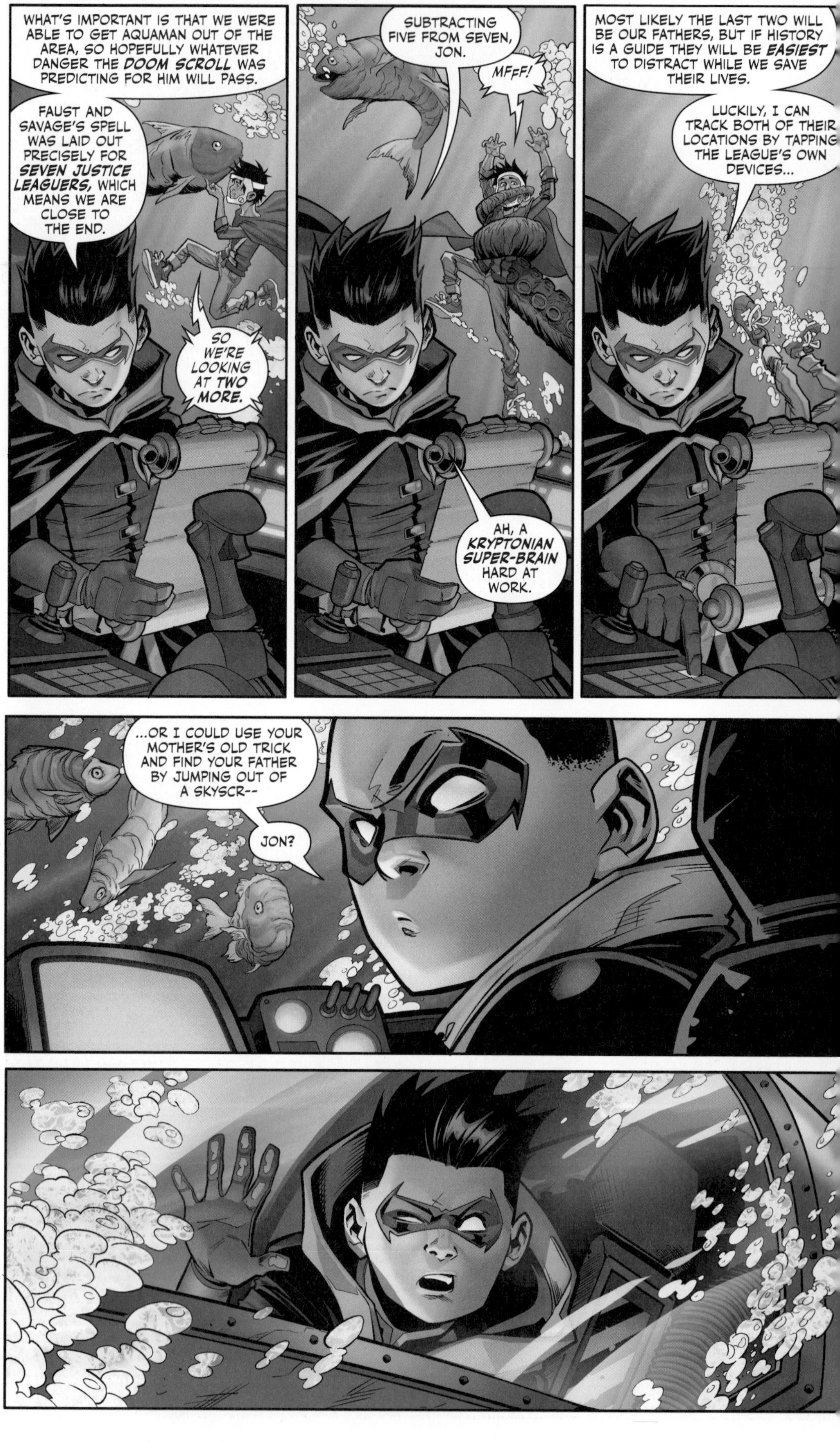

WHAT'S IMPORTANT IS THAT WE WERE ABLE TO GET AQUAMAN OUT OF THE AREA, SO HOPEFULLY WHATEVER DANGER THE DOOM SCROLL WAS PREDICTING FOR HIM WILL PASS.
FAUST AND SAVAGE'S SPELL WAS LAID OUT PRECISELY FOR SEVEN JUSTICE LEAGUERS, WHICH MEANS WE ARE CLOSE TO THE END.
SO WE'RE LOOKING AT TWO MORE.
SUBTRACTING FIVE FROM SEVEN, JON.
MFFF!
AH, A KRYPTONIAN SUPER-BRAIN HARD AT WORK.
MOST LIKELY THE LAST TWO WILL BE OUR FATHERS, BUT IF HISTORY IS A GUIDE THEY WILL BE EASIEST TO DISTRACT WHILE WE SAVE THEIR LIVES.
LUCKILY, I CAN TRACK BOTH OF THEIR LOCATIONS BY TAPPING THE LEAGUE'S OWN DEVICES...
...OR I COULD USE YOUR MOTHER'S OLD TRICK AND FIND YOUR FATHER BY JUMPING OUT OF A SKYSCR--
JON?

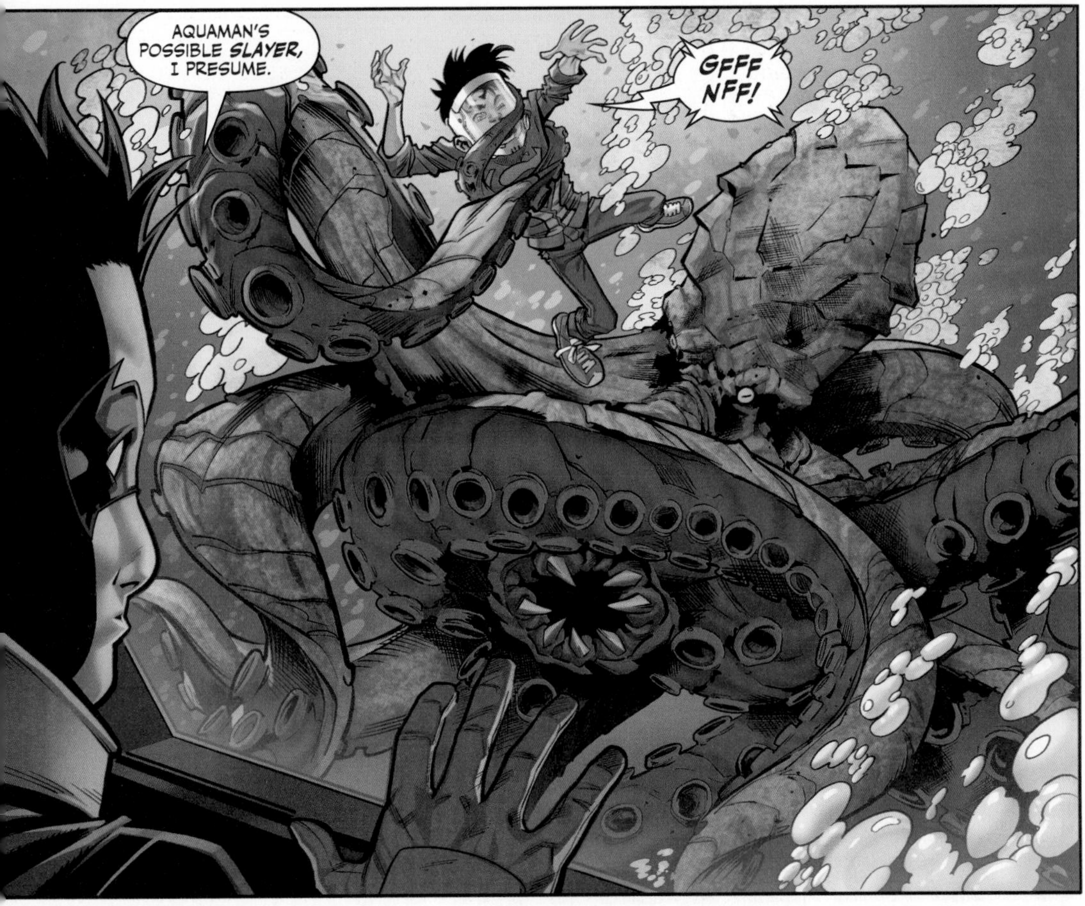
AQUAMAN'S POSSIBLE SLAYER, I PRESUME.
GFFF NFF!

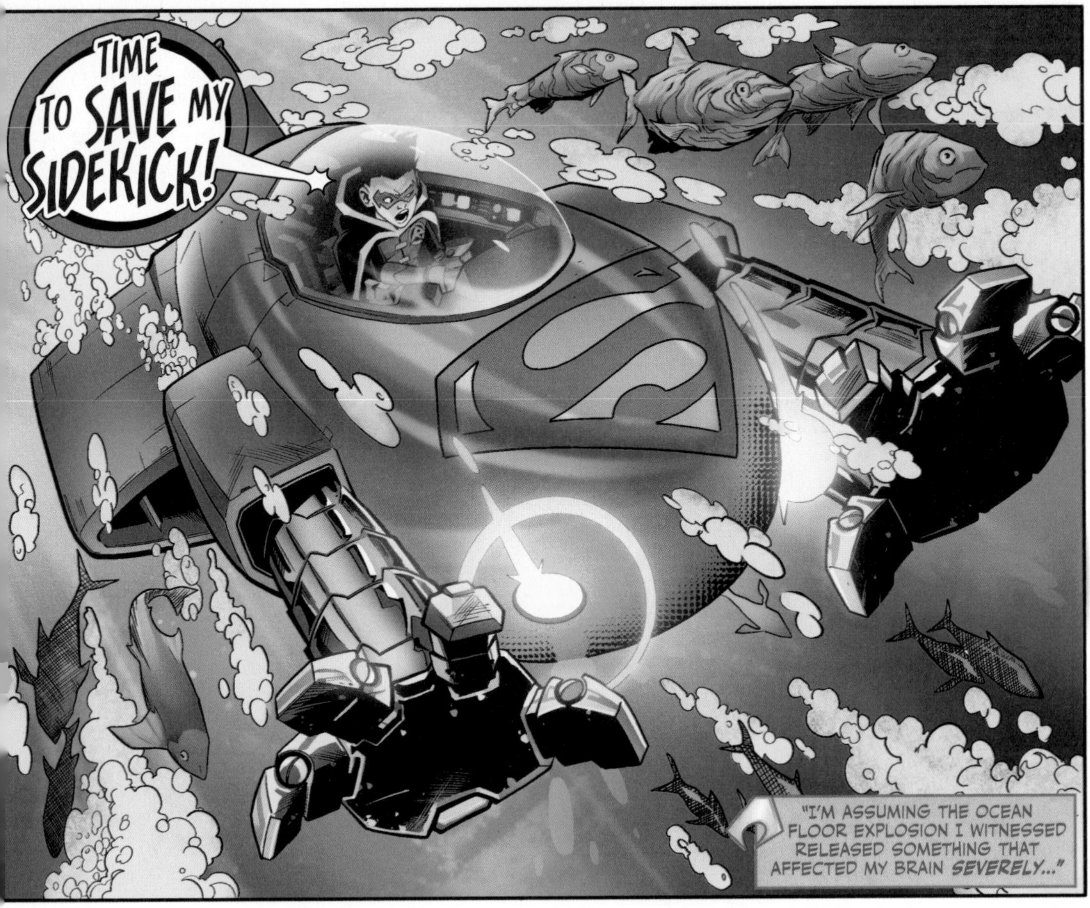
TIME TO SAVE MY SIDEKICK!
"I'M ASSUMING THE OCEAN FLOOR EXPLOSION I WITNESSED RELEASED SOMETHING THAT AFFECTED MY BRAIN SEVERELY..."

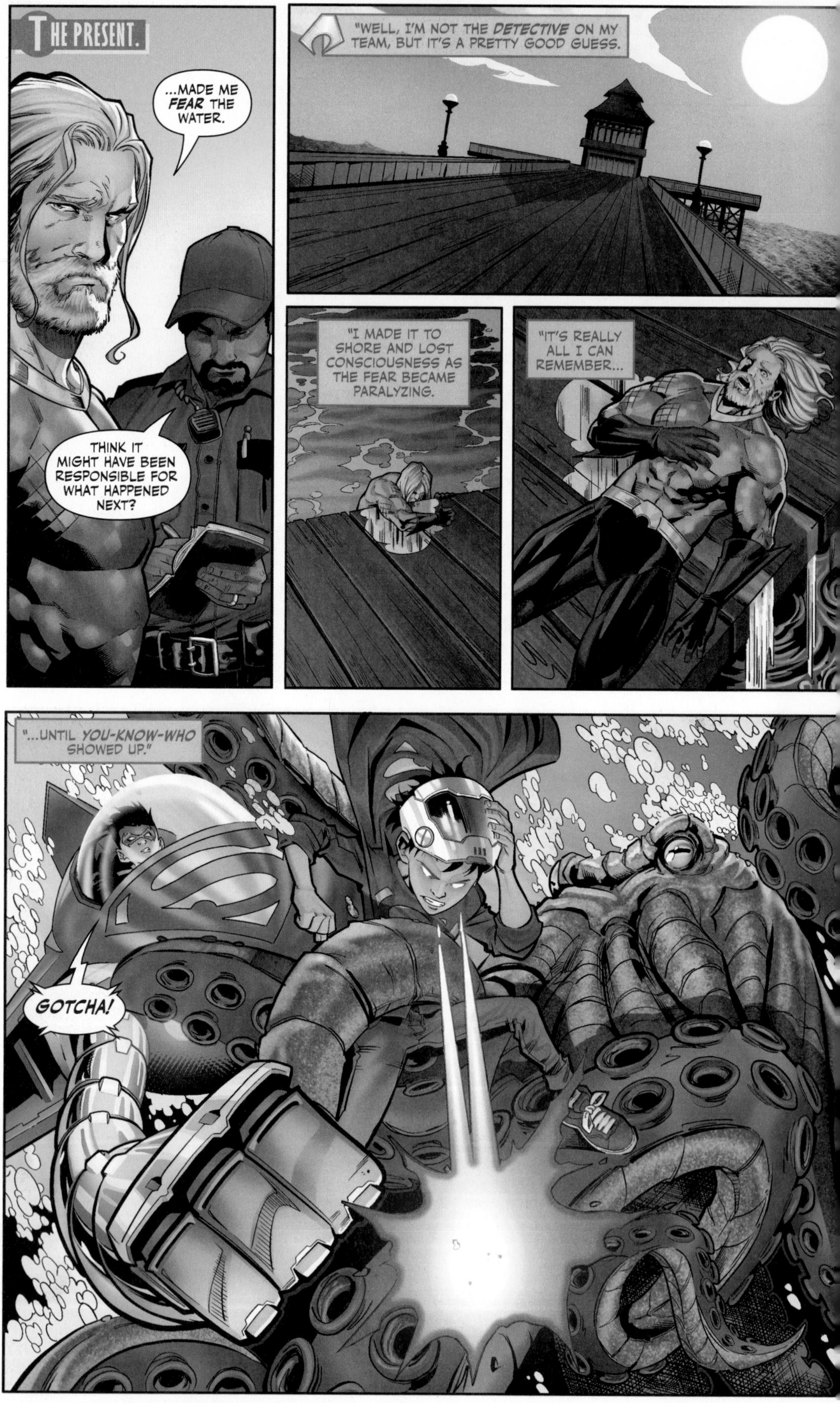
THE PRESENT.
...MADE ME FEAR THE WATER.
THINK IT MIGHT HAVE BEEN RESPONSIBLE FOR WHAT HAPPENED NEXT?
"WELL, I'M NOT THE DETECTIVE ON MY TEAM, BUT IT'S A PRETTY GOOD GUESS.
"I MADE IT TO SHORE AND LOST CONSCIOUSNESS AS THE FEAR BECAME PARALYZING.
"IT'S REALLY ALL I CAN REMEMBER...
"...UNTIL YOU-KNOW-WHO SHOWED UP."
GOTCHA!

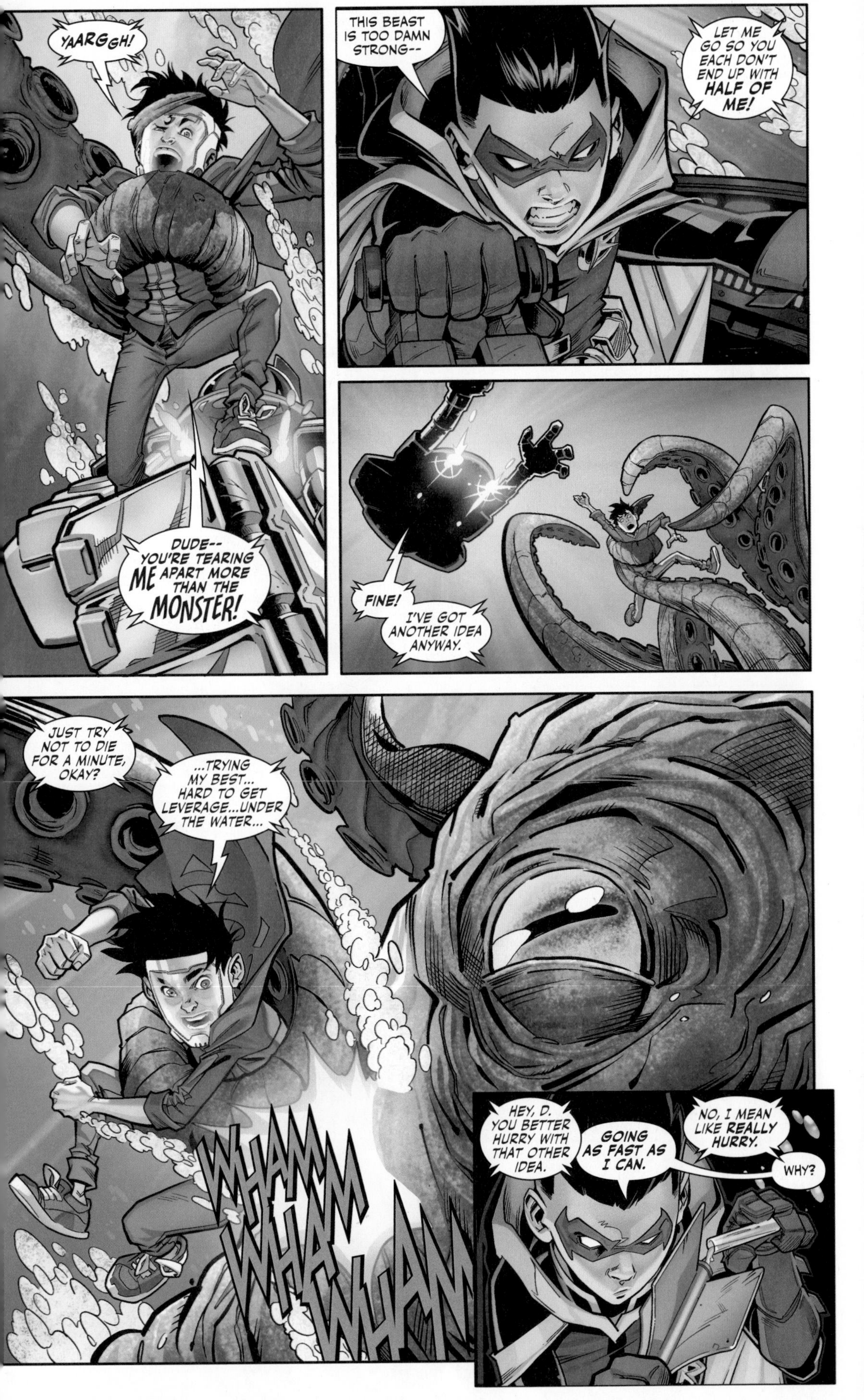
YAARGGH!
DUDE-- YOU'RE TEARING ME APART MORE THAN THE MONSTER!
THIS BEAST IS TOO DAMN STRONG--
LET ME GO SO YOU EACH DON'T END UP WITH HALF OF ME!
FINE!
I'VE GOT ANOTHER IDEA ANYWAY.
JUST TRY NOT TO DIE FOR A MINUTE, OKAY?
...TRYING MY BEST... HARD TO GET LEVERAGE...UNDER THE WATER...
WHAM WHAM WHAM
HEY, D. YOU BETTER HURRY WITH THAT OTHER IDEA.
GOING AS FAST AS I CAN.
NO, I MEAN LIKE REALLY HURRY.
WHY?

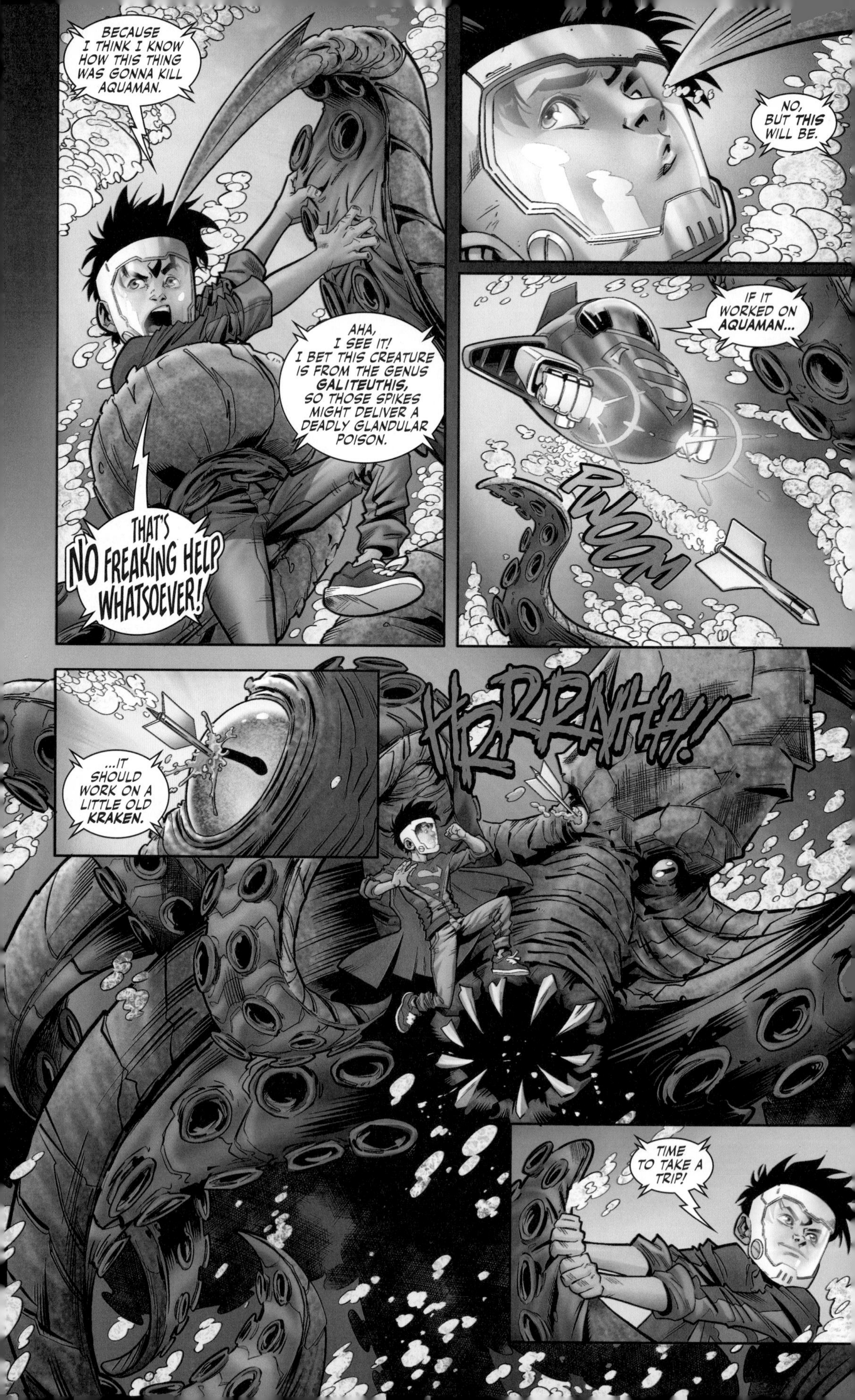
BECAUSE I THINK I KNOW HOW THIS THING WAS GONNA KILL AQUAMAN.
AHA, I SEE IT! I BET THIS CREATURE IS FROM THE GENUS GALITEUTHIS, SO THOSE SPIKES MIGHT DELIVER A DEADLY GLANDULAR POISON.
THAT'S NO FREAKING HELP WHATSOEVER!
NO, BUT THIS WILL BE.
IF IT WORKED ON AQUAMAN...
FWOOOM
...IT SHOULD WORK ON A LITTLE OLD KRAKEN.
HRRRAHHH!
TIME TO TAKE A TRIP!

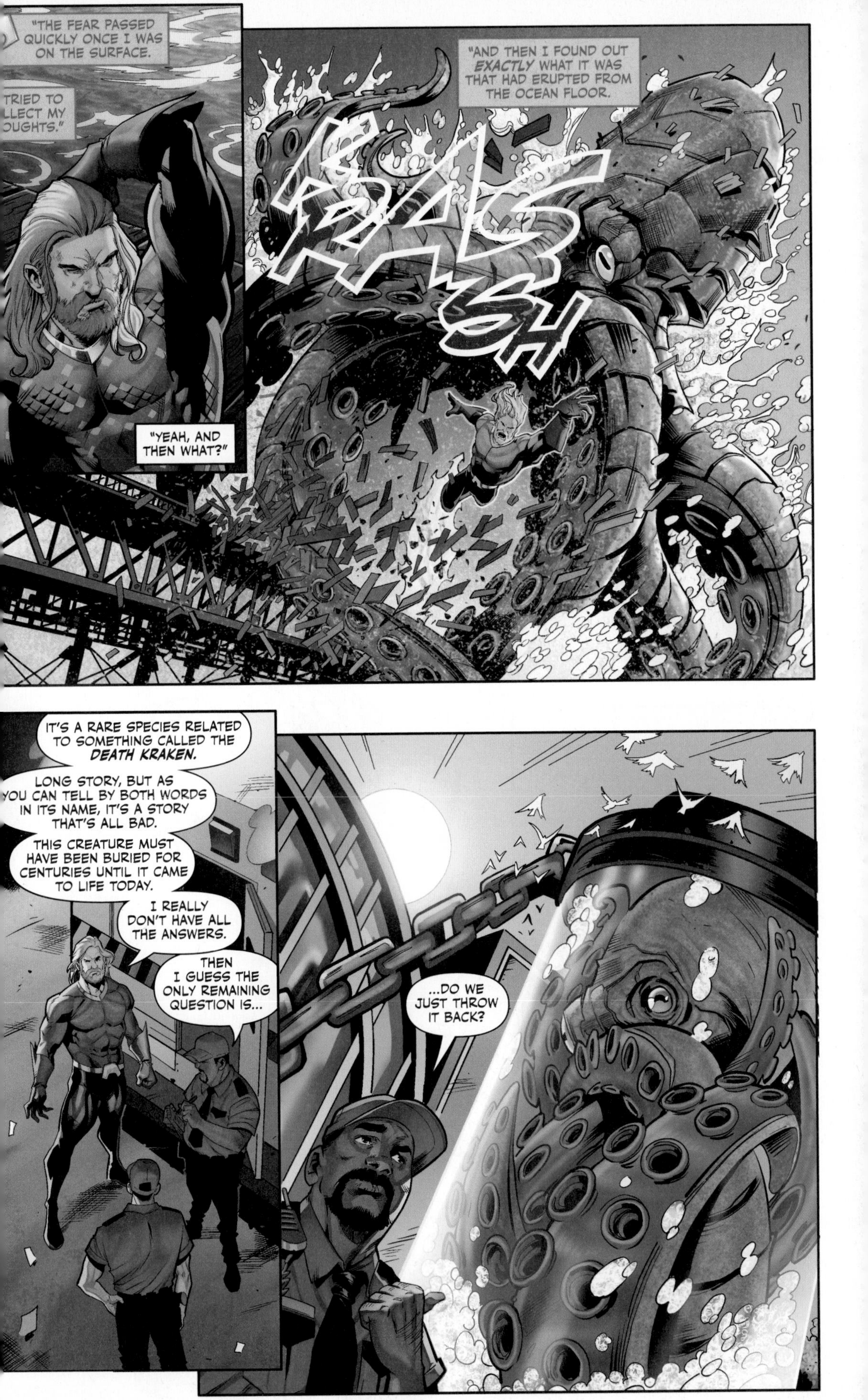
"THE FEAR PASSED QUICKLY ONCE I WAS ON THE SURFACE.
TRIED TO LLECT MY OUGHTS."
"AND THEN I FOUND OUT *EXACTLY* WHAT IT WAS THAT HAD ERUPTED FROM THE OCEAN FLOOR.
"YEAH, AND THEN WHAT?"
IT'S A RARE SPECIES RELATED TO SOMETHING CALLED THE *DEATH KRAKEN.*
LONG STORY, BUT AS YOU CAN TELL BY BOTH WORDS IN ITS NAME, IT'S A STORY THAT'S ALL BAD.
THIS CREATURE MUST HAVE BEEN BURIED FOR CENTURIES UNTIL IT CAME TO LIFE TODAY.
I REALLY DON'T HAVE ALL THE ANSWERS.
THEN I GUESS THE ONLY REMAINING QUESTION IS...
...DO WE JUST THROW IT BACK?

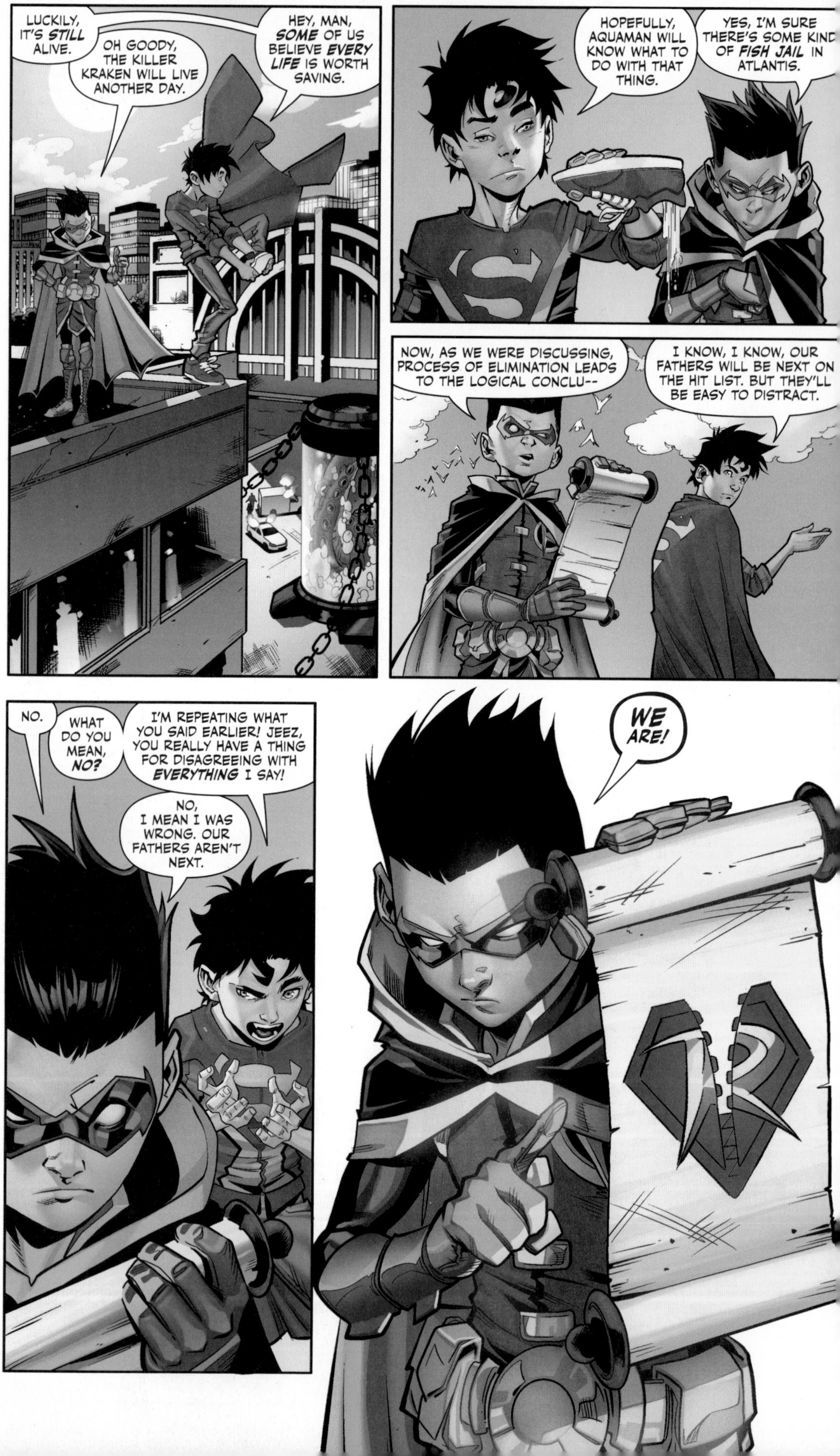
LUCKILY, IT'S STILL ALIVE.
OH GOODY, THE KILLER KRAKEN WILL LIVE ANOTHER DAY.
HEY, MAN, SOME OF US BELIEVE EVERY LIFE IS WORTH SAVING.
HOPEFULLY, AQUAMAN WILL KNOW WHAT TO DO WITH THAT THING.
YES, I'M SURE THERE'S SOME KIND OF FISH JAIL IN ATLANTIS.
NOW, AS WE WERE DISCUSSING, PROCESS OF ELIMINATION LEADS TO THE LOGICAL CONCLU--
I KNOW, I KNOW, OUR FATHERS WILL BE NEXT ON THE HIT LIST. BUT THEY'LL BE EASY TO DISTRACT.
NO.
WHAT DO YOU MEAN, NO?
I'M REPEATING WHAT YOU SAID EARLIER! JEEZ, YOU REALLY HAVE A THING FOR DISAGREEING WITH EVERYTHING I SAY!
NO, I MEAN I WAS WRONG. OUR FATHERS AREN'T NEXT.
WE ARE!

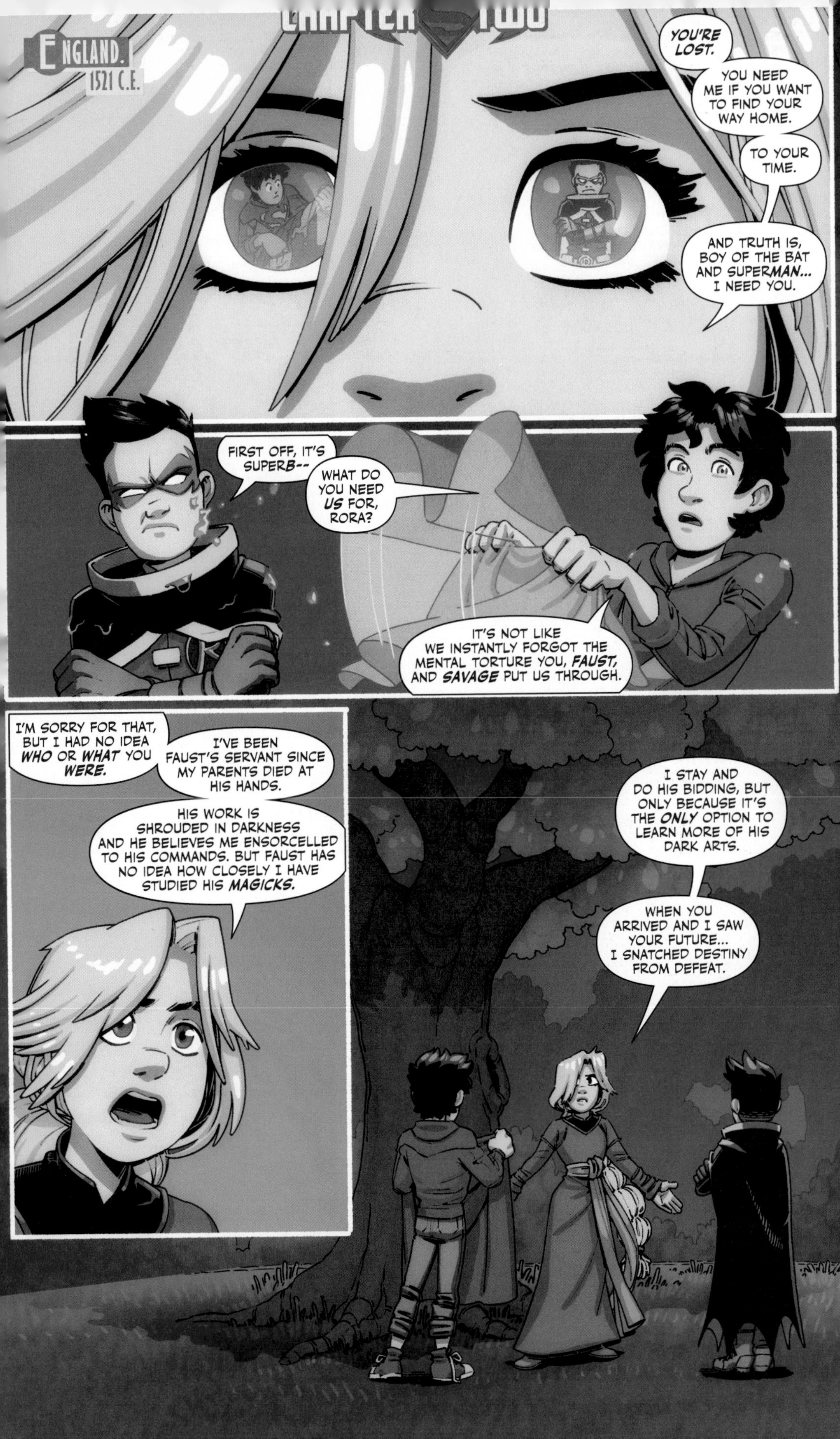
CHAPTER TWO
ENGLAND. 1521 C.E.
YOU'RE LOST.
YOU NEED ME IF YOU WANT TO FIND YOUR WAY HOME.
TO YOUR TIME.
AND TRUTH IS, BOY OF THE BAT AND SUPERMAN... I NEED YOU.
FIRST OFF, IT'S SUPERB--
WHAT DO YOU NEED US FOR, RORA?
IT'S NOT LIKE WE INSTANTLY FORGOT THE MENTAL TORTURE YOU, FAUST, AND SAVAGE PUT US THROUGH.
I'M SORRY FOR THAT, BUT I HAD NO IDEA WHO OR WHAT YOU WERE.
I'VE BEEN FAUST'S SERVANT SINCE MY PARENTS DIED AT HIS HANDS.
HIS WORK IS SHROUDED IN DARKNESS AND HE BELIEVES ME ENSORCELLED TO HIS COMMANDS. BUT FAUST HAS NO IDEA HOW CLOSELY I HAVE STUDIED HIS MAGICKS.
I STAY AND DO HIS BIDDING, BUT ONLY BECAUSE IT'S THE ONLY OPTION TO LEARN MORE OF HIS DARK ARTS.
WHEN YOU ARRIVED AND I SAW YOUR FUTURE... I SNATCHED DESTINY FROM DEFEAT.

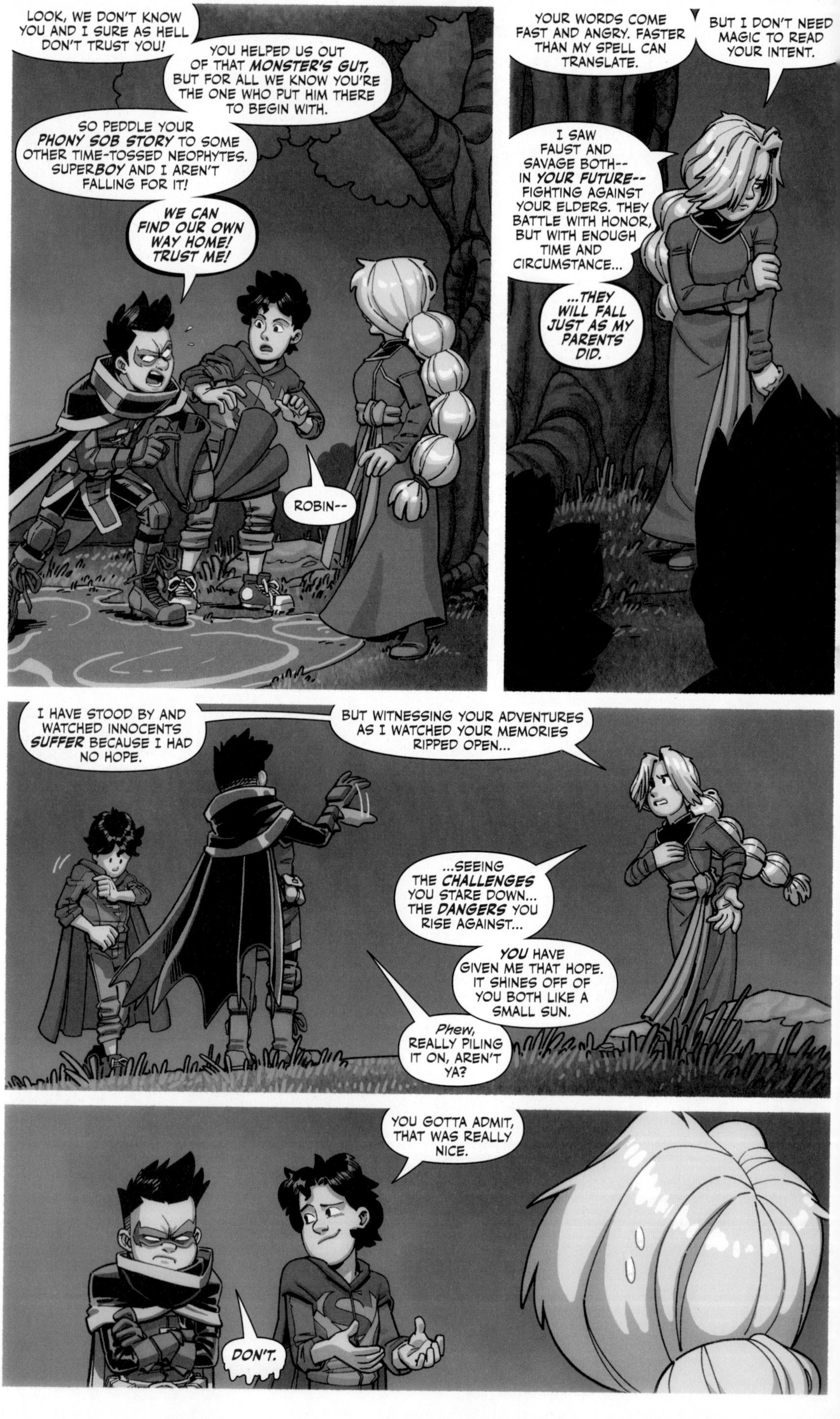

LOOK, WE DON'T KNOW YOU AND I SURE AS HELL DON'T TRUST YOU!
YOU HELPED US OUT OF THAT *MONSTER'S GUT*, BUT FOR ALL WE KNOW YOU'RE THE ONE WHO PUT HIM THERE TO BEGIN WITH.
SO PEDDLE YOUR *PHONY SOB STORY* TO SOME OTHER TIME-TOSSED NEOPHYTES. SUPER*BOY* AND I AREN'T FALLING FOR IT!
WE CAN FIND OUR OWN WAY HOME! TRUST ME!
ROBIN--
YOUR WORDS COME FAST AND ANGRY. FASTER THAN MY SPELL CAN TRANSLATE.
BUT I DON'T NEED MAGIC TO READ YOUR INTENT.
I SAW FAUST AND SAVAGE BOTH-- IN *YOUR FUTURE--* FIGHTING AGAINST YOUR ELDERS. THEY BATTLE WITH HONOR, BUT WITH ENOUGH TIME AND CIRCUMSTANCE...
...THEY WILL FALL JUST AS MY PARENTS DID.
I HAVE STOOD BY AND WATCHED INNOCENTS *SUFFER* BECAUSE I HAD NO HOPE.
BUT WITNESSING YOUR ADVENTURES AS I WATCHED YOUR MEMORIES RIPPED OPEN...
...SEEING THE *CHALLENGES* YOU STARE DOWN... THE *DANGERS* YOU RISE AGAINST...
YOU HAVE GIVEN ME THAT HOPE. IT SHINES OFF OF YOU BOTH LIKE A SMALL SUN.
Phew, REALLY PILING IT ON, AREN'T YA?
YOU GOTTA ADMIT, THAT WAS REALLY NICE.
DON'T.

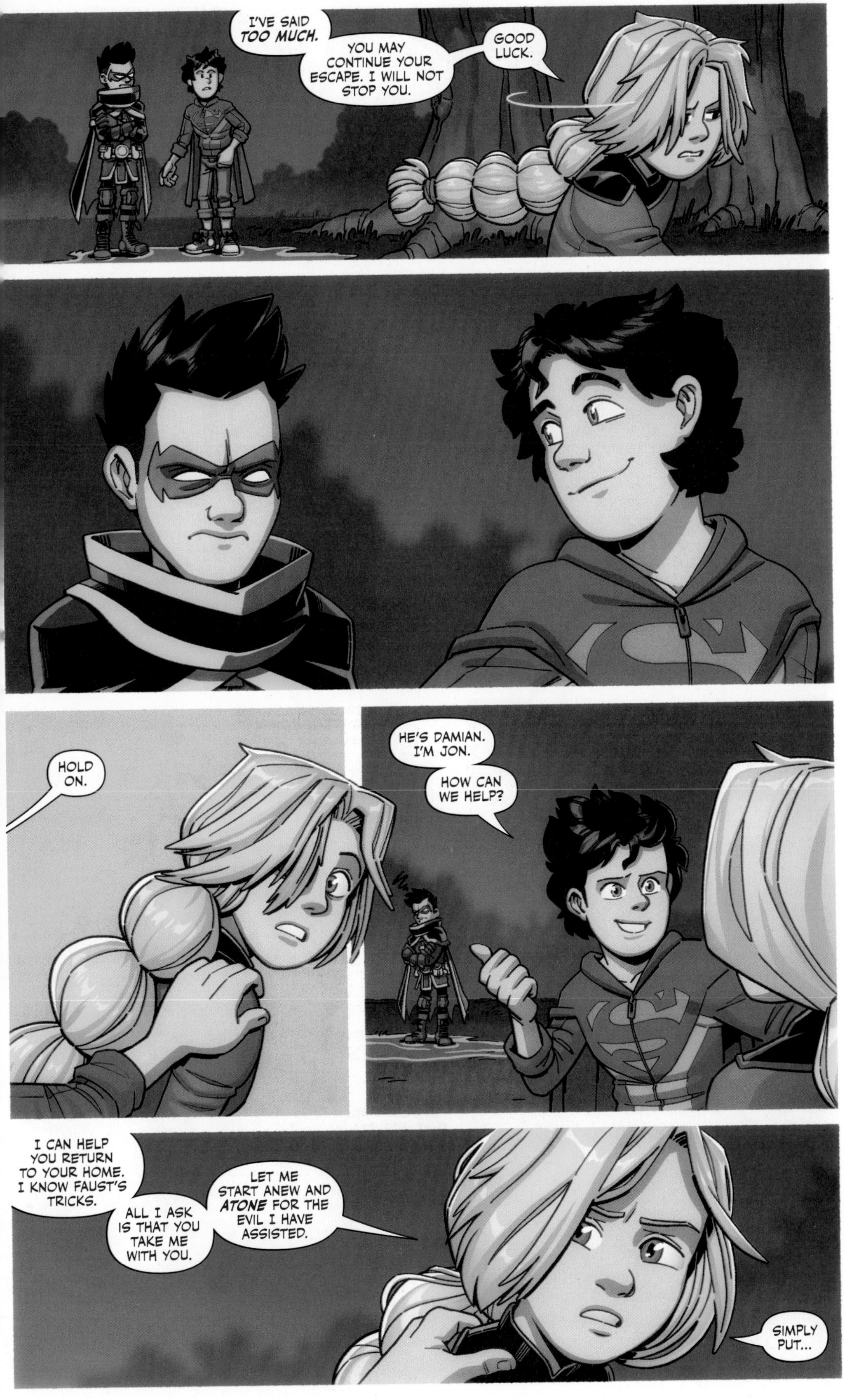
I'VE SAID TOO MUCH.
YOU MAY CONTINUE YOUR ESCAPE. I WILL NOT STOP YOU.
GOOD LUCK.
HOLD ON.
HE'S DAMIAN. I'M JON.
HOW CAN WE HELP?
I CAN HELP YOU RETURN TO YOUR HOME. I KNOW FAUST'S TRICKS.
ALL I ASK IS THAT YOU TAKE ME WITH YOU.
LET ME START ANEW AND ATONE FOR THE EVIL I HAVE ASSISTED.
SIMPLY PUT...

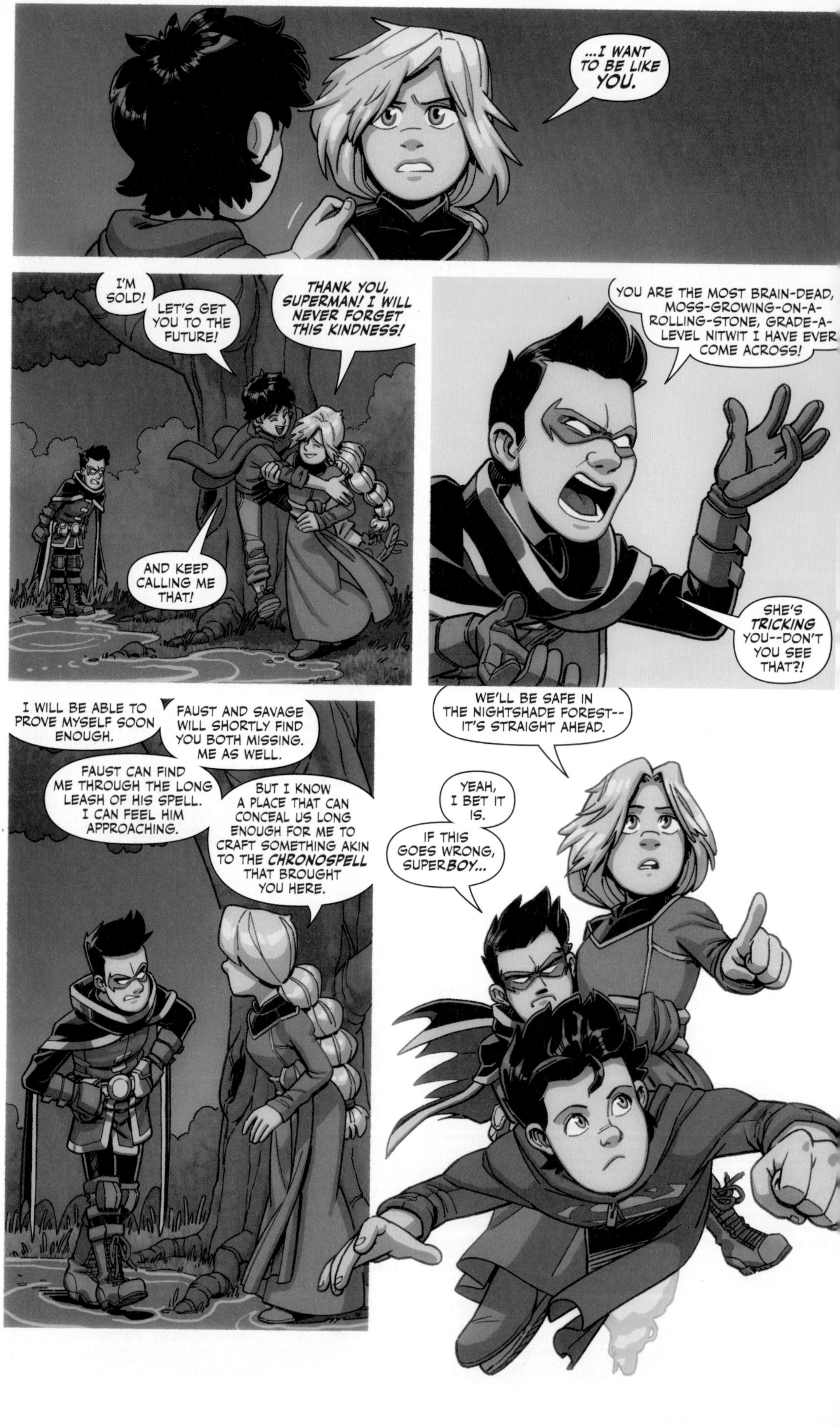
...I WANT TO BE LIKE YOU.
I'M SOLD!
LET'S GET YOU TO THE FUTURE!
THANK YOU, SUPERMAN! I WILL NEVER FORGET THIS KINDNESS!
AND KEEP CALLING ME THAT!
YOU ARE THE MOST BRAIN-DEAD, MOSS-GROWING-ON-A-ROLLING-STONE, GRADE-A-LEVEL NITWIT I HAVE EVER COME ACROSS!
SHE'S TRICKING YOU--DON'T YOU SEE THAT?!
I WILL BE ABLE TO PROVE MYSELF SOON ENOUGH.
FAUST AND SAVAGE WILL SHORTLY FIND YOU BOTH MISSING. ME AS WELL.
FAUST CAN FIND ME THROUGH THE LONG LEASH OF HIS SPELL. I CAN FEEL HIM APPROACHING.
BUT I KNOW A PLACE THAT CAN CONCEAL US LONG ENOUGH FOR ME TO CRAFT SOMETHING AKIN TO THE CHRONOSPELL THAT BROUGHT YOU HERE.
WE'LL BE SAFE IN THE NIGHTSHADE FOREST--IT'S STRAIGHT AHEAD.
YEAH, I BET IT IS.
IF THIS GOES WRONG, SUPERBOY...

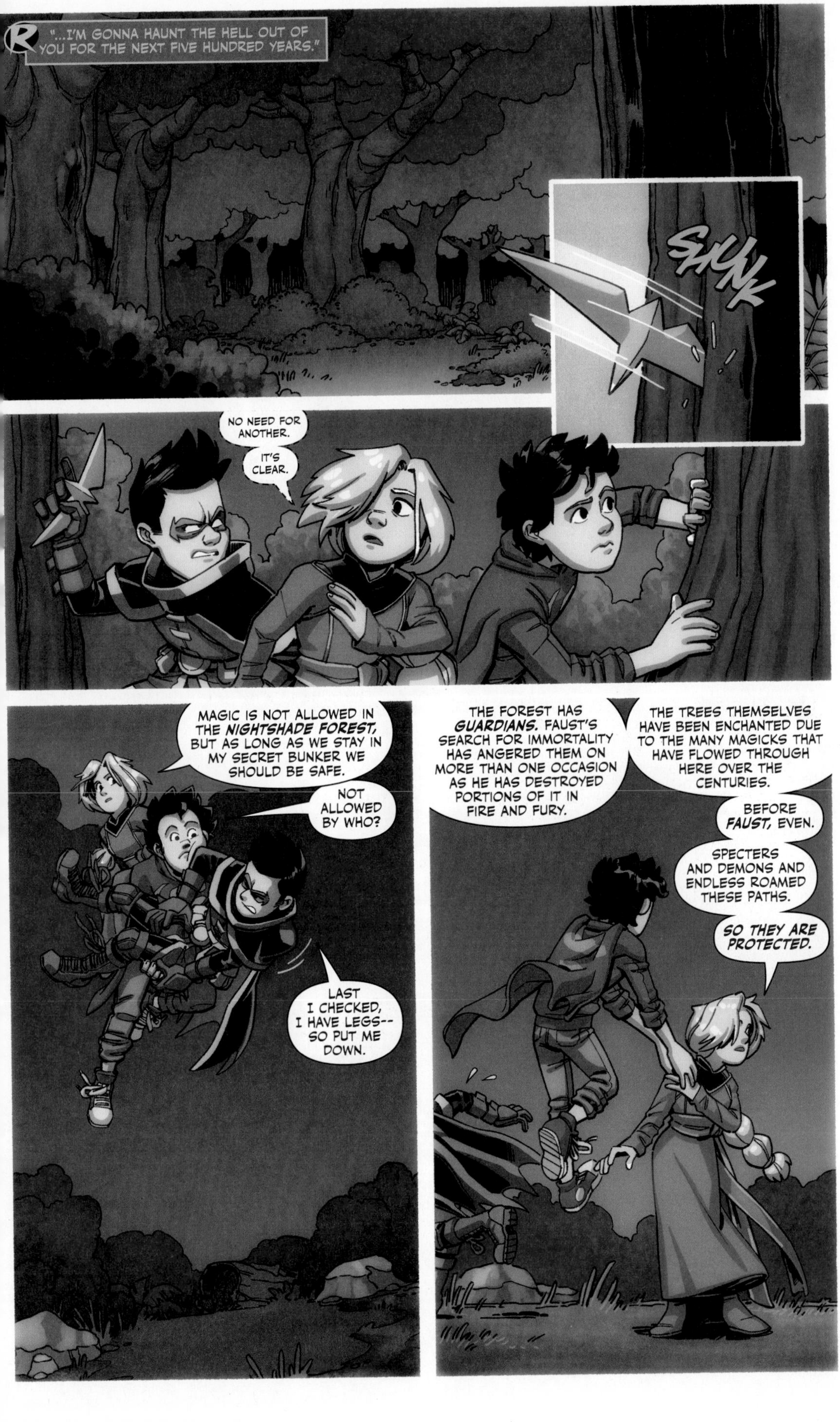
"...I'M GONNA HAUNT THE HELL OUT OF YOU FOR THE NEXT FIVE HUNDRED YEARS."
SHUNK
NO NEED FOR ANOTHER.
IT'S CLEAR.
MAGIC IS NOT ALLOWED IN THE NIGHTSHADE FOREST, BUT AS LONG AS WE STAY IN MY SECRET BUNKER WE SHOULD BE SAFE.
NOT ALLOWED BY WHO?
LAST I CHECKED, I HAVE LEGS-- SO PUT ME DOWN.
THE FOREST HAS GUARDIANS. FAUST'S SEARCH FOR IMMORTALITY HAS ANGERED THEM ON MORE THAN ONE OCCASION AS HE HAS DESTROYED PORTIONS OF IT IN FIRE AND FURY.
THE TREES THEMSELVES HAVE BEEN ENCHANTED DUE TO THE MANY MAGICKS THAT HAVE FLOWED THROUGH HERE OVER THE CENTURIES.
BEFORE FAUST, EVEN.
SPECTERS AND DEMONS AND ENDLESS ROAMED THESE PATHS.
SO THEY ARE PROTECTED.

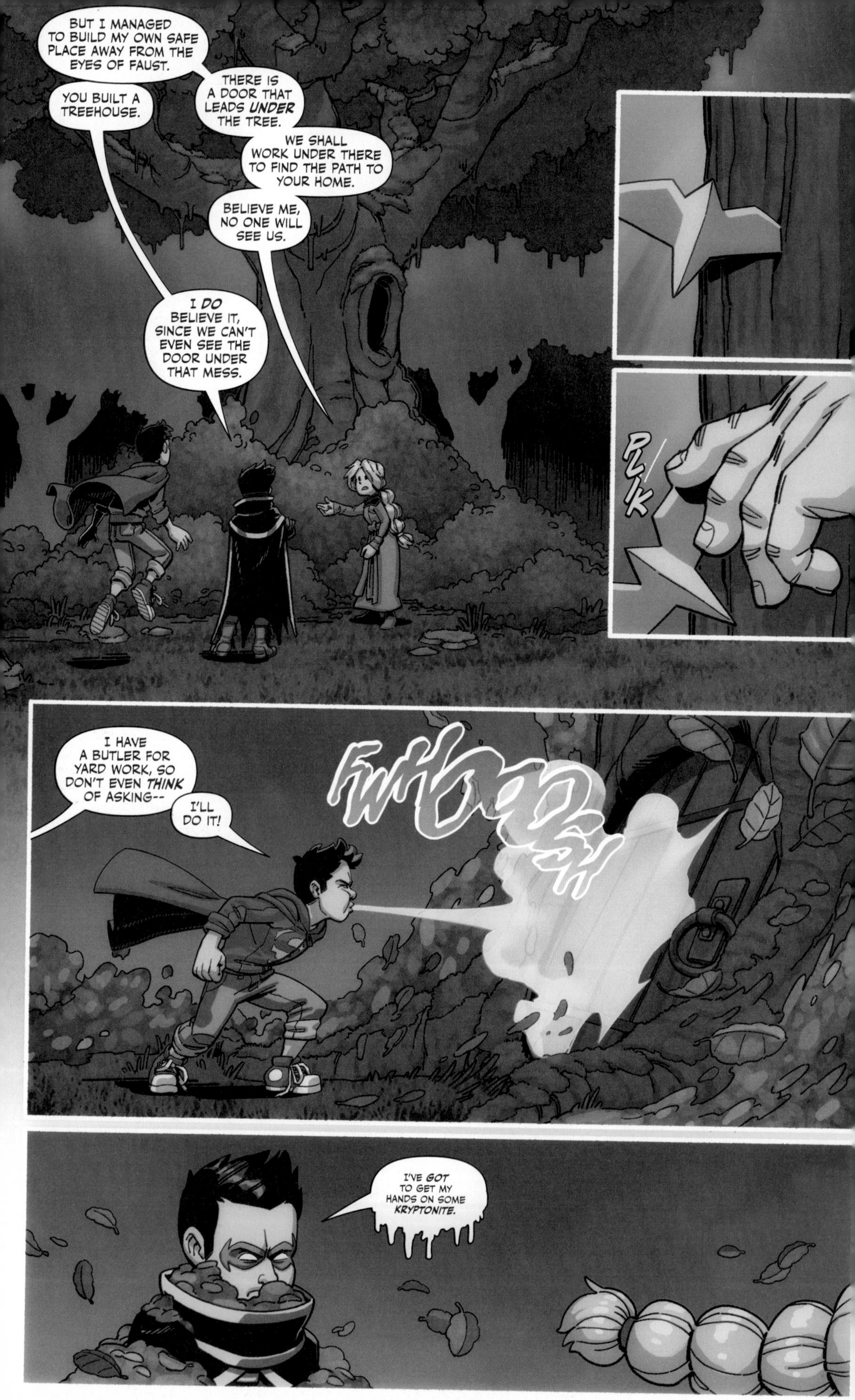
BUT I MANAGED TO BUILD MY OWN SAFE PLACE AWAY FROM THE EYES OF FAUST.
YOU BUILT A TREEHOUSE.
THERE IS A DOOR THAT LEADS UNDER THE TREE.
WE SHALL WORK UNDER THERE TO FIND THE PATH TO YOUR HOME.
BELIEVE ME, NO ONE WILL SEE US.
I DO BELIEVE IT, SINCE WE CAN'T EVEN SEE THE DOOR UNDER THAT MESS.
PLIK
I HAVE A BUTLER FOR YARD WORK, SO DON'T EVEN THINK OF ASKING--
I'LL DO IT!
FWHOOOSH
I'VE GOT TO GET MY HANDS ON SOME KRYPTONITE.

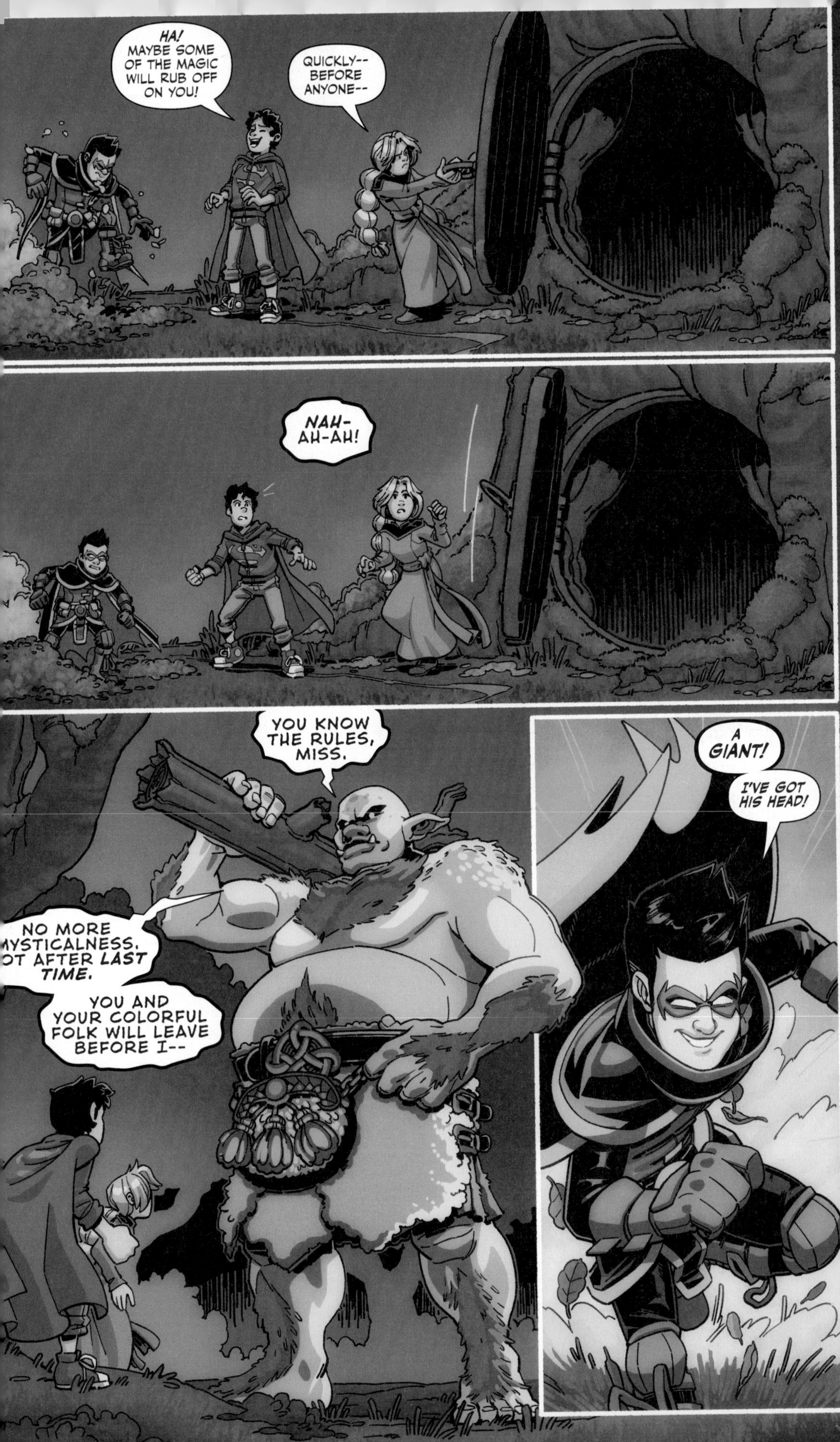
HA! MAYBE SOME OF THE MAGIC WILL RUB OFF ON YOU!
QUICKLY-- BEFORE ANYONE--
NAH-AH-AH!
YOU KNOW THE RULES, MISS.
NO MORE MYSTICALNESS. OT AFTER LAST TIME.
YOU AND YOUR COLORFUL FOLK WILL LEAVE BEFORE I--
A GIANT!
I'VE GOT HIS HEAD!

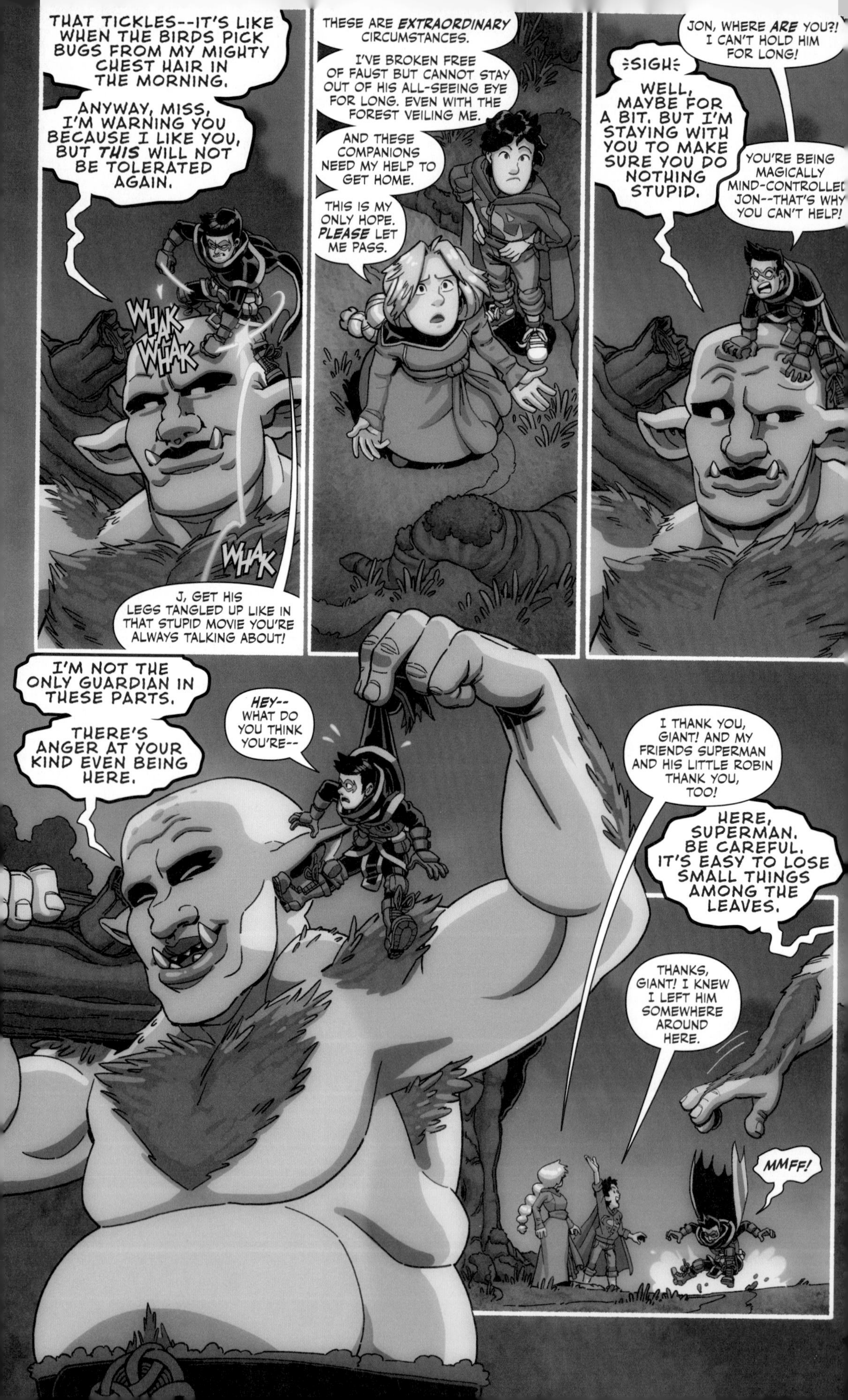
THAT TICKLES--IT'S LIKE WHEN THE BIRDS PICK BUGS FROM MY MIGHTY CHEST HAIR IN THE MORNING.
ANYWAY, MISS, I'M WARNING YOU BECAUSE I LIKE YOU, BUT THIS WILL NOT BE TOLERATED AGAIN.
WHAK WHAK
WHAK
J, GET HIS LEGS TANGLED UP LIKE IN THAT STUPID MOVIE YOU'RE ALWAYS TALKING ABOUT!
THESE ARE EXTRAORDINARY CIRCUMSTANCES.
I'VE BROKEN FREE OF FAUST BUT CANNOT STAY OUT OF HIS ALL-SEEING EYE FOR LONG. EVEN WITH THE FOREST VEILING ME.
AND THESE COMPANIONS NEED MY HELP TO GET HOME.
THIS IS MY ONLY HOPE. PLEASE LET ME PASS.
SIGH
WELL, MAYBE FOR A BIT. BUT I'M STAYING WITH YOU TO MAKE SURE YOU DO NOTHING STUPID.
JON, WHERE ARE YOU?! I CAN'T HOLD HIM FOR LONG!
YOU'RE BEING MAGICALLY MIND-CONTROLLED JON--THAT'S WHY YOU CAN'T HELP!
I'M NOT THE ONLY GUARDIAN IN THESE PARTS.
THERE'S ANGER AT YOUR KIND EVEN BEING HERE.
HEY-- WHAT DO YOU THINK YOU'RE--
I THANK YOU, GIANT! AND MY FRIENDS SUPERMAN AND HIS LITTLE ROBIN THANK YOU, TOO!
HERE, SUPERMAN. BE CAREFUL. IT'S EASY TO LOSE SMALL THINGS AMONG THE LEAVES.
THANKS, GIANT! I KNEW I LEFT HIM SOMEWHERE AROUND HERE.
MMFF!

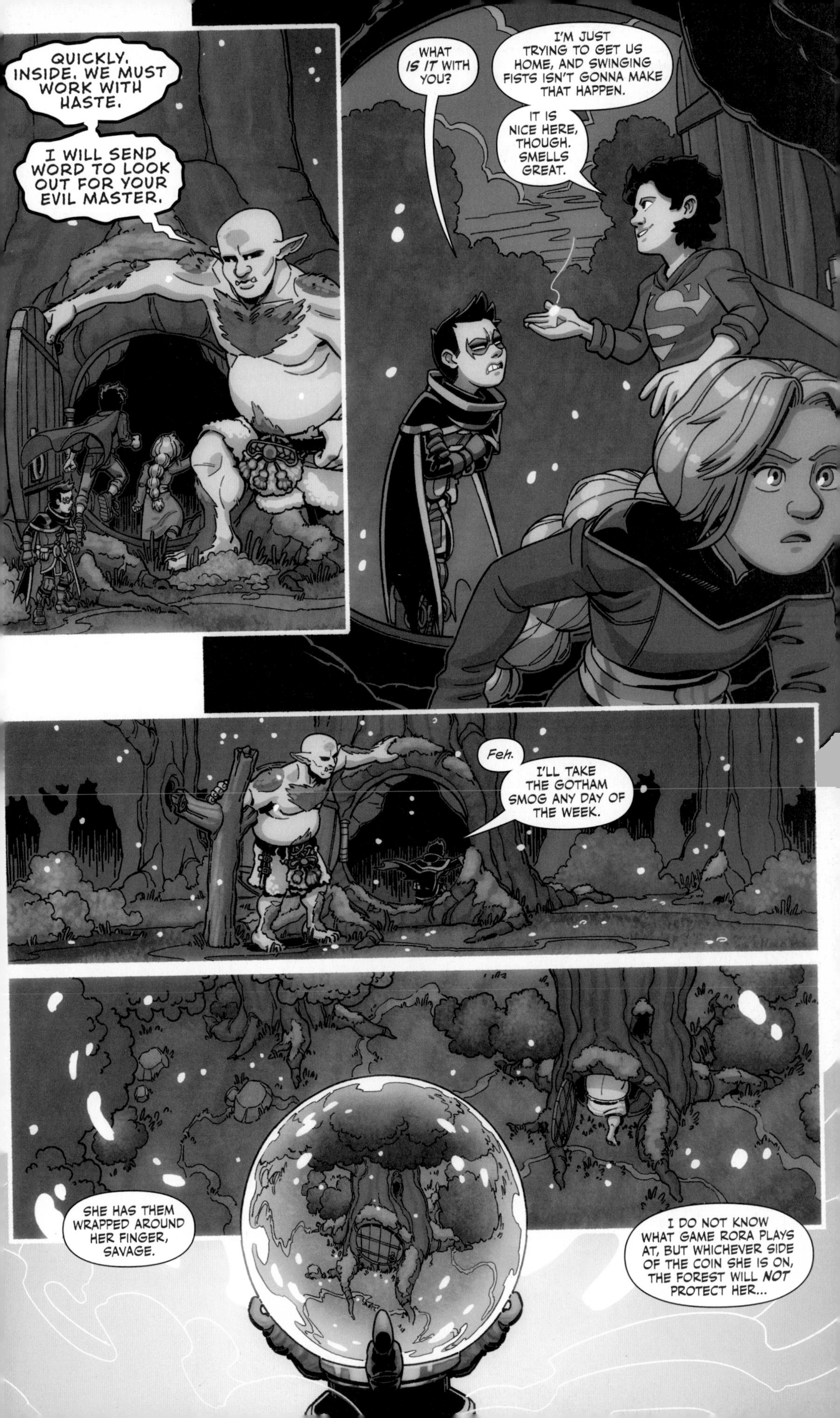
QUICKLY. INSIDE. WE MUST WORK WITH HASTE.
I WILL SEND WORD TO LOOK OUT FOR YOUR EVIL MASTER.
WHAT *IS IT* WITH YOU?
I'M JUST TRYING TO GET US HOME, AND SWINGING FISTS ISN'T GONNA MAKE THAT HAPPEN.
IT IS NICE HERE, THOUGH. SMELLS GREAT.
Feh.
I'LL TAKE THE GOTHAM SMOG ANY DAY OF THE WEEK.
SHE HAS THEM WRAPPED AROUND HER FINGER, SAVAGE.
I DO NOT KNOW WHAT GAME RORA PLAYS AT, BUT WHICHEVER SIDE OF THE COIN SHE IS ON, THE FOREST WILL **NOT** PROTECT HER...

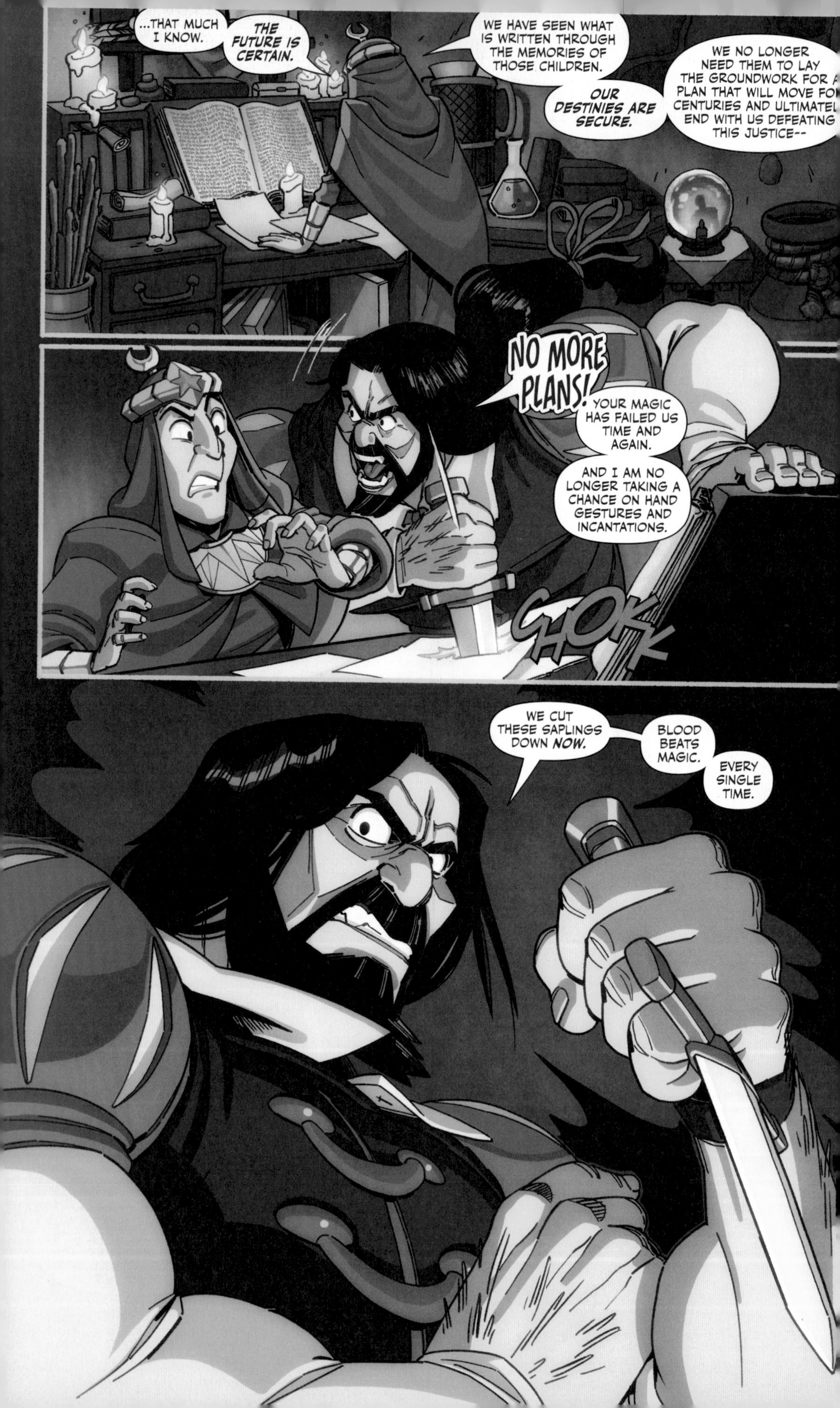

...THAT MUCH I KNOW.
THE FUTURE IS CERTAIN.
WE HAVE SEEN WHAT IS WRITTEN THROUGH THE MEMORIES OF THOSE CHILDREN.
OUR DESTINIES ARE SECURE.
WE NO LONGER NEED THEM TO LAY THE GROUNDWORK FOR A PLAN THAT WILL MOVE FOR CENTURIES AND ULTIMATELY END WITH US DEFEATING THIS JUSTICE--
NO MORE PLANS!
YOUR MAGIC HAS FAILED US TIME AND AGAIN.
AND I AM NO LONGER TAKING A CHANCE ON HAND GESTURES AND INCANTATIONS.
CHOKK
WE CUT THESE SAPLINGS DOWN NOW.
BLOOD BEATS MAGIC.
EVERY SINGLE TIME.

Challenge of the Super Sons #6 cover by **SIMONE DI MEO**

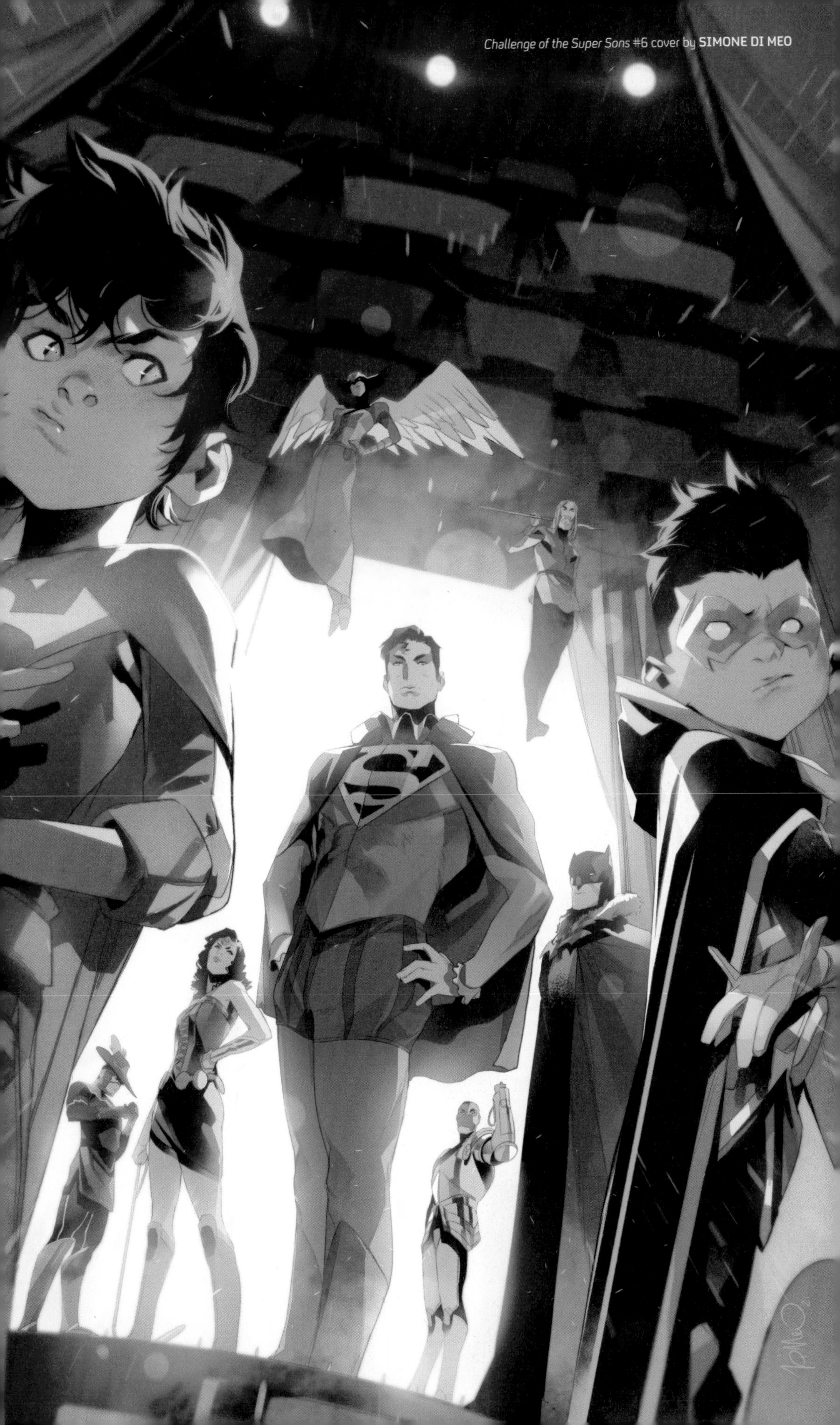

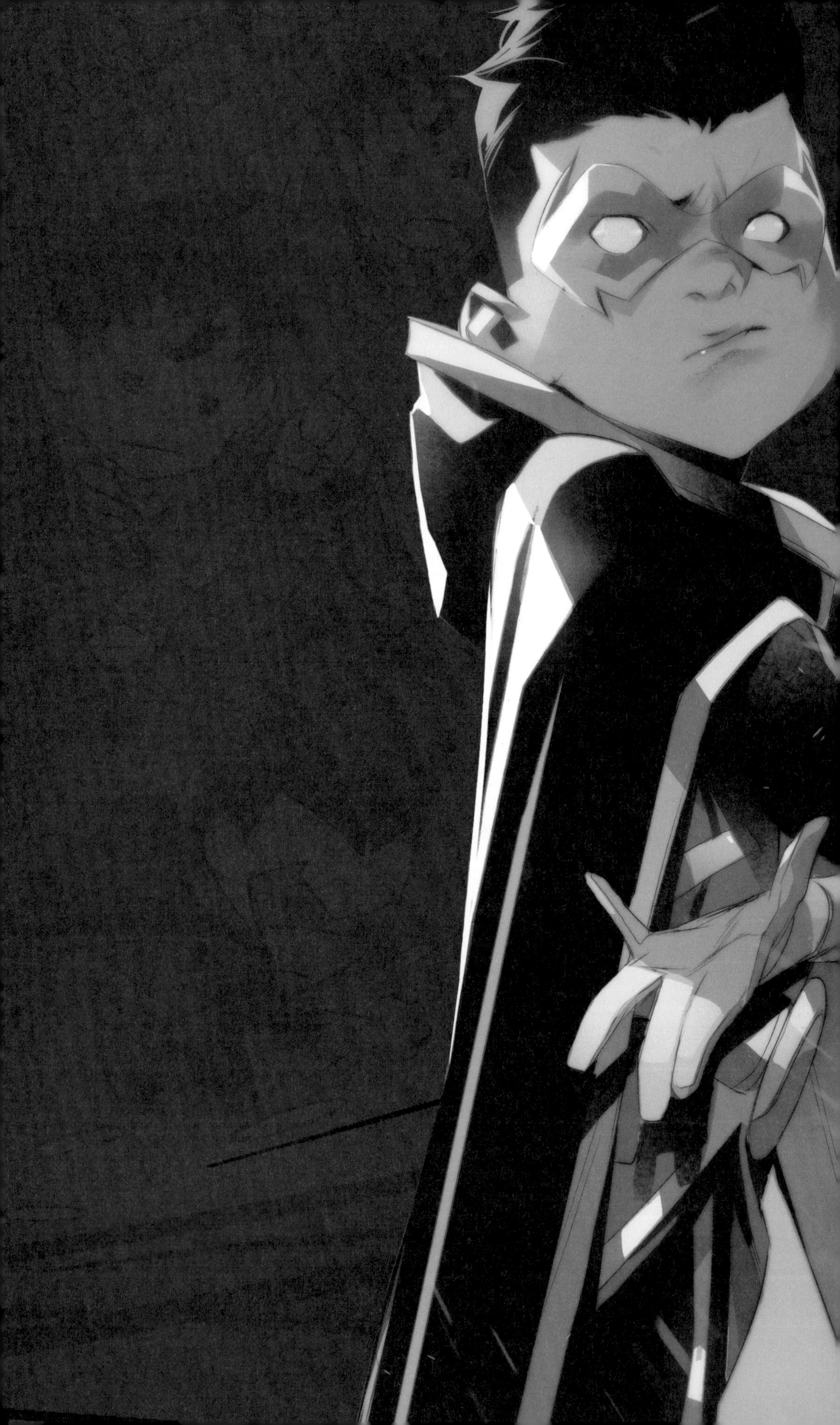

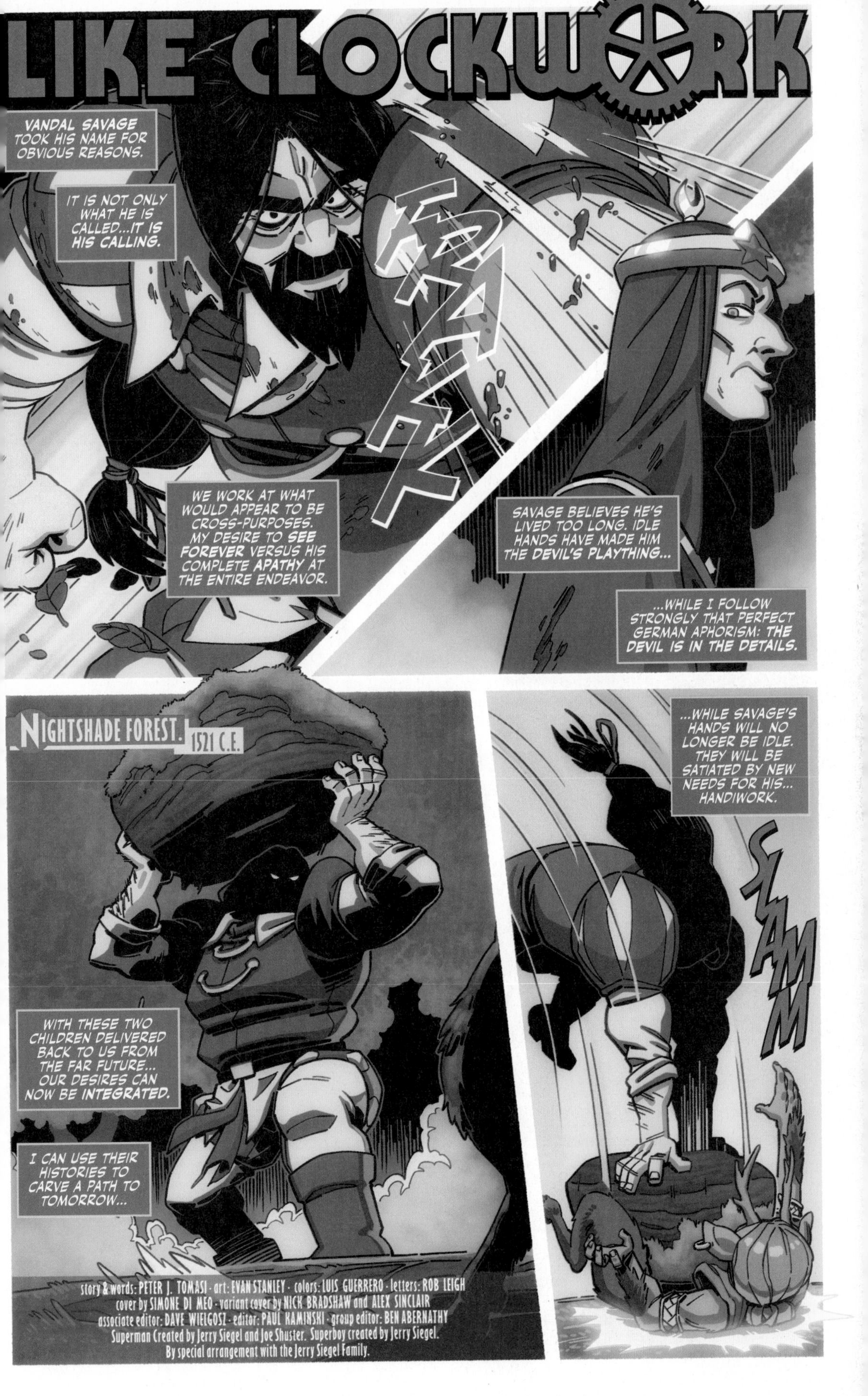
LIKE CLOCKWORK
VANDAL SAVAGE TOOK HIS NAME FOR OBVIOUS REASONS.
IT IS NOT ONLY WHAT HE IS CALLED...IT IS HIS CALLING.
KRAAAKK
WE WORK AT WHAT WOULD APPEAR TO BE CROSS-PURPOSES. MY DESIRE TO SEE FOREVER VERSUS HIS COMPLETE APATHY AT THE ENTIRE ENDEAVOR.
SAVAGE BELIEVES HE'S LIVED TOO LONG. IDLE HANDS HAVE MADE HIM THE DEVIL'S PLAYTHING...
...WHILE I FOLLOW STRONGLY THAT PERFECT GERMAN APHORISM: THE DEVIL IS IN THE DETAILS.
NIGHTSHADE FOREST. 1521 C.E.
WITH THESE TWO CHILDREN DELIVERED BACK TO US FROM THE FAR FUTURE... OUR DESIRES CAN NOW BE INTEGRATED.
I CAN USE THEIR HISTORIES TO CARVE A PATH TO TOMORROW...
...WHILE SAVAGE'S HANDS WILL NO LONGER BE IDLE. THEY WILL BE SATIATED BY NEW NEEDS FOR HIS... HANDIWORK.
SLAMM
story & words: PETER J. TOMASI · art: EVAN STANLEY · colors: LUIS GUERRERO · letters: ROB LEIGH
cover by SIMONE DI MEO · variant cover by NICK BRADSHAW and ALEX SINCLAIR
associate editor: DAVE WIELGOSZ · editor: PAUL KAMINSKI · group editor: BEN ABERNATHY
Superman Created by Jerry Siegel and Joe Shuster. Superboy created by Jerry Siegel.
By special arrangement with the Jerry Siegel Family.

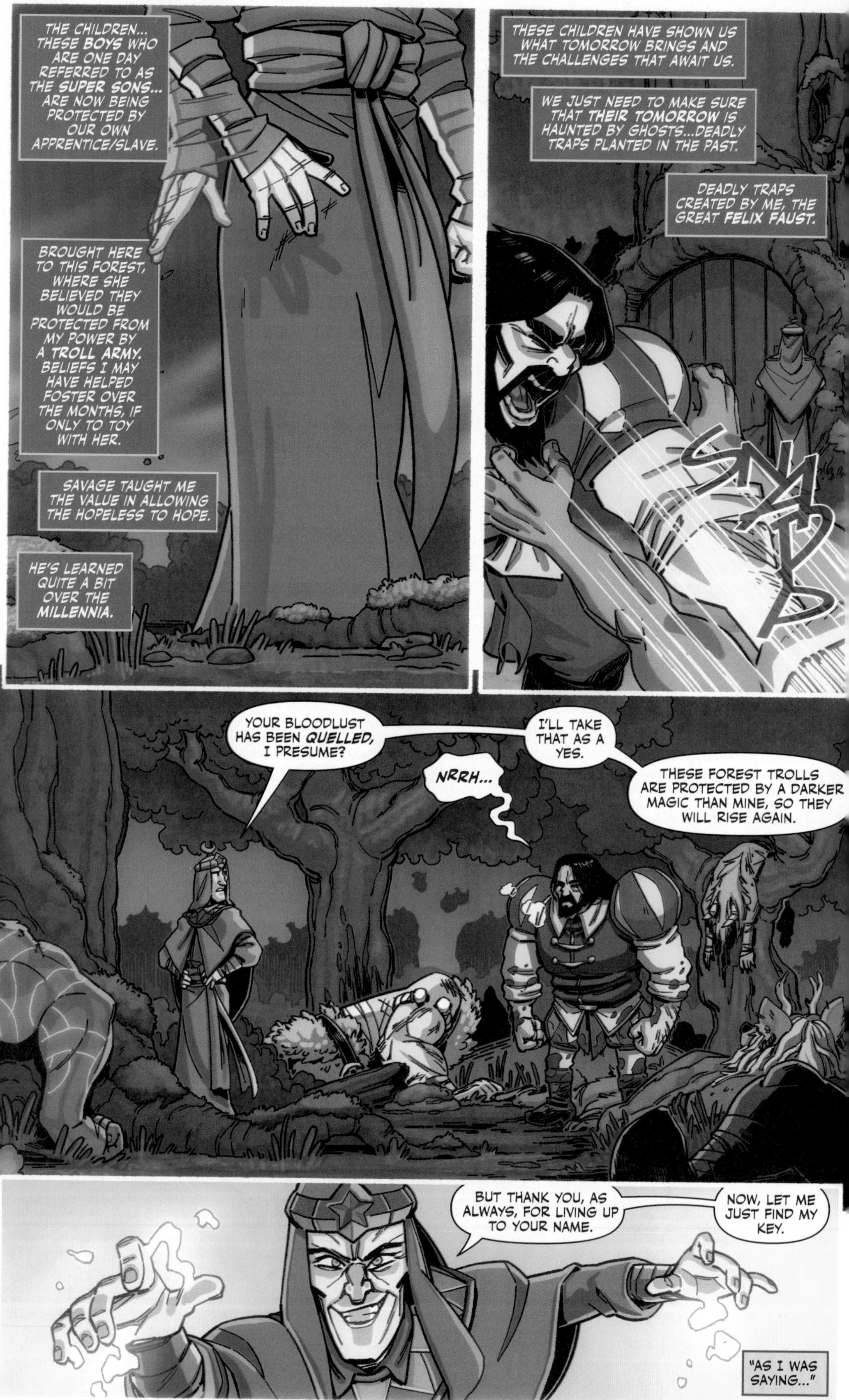
THE CHILDREN... THESE BOYS WHO ARE ONE DAY REFERRED TO AS THE SUPER SONS... ARE NOW BEING PROTECTED BY OUR OWN APPRENTICE/SLAVE.
BROUGHT HERE TO THIS FOREST, WHERE SHE BELIEVED THEY WOULD BE PROTECTED FROM MY POWER BY A TROLL ARMY. BELIEFS I MAY HAVE HELPED FOSTER OVER THE MONTHS, IF ONLY TO TOY WITH HER.
SAVAGE TAUGHT ME THE VALUE IN ALLOWING THE HOPELESS TO HOPE.
HE'S LEARNED QUITE A BIT OVER THE MILLENNIA.
THESE CHILDREN HAVE SHOWN US WHAT TOMORROW BRINGS AND THE CHALLENGES THAT AWAIT US.
WE JUST NEED TO MAKE SURE THAT THEIR TOMORROW IS HAUNTED BY GHOSTS...DEADLY TRAPS PLANTED IN THE PAST.
DEADLY TRAPS CREATED BY ME, THE GREAT FELIX FAUST.
SNAP
YOUR BLOODLUST HAS BEEN QUELLED, I PRESUME?
NRRH...
I'LL TAKE THAT AS A YES.
THESE FOREST TROLLS ARE PROTECTED BY A DARKER MAGIC THAN MINE, SO THEY WILL RISE AGAIN.
BUT THANK YOU, AS ALWAYS, FOR LIVING UP TO YOUR NAME.
NOW, LET ME JUST FIND MY KEY.
"AS I WAS SAYING..."

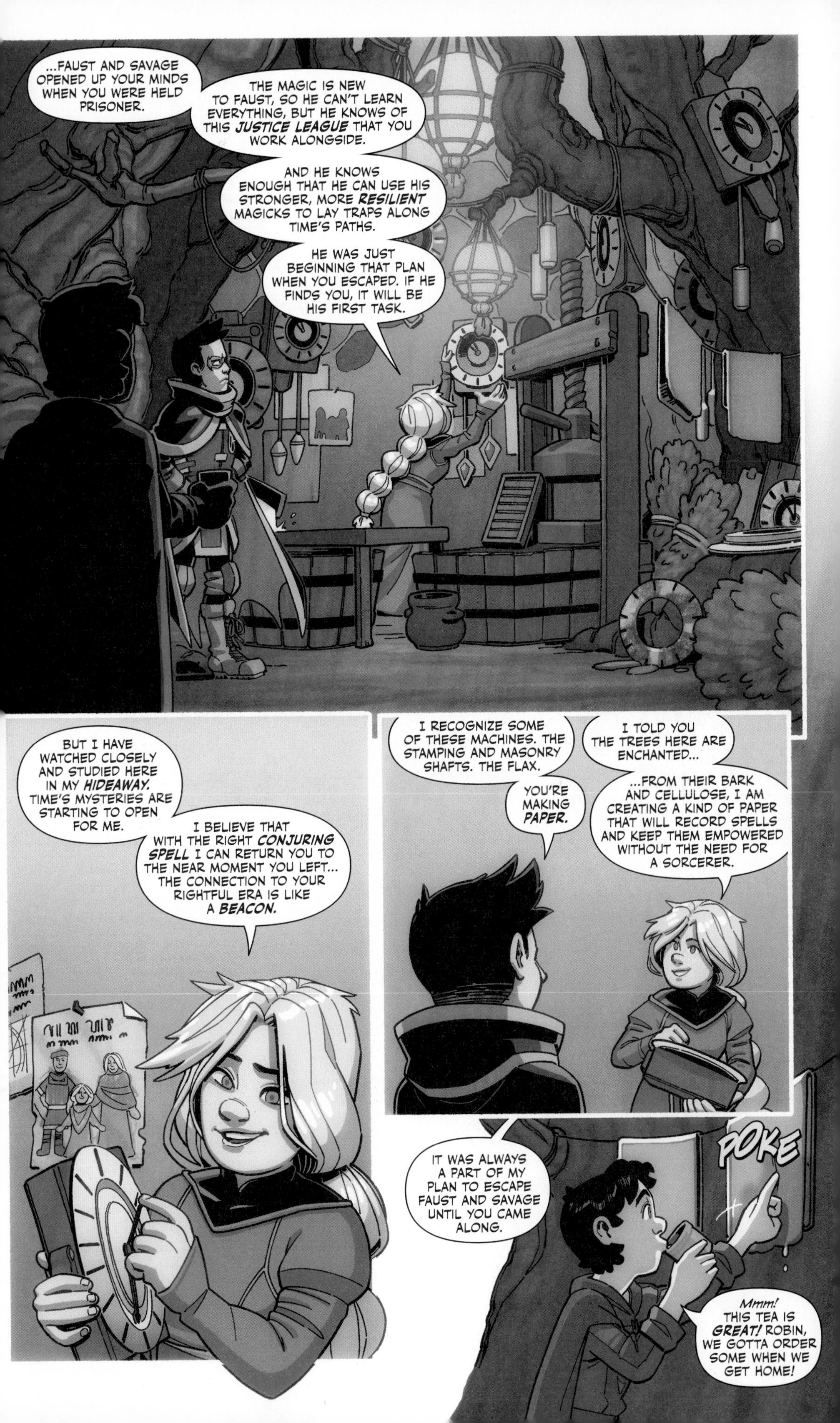
...FAUST AND SAVAGE OPENED UP YOUR MINDS WHEN YOU WERE HELD PRISONER.
THE MAGIC IS NEW TO FAUST, SO HE CAN'T LEARN EVERYTHING, BUT HE KNOWS OF THIS *JUSTICE LEAGUE* THAT YOU WORK ALONGSIDE.
AND HE KNOWS ENOUGH THAT HE CAN USE HIS STRONGER, MORE *RESILIENT* MAGICKS TO LAY TRAPS ALONG TIME'S PATHS.
HE WAS JUST BEGINNING THAT PLAN WHEN YOU ESCAPED. IF HE FINDS YOU, IT WILL BE HIS FIRST TASK.
BUT I HAVE WATCHED CLOSELY AND STUDIED HERE IN MY *HIDEAWAY.* TIME'S MYSTERIES ARE STARTING TO OPEN FOR ME.
I BELIEVE THAT WITH THE RIGHT *CONJURING SPELL* I CAN RETURN YOU TO THE NEAR MOMENT YOU LEFT... THE CONNECTION TO YOUR RIGHTFUL ERA IS LIKE A *BEACON.*
I RECOGNIZE SOME OF THESE MACHINES. THE STAMPING AND MASONRY SHAFTS. THE FLAX.
YOU'RE MAKING *PAPER.*
I TOLD YOU THE TREES HERE ARE ENCHANTED...
...FROM THEIR BARK AND CELLULOSE, I AM CREATING A KIND OF PAPER THAT WILL RECORD SPELLS AND KEEP THEM EMPOWERED WITHOUT THE NEED FOR A SORCERER.
IT WAS ALWAYS A PART OF MY PLAN TO ESCAPE FAUST AND SAVAGE UNTIL YOU CAME ALONG.
POKE
Mmm! THIS TEA IS *GREAT!* ROBIN, WE GOTTA ORDER SOME WHEN WE GET HOME!

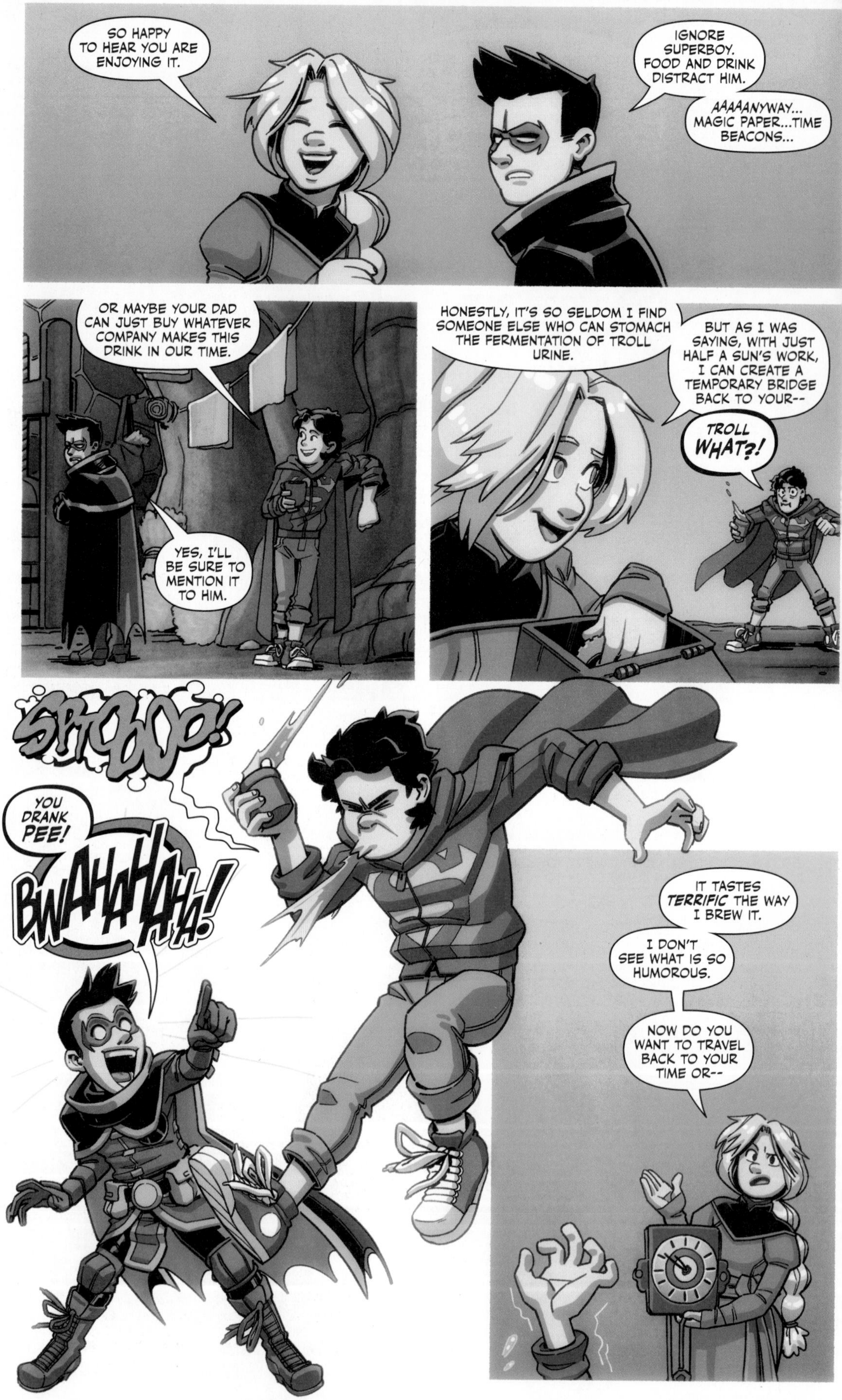
SO HAPPY TO HEAR YOU ARE ENJOYING IT.
IGNORE SUPERBOY. FOOD AND DRINK DISTRACT HIM.
AAAAANYWAY... MAGIC PAPER...TIME BEACONS...
OR MAYBE YOUR DAD CAN JUST BUY WHATEVER COMPANY MAKES THIS DRINK IN OUR TIME.
YES, I'LL BE SURE TO MENTION IT TO HIM.
HONESTLY, IT'S SO SELDOM I FIND SOMEONE ELSE WHO CAN STOMACH THE FERMENTATION OF TROLL URINE.
BUT AS I WAS SAYING, WITH JUST HALF A SUN'S WORK, I CAN CREATE A TEMPORARY BRIDGE BACK TO YOUR--
TROLL WHAT?!
SPTOOO!
YOU DRANK PEE!
BWAHAHAHA!
IT TASTES *TERRIFIC* THE WAY I BREW IT.
I DON'T SEE WHAT IS SO HUMOROUS.
NOW DO YOU WANT TO TRAVEL BACK TO YOUR TIME OR--

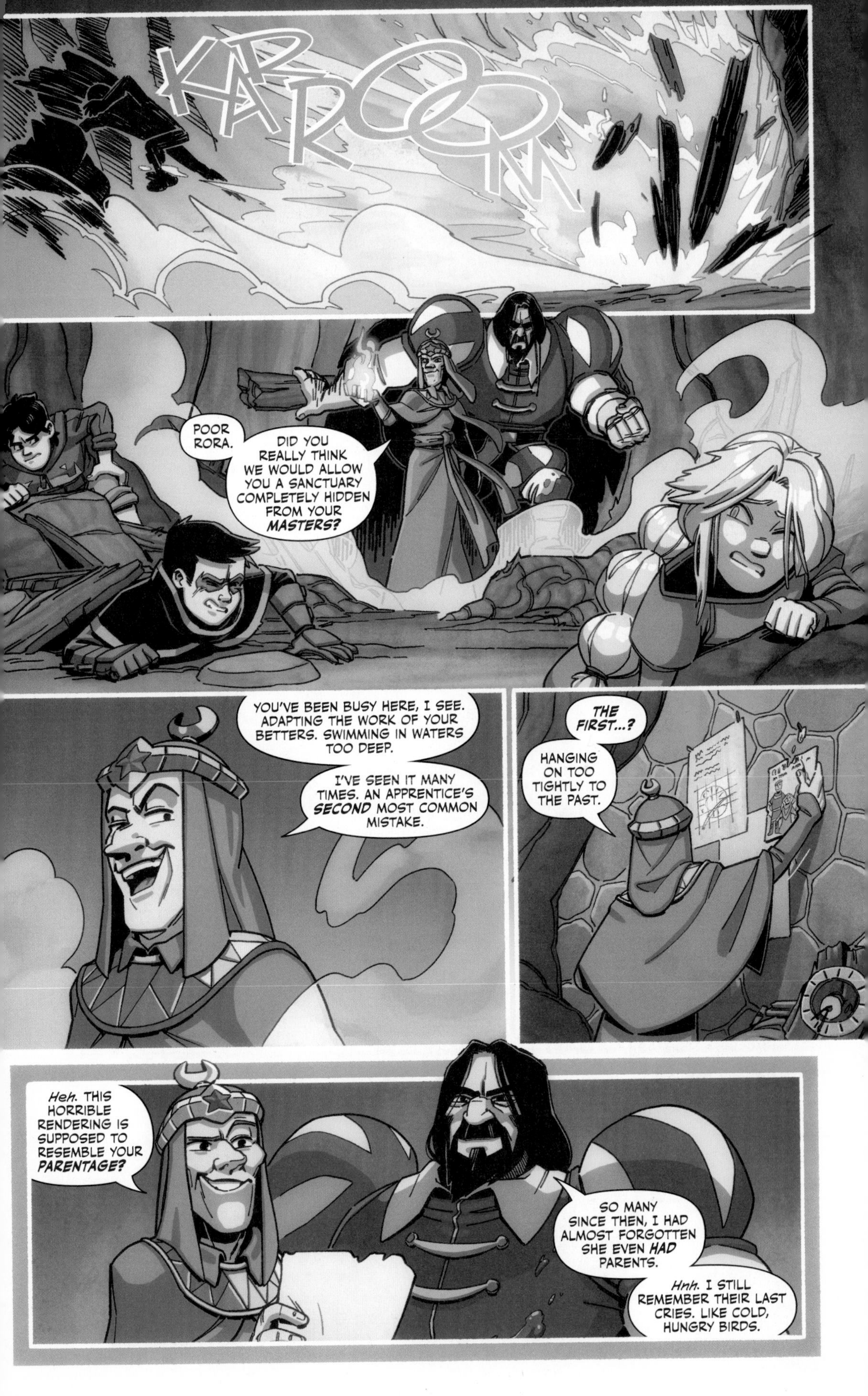
KARROOOM
POOR RORA.
DID YOU REALLY THINK WE WOULD ALLOW YOU A SANCTUARY COMPLETELY HIDDEN FROM YOUR MASTERS?
YOU'VE BEEN BUSY HERE, I SEE. ADAPTING THE WORK OF YOUR BETTERS. SWIMMING IN WATERS TOO DEEP.
I'VE SEEN IT MANY TIMES. AN APPRENTICE'S SECOND MOST COMMON MISTAKE.
THE FIRST...?
HANGING ON TOO TIGHTLY TO THE PAST.
Heh. THIS HORRIBLE RENDERING IS SUPPOSED TO RESEMBLE YOUR PARENTAGE?
SO MANY SINCE THEN, I HAD ALMOST FORGOTTEN SHE EVEN HAD PARENTS.
Hnh. I STILL REMEMBER THEIR LAST CRIES. LIKE COLD, HUNGRY BIRDS.

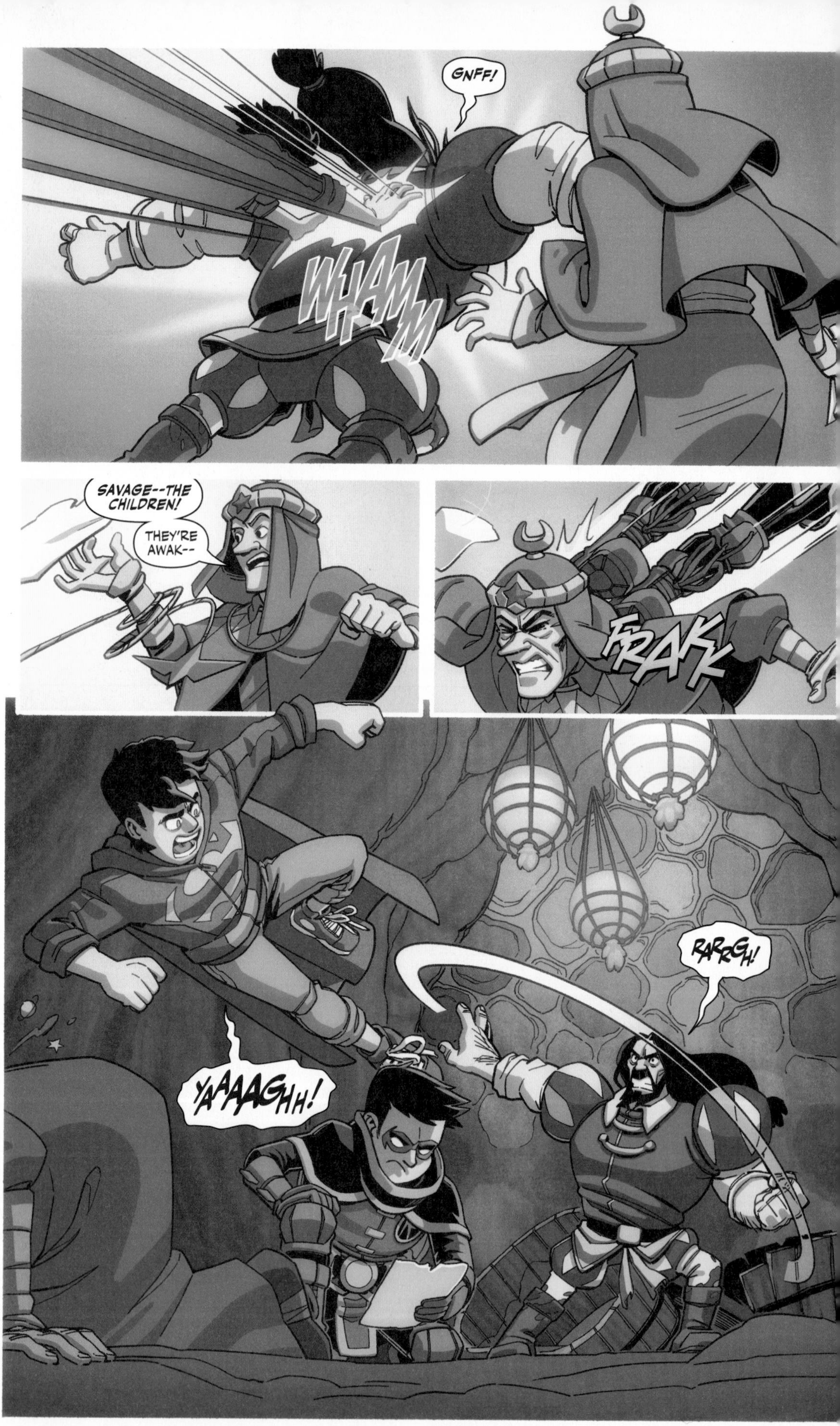
GNFF!
WHAMM
SAVAGE--THE CHILDREN!
THEY'RE AWAK--
FRAK
RARRGH!
YAAAAGHH!

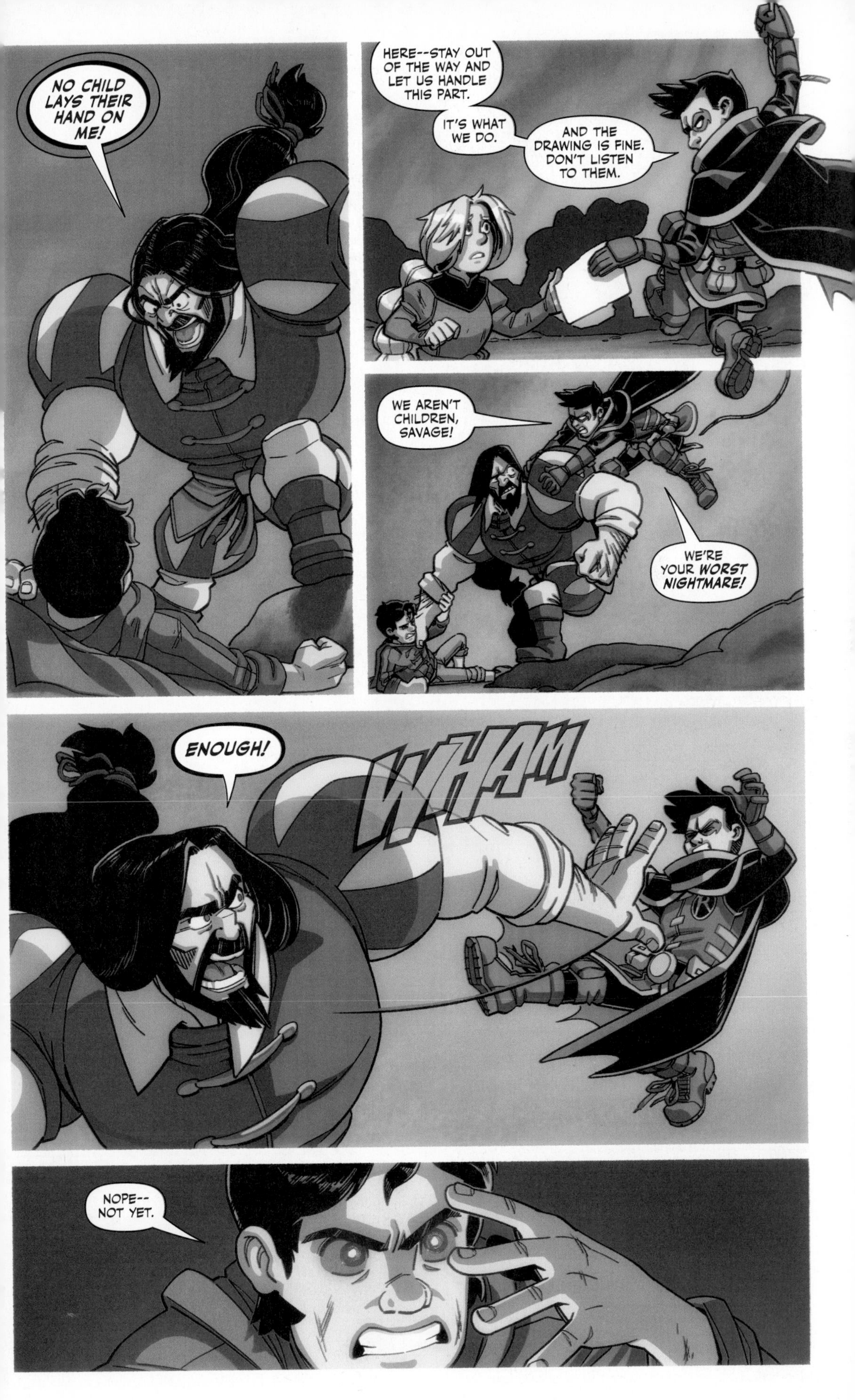
NO CHILD LAYS THEIR HAND ON ME!
HERE--STAY OUT OF THE WAY AND LET US HANDLE THIS PART.
IT'S WHAT WE DO.
AND THE DRAWING IS FINE. DON'T LISTEN TO THEM.
WE AREN'T CHILDREN, SAVAGE!
WE'RE YOUR WORST NIGHTMARE!
ENOUGH!
WHAM
NOPE-- NOT YET.

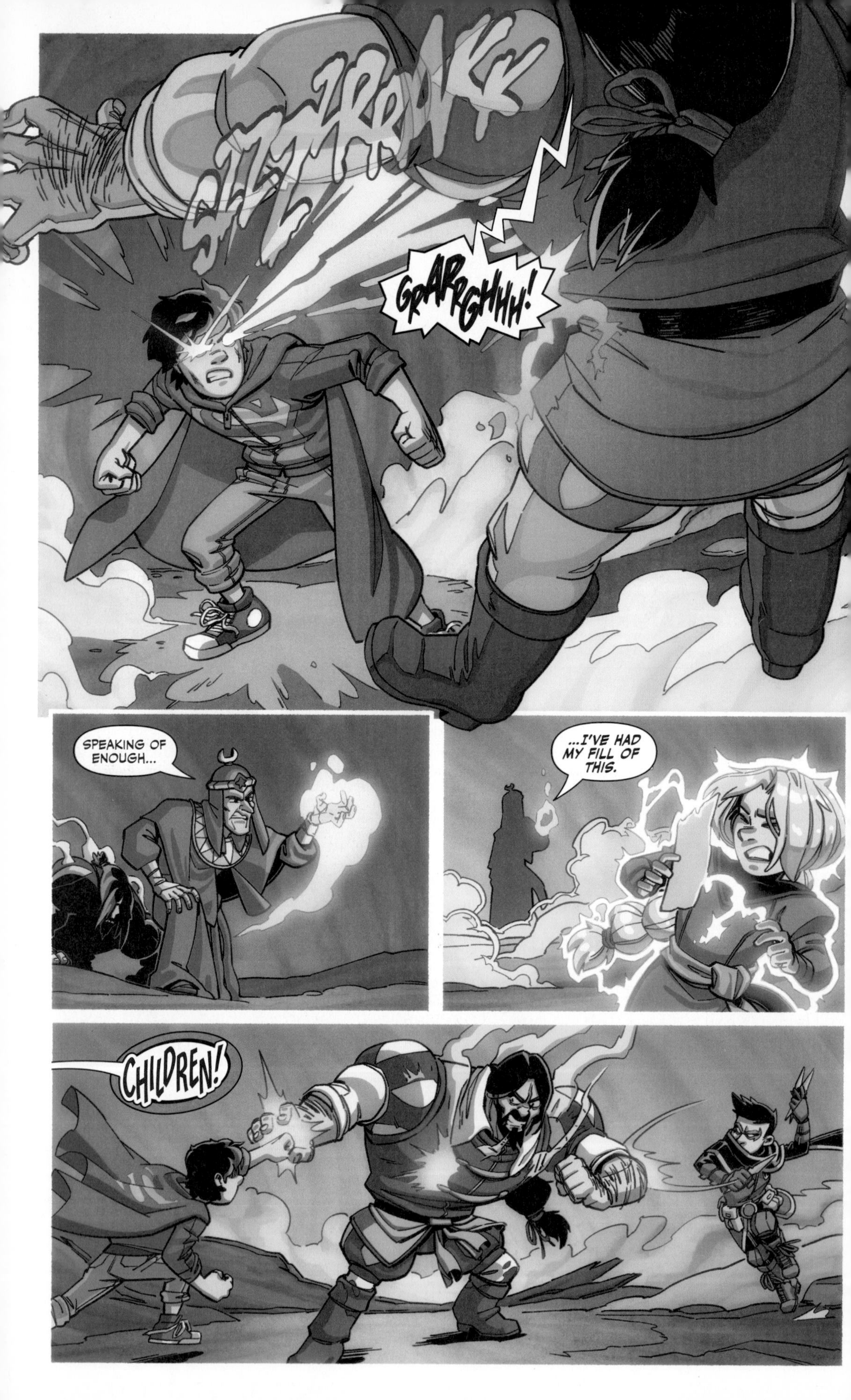
SZZZRRAKK
GRARRGHHH!
SPEAKING OF ENOUGH...
...I'VE HAD MY FILL OF THIS.
CHILLDREN!

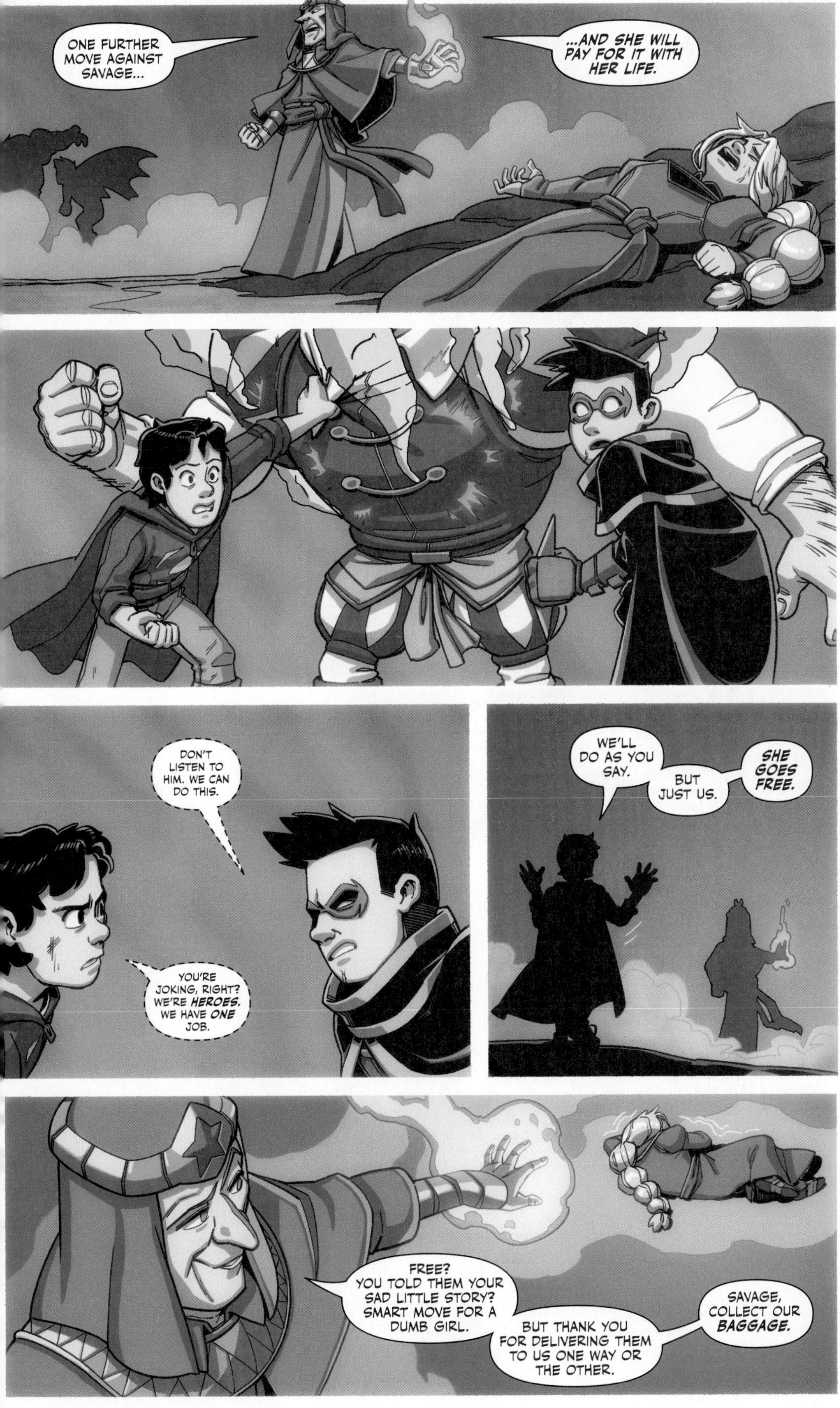
ONE FURTHER MOVE AGAINST SAVAGE...
...AND SHE WILL PAY FOR IT WITH HER LIFE.
DON'T LISTEN TO HIM. WE CAN DO THIS.
YOU'RE JOKING, RIGHT? WE'RE HEROES. WE HAVE ONE JOB.
WE'LL DO AS YOU SAY.
BUT JUST US.
SHE GOES FREE.
FREE? YOU TOLD THEM YOUR SAD LITTLE STORY? SMART MOVE FOR A DUMB GIRL.
BUT THANK YOU FOR DELIVERING THEM TO US ONE WAY OR THE OTHER.
SAVAGE, COLLECT OUR BAGGAGE.

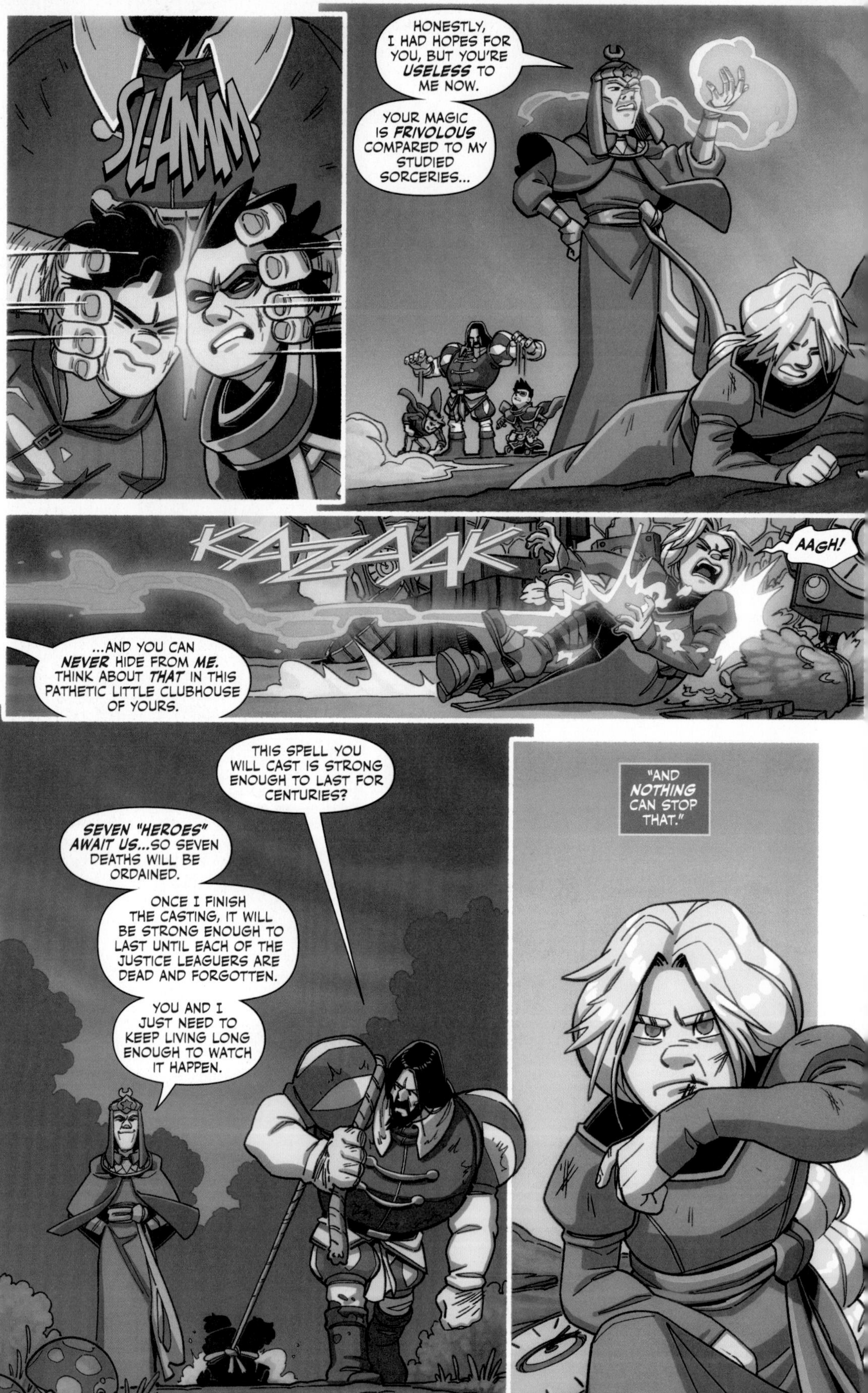
SLAMM
HONESTLY, I HAD HOPES FOR YOU, BUT YOU'RE USELESS TO ME NOW.
YOUR MAGIC IS FRIVOLOUS COMPARED TO MY STUDIED SORCERIES...
KAZAAK
AAGH!
...AND YOU CAN NEVER HIDE FROM ME. THINK ABOUT THAT IN THIS PATHETIC LITTLE CLUBHOUSE OF YOURS.
THIS SPELL YOU WILL CAST IS STRONG ENOUGH TO LAST FOR CENTURIES?
SEVEN "HEROES" AWAIT US...SO SEVEN DEATHS WILL BE ORDAINED.
ONCE I FINISH THE CASTING, IT WILL BE STRONG ENOUGH TO LAST UNTIL EACH OF THE JUSTICE LEAGUERS ARE DEAD AND FORGOTTEN.
YOU AND I JUST NEED TO KEEP LIVING LONG ENOUGH TO WATCH IT HAPPEN.
"AND NOTHING CAN STOP THAT."

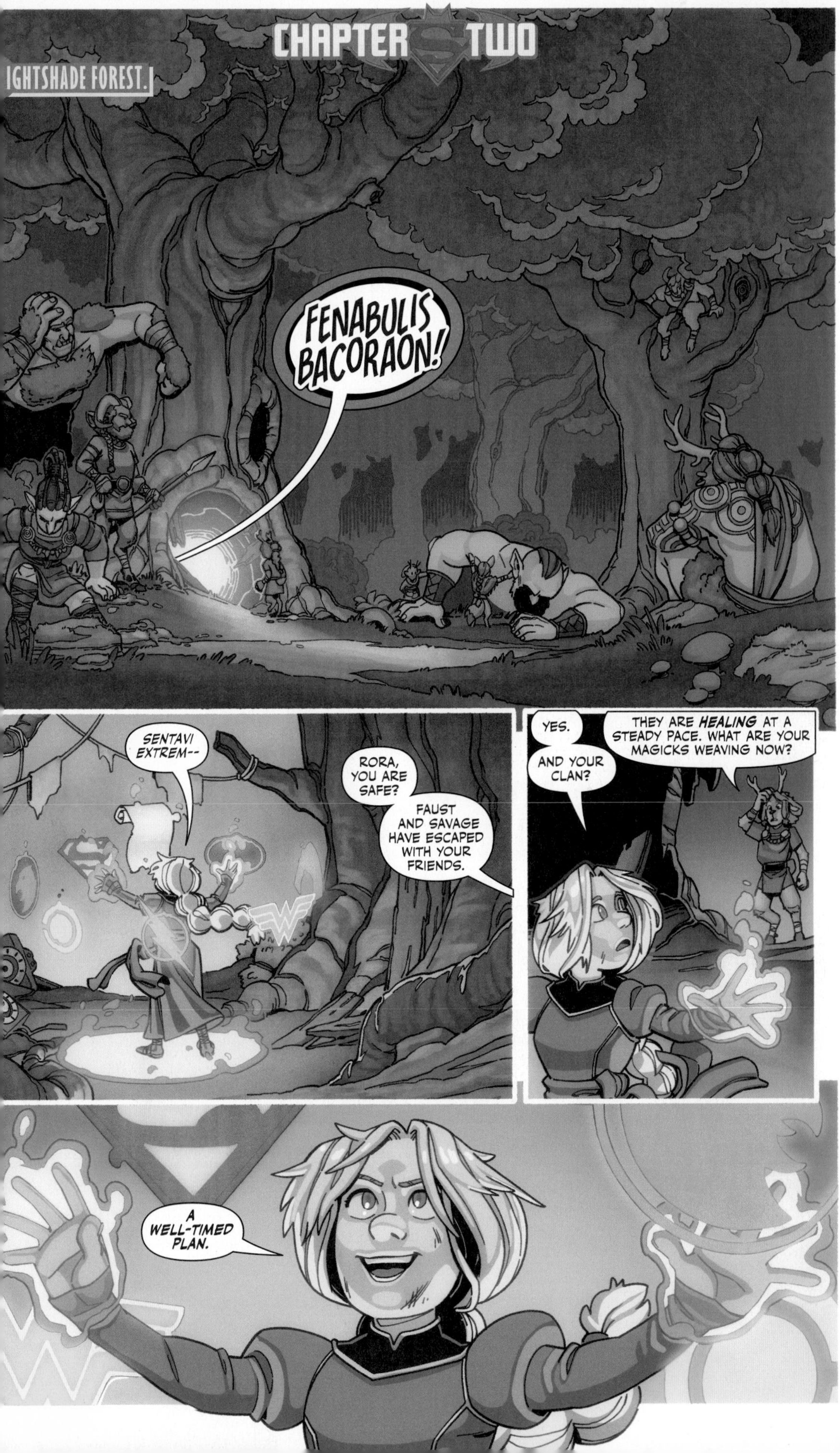
CHAPTER TWO
IGHTSHADE FOREST.
FENABULIS BACORAON!
SENTAVI EXTREM--
RORA, YOU ARE SAFE?
FAUST AND SAVAGE HAVE ESCAPED WITH YOUR FRIENDS.
YES.
AND YOUR CLAN?
THEY ARE HEALING AT A STEADY PACE. WHAT ARE YOUR MAGICKS WEAVING NOW?
A WELL-TIMED PLAN.

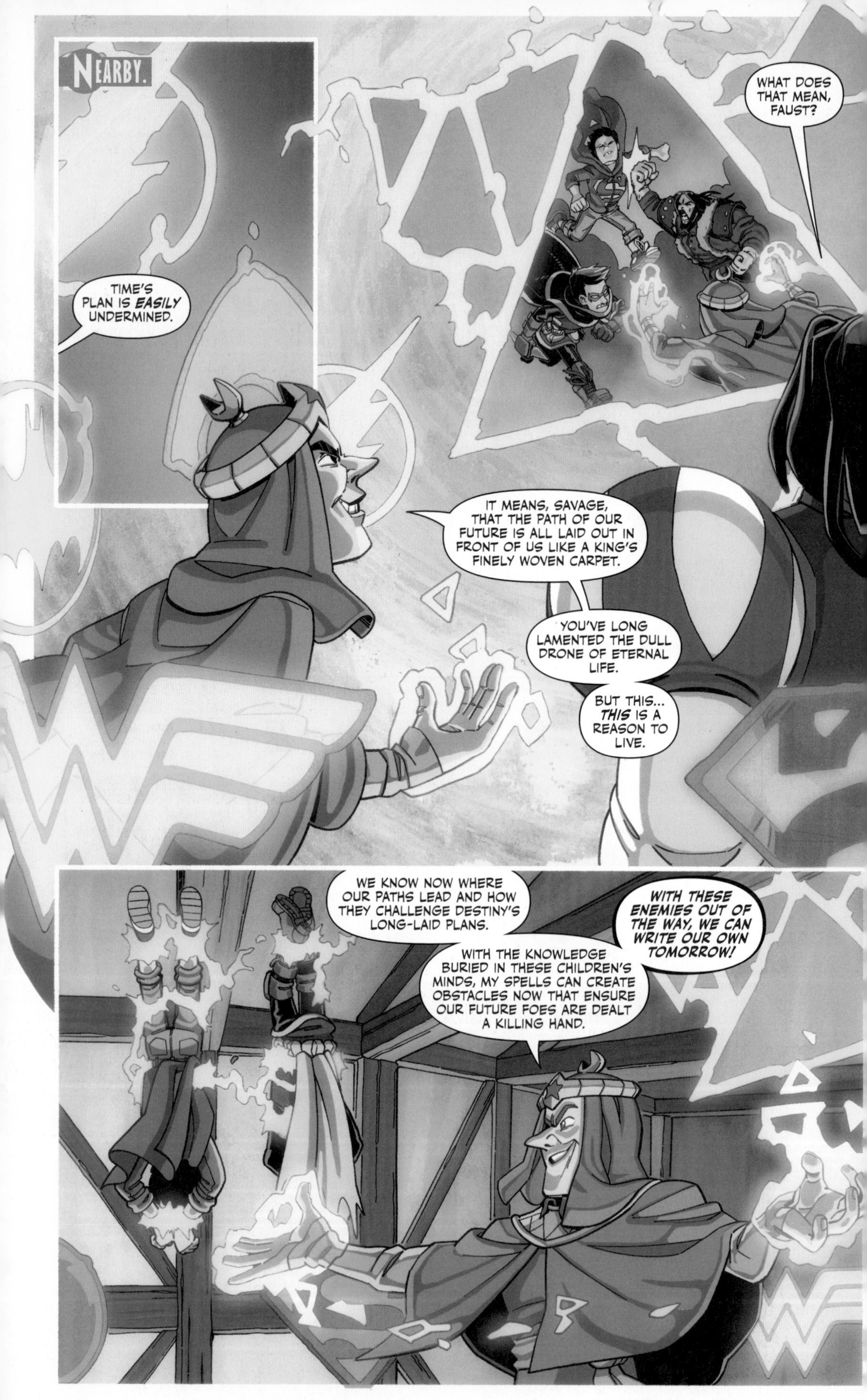
NEARBY.
TIME'S PLAN IS *EASILY* UNDERMINED.
WHAT DOES THAT MEAN, FAUST?
IT MEANS, SAVAGE, THAT THE PATH OF OUR FUTURE IS ALL LAID OUT IN FRONT OF US LIKE A KING'S FINELY WOVEN CARPET.
YOU'VE LONG LAMENTED THE DULL DRONE OF ETERNAL LIFE.
BUT THIS... *THIS* IS A REASON TO LIVE.
WE KNOW NOW WHERE OUR PATHS LEAD AND HOW THEY CHALLENGE DESTINY'S LONG-LAID PLANS.
WITH THE KNOWLEDGE BURIED IN THESE CHILDREN'S MINDS, MY SPELLS CAN CREATE OBSTACLES NOW THAT ENSURE OUR FUTURE FOES ARE DEALT A KILLING HAND.
WITH THESE ENEMIES OUT OF THE WAY, WE CAN WRITE OUR OWN TOMORROW!

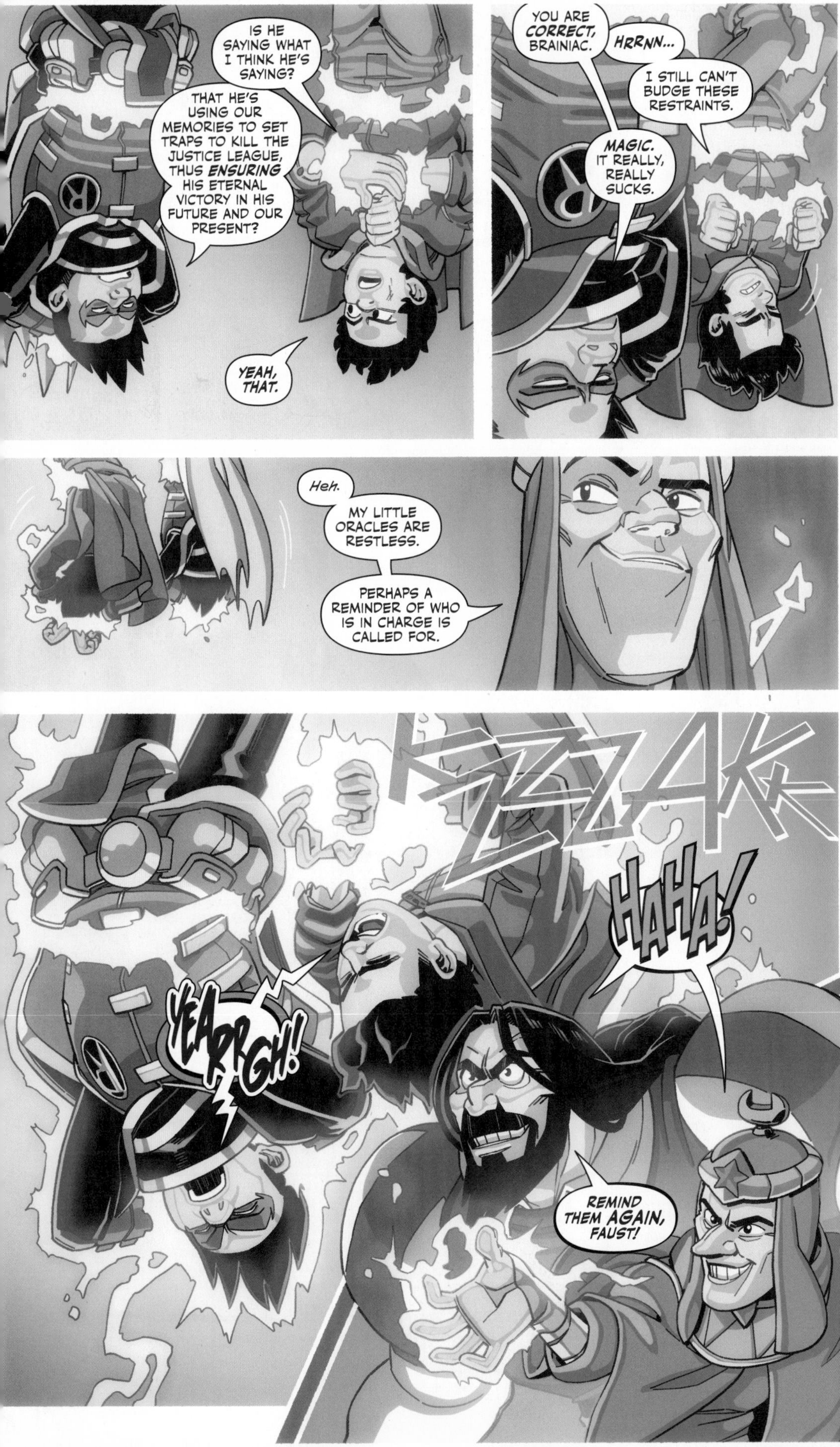
IS HE SAYING WHAT I THINK HE'S SAYING?
THAT HE'S USING OUR MEMORIES TO SET TRAPS TO KILL THE JUSTICE LEAGUE, THUS ENSURING HIS ETERNAL VICTORY IN HIS FUTURE AND OUR PRESENT?
YEAH, THAT.
YOU ARE CORRECT, BRAINIAC.
HRRNN...
I STILL CAN'T BUDGE THESE RESTRAINTS.
MAGIC. IT REALLY, REALLY SUCKS.
Heh.
MY LITTLE ORACLES ARE RESTLESS.
PERHAPS A REMINDER OF WHO IS IN CHARGE IS CALLED FOR.
KZZZAKK
HAHA!
YEAARRGH!
REMIND THEM AGAIN, FAUST!

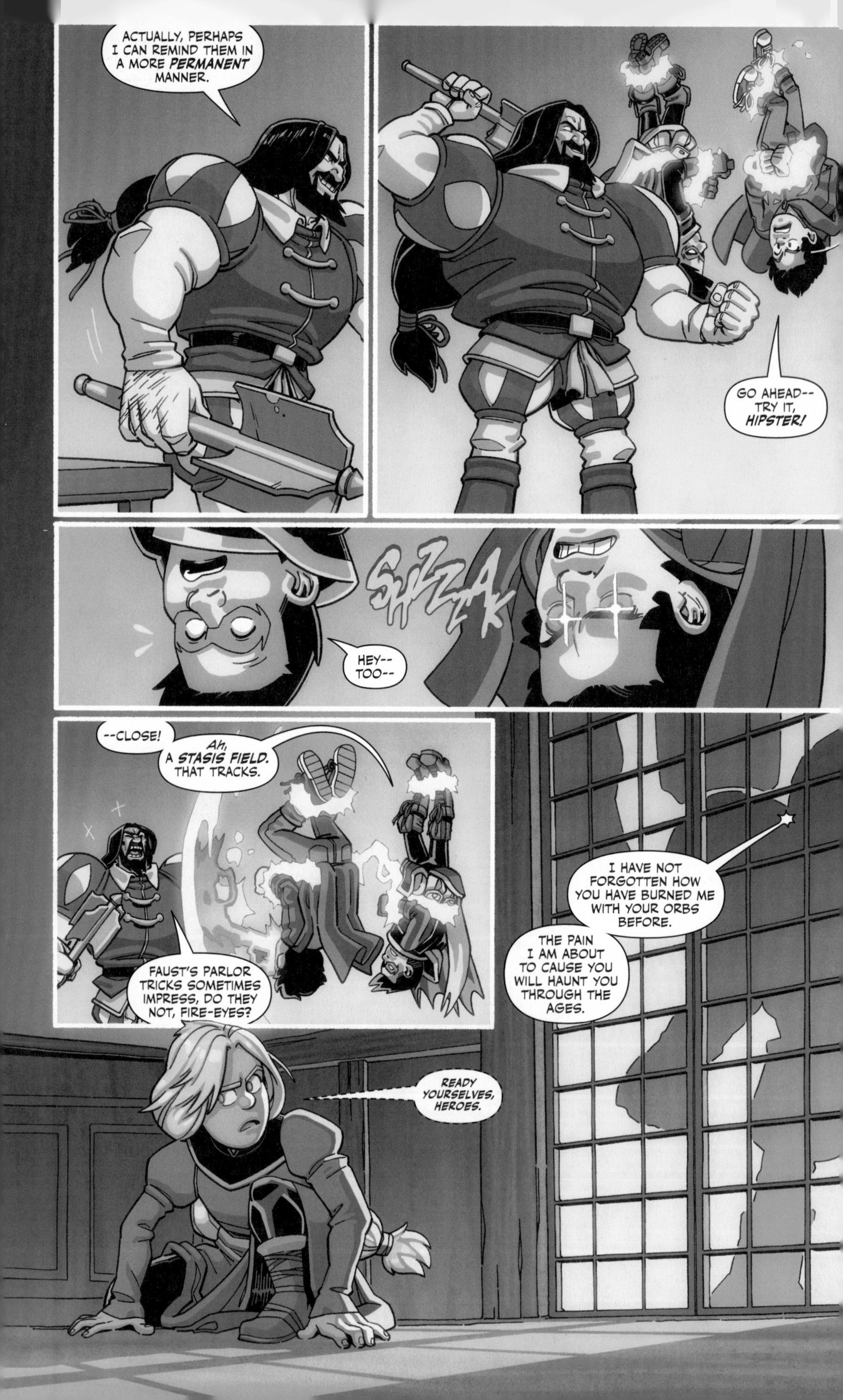

ACTUALLY, PERHAPS I CAN REMIND THEM IN A MORE *PERMANENT* MANNER.
GO AHEAD--TRY IT, ***HIPSTER!***
SHZZZAK
HEY--TOO--
--CLOSE!
Ah, A ***STASIS FIELD.*** THAT TRACKS.
FAUST'S PARLOR TRICKS SOMETIMES IMPRESS, DO THEY NOT, FIRE-EYES?
I HAVE NOT FORGOTTEN HOW YOU HAVE BURNED ME WITH YOUR ORBS BEFORE.
THE PAIN I AM ABOUT TO CAUSE YOU WILL HAUNT YOU THROUGH THE AGES.
READY YOURSELVES, HEROES.

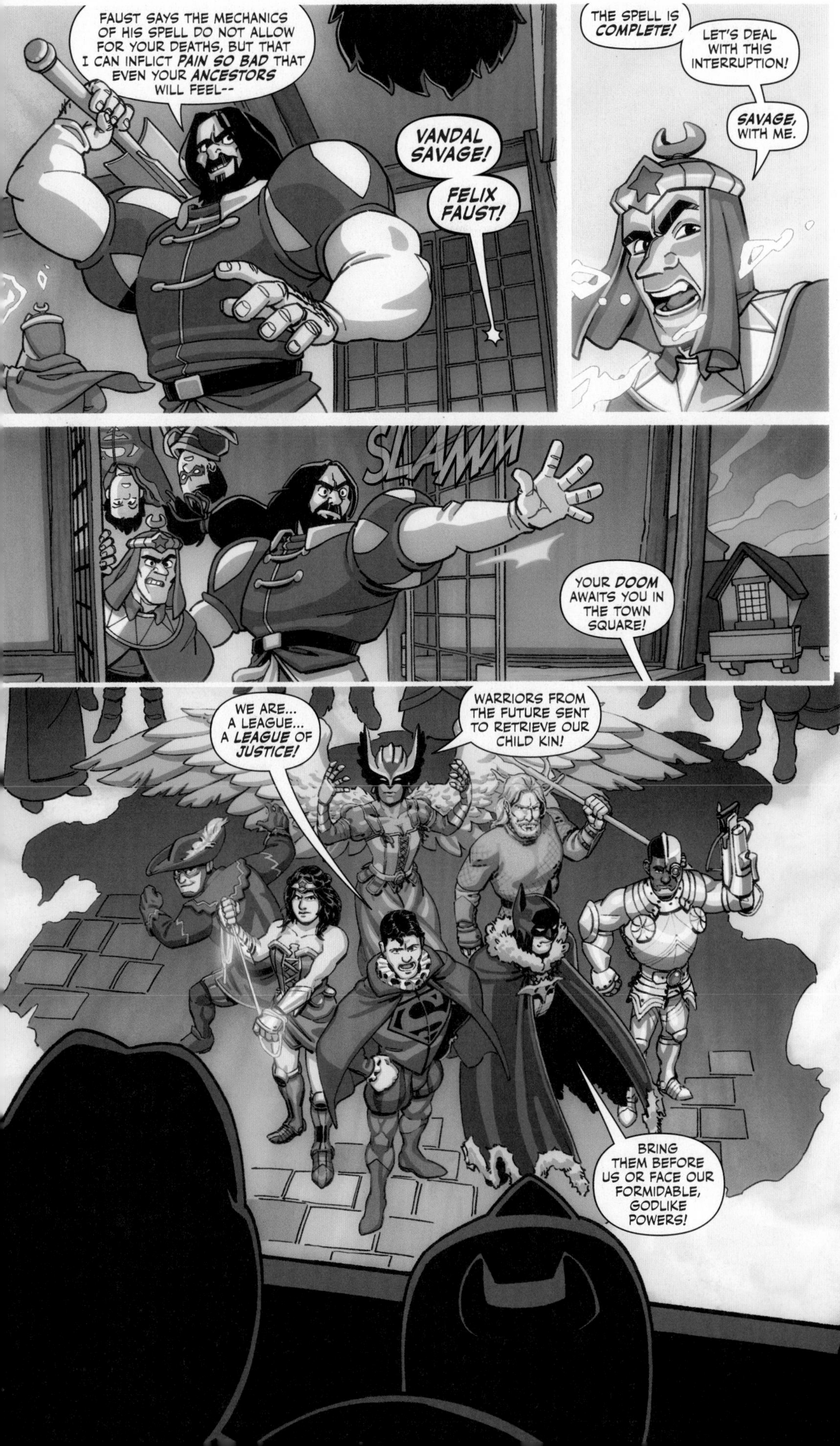
FAUST SAYS THE MECHANICS OF HIS SPELL DO NOT ALLOW FOR YOUR DEATHS, BUT THAT I CAN INFLICT PAIN SO BAD THAT EVEN YOUR ANCESTORS WILL FEEL--
VANDAL SAVAGE!
FELIX FAUST!
THE SPELL IS COMPLETE!
LET'S DEAL WITH THIS INTERRUPTION!
SAVAGE, WITH ME.
SLAMM
YOUR DOOM AWAITS YOU IN THE TOWN SQUARE!
WE ARE... A LEAGUE... A LEAGUE OF JUSTICE!
WARRIORS FROM THE FUTURE SENT TO RETRIEVE OUR CHILD KIN!
BRING THEM BEFORE US OR FACE OUR FORMIDABLE, GODLIKE POWERS!

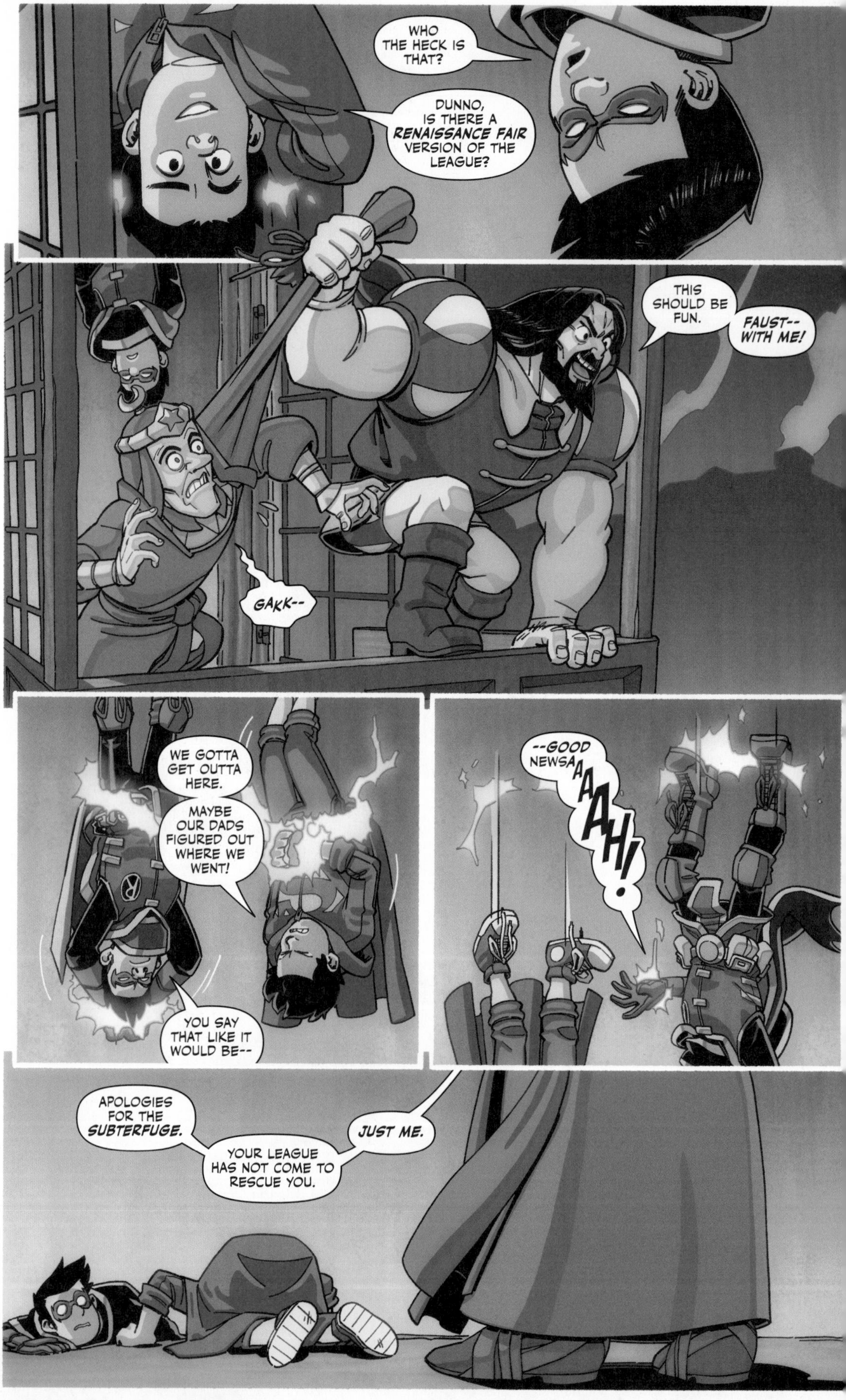
WHO THE HECK IS THAT?
DUNNO, IS THERE A *RENAISSANCE FAIR* VERSION OF THE LEAGUE?
THIS SHOULD BE FUN.
FAUST-- WITH ME!
GAKK--
WE GOTTA GET OUTTA HERE.
MAYBE OUR DADS FIGURED OUT WHERE WE WENT!
YOU SAY THAT LIKE IT WOULD BE--
--GOOD NEWSAAAAH!
APOLOGIES FOR THE *SUBTERFUGE.*
YOUR LEAGUE HAS NOT COME TO RESCUE YOU.
JUST ME.

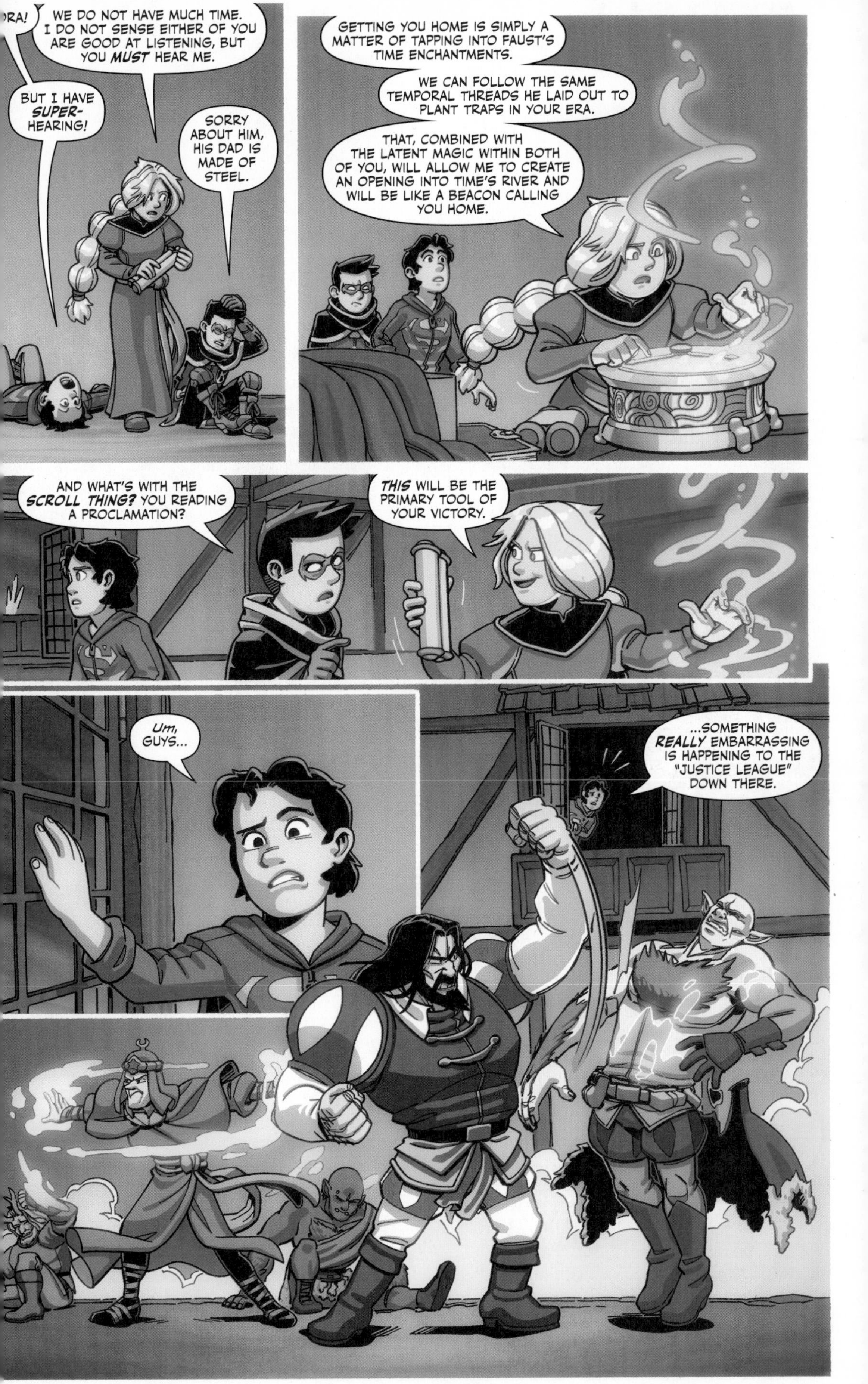

...RA!
WE DO NOT HAVE MUCH TIME. I DO NOT SENSE EITHER OF YOU ARE GOOD AT LISTENING, BUT YOU *MUST* HEAR ME.
BUT I HAVE *SUPER*-HEARING!
SORRY ABOUT HIM, HIS DAD IS MADE OF STEEL.
GETTING YOU HOME IS SIMPLY A MATTER OF TAPPING INTO FAUST'S TIME ENCHANTMENTS.
WE CAN FOLLOW THE SAME TEMPORAL THREADS HE LAID OUT TO PLANT TRAPS IN YOUR ERA.
THAT, COMBINED WITH THE LATENT MAGIC WITHIN BOTH OF YOU, WILL ALLOW ME TO CREATE AN OPENING INTO TIME'S RIVER AND WILL BE LIKE A BEACON CALLING YOU HOME.
AND WHAT'S WITH THE *SCROLL THING?* YOU READING A PROCLAMATION?
THIS WILL BE THE PRIMARY TOOL OF YOUR VICTORY.
Um, GUYS...
...SOMETHING *REALLY* EMBARRASSING IS HAPPENING TO THE "JUSTICE LEAGUE" DOWN THERE.

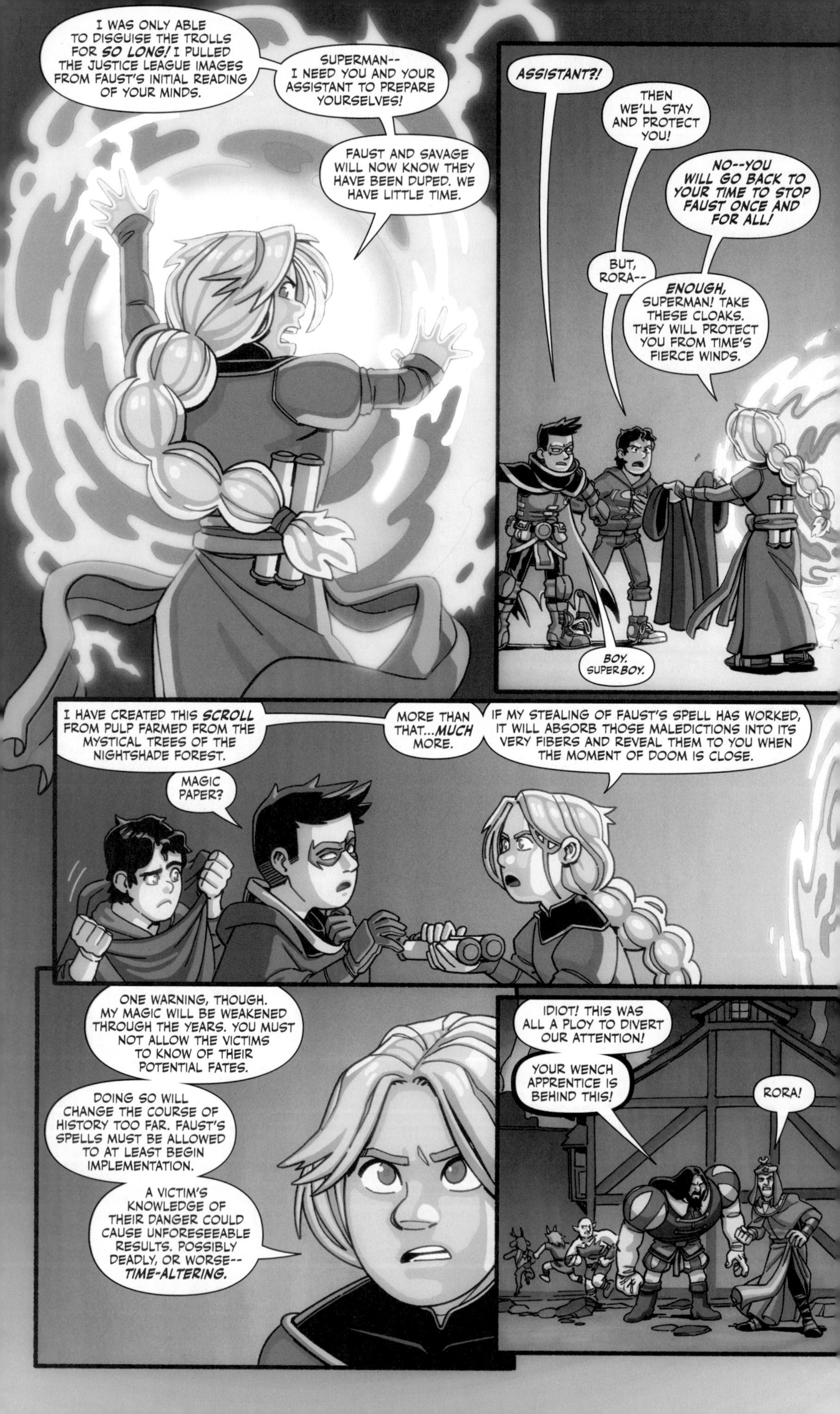
I WAS ONLY ABLE TO DISGUISE THE TROLLS FOR SO LONG! I PULLED THE JUSTICE LEAGUE IMAGES FROM FAUST'S INITIAL READING OF YOUR MINDS.
SUPERMAN-- I NEED YOU AND YOUR ASSISTANT TO PREPARE YOURSELVES!
FAUST AND SAVAGE WILL NOW KNOW THEY HAVE BEEN DUPED. WE HAVE LITTLE TIME.
ASSISTANT?!
THEN WE'LL STAY AND PROTECT YOU!
NO--YOU WILL GO BACK TO YOUR TIME TO STOP FAUST ONCE AND FOR ALL!
BUT, RORA--
ENOUGH, SUPERMAN! TAKE THESE CLOAKS. THEY WILL PROTECT YOU FROM TIME'S FIERCE WINDS.
BOY. SUPERBOY.
I HAVE CREATED THIS SCROLL FROM PULP FARMED FROM THE MYSTICAL TREES OF THE NIGHTSHADE FOREST.
MAGIC PAPER?
MORE THAN THAT...MUCH MORE.
IF MY STEALING OF FAUST'S SPELL HAS WORKED, IT WILL ABSORB THOSE MALEDICTIONS INTO ITS VERY FIBERS AND REVEAL THEM TO YOU WHEN THE MOMENT OF DOOM IS CLOSE.
ONE WARNING, THOUGH. MY MAGIC WILL BE WEAKENED THROUGH THE YEARS. YOU MUST NOT ALLOW THE VICTIMS TO KNOW OF THEIR POTENTIAL FATES.
DOING SO WILL CHANGE THE COURSE OF HISTORY TOO FAR. FAUST'S SPELLS MUST BE ALLOWED TO AT LEAST BEGIN IMPLEMENTATION.
A VICTIM'S KNOWLEDGE OF THEIR DANGER COULD CAUSE UNFORESEEABLE RESULTS. POSSIBLY DEADLY, OR WORSE-- TIME-ALTERING.
IDIOT! THIS WAS ALL A PLOY TO DIVERT OUR ATTENTION!
YOUR WENCH APPRENTICE IS BEHIND THIS!
RORA!

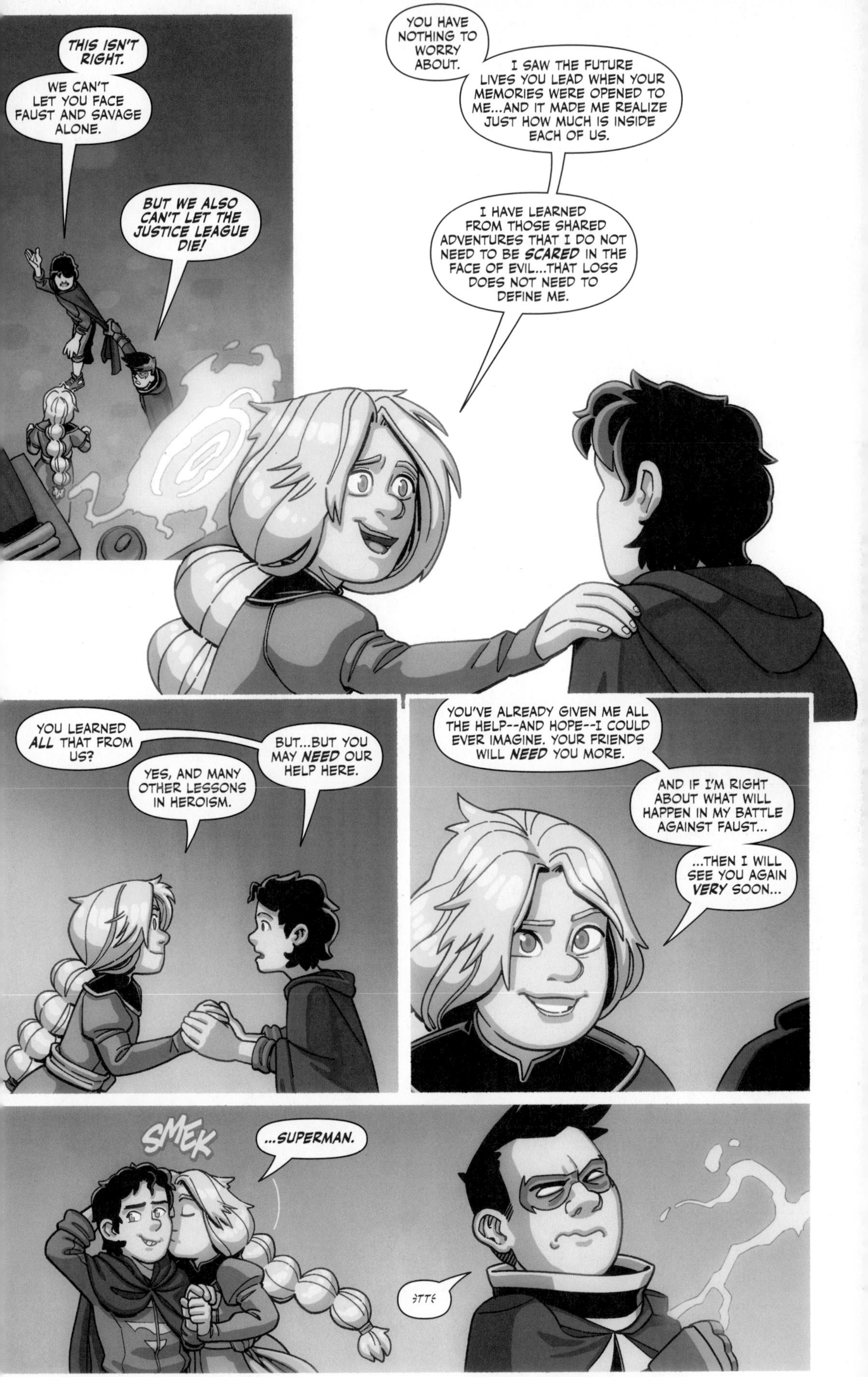
THIS ISN'T RIGHT.
WE CAN'T LET YOU FACE FAUST AND SAVAGE ALONE.
BUT WE ALSO CAN'T LET THE JUSTICE LEAGUE DIE!
YOU HAVE NOTHING TO WORRY ABOUT.
I SAW THE FUTURE LIVES YOU LEAD WHEN YOUR MEMORIES WERE OPENED TO ME...AND IT MADE ME REALIZE JUST HOW MUCH IS INSIDE EACH OF US.
I HAVE LEARNED FROM THOSE SHARED ADVENTURES THAT I DO NOT NEED TO BE SCARED IN THE FACE OF EVIL...THAT LOSS DOES NOT NEED TO DEFINE ME.
YOU LEARNED ALL THAT FROM US?
YES, AND MANY OTHER LESSONS IN HEROISM.
BUT...BUT YOU MAY NEED OUR HELP HERE.
YOU'VE ALREADY GIVEN ME ALL THE HELP--AND HOPE--I COULD EVER IMAGINE. YOUR FRIENDS WILL NEED YOU MORE.
AND IF I'M RIGHT ABOUT WHAT WILL HAPPEN IN MY BATTLE AGAINST FAUST...
...THEN I WILL SEE YOU AGAIN VERY SOON...
SMEK
...SUPERMAN.
TT

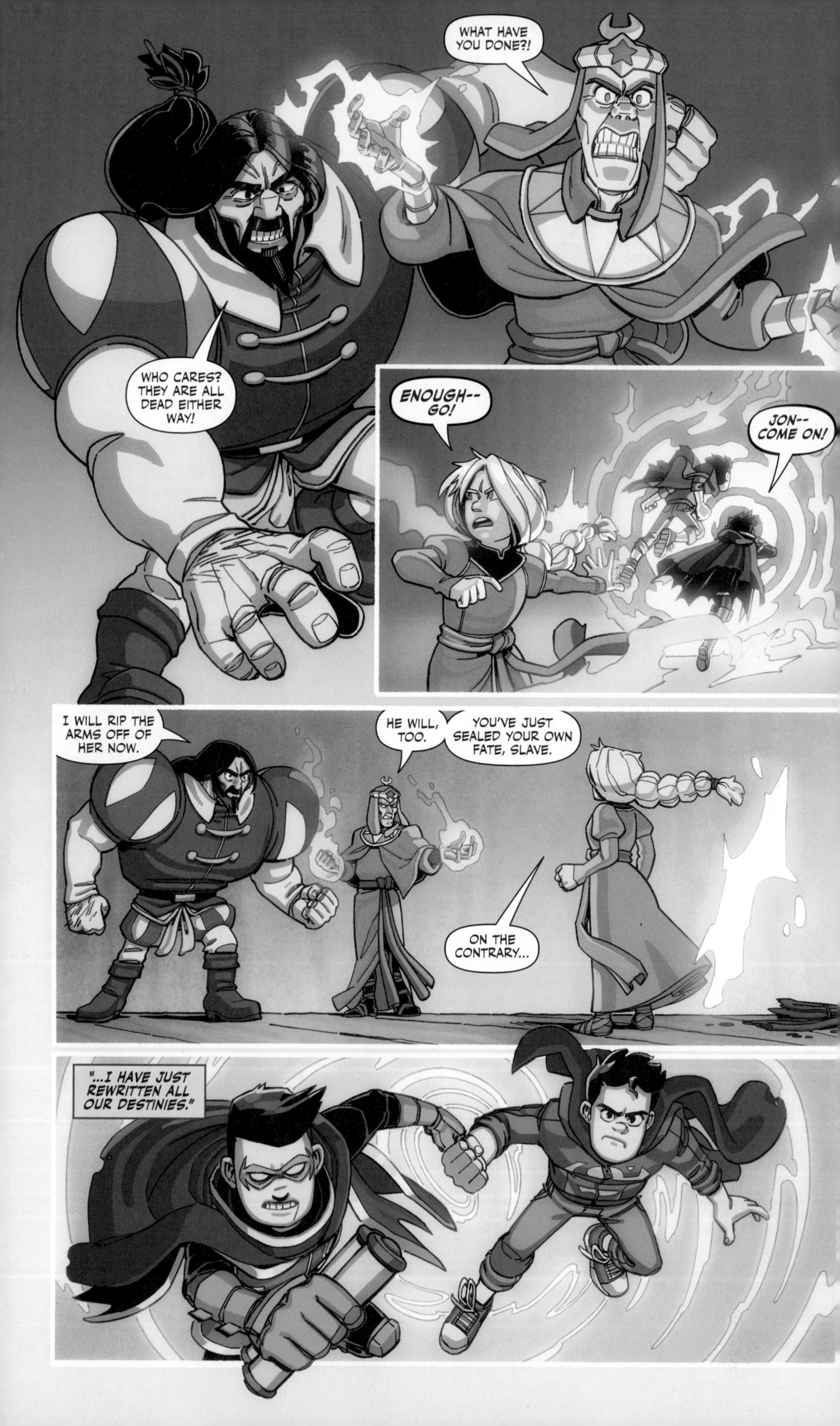
WHAT HAVE YOU DONE?!
WHO CARES? THEY ARE ALL DEAD EITHER WAY!
ENOUGH-- GO!
JON-- COME ON!
I WILL RIP THE ARMS OFF OF HER NOW.
HE WILL, TOO.
YOU'VE JUST SEALED YOUR OWN FATE, SLAVE.
ON THE CONTRARY...
"...I HAVE JUST REWRITTEN ALL OUR DESTINIES."

Challenge of the Super Sons #7 cover by **SIMONE DI MEO**

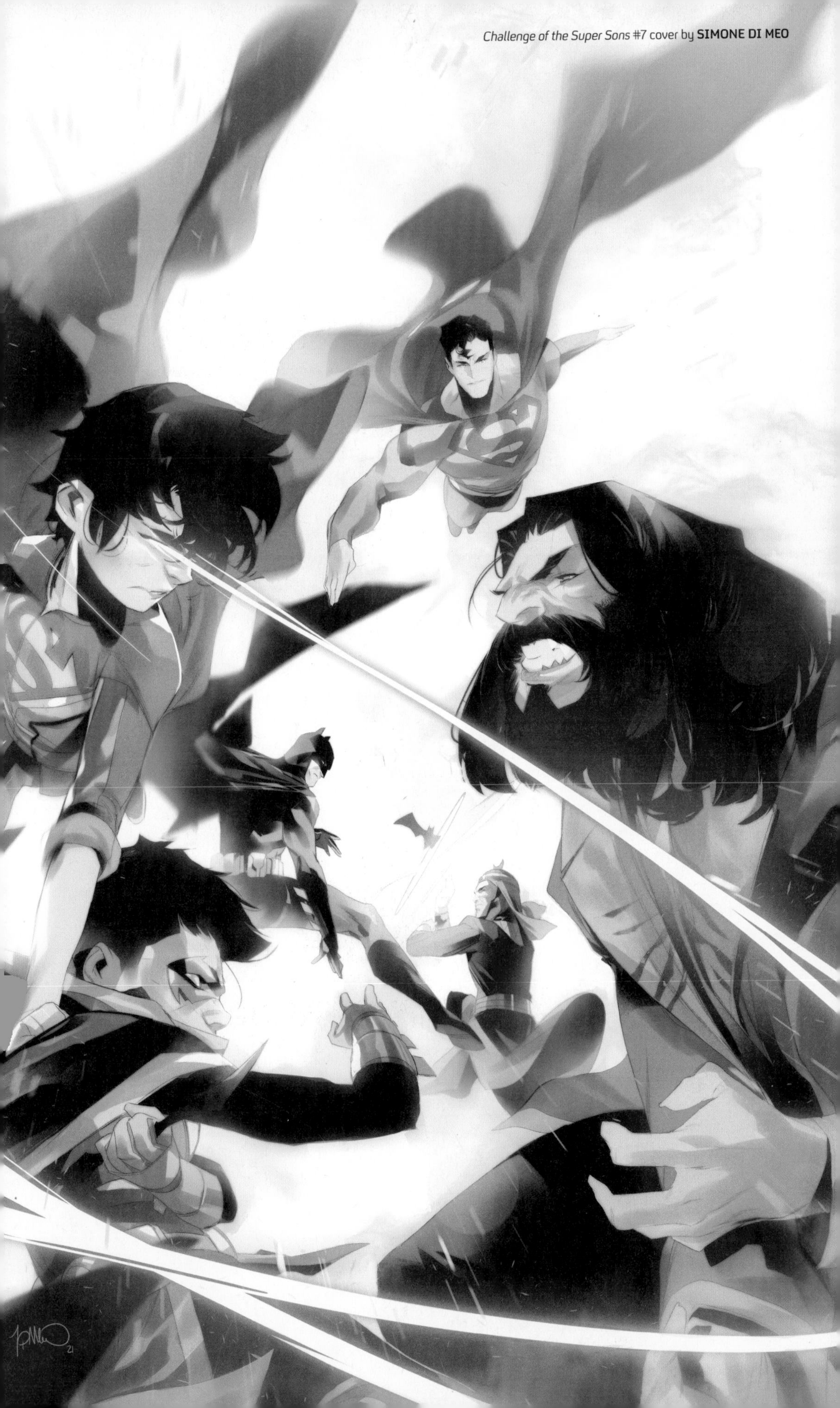

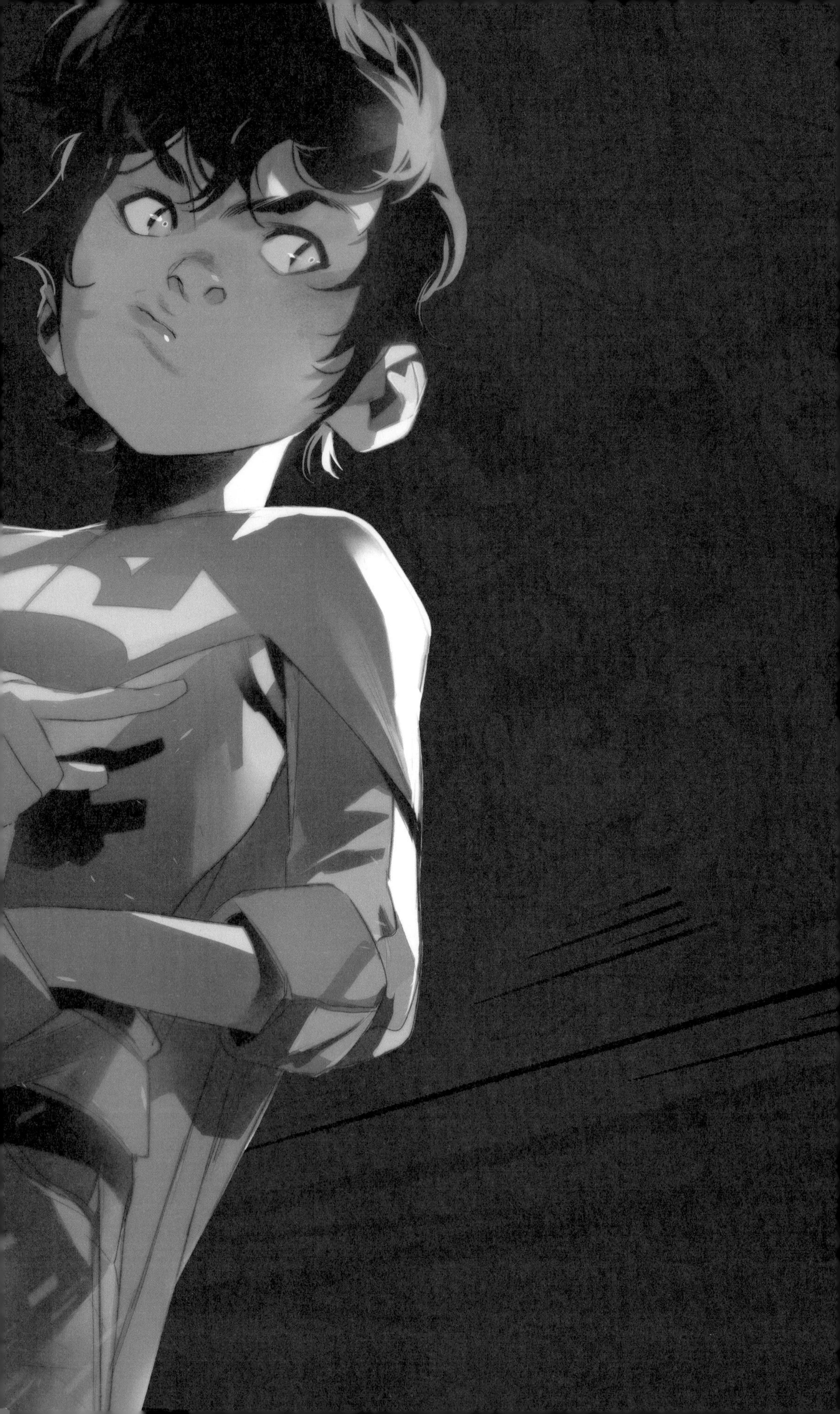

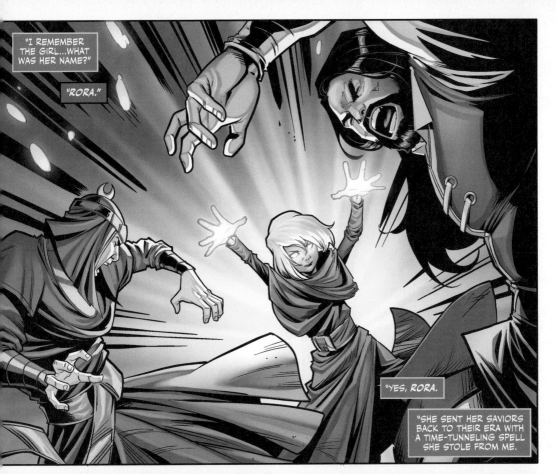

"I REMEMBER THE GIRL...WHAT WAS HER NAME?"
"RORA."
"YES, RORA.
"SHE SENT HER SAVIORS BACK TO THEIR ERA WITH A TIME-TUNNELING SPELL SHE STOLE FROM ME.
"THEN SHE ESCAPED."
"AND AS I RECALL, YOU WERE THE ONE WHO SAID SHE WAS NOT WORTH FOLLOWING."
"WE JUST HAD MORE IMPORTANT MATTERS TO ATTEND TO, SAVAGE.
"MAINLY PREPARING A LONG-TERM SPELL THAT WOULD PAY DIVIDENDS MANY YEARS FROM THEN.
OR, AS YOU AND I CALL IT...
...NOW.
DEATH TO THE DOOM SCROLL!

story & words: PETER J. TOMASI
art: MAX RAYNOR
colors: LUIS GUERRERO
letters: ROB LEIGH
cover by SIMONE DI MEO
variant cover by RILEY ROSSMO and IVAN PLASCENCIA
associate editor: DAVE WIELGOSZ
editor: PAUL KAMINSKI
group editor: BEN ABERNATHY

Superman Created by Jerry Siegel and Joe Shuster. Superboy created by Jerry Siegel. By special arrangement with the Jerry Siegel Family.

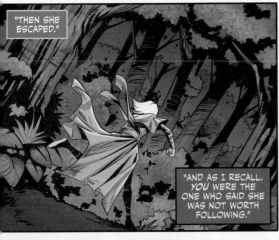

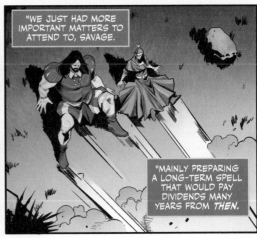

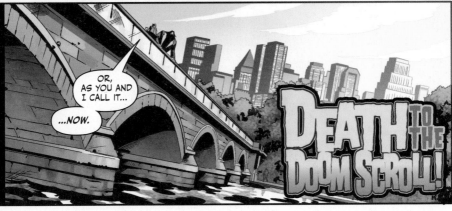

I HAD COMPLETELY FORGOTTEN THIS FOOLISH *GAMESMANSHIP* WITH THE PASSING OF THE CENTURIES.

I BARELY EVEN REMEMBERED KNOWING *YOU*, TRUTH BE TOLD.

WHAT A NICE THING TO SAY TO SOMEONE YOU CAME RUNNING TO AFTER BEING *HUMILIATED* BY TWO BOYS BARELY OUT OF DIAPERS.

I CAME TO YOU BECAUSE *YOU* STARTED THIS.

REMEMBER, I HELD UP *MY* END OF OUR BARGAIN. YOU LIVED TO SEE THE *FUTURE*, FAUST.

AND I GAVE YOU A REASON TO KEEP *LIVING*, SAVAGE.

FOREVER IS SHORTER THAN YOU THINK. MIGHT AS WELL STAY ENTERTAINED.

I'D CALL US *EVEN*.

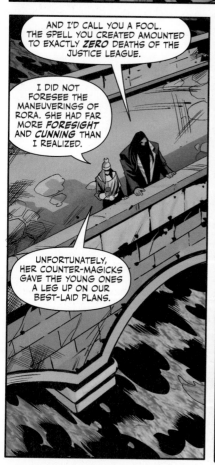

AND I'D CALL YOU A FOOL. THE SPELL YOU CREATED AMOUNTED TO EXACTLY *ZERO* DEATHS OF THE JUSTICE LEAGUE.

I DID NOT FORESEE THE MANEUVERINGS OF RORA. SHE HAD FAR MORE *FORESIGHT* AND *CUNNING* THAN I REALIZED.

UNFORTUNATELY, HER COUNTER-MAGICKS GAVE THE YOUNG ONES A LEG UP ON OUR BEST-LAID PLANS.

BUT YOU SEE THAT LIGHT? IS IT COMING BACK TO YOU? YOU REMEMBER NOW WHAT THAT IS?

IT'S ONE MORE CHANCE FOR US TO GET IT *RIGHT*.

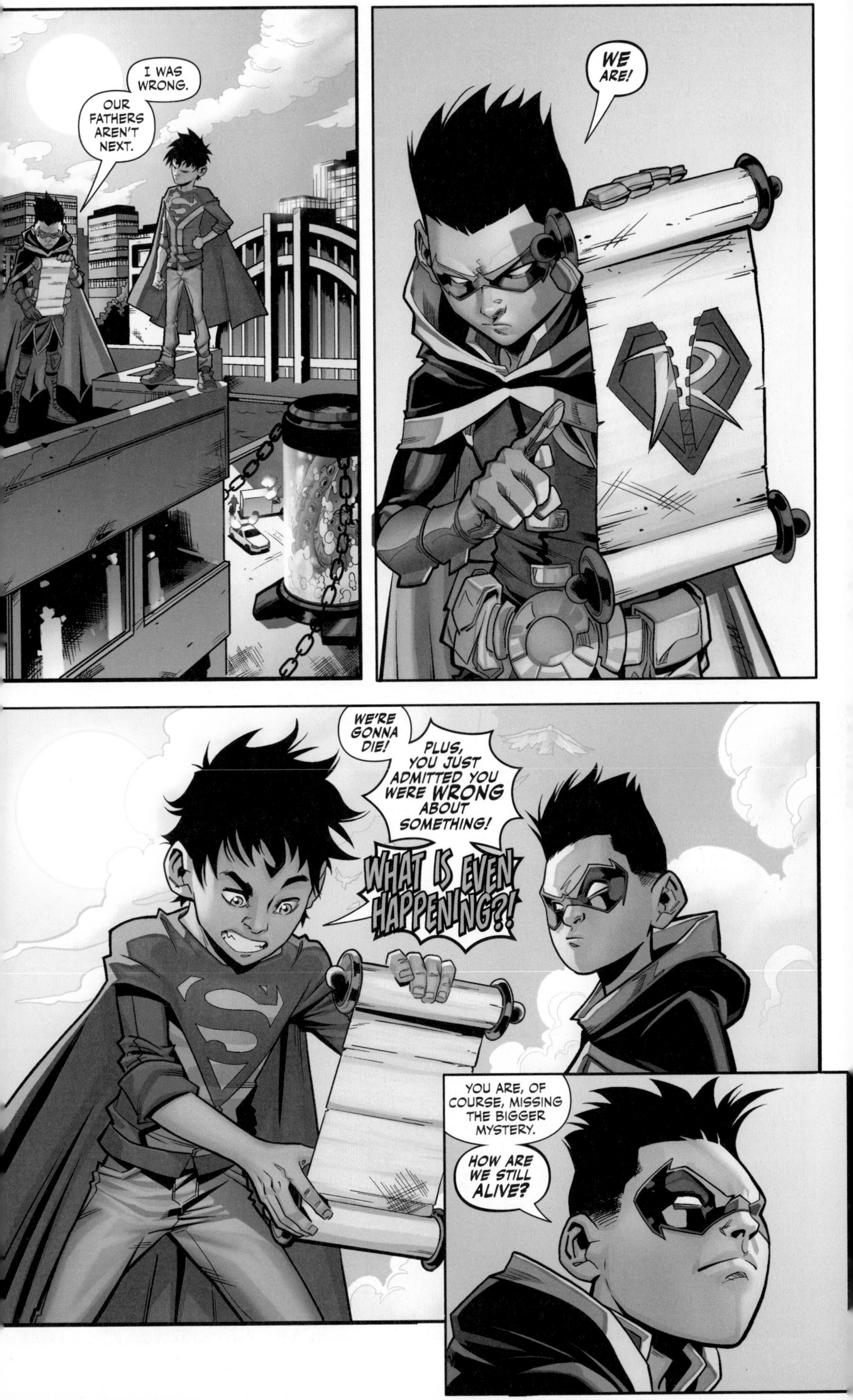
I WAS WRONG.
OUR FATHERS AREN'T NEXT.
WE ARE!
WE'RE GONNA DIE!
PLUS, YOU JUST ADMITTED YOU WERE WRONG ABOUT SOMETHING!
WHAT IS EVEN HAPPENING?!
YOU ARE, OF COURSE, MISSING THE BIGGER MYSTERY.
HOW ARE WE STILL ALIVE?

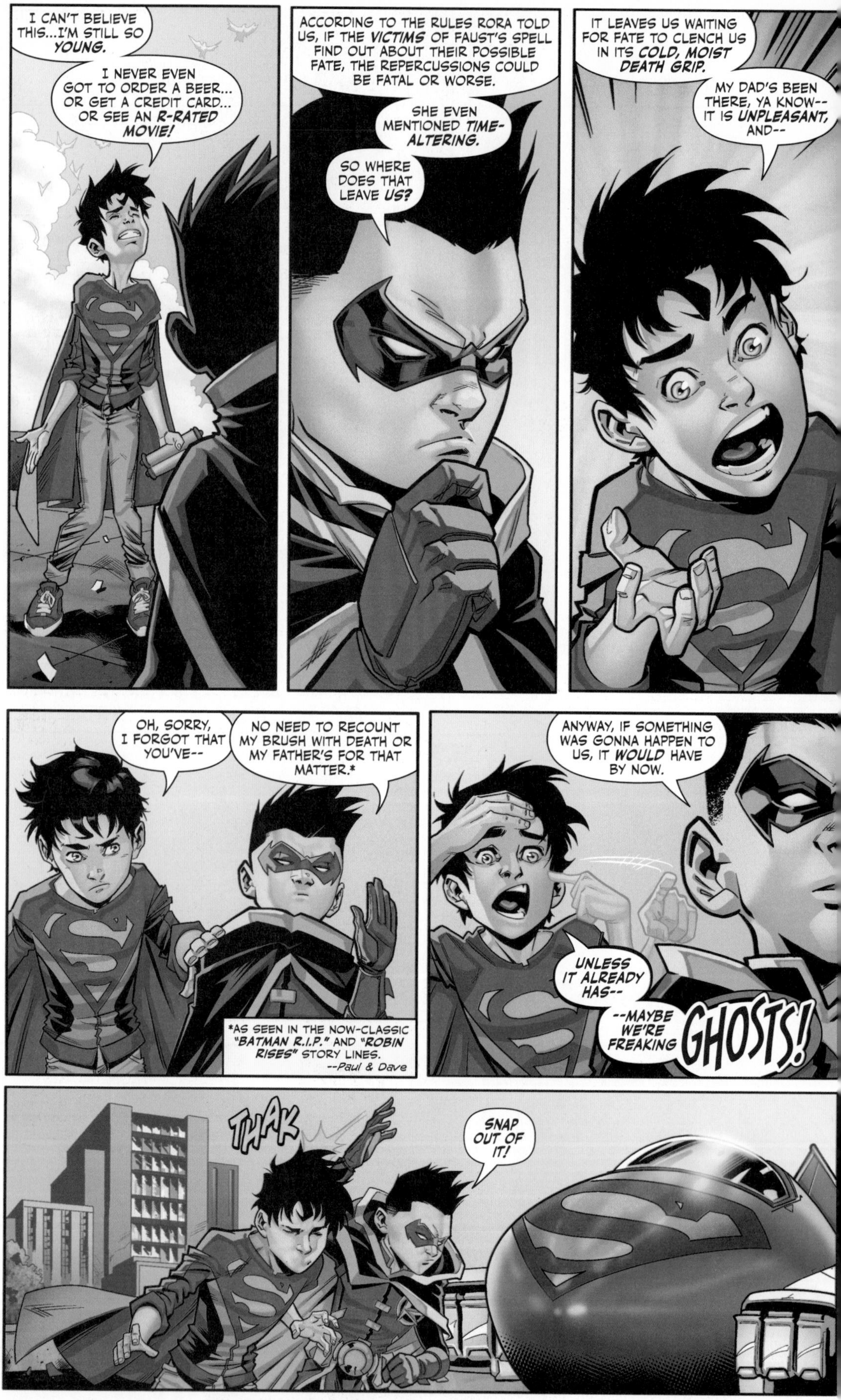
I CAN'T BELIEVE THIS...I'M STILL SO YOUNG.
I NEVER EVEN GOT TO ORDER A BEER... OR GET A CREDIT CARD... OR SEE AN R-RATED MOVIE!
ACCORDING TO THE RULES RORA TOLD US, IF THE VICTIMS OF FAUST'S SPELL FIND OUT ABOUT THEIR POSSIBLE FATE, THE REPERCUSSIONS COULD BE FATAL OR WORSE.
SHE EVEN MENTIONED TIME-ALTERING.
SO WHERE DOES THAT LEAVE US?
IT LEAVES US WAITING FOR FATE TO CLENCH US IN ITS COLD, MOIST DEATH GRIP.
MY DAD'S BEEN THERE, YA KNOW--IT IS UNPLEASANT, AND--
OH, SORRY, I FORGOT THAT YOU'VE--
NO NEED TO RECOUNT MY BRUSH WITH DEATH OR MY FATHER'S FOR THAT MATTER.*
*AS SEEN IN THE NOW-CLASSIC "BATMAN R.I.P." AND "ROBIN RISES" STORY LINES. --Paul & Dave
ANYWAY, IF SOMETHING WAS GONNA HAPPEN TO US, IT WOULD HAVE BY NOW.
UNLESS IT ALREADY HAS--
--MAYBE WE'RE FREAKING GHOSTS!
THAK
SNAP OUT OF IT!

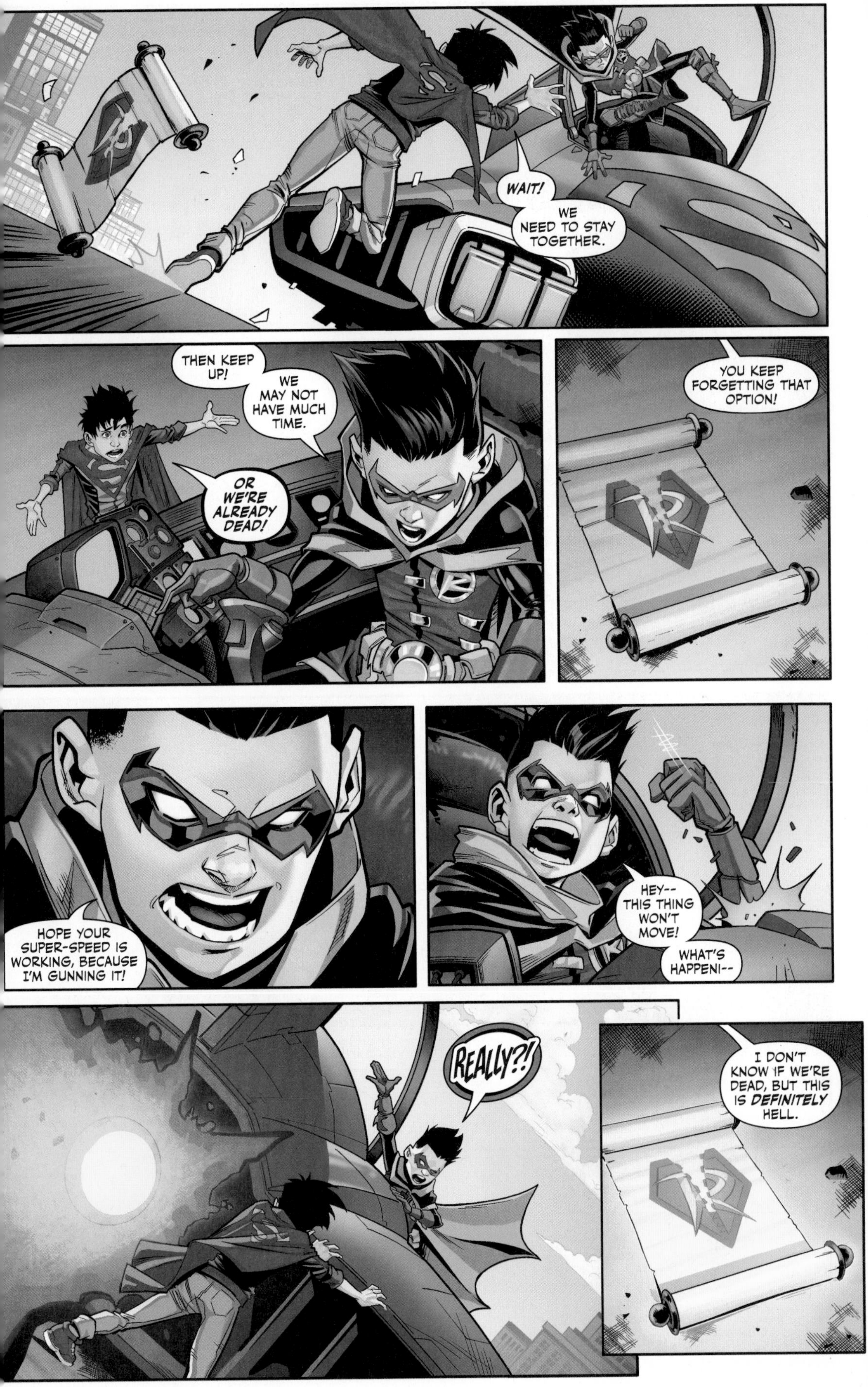
WAIT!
WE NEED TO STAY TOGETHER.
THEN KEEP UP!
WE MAY NOT HAVE MUCH TIME.
OR WE'RE ALREADY DEAD!
YOU KEEP FORGETTING THAT OPTION!
HOPE YOUR SUPER-SPEED IS WORKING, BECAUSE I'M GUNNING IT!
HEY-- THIS THING WON'T MOVE!
WHAT'S HAPPENI--
REALLY?!
I DON'T KNOW IF WE'RE DEAD, BUT THIS IS *DEFINITELY* HELL.

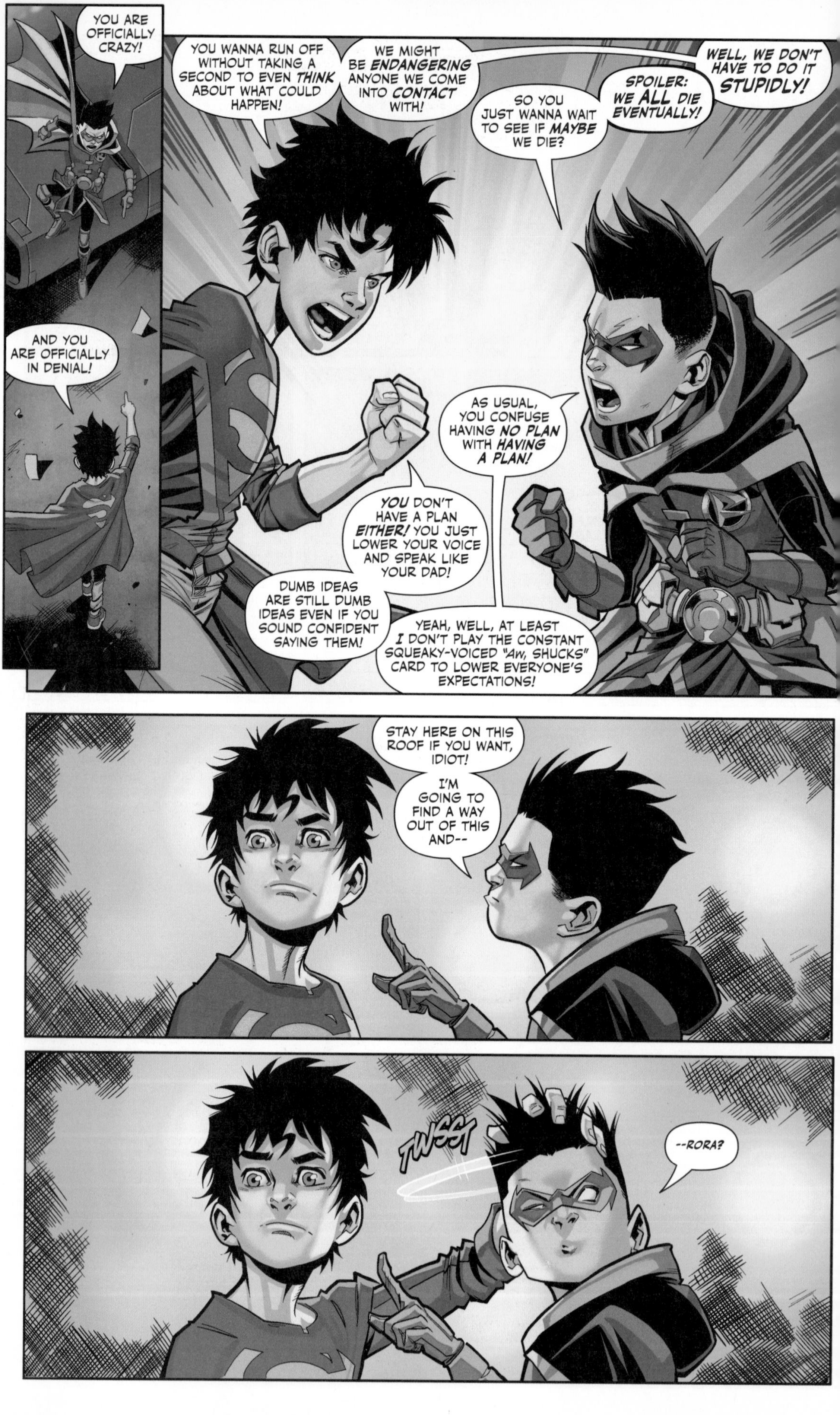
YOU ARE OFFICIALLY CRAZY!
AND YOU ARE OFFICIALLY IN DENIAL!
YOU WANNA RUN OFF WITHOUT TAKING A SECOND TO EVEN THINK ABOUT WHAT COULD HAPPEN!
WE MIGHT BE ENDANGERING ANYONE WE COME INTO CONTACT WITH!
SO YOU JUST WANNA WAIT TO SEE IF MAYBE WE DIE?
SPOILER: WE ALL DIE EVENTUALLY!
WELL, WE DON'T HAVE TO DO IT STUPIDLY!
AS USUAL, YOU CONFUSE HAVING NO PLAN WITH HAVING A PLAN!
YOU DON'T HAVE A PLAN EITHER! YOU JUST LOWER YOUR VOICE AND SPEAK LIKE YOUR DAD!
DUMB IDEAS ARE STILL DUMB IDEAS EVEN IF YOU SOUND CONFIDENT SAYING THEM!
YEAH, WELL, AT LEAST I DON'T PLAY THE CONSTANT SQUEAKY-VOICED "Aw, SHUCKS" CARD TO LOWER EVERYONE'S EXPECTATIONS!
STAY HERE ON THIS ROOF IF YOU WANT, IDIOT!
I'M GOING TO FIND A WAY OUT OF THIS AND--
TWSST
--RORA?

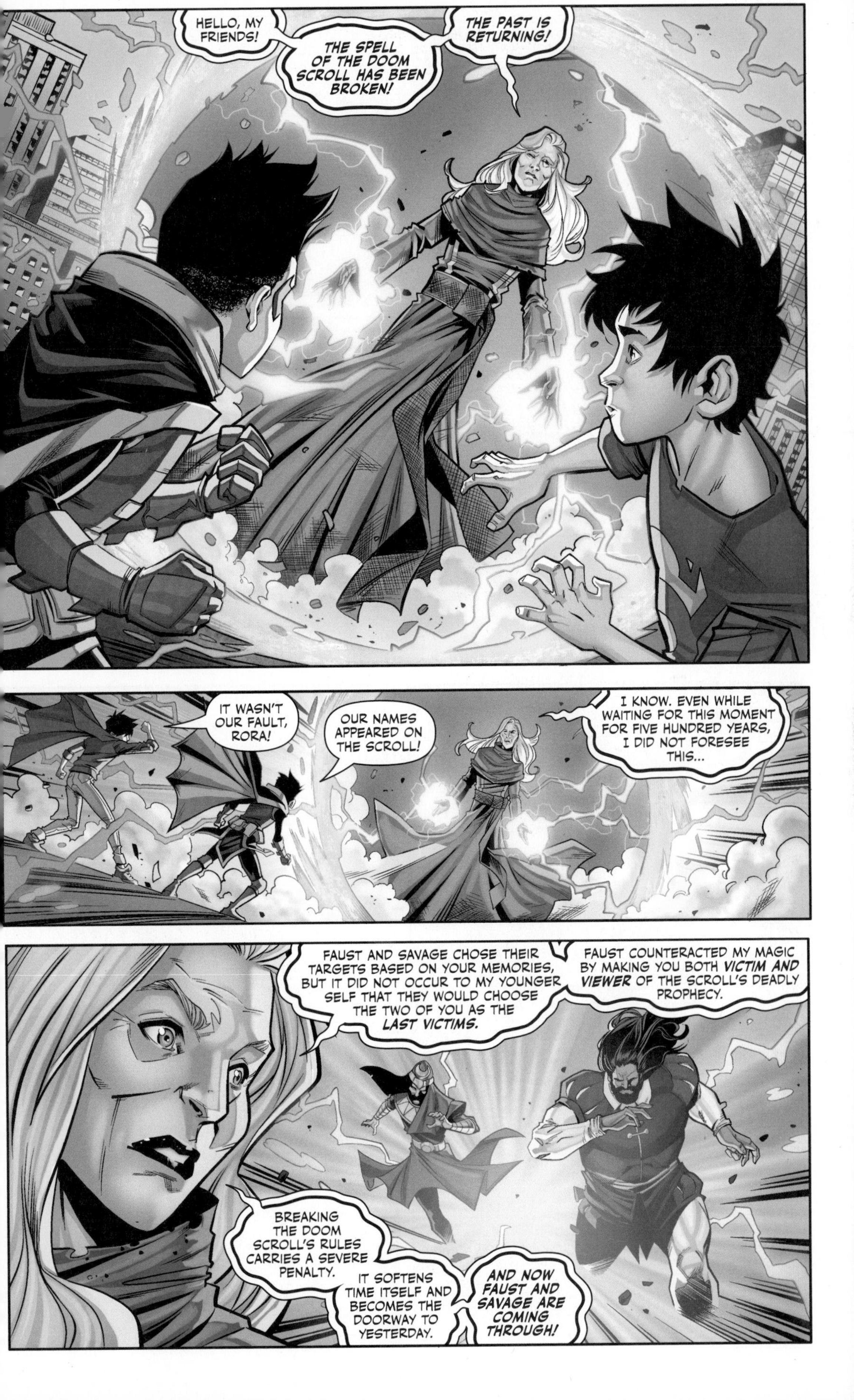
HELLO, MY FRIENDS!
THE SPELL OF THE DOOM SCROLL HAS BEEN BROKEN!
THE PAST IS RETURNING!
IT WASN'T OUR FAULT, RORA!
OUR NAMES APPEARED ON THE SCROLL!
I KNOW. EVEN WHILE WAITING FOR THIS MOMENT FOR FIVE HUNDRED YEARS, I DID NOT FORESEE THIS...
FAUST AND SAVAGE CHOSE THEIR TARGETS BASED ON YOUR MEMORIES, BUT IT DID NOT OCCUR TO MY YOUNGER SELF THAT THEY WOULD CHOOSE THE TWO OF YOU AS THE LAST VICTIMS.
FAUST COUNTERACTED MY MAGIC BY MAKING YOU BOTH VICTIM AND VIEWER OF THE SCROLL'S DEADLY PROPHECY.
BREAKING THE DOOM SCROLL'S RULES CARRIES A SEVERE PENALTY.
IT SOFTENS TIME ITSELF AND BECOMES THE DOORWAY TO YESTERDAY.
AND NOW FAUST AND SAVAGE ARE COMING THROUGH!

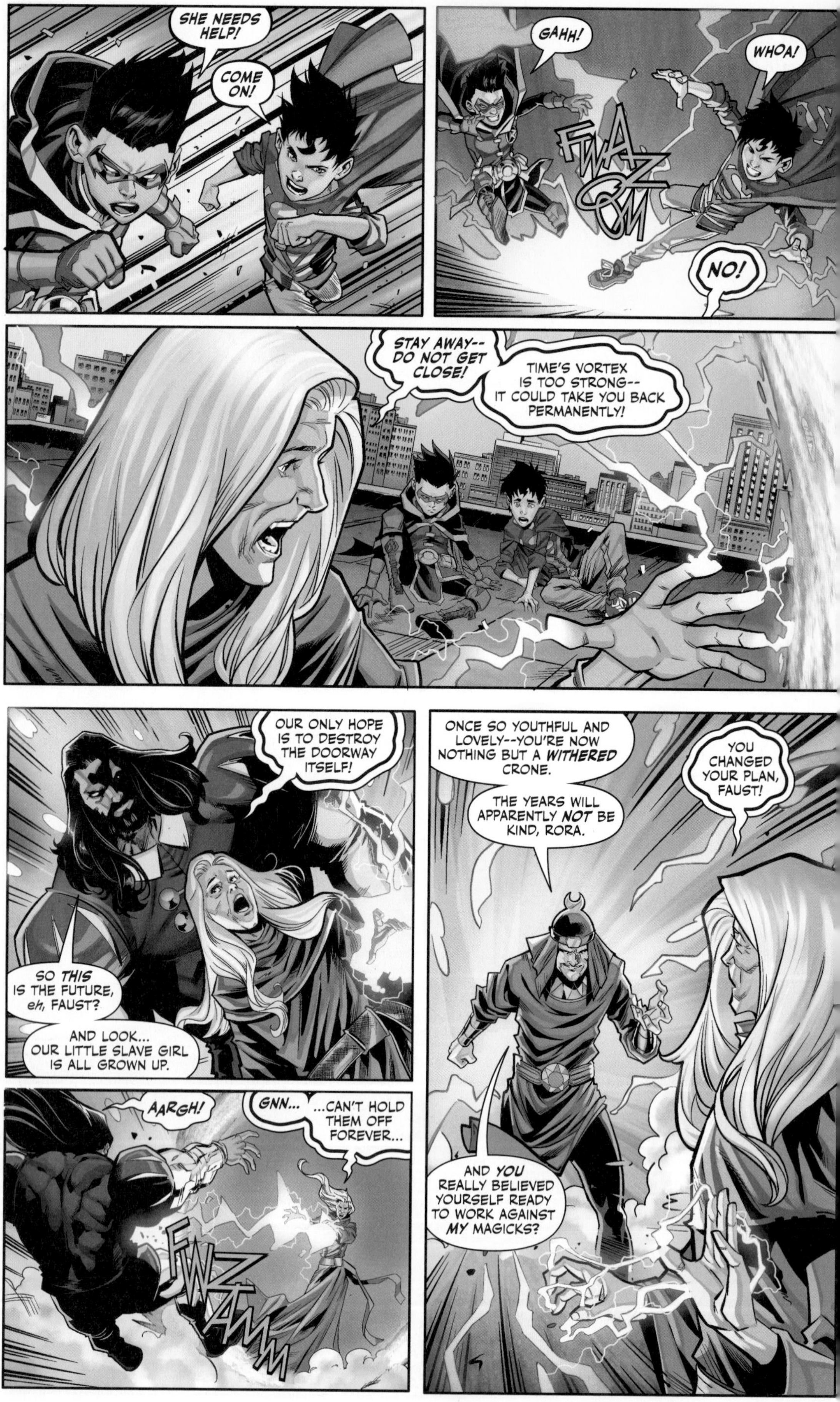
SHE NEEDS HELP!
COME ON!
GAHH!
WHOA!
FWAZOM
NO!
STAY AWAY-- DO NOT GET CLOSE!
TIME'S VORTEX IS TOO STRONG-- IT COULD TAKE YOU BACK PERMANENTLY!
OUR ONLY HOPE IS TO DESTROY THE DOORWAY ITSELF!
SO THIS IS THE FUTURE, eh, FAUST?
AND LOOK... OUR LITTLE SLAVE GIRL IS ALL GROWN UP.
AARGH!
GNN...
...CAN'T HOLD THEM OFF FOREVER...
FWZZAMM
ONCE SO YOUTHFUL AND LOVELY--YOU'RE NOW NOTHING BUT A WITHERED CRONE.
THE YEARS WILL APPARENTLY NOT BE KIND, RORA.
YOU CHANGED YOUR PLAN, FAUST!
AND YOU REALLY BELIEVED YOURSELF READY TO WORK AGAINST MY MAGICKS?

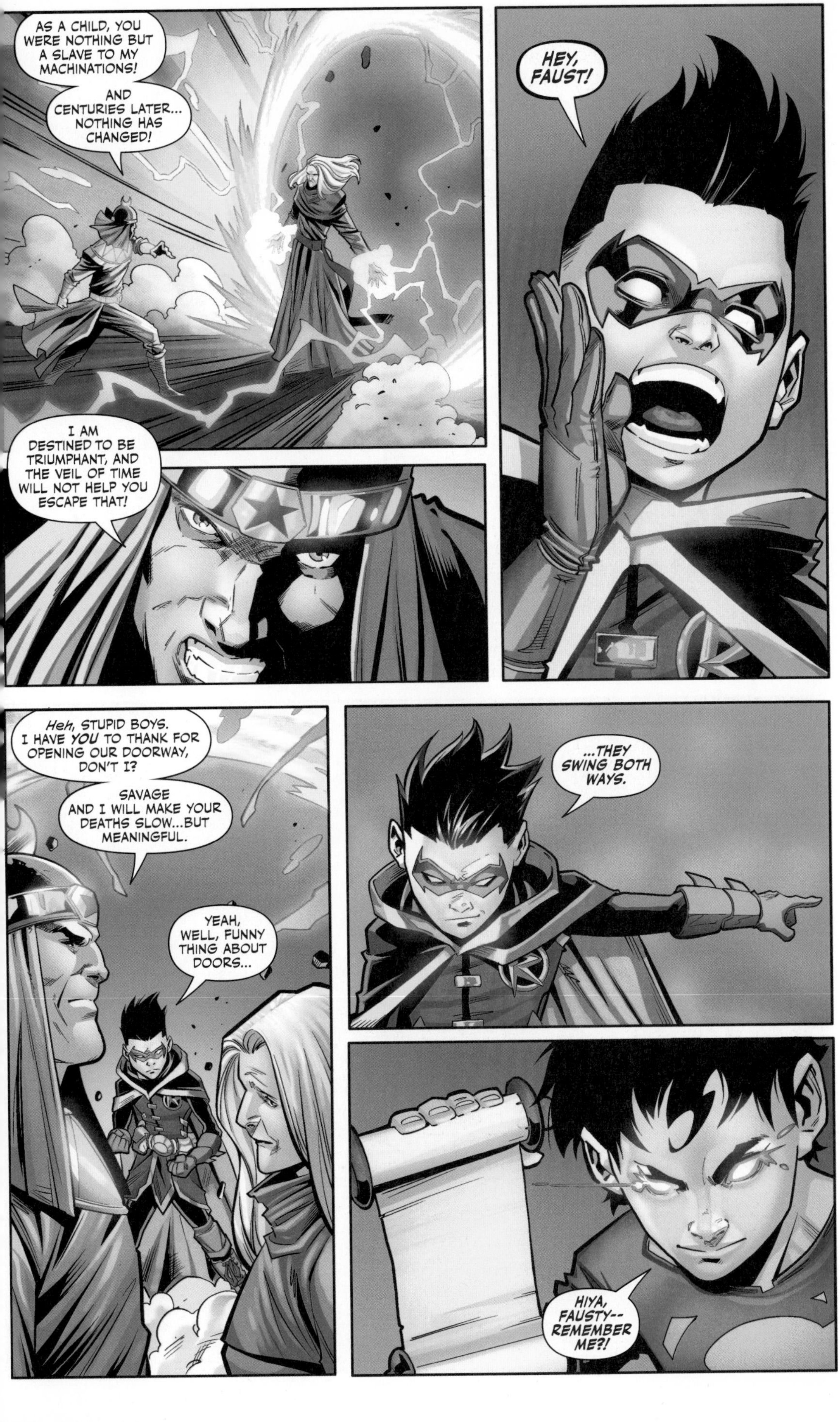

AS A CHILD, YOU WERE NOTHING BUT A SLAVE TO MY MACHINATIONS!
AND CENTURIES LATER... NOTHING HAS CHANGED!
HEY, FAUST!
I AM DESTINED TO BE TRIUMPHANT, AND THE VEIL OF TIME WILL NOT HELP YOU ESCAPE THAT!
Heh, STUPID BOYS. I HAVE *YOU* TO THANK FOR OPENING OUR DOORWAY, DON'T I?
SAVAGE AND I WILL MAKE YOUR DEATHS SLOW...BUT MEANINGFUL.
YEAH, WELL, FUNNY THING ABOUT DOORS...
...THEY SWING BOTH WAYS.
HIYA, FAUSTY--REMEMBER ME?!

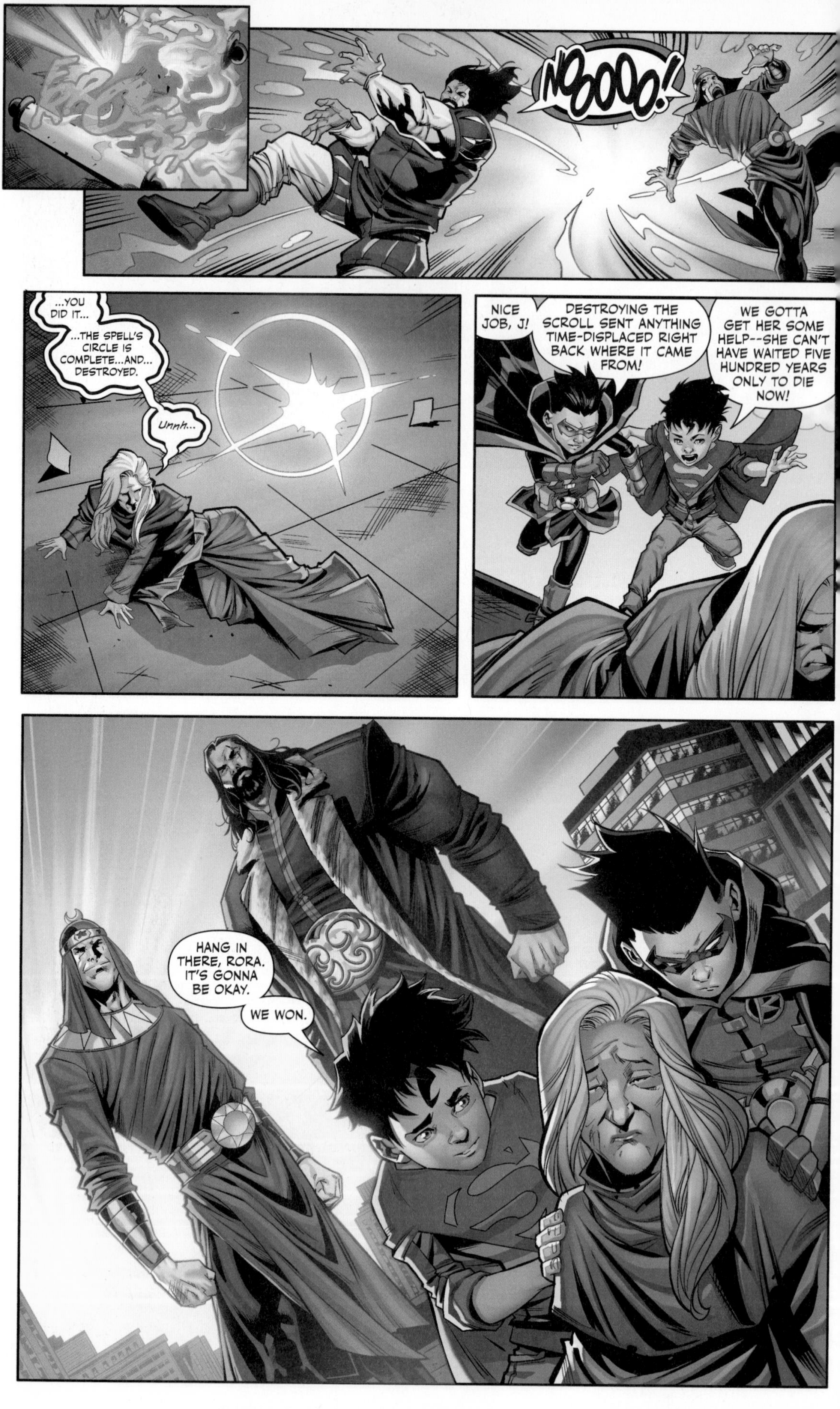

NOOOO!
...YOU DID IT...
...THE SPELL'S CIRCLE IS COMPLETE...AND... DESTROYED.
Unnh...
NICE JOB, J!
DESTROYING THE SCROLL SENT ANYTHING TIME-DISPLACED RIGHT BACK WHERE IT CAME FROM!
WE GOTTA GET HER SOME HELP--SHE CAN'T HAVE WAITED FIVE HUNDRED YEARS ONLY TO DIE NOW!
HANG IN THERE, RORA. IT'S GONNA BE OKAY.
WE WON.

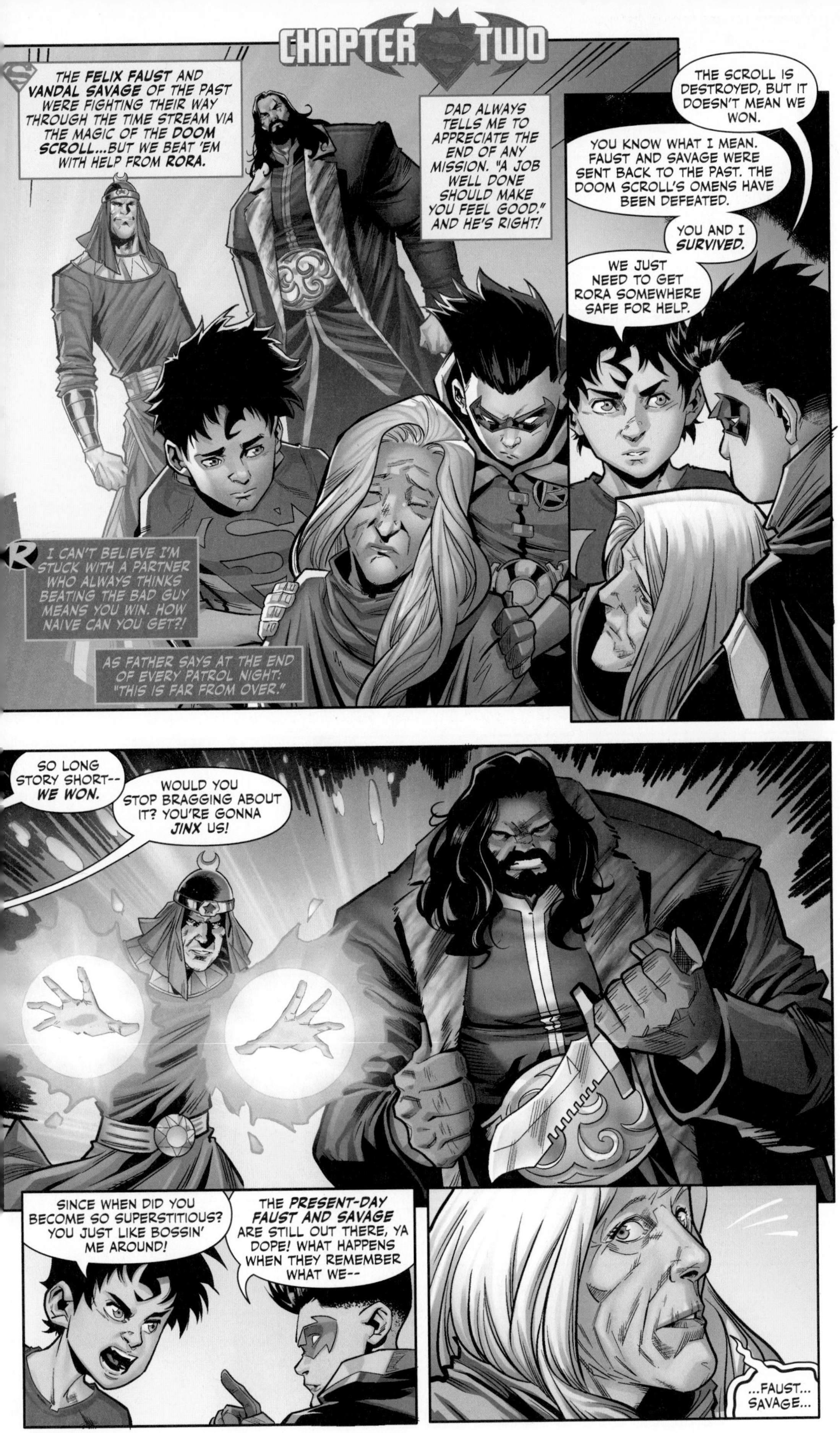
CHAPTER TWO
THE FELIX FAUST AND VANDAL SAVAGE OF THE PAST WERE FIGHTING THEIR WAY THROUGH THE TIME STREAM VIA THE MAGIC OF THE DOOM SCROLL...BUT WE BEAT 'EM WITH HELP FROM RORA.
DAD ALWAYS TELLS ME TO APPRECIATE THE END OF ANY MISSION. "A JOB WELL DONE SHOULD MAKE YOU FEEL GOOD." AND HE'S RIGHT!
I CAN'T BELIEVE I'M STUCK WITH A PARTNER WHO ALWAYS THINKS BEATING THE BAD GUY MEANS YOU WIN. HOW NAIVE CAN YOU GET?!
AS FATHER SAYS AT THE END OF EVERY PATROL NIGHT: "THIS IS FAR FROM OVER."
THE SCROLL IS DESTROYED, BUT IT DOESN'T MEAN WE WON.
YOU KNOW WHAT I MEAN. FAUST AND SAVAGE WERE SENT BACK TO THE PAST. THE DOOM SCROLL'S OMENS HAVE BEEN DEFEATED.
YOU AND I SURVIVED.
WE JUST NEED TO GET RORA SOMEWHERE SAFE FOR HELP.
SO LONG STORY SHORT-- WE WON.
WOULD YOU STOP BRAGGING ABOUT IT? YOU'RE GONNA JINX US!
SINCE WHEN DID YOU BECOME SO SUPERSTITIOUS? YOU JUST LIKE BOSSIN' ME AROUND!
THE PRESENT-DAY FAUST AND SAVAGE ARE STILL OUT THERE, YA DOPE! WHAT HAPPENS WHEN THEY REMEMBER WHAT WE--
...FAUST... SAVAGE...

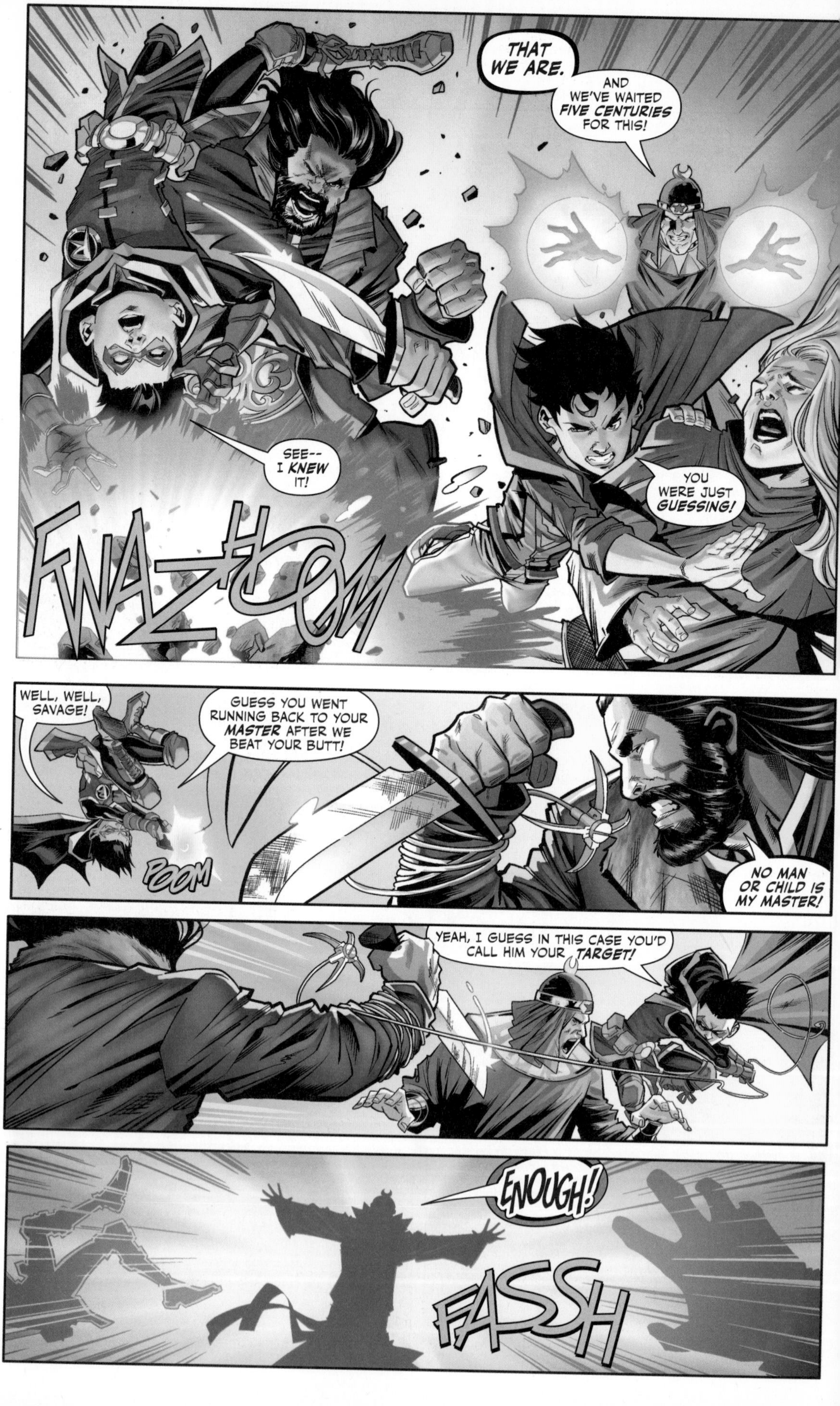
THAT WE ARE.
AND WE'VE WAITED FIVE CENTURIES FOR THIS!
SEE-- I KNEW IT!
YOU WERE JUST GUESSING!
FWAZHOOM
WELL, WELL, SAVAGE!
GUESS YOU WENT RUNNING BACK TO YOUR MASTER AFTER WE BEAT YOUR BUTT!
POOM
NO MAN OR CHILD IS MY MASTER!
YEAH, I GUESS IN THIS CASE YOU'D CALL HIM YOUR TARGET!
ENOUGH!
FASSH

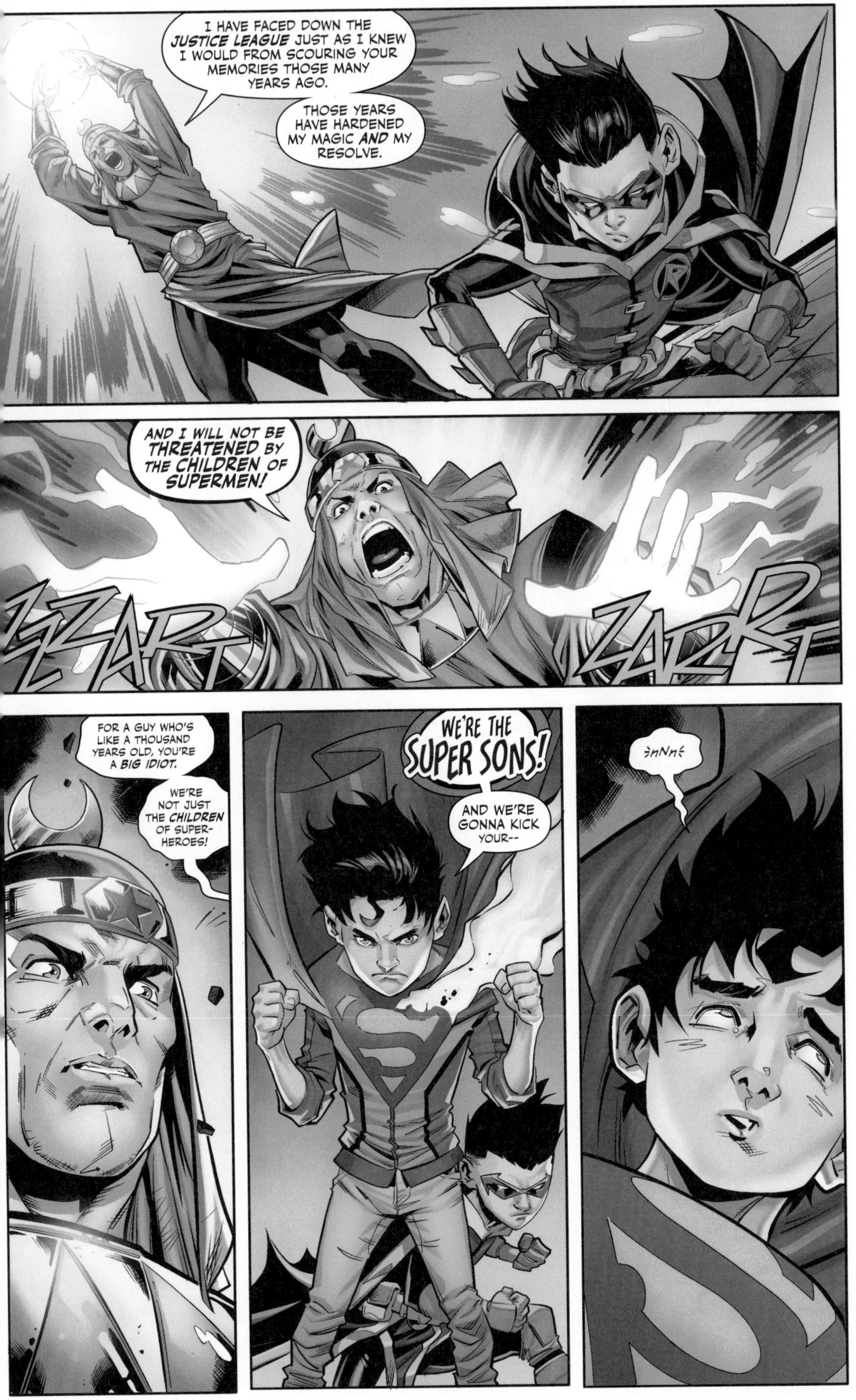
I HAVE FACED DOWN THE JUSTICE LEAGUE JUST AS I KNEW I WOULD FROM SCOURING YOUR MEMORIES THOSE MANY YEARS AGO.
THOSE YEARS HAVE HARDENED MY MAGIC AND MY RESOLVE.
AND I WILL NOT BE THREATENED BY THE CHILDREN OF SUPERMEN!
ZZZART
ZAKRT
FOR A GUY WHO'S LIKE A THOUSAND YEARS OLD, YOU'RE A BIG IDIOT.
WE'RE NOT JUST THE CHILDREN OF SUPER-HEROES!
WE'RE THE SUPER SONS!
AND WE'RE GONNA KICK YOUR--
nNn

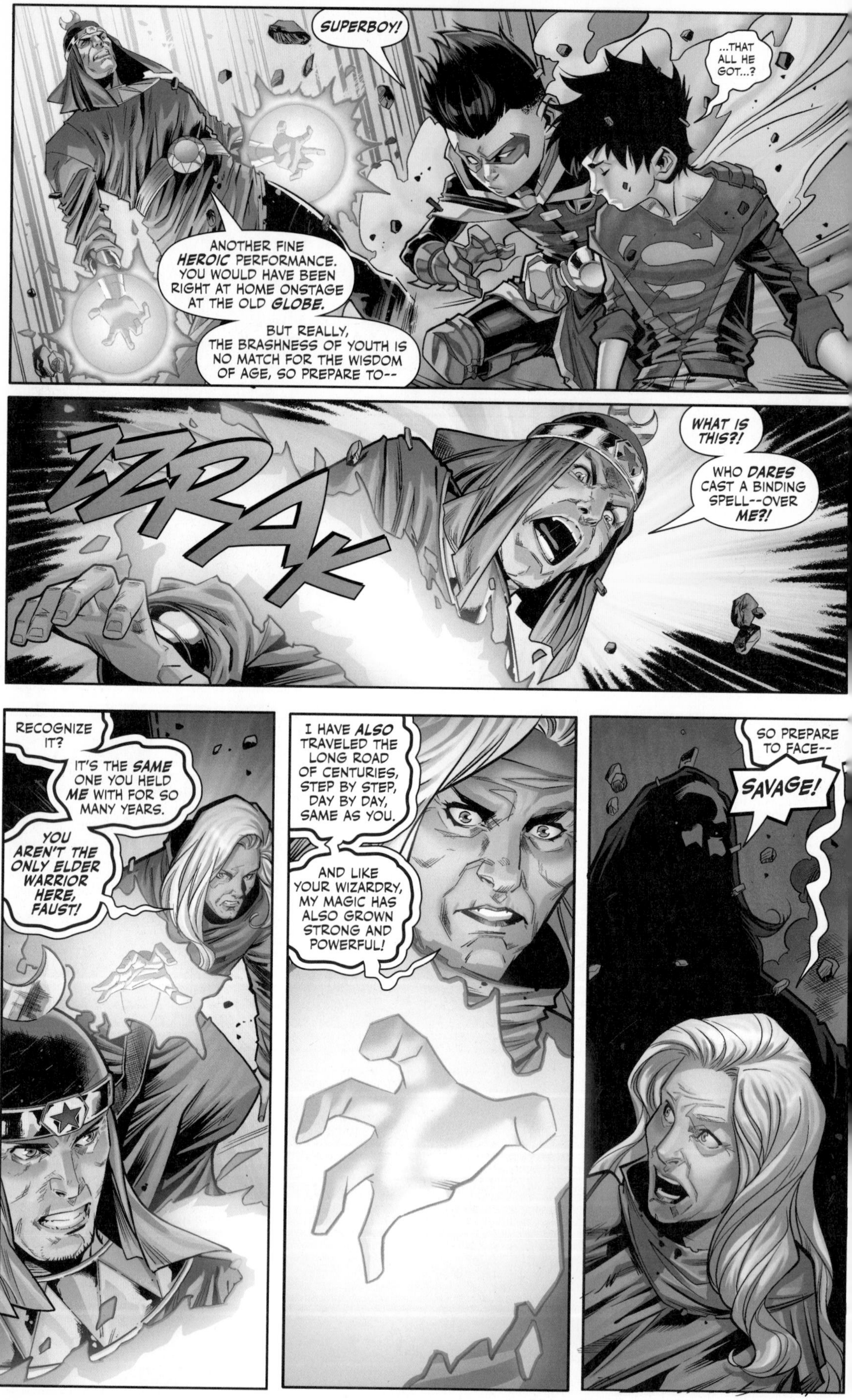
SUPERBOY!
...THAT ALL HE GOT...?
ANOTHER FINE HEROIC PERFORMANCE. YOU WOULD HAVE BEEN RIGHT AT HOME ONSTAGE AT THE OLD GLOBE.
BUT REALLY, THE BRASHNESS OF YOUTH IS NO MATCH FOR THE WISDOM OF AGE, SO PREPARE TO--
ZZRAK
WHAT IS THIS?!
WHO DARES CAST A BINDING SPELL--OVER ME?!
RECOGNIZE IT?
IT'S THE SAME ONE YOU HELD ME WITH FOR SO MANY YEARS.
YOU AREN'T THE ONLY ELDER WARRIOR HERE, FAUST!
I HAVE ALSO TRAVELED THE LONG ROAD OF CENTURIES, STEP BY STEP, DAY BY DAY, SAME AS YOU.
AND LIKE YOUR WIZARDRY, MY MAGIC HAS ALSO GROWN STRONG AND POWERFUL!
SO PREPARE TO FACE--
SAVAGE!

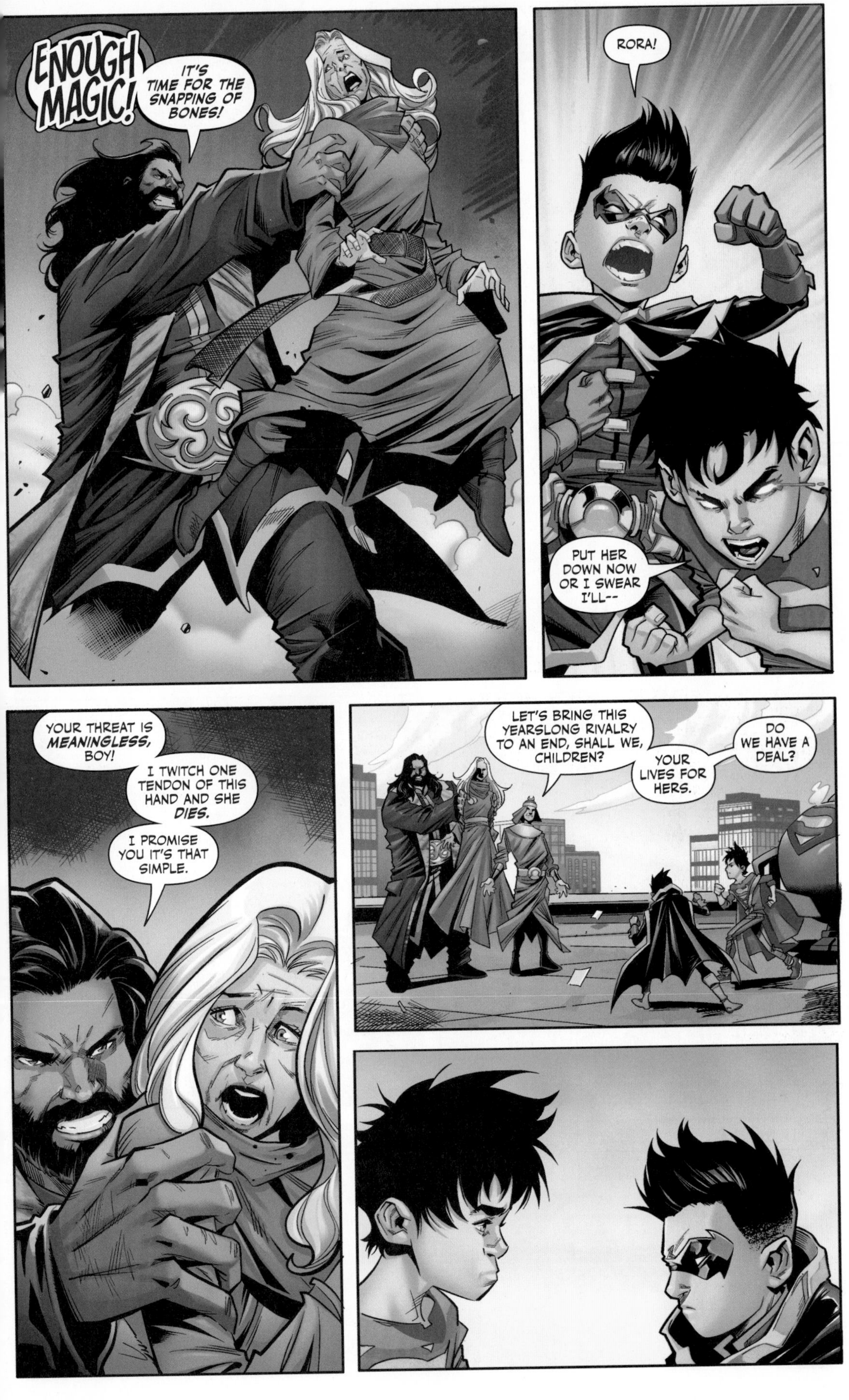
ENOUGH MAGIC!
IT'S TIME FOR THE SNAPPING OF BONES!
RORA!
PUT HER DOWN NOW OR I SWEAR I'LL--
YOUR THREAT IS *MEANINGLESS*, BOY!
I TWITCH ONE TENDON OF THIS HAND AND SHE *DIES*.
I PROMISE YOU IT'S THAT SIMPLE.
LET'S BRING THIS YEARSLONG RIVALRY TO AN END, SHALL WE, CHILDREN?
YOUR LIVES FOR HERS.
DO WE HAVE A DEAL?

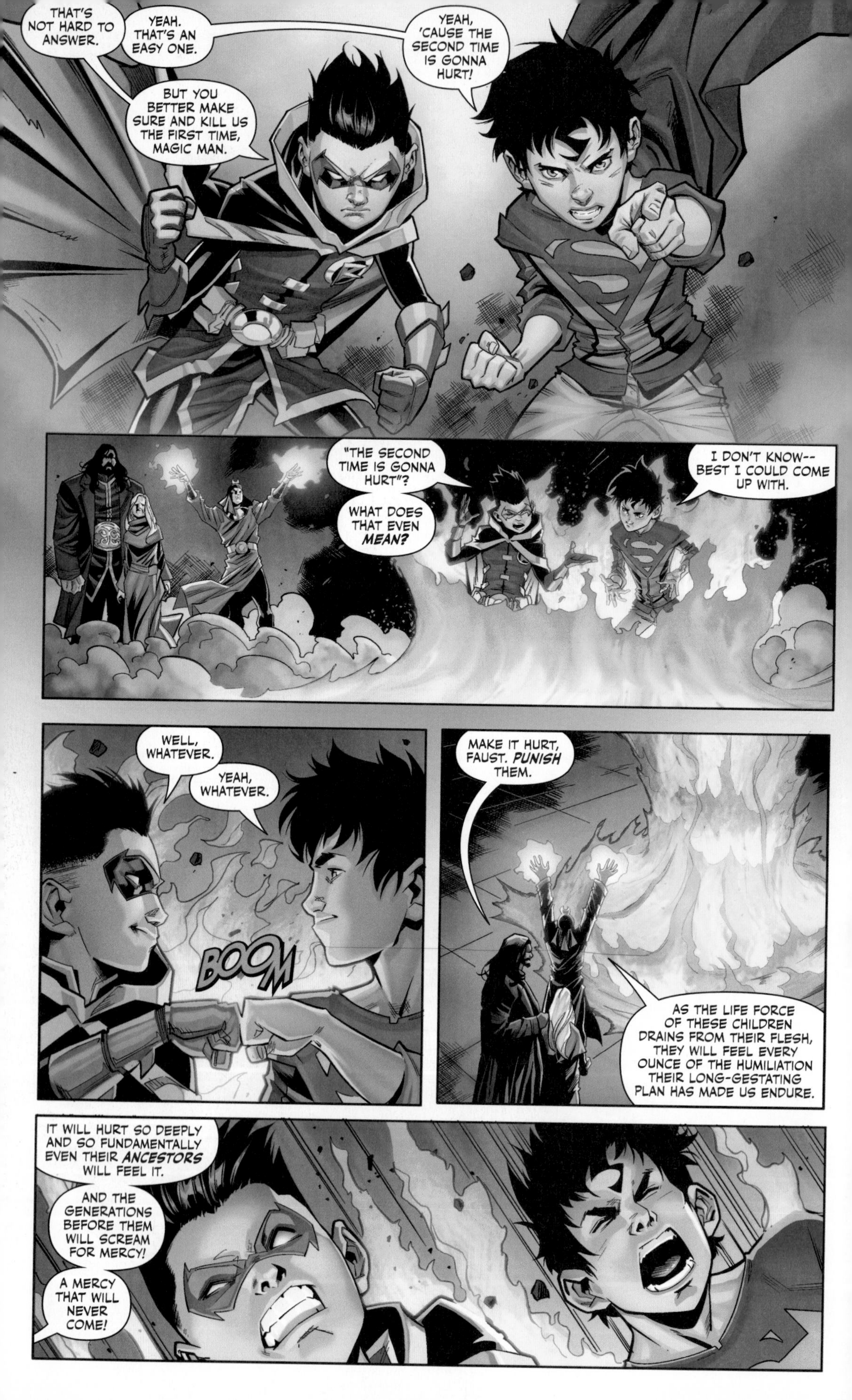
THAT'S NOT HARD TO ANSWER.
YEAH. THAT'S AN EASY ONE.
YEAH, 'CAUSE THE SECOND TIME IS GONNA HURT!
BUT YOU BETTER MAKE SURE AND KILL US THE FIRST TIME, MAGIC MAN.
"THE SECOND TIME IS GONNA HURT"?
WHAT DOES THAT EVEN MEAN?
I DON'T KNOW-- BEST I COULD COME UP WITH.
WELL, WHATEVER.
YEAH, WHATEVER.
BOOM
MAKE IT HURT, FAUST. PUNISH THEM.
AS THE LIFE FORCE OF THESE CHILDREN DRAINS FROM THEIR FLESH, THEY WILL FEEL EVERY OUNCE OF THE HUMILIATION THEIR LONG-GESTATING PLAN HAS MADE US ENDURE.
IT WILL HURT SO DEEPLY AND SO FUNDAMENTALLY EVEN THEIR ANCESTORS WILL FEEL IT.
AND THE GENERATIONS BEFORE THEM WILL SCREAM FOR MERCY!
A MERCY THAT WILL NEVER COME!

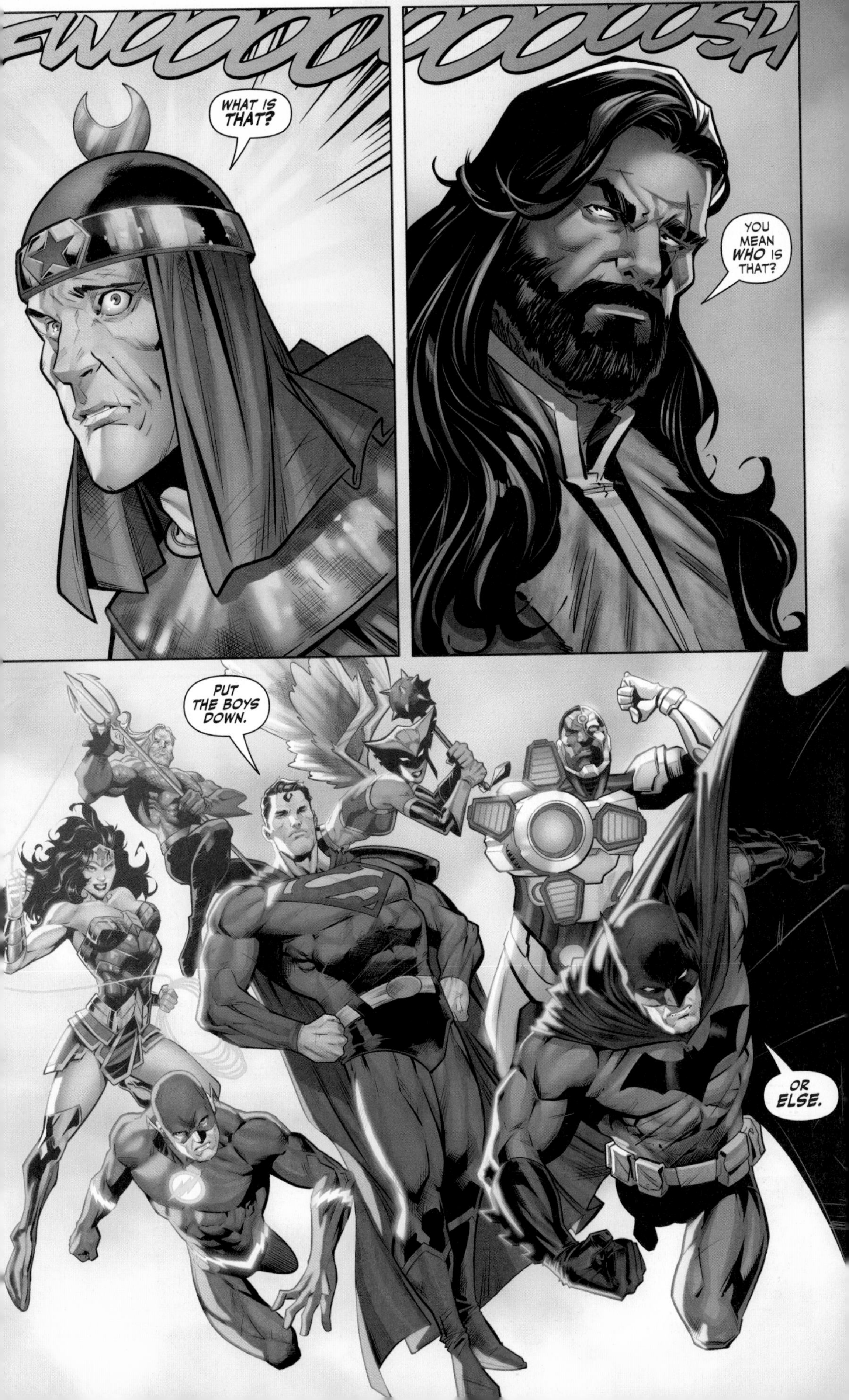
FWOOOOOOOOOOOSH
WHAT IS THAT?
YOU MEAN WHO IS THAT?
PUT THE BOYS DOWN.
OR ELSE.

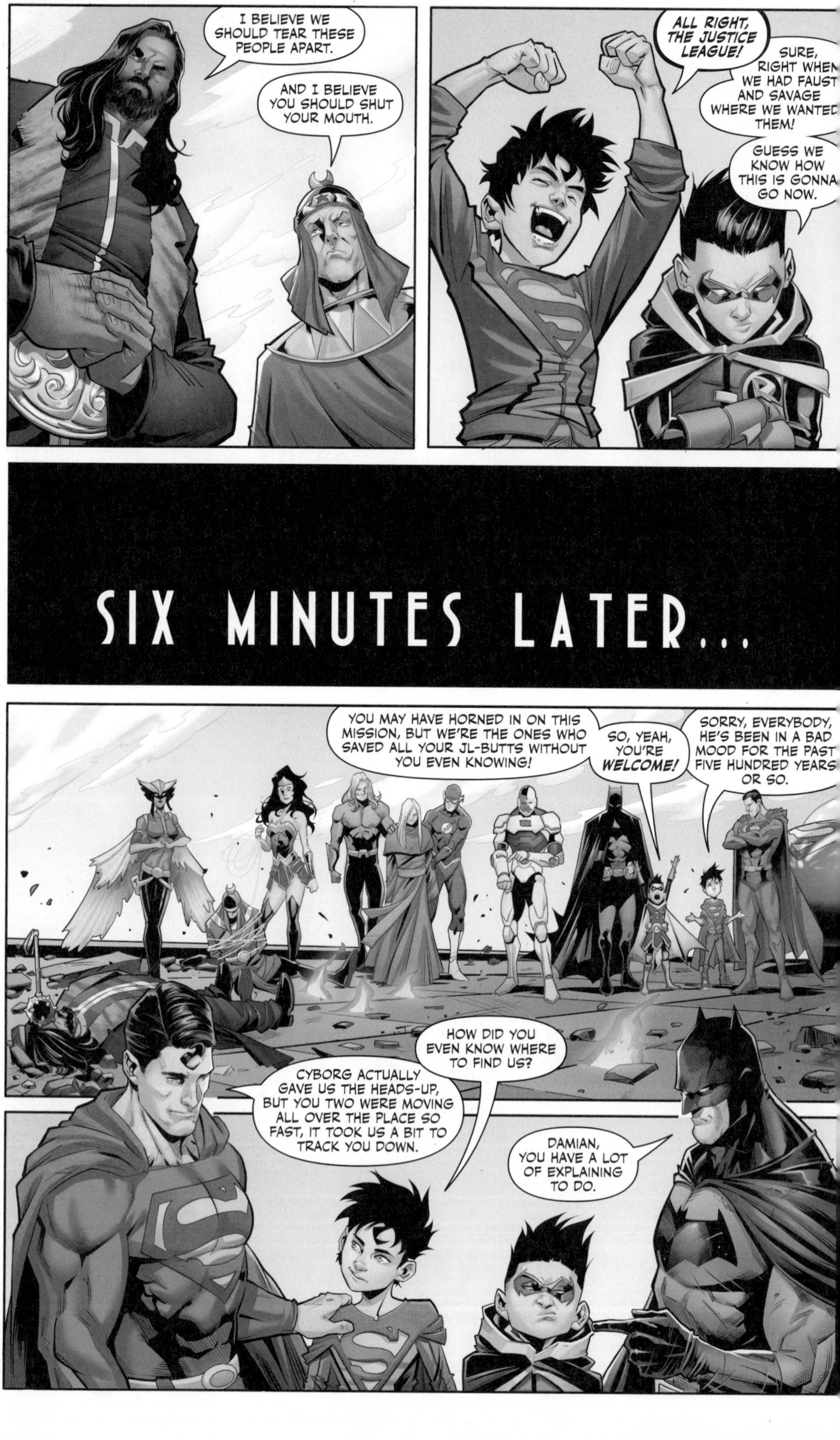
I BELIEVE WE SHOULD TEAR THESE PEOPLE APART.
AND I BELIEVE YOU SHOULD SHUT YOUR MOUTH.
ALL RIGHT, THE JUSTICE LEAGUE!
SURE, RIGHT WHEN WE HAD FAUST AND SAVAGE WHERE WE WANTED THEM!
GUESS WE KNOW HOW THIS IS GONNA GO NOW.
SIX MINUTES LATER...
YOU MAY HAVE HORNED IN ON THIS MISSION, BUT WE'RE THE ONES WHO SAVED ALL YOUR JL-BUTTS WITHOUT YOU EVEN KNOWING!
SO, YEAH, YOU'RE WELCOME!
SORRY, EVERYBODY, HE'S BEEN IN A BAD MOOD FOR THE PAST FIVE HUNDRED YEARS OR SO.
HOW DID YOU EVEN KNOW WHERE TO FIND US?
CYBORG ACTUALLY GAVE US THE HEADS-UP, BUT YOU TWO WERE MOVING ALL OVER THE PLACE SO FAST, IT TOOK US A BIT TO TRACK YOU DOWN.
DAMIAN, YOU HAVE A LOT OF EXPLAINING TO DO.

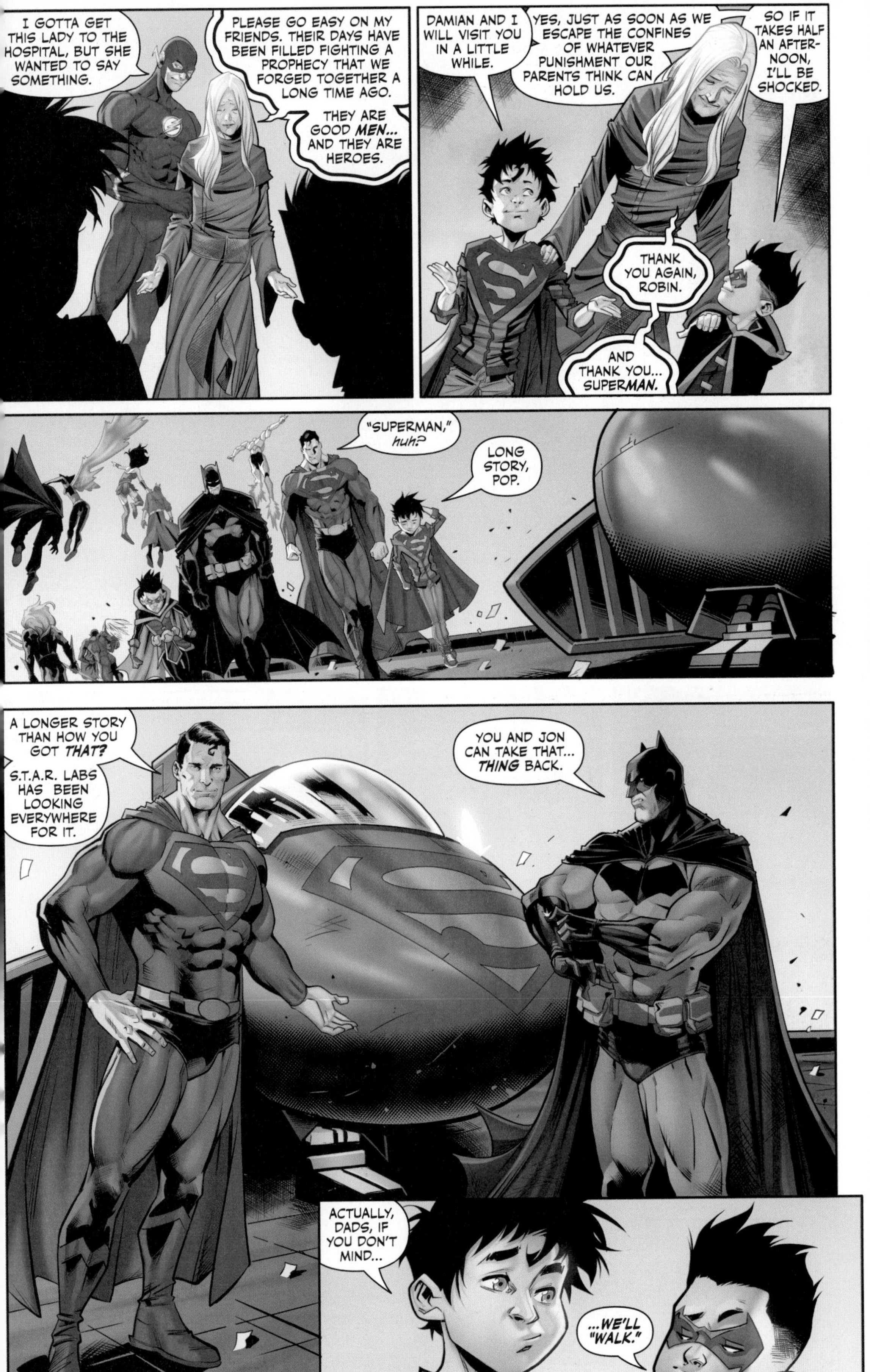
I GOTTA GET THIS LADY TO THE HOSPITAL, BUT SHE WANTED TO SAY SOMETHING.
PLEASE GO EASY ON MY FRIENDS. THEIR DAYS HAVE BEEN FILLED FIGHTING A PROPHECY THAT WE FORGED TOGETHER A LONG TIME AGO.
THEY ARE GOOD *MEN...* AND THEY ARE HEROES.
DAMIAN AND I WILL VISIT YOU IN A LITTLE WHILE.
YES, JUST AS SOON AS WE ESCAPE THE CONFINES OF WHATEVER PUNISHMENT OUR PARENTS THINK CAN HOLD US.
SO IF IT TAKES HALF AN AFTER-NOON, I'LL BE SHOCKED.
THANK YOU AGAIN, ROBIN.
AND THANK YOU... SUPER*MAN.*
"SUPERMAN," *huh?*
LONG STORY, POP.
A LONGER STORY THAN HOW YOU GOT *THAT?*
S.T.A.R. LABS HAS BEEN LOOKING EVERYWHERE FOR IT.
YOU AND JON CAN TAKE THAT... *THING* BACK.
ACTUALLY, DADS, IF YOU DON'T MIND...
...WE'LL "WALK."

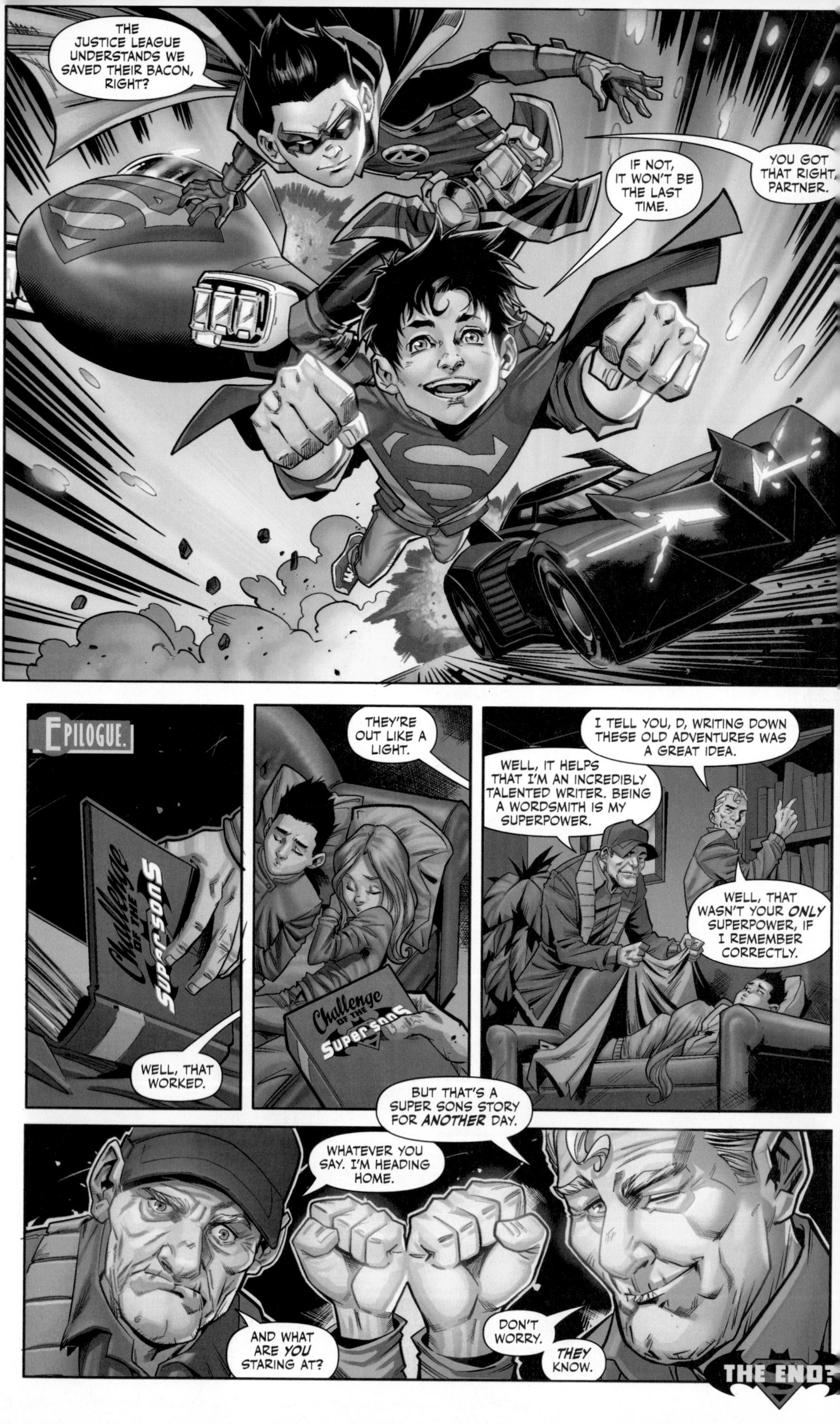
THE JUSTICE LEAGUE UNDERSTANDS WE SAVED THEIR BACON, RIGHT?
IF NOT, IT WON'T BE THE LAST TIME.
YOU GOT THAT RIGHT, PARTNER.
EPILOGUE.
Challenge OF THE Super Sons
WELL, THAT WORKED.
THEY'RE OUT LIKE A LIGHT.
Challenge OF THE Super Sons
I TELL YOU, D, WRITING DOWN THESE OLD ADVENTURES WAS A GREAT IDEA.
WELL, IT HELPS THAT I'M AN INCREDIBLY TALENTED WRITER. BEING A WORDSMITH IS MY SUPERPOWER.
WELL, THAT WASN'T YOUR *ONLY* SUPERPOWER, IF I REMEMBER CORRECTLY.
BUT THAT'S A SUPER SONS STORY FOR *ANOTHER* DAY.
WHATEVER YOU SAY. I'M HEADING HOME.
AND WHAT ARE *YOU* STARING AT?
DON'T WORRY. *THEY* KNOW.
THE END?

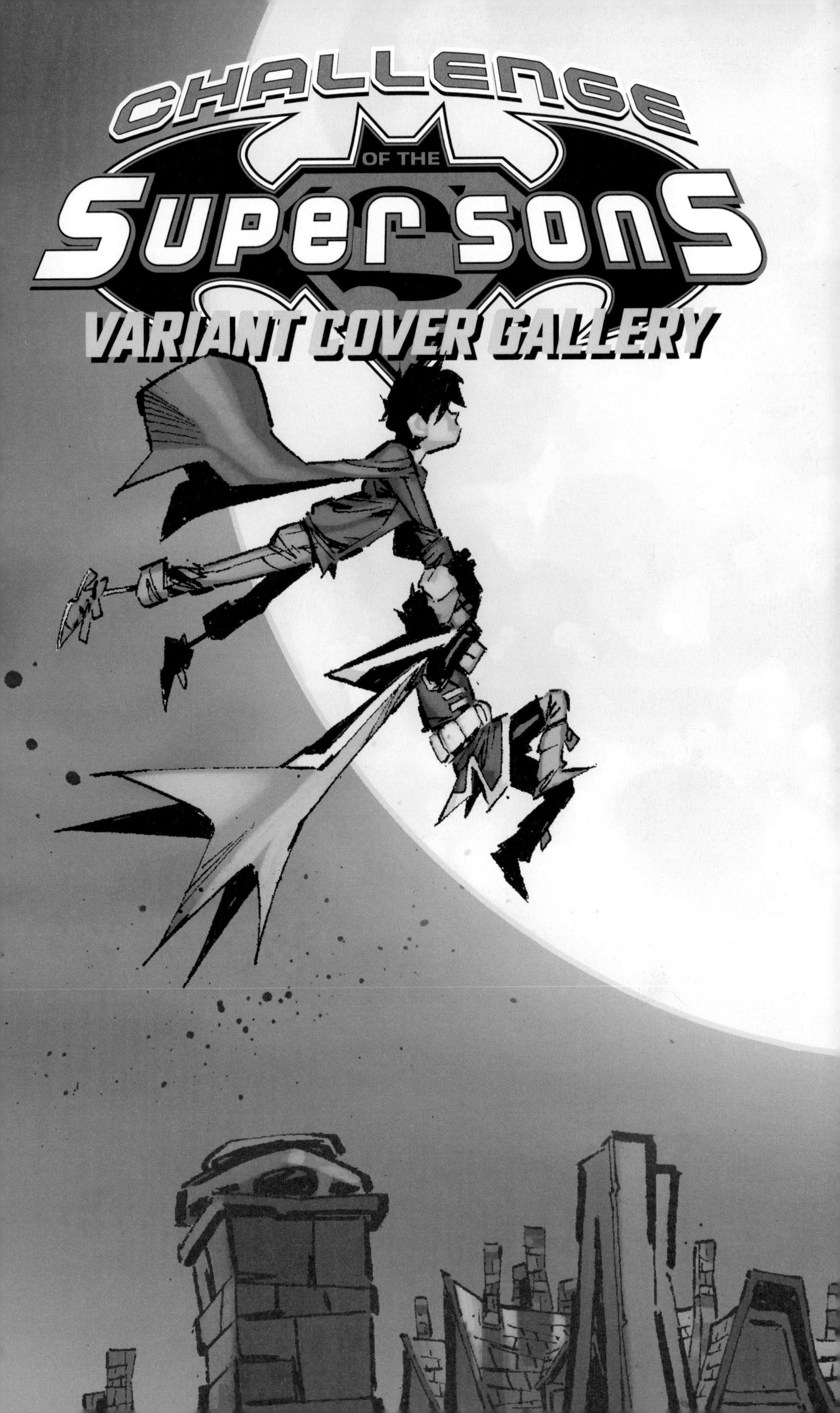
CHALLENGE
OF THE
SUPER SONS
VARIANT COVER GALLERY

Challenge of the Super Sons #1 variant cover by **SIMONE DI MEO**

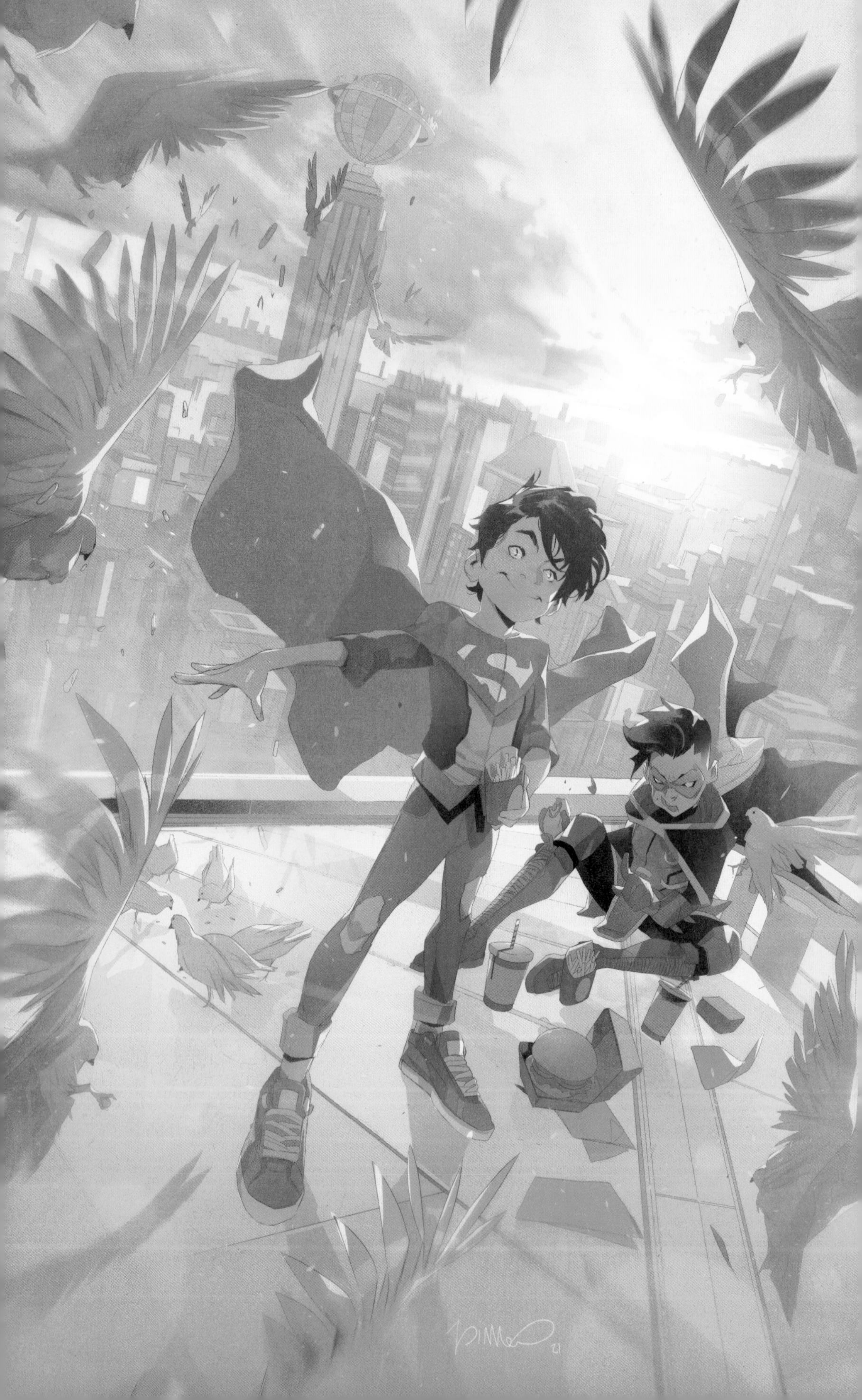

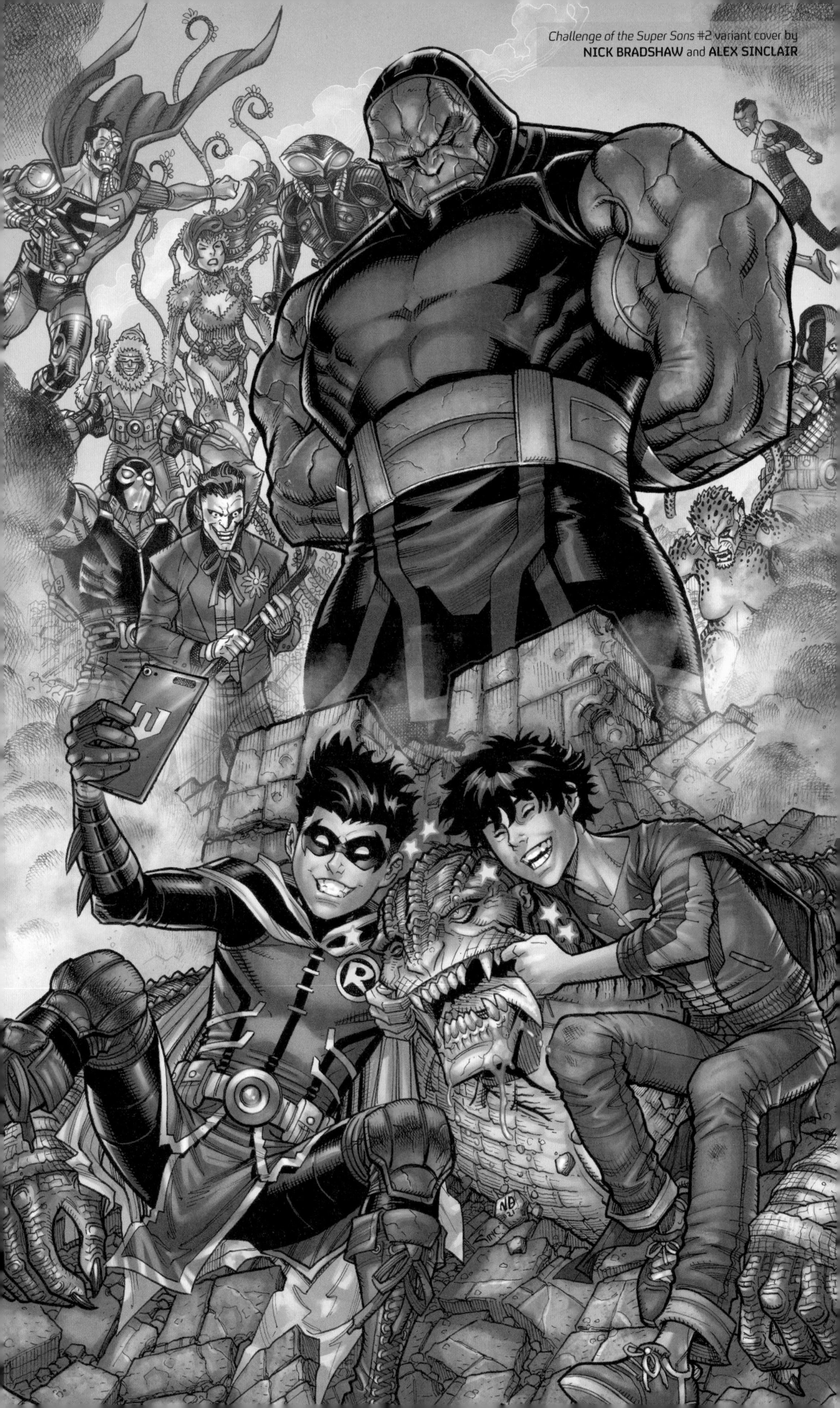

Challenge of the Super Sons #2 variant cover by
NICK BRADSHAW and **ALEX SINCLAIR**

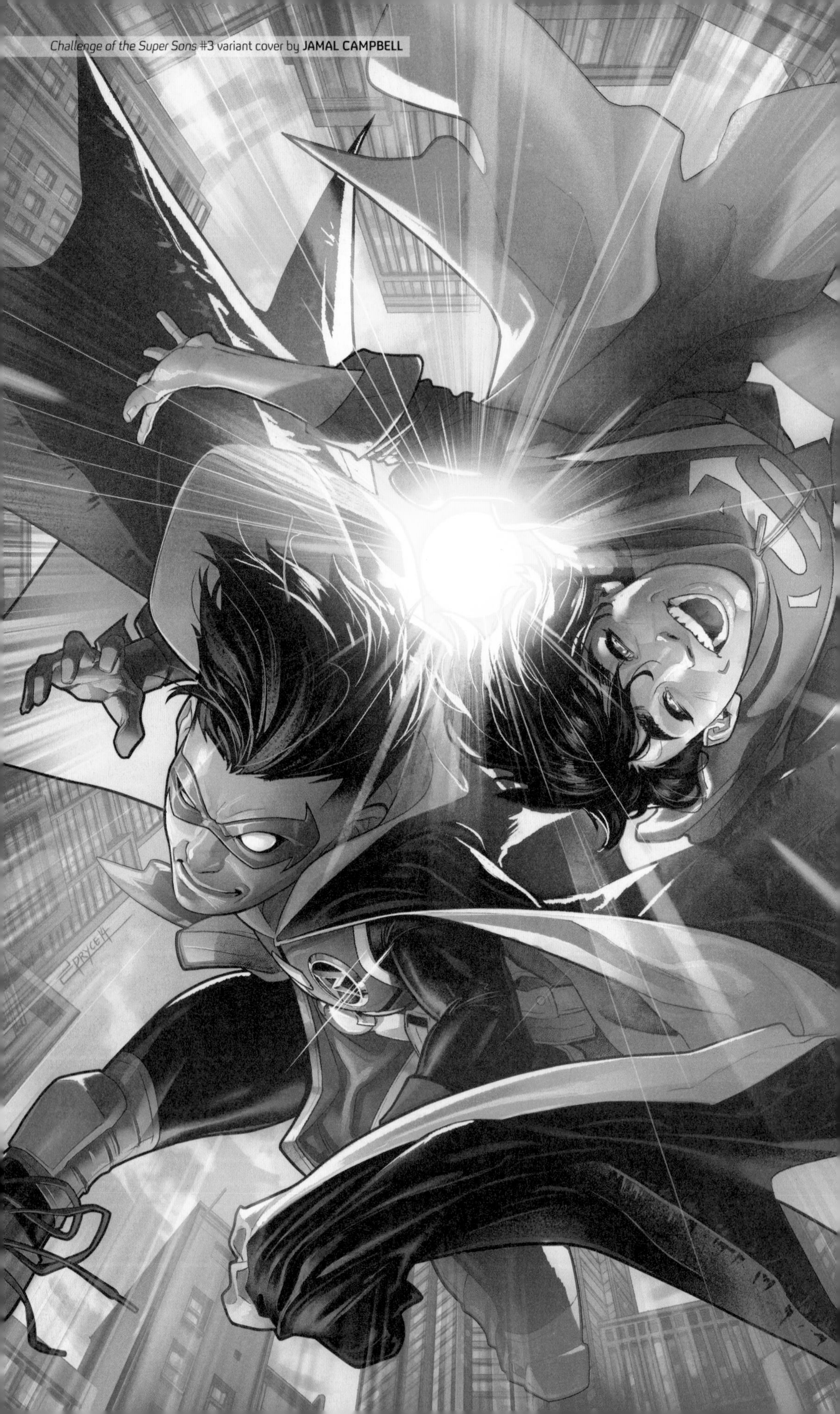

Challenge of the Super Sons #3 variant cover by **JAMAL CAMPBELL**

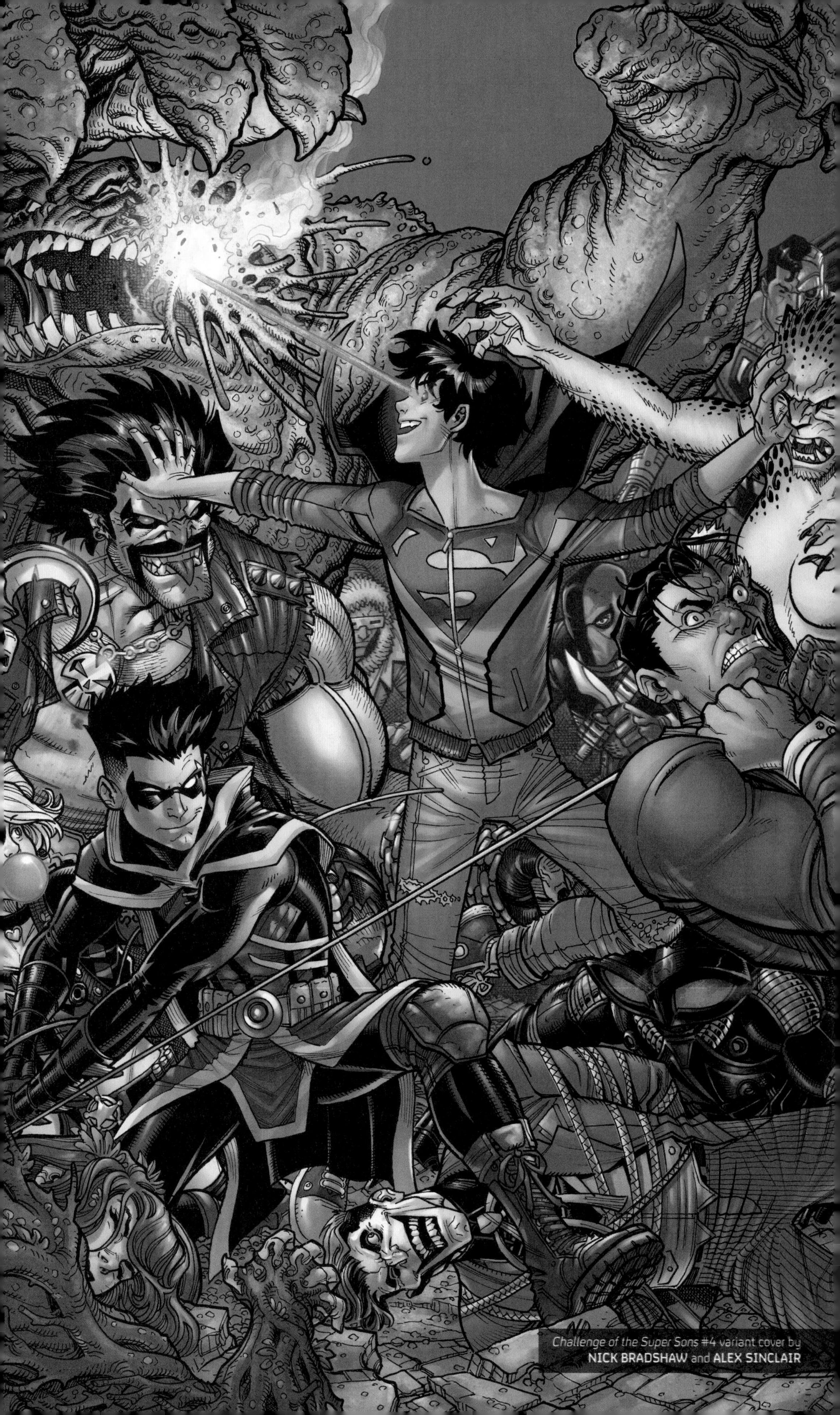

Challenge of the Super Sons #4 variant cover by
NICK BRADSHAW and **ALEX SINCLAIR**

Challenge of the Super Sons #5 variant cover by **JAMAL CAMPBELL**

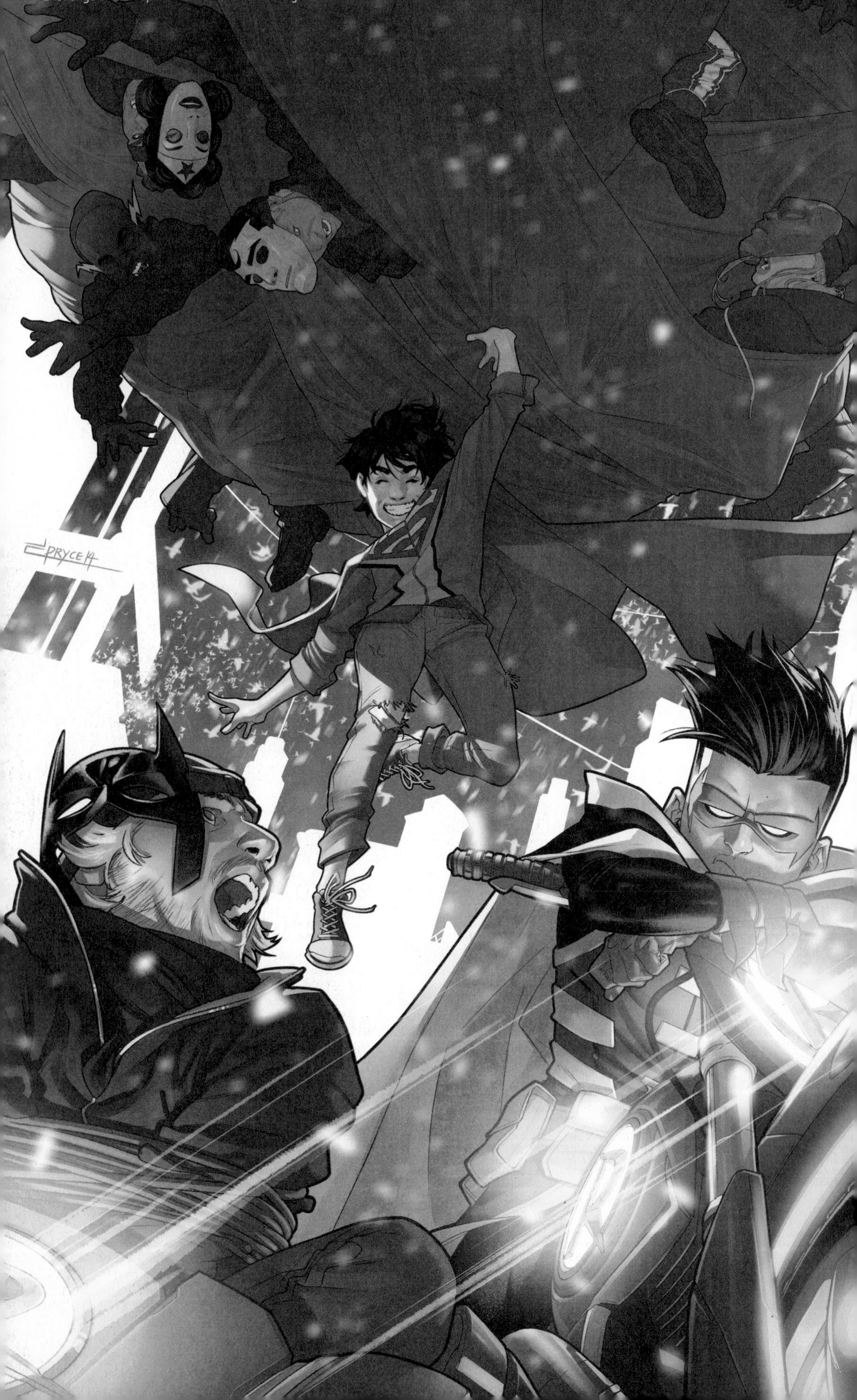

DPRYCE 14

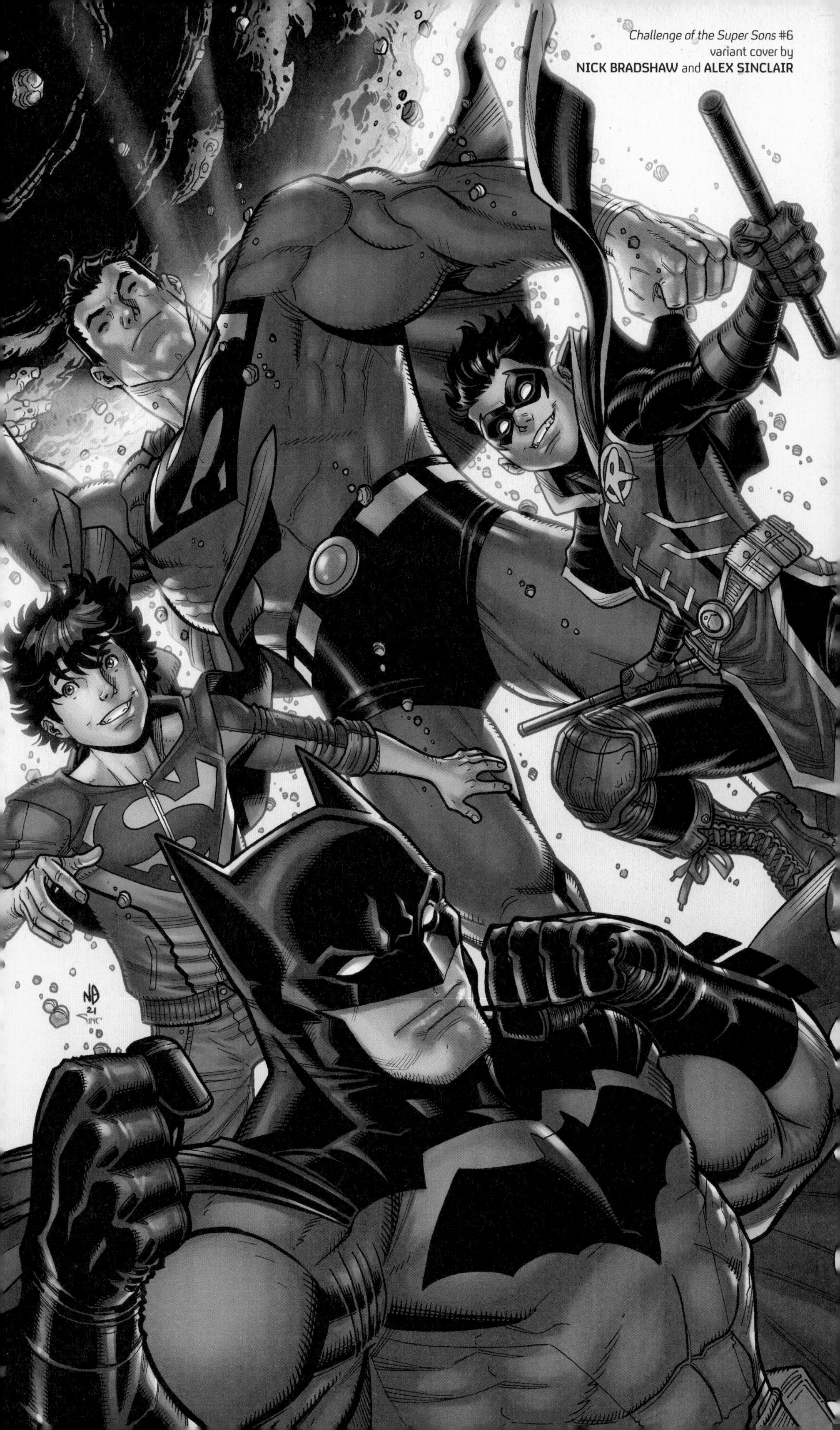

Challenge of the Super Sons #6
variant cover by
NICK BRADSHAW and **ALEX SINCLAIR**

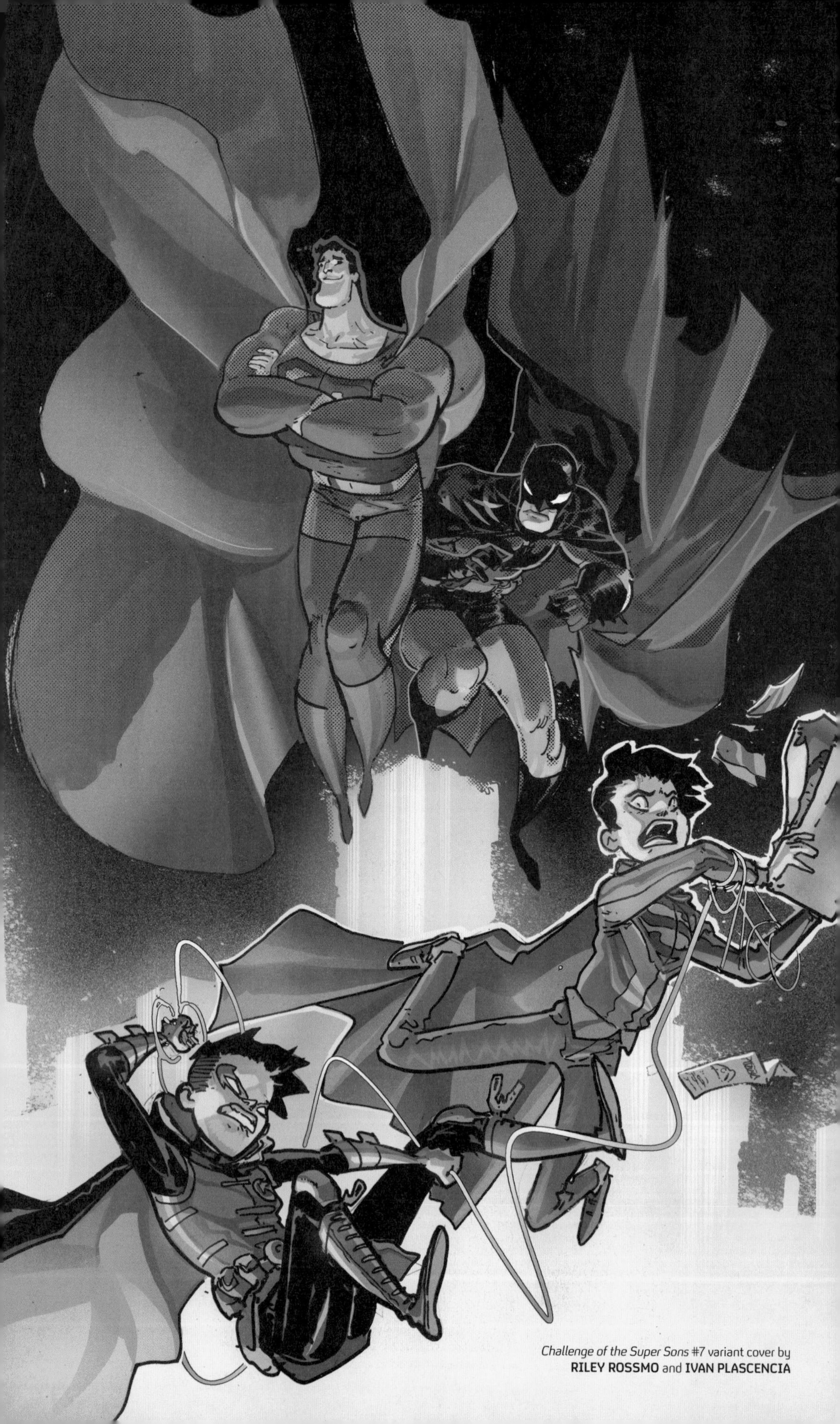

Challenge of the Super Sons #7 variant cover by
RILEY ROSSMO and **IVAN PLASCENCIA**

Challenge of the Super Sons #1 variant cover process by **SIMONE DI MEO**

Challenge of the Super Sons #2 variant cover sketches by **NICK BRADSHAW**

A   B   C   D

Challenge of the Super Sons #3 variant cover sketches by **JAMAL CAMPBELL**

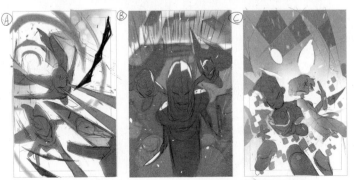

Challenge of the Super Sons #4 cover sketches by **SIMONE DI MEO**

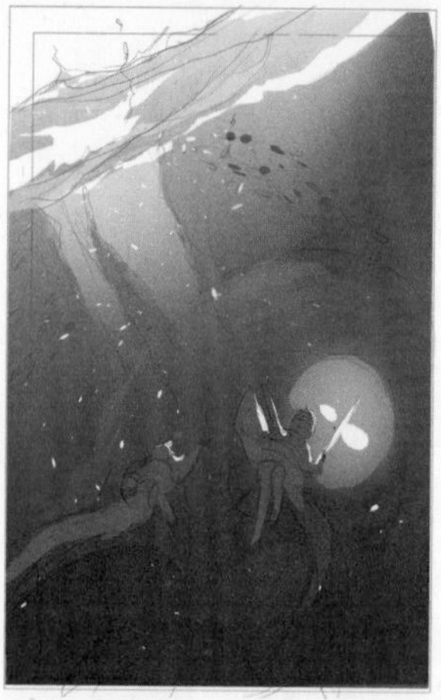

Challenge of the Super Sons #5 cover sketch by **SIMONE DI MEO**

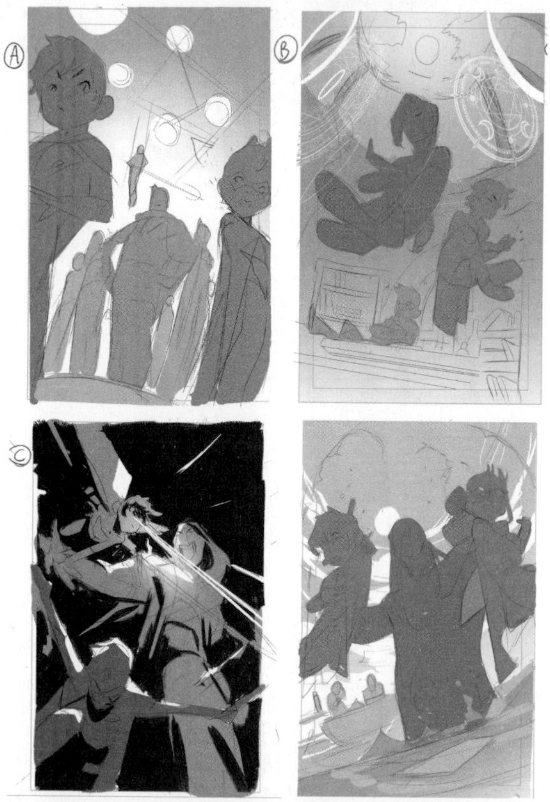
A
B
C

Challenge of the Super Sons #6 cover sketches by **SIMONE DI MEO**

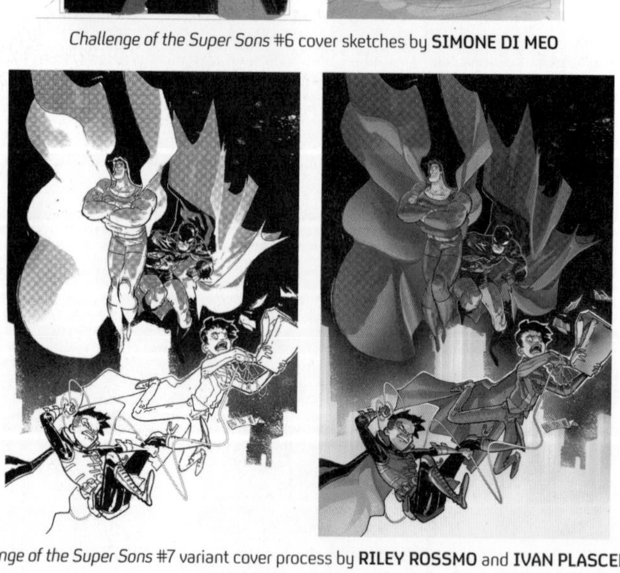

Challenge of the Super Sons #7 variant cover process by **RILEY ROSSMO** and **IVAN PLASCENCIA**